The Micro-Analysis of Regional Economy in China

A Perspective of Firm Relocation

Series on Chinese Economics Research

(ISSN: 2251-1644)

Series Editors: Yang Mu *(National University of Singapore, Singapore)*
Fan Gang *(Peking University, China)*

Series on Chinese Economics Research – Vol. 3

The Micro-Analysis of Regional Economy in China

A Perspective of Firm Relocation

Wei Houkai

Wang Yeqiang

Bai Mei

Chinese Academy of Social Sciences, China

 Unirule Institute of Economics

 World Scientific

Published by

World Scientific Publishing Co. Pte. Ltd.

5 Toh Tuck Link, Singapore 596224

USA office: 27 Warren Street, Suite 401-402, Hackensack, NJ 07601

UK office: 57 Shelton Street, Covent Garden, London WC2H 9HE

Library of Congress Cataloging-in-Publication Data
Wei, Houkai.
    The micro-analysis of regional economy in China : a perspective of firm relocation /
Wei Houkai, Chinese Academy of Social Sciences, Wang Yeqiang, Chinese Academy of Social
Sciences, Bai Mei, Chinese Academy of Social Sciences.
        pages cm. -- (Series on Chinese economics research ; v.3)
        ISBN 978-9814452250 -- ISBN 9814452254
        1. Industrial location--China. 2. Industries--China. 3. Regional planning--Chin
    4. Regional economics--China. I. Wang, Yeqiang, 1972– II. Mei, Bai. III. Titl
        HC430.D5W447 2013
        338.50951--dc23
                                                    2013007837

British Library Cataloguing-in-Publication Data
A catalogue record for this book is available from the British Library.

《中国区域经济的微观透析：企业迁移的视角》
Originally published in Chinese by Economy & Management Publishing House of Beijing
经济管理出版社，北京
Copyright@经济管理出版社，北京 2010

In-house Editor: Lum Pui Yee

Typeset by Stallion Press
Email: enquiries@stallionpress.com

Printed in Singapore

Contents

**Chapter 9.   Corporate Headquarters Relocation of Listed
               Companies and Wealth Transfer in China   247**

Wei Houkai and Bai Mei

**Chapter 10. Relocation Mechanism and Spatial
               Agglomeration of Enterprise R&D Activities   283**

Liu Changquan

**Chapter 11. New Industrial Division and Conflict
Management in Metropolitan Area — Based
on the Perspective of Industrial Chain Division   309**

Wei Houkai

**Chapter 12. Analysis of Urban Industrial Relocation's
Incentive, Approaches and Effects — Taking
Beijing as an Example   327**

Fu Xiaoxia, Wei Houkai and Wu Lixue

Preface

(I)

Since the reform and opening-up, the Chinese economy has grown at a rapid and continuous pace. From 1979 to 2011, China's Gross Domestic Product (GDP) grew by 9.9% annually. Even when faced with the impact of the global financial crisis and the European debt crisis, the growth rate of China's GDP between 2009 and 2011 was as high as 9.6%. If we calculate according to the speed of growth of each province, autonomous region, and municipality, the average growth rate of Gross Regional Product (GRP) of each region has reached 12.2% among the three years. With the rapid growth of economy, the living standard of the people has significantly improved. The comprehensive national power and competitiveness have been strengthened incessantly. The national economic aggregate rose from the tenth place globally to the second place in 2010. Impoverished population numbers were substantially reduced, decreasing from 0.25 billion at the early stage of the reform and opening-up to 26.88 million[1] in 2010. The academia at home and abroad term the stunning accomplishment and rapid growth of Chinese economy since the reform and opening-up alternatively as "Chinese miracle", "Chinese model", and "Chinese experience".

Obviously, the fast growth of the Chinese economy is supported by regional economic prosperity. We can safely state that, without the common prosperity of each region's economy, the unrelenting rapid growth of the national economy cannot be sustained. Since the reform and opening-up, although the regional economic growth rate differs from region to region, large-scale growth on the whole has been achieved, and every regional economy has the tendency to grow rapidly. Based on our measurement, from 1980 to 2009, the annual average growth rate of the 31 provinces, autonomous regions, and municipalities has reached 11.1%, among which the eastern region's growth rate stands at 12.1%, the northeastern region

---

[1] Measured according to the 1274 Yuan poverty standard in 2010.

9.6%, the central region 10.5%, and the western region 10.2%. This illustrates that since the reform and opening-up, no matter whether eastern region, the central and western region, or the northeastern region, the economic growth rate is fairly rapid, presenting the feature of typical high growth. The rapid growth rate of more than 9% for the past 30 years in each region is unprecedented, which is very rare from an international perspective.

It is predictable that, in the coming decade or two, the Chinese regional economy will maintain this fast growth. First, influenced by the lack of industrial land and increase of factor price and environmental protection standards, although the eastern region slacks off its economic growth, with the acceleration of the economic transition and upgrade, it will soon enter a new round of sustainable fast growth. Second, the central and western region's resources are rich, the cost of the factor price is low, the supply of labor is adequate, and the space and potential for future development is ample; thus, in recent years, this region shows a strong growth. The GRP growth rate of central and western regions, respectively, reached up to 12.7% and 13.7% from 2008 to 2011, which were much high than that of the eastern region (11.2%) and the entire country (12.1%). Third, with the powerful support of the national policy, the Northeast Industrial Base was pulled out of "relative degradation" since the reform and opening-up. The annual average GRP growth rate reached 13.4% during 2006–2011 and 13.1% during 2008–2011. It's quite hopeful to realize the goal of overall revitalization. Fourth, in the past, the rapid economic growth of the Chinese was supported mainly by the few regions like Yangtze River Delta (YRD) region and the Pearl River Delta (PRD) region. In recent years, with the promotion of the urbanization and industrialization, a climax of boosting urban agglomeration development has swept the whole nation. The Beijing–Tianjin–Hebei metropolitan area, Shandong peninsula urban agglomeration, Liaoning coastal economic belt, Zhongyuan urban agglomeration, Wanjiang urban belt, Changsha-Zhuzhou-Xiangtan "3 + 5" urban agglomeration, Chengdu–Chongqing economic region, Guanzhong–Tianshui economic region, Beibu Gulf economic region, etc., have the potential to become the pillars of rapid growth of Chinese economy as the new dominant regions, thereby forming a diversified competitive pattern of "rise of various regions".

(II)

However, we should understand that the fast growth of regional economy since the reform and opening-up has been realized at the expense of high consumption, high emission, in coordination, and unplanned exploitation, of which high consumption comes at the top. In 2010, China's GDP accounted for 9.5% of the world's total, yet the consumption of cements took up 56.2% of the global quantity,[2] the primary energy consumption took up 20.3%, among which the coal occupied 48.2%,[3] the apparent consumption of the steel took up 44.9%.[4] According to the WDI database of the World Bank, in 2007, China's energy consumption per ten thousand USD of GDP reached 7.96 ton oil equivalent, which is 2.71 times the average level of the world, and 4.28 times of the high-income countries.[5] Especially in the central and western region and northeastern region, influenced by the industrial structure and the technologic and management level, the feature of high consumption of resources and energy is more manifest. In 2009, energy consumption per 10,000 Yuan of GDP in the western region takes up 1.57 ton coal equivalent, which is 41.4% higher than the national average and 80.5% higher than the eastern region. Even in the developed eastern region, the per unit GDP's consumption strength of resources and energy is a far cry from the developed countries.

What comes second is the high emission. According to the data issued by the International Energy Agency (IEA), the emission of carbon dioxide of China in 2009 has taken up 23.6% of the world's total. Although the per capita carbon dioxide emission of China equals that of the world average and it is equivalent to 52.2% of the OECD countries, its emission strength per unit GDP is 3.19 times that of the world average and 5.68 times that of the OECD countries.[6] Per unit GDP's emission strength of sulfur dioxide is far higher than the level of the developed countries. In 2006, China's sulfur dioxide emission per 10,000 Yuan of GDP is 0.012015 tons, which

---

[2]International Cement Review (ICR) (2011). *Global Cement Report*, (10).

[3]BP Company (2011). *BP World Energy Statistics 2011*, June.

[4]World Steel Association (WSA) (2011). World Steel Short Range Outlook, WSA.

[5]National Bureau of Statistics of China (NBSC) (2011). *International Statistical Yearbook*, China: China Statistics Press.

[6]International Energy Agency, Key World Energy Statistics 2011, OECD/IEA, 2011.

is 59.6 times that of the US and 19.8 times that of Japan.[7] If judged from region to region, although 50% of the total quantity of industrial waste air and waste water is concentrated in the eastern region, the "three wastes" emission per unit industrial value-added in the central and western region is far higher than that of the eastern region, presenting a typical high emission feature. In 2007, the waste water, waste air, and waste solid's emission per 100 million Yuan industrial value-added in the western region is 1.79 times, 2.46 times, and 48 times that of the eastern region, respectively. Thus, we can conclude that the task of emission reduction of the central and western region is arduous.

The third is the in coordination, mainly shown in the following aspects: (1) Pursuing the GDP growth blindly and ignoring the structural upgrade, technologic innovation, social development, and construction of ecological environment, which gives rise to the in coordination of the economic and social development and the construction of ecological environment; (2) The in coordination of regional development: Since the reform and opening-up, the developmental difference between the eastern region and the central and western region is widening and has been improved in recent years; (3) The in coordination of urban and rural development: Since the mid 1980s, apart from few years, the income difference between urban and rural residents is always widening. In 2011, the ratio of the per capita disposable income of the urban households to per capita net income of rural households reaches 3.13:1, much higher than the 2.48:1 in 1997 and 1.86:1 in 1985; (4) The in coordination between the population and industry distribution: In recent years, while industries have concentrated in some cities and metropolitan areas, the population does not concentrate accordingly, which has given rise to a serious mismatching between the job vacancies and population distribution. Although 150 million rural migrant workers have worked in urban region,[8] they have not received a fair share of the accomplishments of urbanization. For example, in 2010, the population of

---

[7]Tie, Z. (2010). China's Ecological Civilization Construction Enters Quantization Age, *Scientific Times*, 5, February.

[8]In 2011, according to the calculation of the sampling investigation data of the NBSC, the amount of national migrant workers is 252.78 million, among which the out-migrant workers are 158.63 million. These out-migrant workers mainly work in urban regions.

China's three metropolitan areas (the YRD, the PRD, and Beijing–Tianjin–Hebei regions) took up 16.57% of the total, but the GRP took up 33.78%, the ratio between which was 1:2.04. However, the northeast mega-region' population took up 17% of the US, the GDP 20%, the ratio between which was only 1:1.18. In developed countries like Japan, the national population distribution basically matches the allocation of economic activities.

Fourth is unplanned exploitation as revealed in the following aspects: (1) Blind exploitation of the countryside causes the sharp decrease of the arable land and the supply of the agricultural products faced with threat; (2) Reckless exploitation of the ecological area has aggravates the integral function of the ecological system, with the result that more and more land is becoming non-inhabitable space; (3) the over-exploitation of the urban areas makes the pressure of resources and environment bigger and bigger. The result of unplanned exploitation is the disorder of territorial development and inappropriateness of spatial structure. From the perspective of production and its impact on ecology and life, the former takes up more space, leaving little to the ecology and life. From the angle of countryside and urban area, the habitancy space of countryside becomes more and that of the urban areas becomes less. Judging from the interior of the city, the industrial space is more and the habitable space becomes less.[9] Especially in recent years, some areas produce "garden factories" and conduct "land enclosure" and the rapid economic growth is mainly dependant on the usage of land expansion. Therefore, from the angle of land exploitation, we can state that, in the past, the industrialization of not a few regions was at the expense of the inhabitant welfare. The industrial land's scale is too big, the proportion is high and the use efficiency is too low.

(III)

Recalling the process of the regional development since the reform and opening-up, we can clearly see that, in the past, each regional development was on the traditional development path of high growth rate, high consumption, high emission, unplanned exploitation, and in coordination. Under the restriction of the resources and environment, this traditional

---

[9]Yang W. (2008). Promote the Establishment of Main Functional Area, Optimize the Pattern of Spatial Exploitation. *Economic Review*, (5).

development model is at its wits end. It is neither sustainable nor in compliance with the spirit of the scientific outlook on development. In particular, the international financial crisis since the second half of 2008 has accelerated the collapse of the traditional development model. Under new circumstances, the regions cannot and should not pursue development depending on the large consumption, high emission of "three wastes", and great exportation of cheap products. They must establish a new scientific outlook on development and continue to developing scientifically and unswervingly. It is safe to state that the regional development with a scientific view will become the core concept of China's regional development in the future. Future regional development will enter into a new epoch, highlighting development with scientific view.

Aiming at the past traditional development model, early in October 2003, the Third Plenary Session of the 16th Central Committee of Communist Party of China (CPC) proposed scientific outlook on overall development that is human-oriented, harmonious, and sustainable. Overall development, harmonious development, and sustainable development are the three core concepts of scientific outlook on development. Therefore, the path of regional development with scientific view insists upon the overall, harmonious, and sustainable development based on human-oriented. It underscores the intensive development, innovation development, harmonious development, and improvement of the regional sustainable development ability. From the perspective of scientific outlook on development, we must accelerate the transformation of regional development pattern and the transition of development model, changing from the traditional development model into the new development model with scientific view as soon as possible. This regional development transition includes the diversified and comprehensive transition of economic, social, cultural, and thinking concepts, the development strategy, and policies. On the whole, the regional development transition in present-day China includes six aspects: First, the transition of growth pattern from the extensive to intensive; Second, the transition of development focus from the economic growth to the improvement of quality, the social development and the improvement of livelihood; Third, the transition of industrial structure from the lower end of industrial chain to the middle and higher end; Fourth, the transition of urban and rural relations from dual division to integration; Fifth, the transition of motivation source from the input-driven to innovation-driven (including the technological innovation, institutional innovation, management innovation and brand innovation); Sixthly, the transition of spatial structure from unplanned exploitation to orderly exploitation.

Hence, we must implement five new strategies, accelerating the overall transition of regional development strategy. First is the implementation of new industrialization strategy. Judging from the large area, the regions suitable for industrialization can be identified from the local situation, highlight its features and advantages, and embark on the resource-saving, environmentally-friendly, high productivity, creativity-oriented industrialization path which gives full play to human resources and shares the development accomplishment.[10] Second is the implementation of the new urbanization strategy. The key is to establish a new urban ecological outlook, to highlight the urban features, to underscore the improvement of urban efficiency, and to persist with balancing urban and rural development. It must emphasize the improvement of the urban spatial structure and embark on the new, human-based, intensive, open, harmonious, diversified, and sustainable urbanization path. Third is the implementation of new exploitation strategy. On one hand, we should divide the control line of spatial exploitation scientifically, implement strict spatial governance and plan the spatial exploitation order reasonably; on the other, we should promote the synergistic agglomeration of population and industries, the coordination between population distribution and economic activity allocation, as well as the adaptability of population, economy and carrying capacity of resources and environment. Fourth is the implementation of a new opening strategy. The key is to balance opening-up to the outside world and domestic development is to start with the promotion of reform, development, upgrade, coordination, and harmony by opening-up, comprehensively improving the open economy level and promoting the economic and social development and the construction of a harmonious society. Fifth is the strengthening of the new social management. We should highlight the community management, give full play to the important role of intermediary organizations and public

---

[10]In China, the industrialization strategy is not suited for every region. At the same time, the industrialization strategy aims at the bigger areas, for the smaller areas, especially the geographic units below counties shall emphasize the thinking of functional division and specialization.

participation, and explore the new social management system which adapts to the scientific outlook on development.

(IV)

Since the reform and opening-up, China's regional development has achieved quite a few accomplishments, but there are several problems pertaining to development. In the course of development, we shall not underplay the considerable achievement of reform and opening-up because of these problems. It is just because of the new problems and new phenomena which crop up in the pursuance of regional development, do various regions explore and innovate in the reform and opening-up practice, creating positively new models, experience, and ways; in reality, these have provided colorful and rich materials for the research of China's and even world's regional development theories. It has also offered favorable conditions for the China's regional economics to stand at the summit of the world.

Chinese academia has always highlighted the research of China's regional development. In recent years, this kind of research is conducted in three directions, the first is the comprehensive research at the national level, which mainly explores the basic features, evolution tendency, and existing problems, dynamic mechanisms, strategy models, policy choice, and so on; the second is the specific study of each field, which covers almost every field concerning the whole regional economic, social, scientific, education, and cultural development and the construction of ecological environment, and so on. The third is research at the local level, the four levels of regional development: provincial development, municipal development; and county-level development; and township, village, and industrial zone development, which have become the hot subjects of the academic research. The research of development strategy planning on various-level region is always on the bloom.

The Chinese Academy of Social Sciences (CASS) has the tradition of highlighting the problems faced in reality. The construction of the regional economics discipline has underscored the positive exploration on the reality problems in China's regional development. From 2003 to 2008, I was honored to chair the construction project of regional economics discipline of "Key Discipline Construction Projects" at the CASS. Since 2008, based on the key discipline construction, the specialists and scholars of the CASS as the main body, with the enormous support of the Economy and Management Publishing House, jointly compiled China's Modern Regional Development Series. The first batch has 12 books. The smooth publication of the series is the result of the enormous support of the Chief Editor Zhiyu Shen, the President Shixian Zhang of the Economy and Management Publishing House, and friends and scholars from domestic and overseas academia. To them I present my sincere thanks!

This book is part of China's Modern Regional Development Series and the final outcome of the National Natural Science Foundation project — "The Determinants of Firm Relocation and Location Policy in China" chaired by me, and it is also the collective wisdom of the group members.

The creation and publication of the book in the Chinese version has obtained strong support from the Institute of Industrial Economics, the Economy and Management Publishing House, and other institutes and departments at the CASS, and also of the academic colleagues in China. As for the English version of this book, I should firstly give my great thanks to Professor Dr. Mu Yang of East Asian Institute (EAI) at the National University of Singapore (NUS) for including this book into the *Chinese Economy Series*. I am also extremely thankful to the World Scientific Publishing Co. Pte. Ltd, especially to the editor Ms Lum Pui Yee. Besides, the smooth publication of the English version of this book has received the support of the Philosophy and Social Science Innovation Programme at the CASS. The Postdoctoral candidates Hongjian Su and Zhanyun Wu, and doctoral candidates Yan Zhang, Yebo Guo, Lianlei Bai, and Ning Wang are partly responsible for the proofreading and typesetting of the English text. I am grateful for their support!

Wei Houkai
5 March 2009, Revised 22 October 2012
Zhonghai Andrews Manor, Beijing

List of Tables

List of Figures

List of Abbreviations

BSR	Bohai Sea Rim
CASS	Chinese Academy of Social Sciences
CPC	Communist Party of China
CV	Coefficient of Variation
FDI	Foreign Direct Investment
GDP	Gross Domestic Product
GRP	Gross Regional Product
HQs	Headquarters
ICR	International Cement Review
IEA	International Energy Agency
NBSC	National Bureau of Statistics of China
NDRC	National Development and Reform Commission
ODM	Original Design Manufacturer
OEM	Original Equipment Manufacturer
PRC	People's Republic of China
PRD	Pearl River Delta
R&D	Research and Development
S&T	Science and Technology
SIC	Standard Industrial Classification
SMEs	Small and Medium Enterprises
UNIDO	United Nations Industrial Development Organization
WSA	World Steel Association
YRD	Yangtze River Delta
ZSP	Zhongguancun Science Park

Chapter 1

Regional Economic Development in China: Agglomeration and Relocation

Wei Houkai

Regional economic development in China has been undergoing a strategic transition from disequilibrium to coordination since 1978, the year the nation adopted the reform and opening-up policy. In light of the major changes that have taken place in the nation's guidelines for regional development in the intervening years, we can roughly divide the metamorphosis of relevant strategies and policies into three periods: 1979–1990, in which the economy developed in favor of east region; 1991–1998, when strategies were initiated to coordinate the economic development of central and western region; and the post-1999 period, when strategies have come into full swing to coordinate the regional economic development. In the Eighth Five-Year Plan, published in March 1991, the Chinese government put a premium on coordinated regional development from the height of national strategy. Then the government adopted a strategy in September 1999 to develop the western region, initiated another strategy in October 2003 to revitalize old industrial bases in northeastern region and other regions, and issued a call in January 2004 to hasten the rise of the central region, which indicates that the decision to achieve equilibrium in regional economic development entered a period of all-round implementation.

From the perspectives of industrial agglomeration and corporate relocation, this chapter follows the changes in China's regional economic development since the reform and opening-up. Section 1.1 succinctly discusses the regional division in the Chinese economy and the salient features of economic growth in each region. Section 1.2 analyses the trend and characteristics of the pattern for regional economic growth. Section 1.3 examines the course of changes in regional economic disparity in this country. Section 1.4 elaborates on the trend of concentration of economic activities and its impact on regional growth and disparity. Section 1.5 examines the new tendency of the Chinese industrial relocation from concentration to diffusion. Some conclusions are given in the end.

1.1 Division of Economic Regions and Characteristics of Regional Economic Development in China

China is a large developing nation with a comparatively large economic disparity among its regions. In the Sixth Five-Year Plan (1981–1985), which came underway shortly after the adoption of the reform and opening-up, the government followed the old tradition and dichotomized the country into coastal and inland regions to reflect the difference (see Table 1-1).[1] On the basis of the traditional dichotomous method, and in light of different geographic locations and regional economic development levels, the Seventh Five-Year Plan (1986–1990) divided the nation into three economic regions — eastern, central, and western regions — to provide the government with something to go by when determining economic development priorities and setting up a pecking order for allocating industrial activity. This division of three economic regions, though somewhat simplistic and rough, has had a major impact on regional statistical work and policy making. The central and western regions used to be mentioned as the "inland region", and this is why they are usually collectively called the "central and western region". Under the Eighth Five-Year Plan (1991–1995), the old dichotomous method was inherited, so that the division of the nation into coastal and inland regions continued. The Ninth Five-Year Plan (1996–2000) renamed the two regions as the "eastern region" and "central and western region". What is noteworthy is that, in the Ninth Five-Year Plan, the government planned to set up seven economic regions by bypassing provincial, municipal, and autonomous regional boundaries, but

---

[1]China adopted this method of dichotomy as early as the First Five-Year Plan period (1952–1957). Mao Tse-tung elaborated on the relationship between the coastal and the inland regions in his 1956 thesis *On Ten Major Relationships*. See Mao (1999).

the plan fell through because of its questionable wisdom and, more importantly, because of its ill-defined purposes. Moreover, the seven-region plan was patterned after the former Soviet Union's blueprint for synthesized economic regions under central planning, whereas China was already in transition from central planning to a market economic system, with the central government having practically lost its ability to construct the synthesized economic regions.

Table 1-1 Division of Chinese Economic Regions Since the Reform and Opening-Up.

State plan	Period	Regional division
Sixth Five-Year Plan	1981–1985	Coastal region and inland region
Seventh Five-Year Plan	1986–1990	Eastern coastal region, central region, and western region
Eighth Five-Year Plan	1991–1995	Coastal region and inland region
Ninth Five-Year Plan	1996–2000	(1) The YRD and the areas along the river, Bohai Sea Rim (BSR) region, southeast coastal region, southwest region, and some provinces and autonomous regions in south China, northeastern region, five provinces and autonomous regions in central region, and northwest region; (2) eastern region and central and western region.
Tenth Five-Year Plan	2001–2005	Eastern region, central region, and western region
Eleventh Five-Year Plan	2006–2010	(1) Western region, northeastern region, central region, and eastern region; (2) four categories of main functional areas including optimized, key, restricted, and prohibited development areas.

Source: The Five-Year Plans for National Economic and Social Development of the People's Republic of China.

To coordinate regional economic development, the government adopted a strategy to develop the western region in 1999. Apart from the 10 western provinces (municipalities and autonomous regions included, thereafter shortened as "provinces") listed in the Seventh Five-Year Plan, the policy covered Guangxi (originally part of eastern region), Inner Mongolia (originally part of central region), the Yanbian Korean autonomous prefecture of Jilin province, the Enshi Tujia and Miao autonomous prefecture of Hubei province, and the Xiangxi Tujia and Miao autonomous prefecture of Hunan province. In the administrative unit of provincial level, this arrangement gave rise to the concept of "10 + 2" great western region and formed the division of the nation into new three major regions in the aforementioned strategy. The government thereafter adopted a strategy to revitalize the northeastern region and another strategy to facilitate the rise of the central region. By the time of the Eleventh Five-Year Plan (2006–2010), the nation has been divided into four regions: eastern region, central region, western region, and northeastern region, with 10 provinces in eastern region, and 6 provinces in central region (see Figure 1-1).

Judging from the economic relations and the degree of economic integration, the central region, as it stands today, cannot be counted as an integral region, still less an economic region. Economic disparity is an outstanding problem in both the eastern and western regions. In the western region, there is a yawning gap between its southwest and northwest regions, while in the eastern region, development is lopsided among the Yangtze River Delta (YRD), the Pearl River Delta (PRD), the Shandong Peninsula, and the Beijing–Tianjin–Hebei region.[2] Only the northeastern region appears to be a relatively integral economic region.[3]

In this chapter, I adopt the Eleventh Five-Year Plan's division of China into four regions. The eastern region includes Hebei, Beijing, Tianjin,

---

[2]In the past, the "BSR Economic Region" was a much-vaunted concept in the academic circles. The region consists of Shandong Peninsula, Liaodong Peninsular, and the Beijing–Tianjin–Hebei regions, which are distinctively different from, and independent of, each other, and in a loose economic relationship. For this reason, BSR region is unlikely to become an economic region in the immediate future.

[3]According to the Program on Revitalization of the Northeastern Region, endorsed by the State Council in August 2007, the region covers Liaoning province, Jilin province, Heilongjiang province, as well as the Inner Mongolia autonomous region's Hulun Boir city, Hinggan (Xing'an) league, Tongliao city, Chifeng city, and Xilin Gol league.

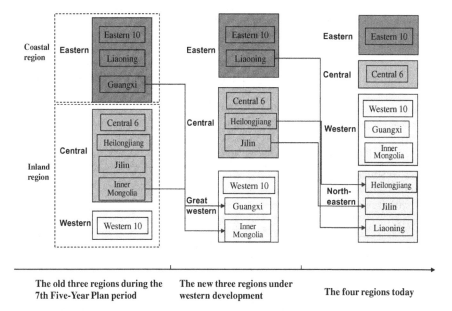

The old three regions during the 7th Five-Year Plan period

The new three regions under western development

The four regions today

Figure 1-1   Three Times Main Changes in the Economic Division of China in Recent Years. This comprises the 10 eastern provinces (Eastern 10): Beijing, Tianjin, Hebei, Shandong, Jiangsu, Shanghai, Zhejiang, Fujian, Guangdong, and Hainan; the six central provinces (Central 6): Shanxi, Henan, Anhui, Hubei, Hunan, and Jiangxi; the 10 western provinces (Western 10): Sichuan, Chongqing, Guizhou, Yunnan, Tibet, Shaanxi, Gansu, Ningxia, Qinghai, and Xinjiang.

Source: Wei Houkai *et al.* (2005). *A Study On the Readjustments of Industrial Location in China*, Institute of Industrial Economics, CASS.

Shandong, Shanghai, Jiangsu, Zhejiang, Fujian, Guangdong, and Hainan; the northeastern region spans Liaoning, Jilin, and Heilongjiang; the central region covers six provinces: Shanxi, Henan, Anhui, Hubei, Hunan, and Jiangxi; and the western region consists of 12 provinces: Inner Mongolia, Guangxi, Shaanxi, Gansu, Ningxia, Qinghai, Xinjiang, Chongqing, Sichuan, Guizhou, Yunnan, and Tibet. According to Table 1-2, the eastern region has 38.0% of the country's total population but makes up 53.1% of the nation's total gross regional product (GRP) and 52.9% of the total industrial value added, 41.7% of the total investment in fixed assets, 63.7% of the total value of Foreign Direct Investment (FDI) actually utilized, and 87.4% of the nation's total exports. In contrast, the percentages of economic aggregates of both central and western regions in the national total are much smaller

Table 1-2 Percentages of Major Economic Indicators for China's Four Regions in National Total in 2010 (%).

	Nation	Eastern region	Northeastern region	Central region	Western region
Population	100	38.0	8.2	26.8	27.0
Gross regional product (GRP)	100	53.1	8.6	19.7	18.6
Industrial value added	100	52.9	9.0	20.3	17.8
Total investment in fixed assets[a]	100	41.7	11.0	22.6	22.3
FDI actually utilized[b]	100	63.7	12.2	14.4	9.6
Exports[c]	100	87.4	4.0	4.0	4.6

[a]Investment not classified by regions account for 2.4%.
[b]Data in 2009.
[c]Computed by the origin of commodity supplies.

Source: *China Statistical Yearbook* (2011) and *Support System for China Statistics Application*. FDI actually utilized in 2009 for Beijing is missing and that of Shaanxi and Xinjiang from statistical bulletin.

than their respective portions in the nation's total population. This disequilibrium in the distribution of economic activity and population is a major cause behind the serious lopsidedness in regional economic development and the glaring regional disparity in China. In 2010, the eastern region registered a per capita GRP of RMB 46,354, as against RMB 34,303 for the northeastern region, RMB 24,242 for the central region, and RMB 22,476 for the western region. A comparison between the provinces reveals that the per capita GRP of Shanghai was the highest in the nation; it is 5.6 times that of Guizhou province. The gap can be even more pronounced when comparisons are drawn among cities and counties and among townships and towns.

1.2 Disequilibrium in Regional Economic Development: A Growing Tendency

A prevalent misconception in the academic world and among government departments is to compare the GRP growth rates of different regions directly with the nation's GDP growth rate announced by the National Bureau of

Statistics of China (NBSC). This unavoidably leads to mistaken judgments because of the incomparability between GRP and GDP statistics. In fact, the total GRP for the 31 provinces, autonomous regions, and municipalities is a lot higher than the GDP released by the NBSC. Before the statistics were adjusted according to economic survey figures, GRP outstripped GDP by 9.7%, 11.7%, 15.5%, and 19.3%, respectively, in 2001, 2002, 2003, and 2004. Even after the statistics were adjusted in the second economic census, GRP still exceeded GDP by 7.7%, 7.6%, 5.2%, 6.1%, 7.2%, and 8.9% from 2005 to 2010. Of the 31 provinces, autonomous regions, and municipalities, the growth rates of most provincial GRPs are higher than the national GDP growth rate from 2005 to 2010, and only Beijing and Shanghai registered a GRP growth rate slightly lower than that of GDP in 2010. Figure 1-2 indicates that the differentials of growth rate between GDP and GRP have kept growing since 1992.[4] According to the NBSC, the nation's 2010 GDP

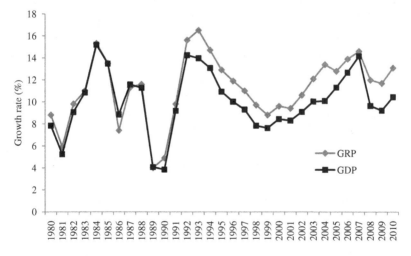

Figure 1-2   Comparisons between GDP and GRP Growth Rates in China during the 1980–2010 Period.

Source: China's Regional Economies in 17 Reform and Opening-up Years, A Compendium of Statistics for New China's 50 Years, and the *China Statistical Yearbook* concerning various years, compiled by the NBSC.

---

[4]The GRP and the growth index of each region in a given year are calculated according to the constant price of the previous year to derive that region's GRP in the previous year. Then the statistics pertaining to all the regions' GRP in both years are collected to derive the nation's average GRP growth rate.

growth rate stood at 10.4%, while the GRP growth rate averaged 13.1%, with a difference of 2.7 percentage points.[5] For this reason, the summarized figures concerning all the 31 provinces, municipalities, and autonomous regions must be used when comparing the GRP growth rate or the per capita GRP of a given region. Failing to do so can only lead to illogical conclusions.

Table 1-3 gives an overview of the GRP growth rates of the four regions during the 1980–2010 period. Over the years, the situation of China's unbalanced regional economic growth until 2006 was that growth was rapid in the eastern region but slow in the central, western, and northeastern regions. The year 2007 was an important turning point, when the western region's GDP growth rate reached 14.9%, higher than that of the eastern region and the regional average of 14.6%. After 2008, the economic growth rate in the northeastern, central, and western regions were all higher than that in the eastern region, showing a relatively balanced growth situation. During the 1980–1990 period, the annual GRP rate averaged 10.2% in the eastern region, 8.8% in the central and western region, and a meager 8.1% in the northeastern region. In the post-1991 years, the growth rate disparity between the eastern region and the other regions began to expand drastically as the nation speeded up its transition toward the market economy. During the 1991–1998 period, the eastern region registered an average annual GRP growth rate of 14.7%, whereas the figures were 12.0% for central region, 10.4% for western region, and 9.5% for northeastern region. The disparity between eastern region and the rest of the country has somewhat narrowed since 1999 as a result of the implementation of the aforementioned government strategies for western, northeastern, and central regions. During the 1999–2006 period, the eastern region's annual GRP growth rate averaged 12.2%, while those of northeastern, central, and western regions

---

[5]There are at least five reasons behind this difference: (1) While most regions used the 1990 constant price in calculating statistics concerning industrial products, the NBSC had already readjusted the relevant data when checking these statistics; (2) Personnel, materials, and funds are transregional, circulating at ever-expanding scales, and difficulties in sorting out the relevant statistics often result in overlapping calculations; (3) Many regions were still using overall report forms on non-state-owned industrial enterprises whose annual sales revenues were below RMB 5 million; (4) China's incomplete statistical network is yet to cover all aspects of the tertiary industry; and (5) While the statistics submitted by regions were doctored to different degrees, the NBSC calculations were as a rule based on adjusted statistics (Li, 2004).

Table 1-3 The Changing GRP Growth Rates in the Eastern, Northeastern, Central, and Western Regions.

Year	Growth rate (%)					Relative growth rate (with the national average rate at 1)			
	Nation	Eastern	Northeastern	Central	Western	Eastern	Northeastern	Central	Western
1980–1990	9.4	10.2	8.1	8.8	8.8	1.09	0.86	0.94	0.94
1991–1998	12.7	14.7	9.5	12.0	10.4	1.16	0.75	0.95	0.82
1999–2006	11.3	12.2	10.6	10.6	10.7	1.08	0.94	0.94	0.95
2007–2010	12.8	12.3	13.5	13.2	13.9	0.96	1.05	1.03	.09
# 1999	8.8	9.9	7.9	7.9	7.3	1.13	0.90	0.90	0.83
2000	9.6	10.5	8.7	8.9	8.5	1.09	0.91	0.93	0.89
2001	9.4	10.2	9.1	9.0	9.0	1.09	0.97	0.96	0.96
2002	10.6	11.6	10.1	9.8	10.3	1.09	0.95	0.92	0.97
2003	12.1	13.4	10.8	10.8	11.5	1.11	0.89	0.89	0.95
2004	13.4	14.4	12.3	13.0	12.9	1.07	0.92	0.97	0.96
2005	12.8	13.5	12.0	12.7	13.1	1.05	0.94	0.99	1.02
2006	13.9	14.3	13.7	13.2	13.5	1.03	0.99	0.95	0.97
2007	14.6	14.6	14.3	14.6	14.9	1.00	0.98	1.00	1.02
2008	12.0	11.2	13.5	12.4	13.1	0.93	1.13	1.03	1.09
2009	11.7	10.9	12.7	11.8	13.5	0.93	1.09	1.01	1.09
2010	13.1	12.4	13.7	13.9	14.2	0.95	1.05	1.06	1.08

Note: All the post-2001 statistics have been revised according to economic survey data. The same is true with the figures and tables below. Annual growth rates for 2006–2010 according to the adjusted data from the *China Statistical Yearbook* (2011).
Source: Same as Figure 1-2.

were 10.6%, 10.6% and 10.7%, respectively. During the 2007–2010 period, the average annual growth rate of eastern region's GDP is 12.3%, while the northeastern, the central, and western regions were as high as 13.2%, 13.5%, and 13.9%, respectively.

We thereby set the average GRP growth rate for all the regions at 1 to calculate the relative GRP growth rate for each region. A comparison between the 1999–2006 period and the 1991–1998 period, as indicated in Table 1-3, shows that the relative GRP growth rate dropped in eastern region, went up in northeastern and western region, and remained stable in central region. By 2006, the relative GRP growth rates for all the four regions gradually approached 1. Obviously, the GRP growth rates of all the regions are closing in on the average level over the last few years, registering a relative balance. Figure 1-3 also clearly indicates that both the GRP growth rate differentials between the four regions and the GRP growth rate disparity between eastern and western regions are dwindling. The GRP growth rate of the western region was lower than that of the eastern region by 2.6 percentage points in 1999, 1.5 percentage points in 2004, and from 2007 to 2010, the GRP growth rate of western region was higher than that of the eastern region 0.3, 1.9, 2.6, and 1.8 percentage points, respectively.

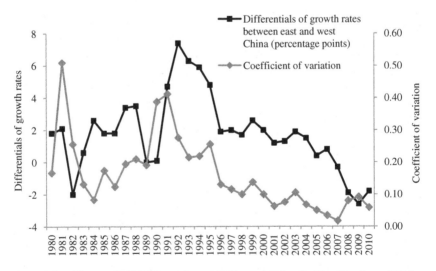

Figure 1-3   Changes in GRP Growth-rate Differentials for the Four Regions of China.
Source: Same as Figure 1-2.

From 1999 to 2010, the coefficient of variation for the GRP growth rates of the four regions went down from 0.138 to 0.059.

All the five provinces with an average annual GRP growth rate of above 14% during the 1991–1998 period were in the eastern region: Fujian at 17.2%, Zhejiang at 16.1%, Guangdong at 15.8%, Jiangsu at 15.7%, and Shandong at 14.3%. These newly rising industrial bases were the dynamos behind the sustained high-speed growth of the Chinese economy throughout the 1990s. In contrast, all the eight provinces whose GRP growth rates averaged below the 10% mark during that period were all located in the western and northeastern regions: Yunnan at 9.8%, Gansu at 9.7%, Liaoning at 9.6%, Shaanxi at 9.5%, Ningxia at 9.3%, Guizhou at 8.7%, Heilongjiang at 8.5%, and Qinghai at 8.1%. Nevertheless, the newly rising industrial bases in the coastal eastern region have been caught in an economic slowdown since 1999, with their average annual GRP growth rates ranging from 11.9% to 12.8%, while some provinces in western and northeastern region have entered a period of gradual economic speedup (see Figure 1-4). This is particularly the case with Inner Mongolia: With its average annual GRP growth rate zooming from 10.0% to 16.0%, the region has led the nation in economic

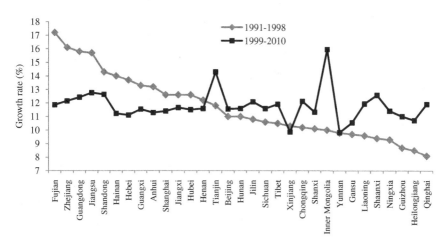

Figure 1-4　Changes in the GRP Growth Rates in 31 Provinces, Municipalities and Autonomous Regions.

Note: In the curve for the 1991–1998 period, the statistics for Chongqing pertain to the 1996–1998 period.

Source: Same as Figure 1-2.

growth for consecutive years. As a matter of fact, Inner Mongolia's recent high economic growth has been generated by local resources, investment, and the rise of local famous brand names — a number of famous local brand names, including Yili, Mengmilk, KingDeer, and Erdos, play a pivotal role in the fast economic growth of this region.

1.3 Metamorphosis of China's Regional Economic Disparity

Imbalanced regional economic development goes hand in hand with an ever-widening regional disparity between the eastern and western regions. Although this disparity did not begin to widen after the reform and opening-up, the transition toward the market economy since 1978 has unquestionably triggered it (Wei, 2007). Figure 1-5 indicates clearly that, during the 1980–2003 period, with the exception of eastern region, whose per capita GRP kept rising steadily, the other three regions all experienced a downturn in their relative per capita GRP growth. The situation with northeastern region was the worst, with its relative per capita GRP level falling from 150.8 to

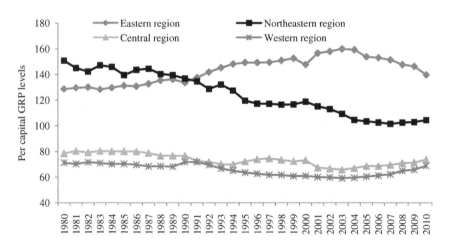

Figure 1-5   Relative Levels of the Per Capita GRP for the Four Regions of China.

Note: The per capita GRPs for the four regions are calculated on the basis of collected data concerning the population and GRP of the provinces in every region; and relative levels are derived by setting the average level of all the regions at 100.

Source: Same as Figure 1-2.

109.3. However, this situation has changed to a certain degree since 2004, when the per capita GRP level began to descend in the eastern region and ascend in the central and western region; northeastern region is the only region whose per capital GRP level dropped further, to 101.5 in 2007, but it reached 104.5 in 2010. During the 2003–2010 period, the relative per capita GRP level went down from 159.8 to 139.8 in the eastern region, and rose from 65.7 to 73.6 in the central region and from 59.2 to 68.9 in the western region.

Figure 1-6 indicates that, with the exception of a few years, the per capita GRP coefficient of the relative disparity between the eastern region and the central and western region has been on an increase since the reform and opening-up. From 1980 to 2003, it grew by 18.7 percentage points, from 44.7% to 63%, between the eastern and western regions, and by 20.0 percentage points, from 38.9% to 58.9%, between the eastern and central regions. The coefficient of variation of the average per capita GPR for all the four regions grew steadily, despite repeated fluctuations, from 0.334 in 1985

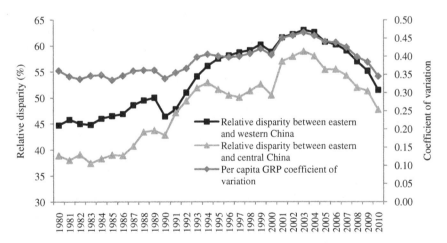

Figure 1-6   Changes in Per Capita GRP Relative Disparity in the Four Regions of China.

Note: Coefficient of relative disparity between eastern region and central and western region = (Targeted value for eastern region — Targeted value for central and western region)/Targeted value for eastern region × 100%. Data for 2005–2010 according to the adjusted data from economic census.

Source: Same as Figure 1-2.

to 0.465 in 2003. The east–west disparity widened by noticeable margins mainly during the 1986–1989, 1991–1994, 1997–1999, and 2001–2003 periods, and began to narrow down after 2004, which was roughly consistent with these regions' per capita GRP levels. Two points must be made here, however. First, the coefficients of variation pertaining to the post-2001 situations have been revised according to economic survey data and are slightly higher than before they were revised. This has resulted in a marked increase in the 2001 figure over what it was in 2000,[6] but it follows basically the same trend of changes. Second, the disparity between eastern and western regions has been widening nonstop since the 1960s, and it was the case even during the period in which third-line strategic areas were being constructed (Liu *et al.*, 1994; Wei *et al.*, 1997). It is fair to say that the widening east–west disparity in the reform years is a continuation of what happened in previous historical periods.

Now let us take a look at the disparities among the provinces in China. Since the reform and opening up, the per capita GRP disparity among the provinces has taken a U-turn with 1990 as the point of inflexion (see Figure 1-7). In the early years of the reform and opening-up, economic stagnation in the high-income northeastern and northern China and in such old industrial bases as Shanghai and Liaoning, plus robust economic growth in the middle- and low-income provinces such as Guangdong, Zhejiang, and Fujian, catalyzed a gradual reduction in the per capita GRP disparity among the provinces. The coefficient of variation for per capita GRP disparity dropped by 38.3% from 0.974 in 1978 to 0.601 in 1990, and the weighted coefficient of variation declined by 33.4% from 0.635 to 0.423. It has been noticed that, with the economies of eastern Chinese provinces growing robustly in a sustained and all-round way, the per capita GRP disparities among the provinces have once again begun to climb up since the 1990s — such disparities' coefficient of variation and weighted coefficient of variation rose by 26.8% and 30.7%, respectively, during the 1990–2003 period before they started to drop to a certain extent in 2004, and the coefficient of

---

[6]Before they were revised according to economic survey data, the coefficients of variation for the per capita GRPs of the four regions in the 2001–2004 period stood at 0.431, 0.440, 0.451, and 0.446, respectively; after they were revised they have increased by roughly 2%–5% to 0.450, 0.457, 0.465, and 0.456.

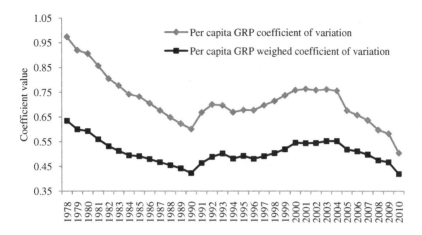

Figure 1-7   Changes in Per Capital GRP Disparities among Provinces in China.

Note: The per capital GRP weighted coefficient of variation is weighted according to populations. Annual growth rates for 2006–2010 according to the adjusted data from the *China Statistical Yearbook* (2011).

Source: Same as Figure 1-2.

variation and the weighted coefficient of variation for inter-provincial per capita GRP dropped to 0.505 and 0.420 in 2010.

Despite the fact that the eastern region continues to grow faster than the central, western, and northeastern regions, the regional disparity benchmarked by per capita GRP has obviously taken on a favorable narrowing trend since 2004. If this trend can stay stable, regional development of China will arrive at a "turning point" or a "point of inflection", thereby entering a new period in which disequilibrium gradually gives way to relative equilibrium. The mitigation of regional disparity since 2004 is attributed to three major reasons. First, government policies and investment continue to boost economic growth in central, western, and northeastern regions; second, under the pressure of rising costs and the needs for industrial upgrading and environment protection, the enterprises and industries of coastal regions are speeding up their northward and westward relocation; and third, the impact of changes in the way statistics on population census and population migration are measured. In the past, the populations in different regions were counted according to official resident registrations. Since 2005, surveys on the basis of 1% sample population have been giving consideration to the

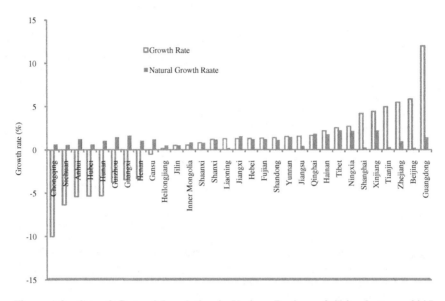

Figure 1-8   Growth Rate of Population in Various Regions of China between 2005 and 2006.

Source: China Statistical Yearbook, 2005–2007.

migrant population — in other words, population statistics are collected according to the actual number of people living permanently in a given region. As a result of this statistical change, the population in 2006 exceeded what it was in 2004 by 12.0% in Guangdong, 5.9% in Beijing, 5.5% in Zhejiang, 5.0% in Tianjin, and 4.2% in Shanghai, and diminished by 10.1% in Chongqing, 6.4% in Sichuan, 5.4% in Anhui and Hubei, 5.3% in Hunan, and 3%–4% in Guizhou, Guangxi, and Henan (see Figure 1-8).

1.4   Concentration of Economic Activities and Its Influences

As is mentioned earlier, for a considerable period of time since the reform and opening-up, regional economies in China had been under the sway of an imbalanced growth pattern, and regional disparity was widening constantly, both of which were the outcome of the relocation and high concentration of economic activities — the manufacturing industry in particular — toward the coastal eastern region. During the 1980–2006 period, the share of GRP in national total increased by 12.1 percentage points, from 43.6% to 55.7% in

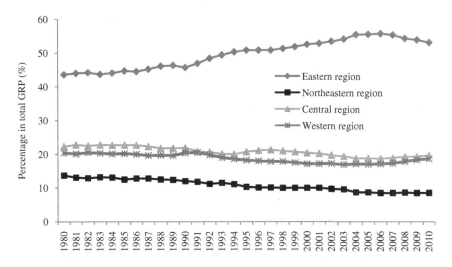

Figure 1-9   Changes in the Share of GRP in Various Regions.

Source: Same as Figure 1-2.

eastern region, but dropped by 5.2 percentage points, from 13.7% to 8.5% in northeastern region, by 3.6 percentage points, from 22.3% to 18.7% in central region, and by 3.3 percent points from 20.4% to 17.1% in western region. Figure 1-9 sheds some light upon the Chinese economic activities' trend of geographical concentration, that is, under the impact of the market force, economic activities are being constantly relocated and agglomerated to the prosperous eastern region. This trend is a result of the nation's transition to the market economy, which finds expression in the gravitation of diverse production factors and industries, the manufacturing industry in particular, toward the eastern region (Wei, 2004). However, it is worth noting that this situation has changed after 2007, the GRP proportion of the eastern region dropped to 53.1% in 2010, while the central and western regions increased to 19.7% and 18.6%, respectively.

According to the study by Wang and Wei (2006), changes were not obvious in the Chinese manufacturing industry's degree of geographical concentration during the 1980s. But at the beginning of the 1990s, the steady acceleration of the market-oriented reform and the vastly increased fluidity of capital and human resources intensified the growing trend of concentration. The gravitation of the manufacturing industry to the eastern region reached a peak after 1991. During the 1991–2003 period, the eastern region's portion in the nation's gross output value snowballed by 19.8 percentage points, from 53.5% to 73.3%. At the same time, the share of the northeastern region in the nation's gross output value plummeted by 5.5 percentage points, from 12.3% to 6.8%; the central region, by 7.4 percentage points from 18.2% to 10.8%; and the western region, by 7.0 percentage points from 16.1% to 9.1%. It goes without saying that Chinese manufacturing industry's agglomerating toward eastern region is incremental — it does not take the form of inventory transfers. As a result, approximately three-fourths of the country's manufacturing industry has been concentrated in a few areas in the eastern region.

The geographical concentration of the manufacturing industry in the eastern region is greatly discrepant. The eastern region maintained a stable share in manufacturing industry's national output value throughout the 1980s, while BSR region saw its share diminish somewhat, and the PRD region's portion expanded to a certain extent. Since 1991, the eastern region's share in the manufacturing industry's national output value rose by a remarkable 21.2 percentage points, from 52.1% in 1990 to 73.3% in 2003. Of this, the increase in the PRD region was the highest as it grew by 13.0 percentage points, from 5.7% to 18.7%; the YRD region came second, rising from 26.4% to 31.6% by 5.2 percentage points; the BSR region remained relatively stable, with its portion hovering between 17.5% and 20.0%. All but one of the 28 branches in the manufacturing industry showed the same tendency of gravitating toward eastern region with varying degrees, during the 1985–2003 period. The only exception is the tobacco industry, which was relocated to Yunnan, Sichuan, and Anhui in the central and western region. Among those branches whose share in the manufacturing industry's national output value expanded by more than 5 percentage points during this period, 18 were located in the PRD region, 13 in the YRD region, and 7 in the BSR region (Wang and Wei, 2006).

In a way, the trend of agglomeration in Chinese economy is conducive to overall resource allocation efficiency under the impact of the market force, but at the same time it tends to aggravate regional economic disparity, to the detriment of regional economic equilibrium. The experiences of developed market economies in Europe and North America prove that high concentration of factors and industries in a few developed regions can cause either over-denseness or over-sparseness in an economy. If this tendency is allowed to run unchecked in China, the benefit from the reform and opening-up and the robust progress of industrialization can be hogged by a few dominant eastern coastal regions, while the underdeveloped regions are in danger of being marginalized. Moreover, over-agglomeration of factors and industrial activities in a narrow geographic space can easily lead to uneconomical scales, thereby boosting costs, straining resource and energy supplies, aggravating the environment, and spoiling local residents' quality of life.

More than anything else, the fact that nationwide distribution of the Chinese population remains largely unchanged while the nation's economic aggregates and manufacturing activities keep relocating to the eastern region in these reform years can lead to spatial disequilibrium in the distribution of population and industrial activities. The high degree of disequilibrium in the distribution of population and economic activities is one of the major causes behind the grave disconnection between processing capacities and resource-producing areas, and behind the major nationwide transfers of resources, the major flow of the labor power, and the widening regional disparity. Especially, as the nation's significant economic regions, the PRD and YRD regions have failed to agglomerate their populations on a large scale when concentrating their industries on a large scale. As a result, the huge armies of immigrant workers in both regions can only be considered as members of a "floating population" or "*Nongmingong*" (migrant workers). In spite of their enormous contributions to the local economic boom, they find it hard to settle down as local residents, join the mainstream of local society, or share the benefits of industrialization they have personally labored and sweated to attain. It is fair to say that disequilibrium in the distribution of jobs (or industry) and population is crucial to the disequilibrium in the Chinese regional economic development.

1.5 From Concentration to Diffusion: A New Trend in Industrial Relocation in China

"Moving up north or going west" has been a spatial pattern for industrial development in China over the last few years. "Moving up north" denotes the relocation of FDI and domestic capital from the PRD region to the YRD region and further north to the BSR and northeastern region. "Going west" describes the move of companies and foreign investors from coastal regions to the central and western region. This trend signals that the regional economic development has entered a watershed period. A prime sign is that, in the distribution of the Chinese economy, the relocation of factors and industrial activities is being steered from the southeast coastal region to the central, western, and northeastern regions.

This new pattern of industrial relocation and diffusion can be observed from three points of view. First, from the viewpoint of the nation's total investment in fixed assets, as a result of the strategies to develop the western region, revitalization of the old industrial bases in northeastern region and other regions, and the rise of the central region, northeastern region, and central and western region have markedly accelerated their rate of growth in investment and steadily expanded their shares in the nation's total investment. In the meanwhile, the eastern region's growth rate of investment in fixed assets, which has been shrinking on a yearly basis after reaching an impressive 33.2% in 2003, has dropped below that of the central and western region and northeastern region. During the 2000–2010 period, the growth rate of investment in fixed assets averaged 26.0% in the central region, 24.8% in the western region, and 26.2% in the northeastern region, as against 19.6% in the eastern region. The northeastern region and central and western region gradually expanded their shares in the nation's total investment in fixed assets, while the shares of eastern region went on a decline (see Table 1-4.)

The second is from the viewpoint of FDI. Since the 1990s, the FDI inflow in China has begun to move from the PRD region to the YRD region and further up north to the BSR region. During the 1999–2003 period, the BSR's share in the nation's total value of FDI actually utilized shrank by 14.4 percentage points from 29.2% to 14.8%, whereas the share of the YRD region rose by 14.3 percentage points from 25.4% to 39.7% (see Figure 1-10) .The share of the BSR region increased from 20.3% in 1999 to 31.5% in 2004. After 2004, the share of the BSR region has somewhat dropped, while those of the PRD and YRD regions have grown to some extent. In the FDI's westward relocation, the share of central region in the nation's total value of FDI actually utilized grew from 7.5% in 1999 to 9.3% in 2004, the share of northeastern region rose from 4.1% to 9.0%, but the share of western region decreased from 4.5% to 2.6%. The FDI

Table 1-4 Growth Rates and Regional Distribution of Investment in Fixed Assets in China.

Year	Growth rate (%)					Regional distribution (%)				
	Nation	Eastern	Northeastern	Central	Western	Eastern	Northeastern	Central	Western	Not-classified by regions
2000	10.3	7.9	14.0	12.7	12.7	53.1	8.2	17.0	18.6	3.1
2001	13.0	11.3	14.2	14.2	17.2	52.3	8.3	17.2	19.2	3.0
2002	16.9	16.1	12.9	16.6	19.0	51.9	8.0	17.1	19.6	3.4
2003	27.7	33.2	20.8	27.2	27.3	54.1	7.6	17.1	19.5	1.7
2004	26.8	24.5	32.5	32.1	26.8	53.1	7.9	17.8	19.5	1.7
2005	26.0	21.9	37.6	28.9	28.3	51.4	8.6	18.2	19.9	1.9
2006	23.9	19.7	37.0	29.4	247	49.7	9.6	19.0	19.9	1.8
2007	24.8	18.7	32.3	32.8	28.4	47.2	10.1	20.2	20.6	1.9
2008	25.9	19.8	34.4	32.3	27.2	45.0	10.8	21.2	20.8	2.2
2009	30.0	22.9	26.8	35.9	38.2	42.5	10.6	22.2	22.1	2.6
2010	23.8	21.3	29.5	26.2	24.6	41.7	11.0	22.6	22.3	2.4
2000–2010	22.5	19.6	26.2	26.0	24.8					

Source: China Statistical Yearbook pertaining to relevant years, compiled by the NBSC.

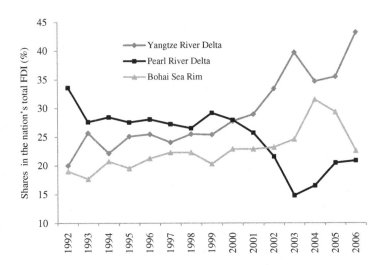

Figure 1-10   The Shares of Three Coastal Regions in China's Total Value of FDI Actually Utilized.

Note: The Bohai Sea Rim (BSR) includes Liaoning, Beijing, Tianjin, Hebei, and Shandong; the Yangtze River Delta (YRD) covers Shanghai, Jiangsu, and Zhejiang; and the Pearl River Delta (PRD) consists of Guangdong.

Source: China Statistical Yearbook pertaining to relevant years, *China Economy & Trade Yearbook* (2007) and statistics from the Ministry of Commerce.

inflow began its relocation from eastern region to central and northeastern region during this period; and it has speeded up its move toward western region since 2005. As a result, the western region's share in the total FDI inflow increased from 2.6% in 2004 to 3.5% in 2006, whereas the shares of the northeastern region and central region declined. A comparison between the 2001–2006 and 1979–2000 periods, however, reveals a certain degree of increase in the FDI shares of both central and northeastern regions (see Table 1-5).

Third, from the perspective of nongovernmental domestic investment, enterprises in coastal regions have raised their speed of relocation to the central and western region in recent years. According to statistics from the Office of the Leading Group for Western Region Development of the State Council (for short Western Development Office of the State Council, 2007), some 200,000 enterprises from eastern region invested a total of RMB 1,500 billion in western region from 2000 to June 2007. Of this, RMB 170 billion

Table 1-5 FDI Actually Utilized in Different Regions of China.

Year	Actually utilized value (billion US dollars)					Geographic distribution (%)				
	Regional total	Eastern	Central	Western	Northeastern	Regional total	Eastern	Central	Western	Northeastern
1999	41.00	34.42	3.06	1.84	1.68	100	83.9	7.5	4.5	4.1
2000	42.38	34.89	2.96	1.85	2.68	100	82.3	7.0	4.4	6.3
2001	48.89	40.34	3.43	1.92	3.20	100	82.5	7.0	3.9	6.6
2002	56.15	45.72	4.40	2.02	4.01	100	81.4	7.9	3.6	7.1
2003	56.32	45.95	5.32	1.72	3.33	100	81.6	9.4	3.1	5.9
2004	65.93	52.10	6.15	1.74	5.94	100	79.0	9.3	2.6	9.0
2005	62.63	53.56	4.09	1.94	3.04	100	85.5	6.5	3.1	4.9
2006	63.02	55.01	3.37	2.18	2.47	100	87.3	5.3	3.5	3.9
2007	79.82	65.64	5.45	3.68	5.05	100	82.3	6.8	4.6	6.3
1979–2000	354.27	292.45	23.21	17.24	21.37	100	82.6	6.6	4.9	6.0
2001–2007	732.39	356.66	32.26	16.38	27.10	100	82.5	7.4	3.8	6.3
1979–2007	786.66	649.11	55.47	33.62	48.47	100	82.5	7.0	4.3	6.2

Note: FDI actually utilized value was US$ 74.47 billion, but the plus sum from all regions was US$ 79.82 billion in 2007.
Source: *China Statistical Yearbook* pertaining to relevant years, *China Economy & Trade Yearbook* (2007), *China Commerce Yearbook* (2008) and statistics from the Ministry of Commerce of the PRC.

came from enterprises in Shanghai, and RMB 130 billion was invested by enterprises from Zhejiang and Fujian. This shows that with government policy support, private businesses in China are quickening their entry into the western region, thereby playing an active role in the great initiative to develop the western region.

The accelerating westward advance of coastal enterprises and foreign investors can be attributed to three reasons. First is the forceful support from government policies. In August 2007, in order to encourage coastal enterprises to move to the western region, the National Development and Reform Commission, Western Development Office of the State Council, and four other ministries and commissions jointly issued the *Proposals on Stepping up Interaction between Eastern and Western Region and Thoroughly Promoting Development of the Western Region*. The Ministry of Commerce has implemented the "Project for Enterprises Going West" (Wanshang Xijin Project), which encourages businesses in the central and western region to accommodate the industrial, processing, and assembling trade to be relocated from the coastal regions, and urges enterprises and economic and technological development zones in the coastal regions to open business in western region. Second is the rising costs of factors in the coastal regions. Large-scale industrial agglomeration over the recent years has markedly boosted the costs of diverse factors, strained land, and energy supplies and reduced the sustainability of the resources and environment in the PRD and YRD region. This has prompted Guangdong, Zhejiang, Jiangsu, and other coastal provinces to raise their entry threshold of industries and step up their industrial upgrading and environment protection efforts, thereby forcing local resource-intensive and labor-intensive processing firms to move to the central and western region. Third is the improved investment environment and efficiency in the central and western region. Thanks to the implementation of strategies to develop the western region and to facilitate the rise of central region, both regions have considerably ameliorated local investment environments and efficiency. In 2006, the ratio of total assets to industrial output value of all state-owned and non–state-owned industrial enterprises above designated size in western region averaged 13.7%, or 1.1 percentage points higher than in eastern region; and their ratio of profits to industrial cost averaged 11.3%, but only 6.2% in eastern region.[7] It can be predicted that, with the reform and opening-up process going in depth in the foreseeable future, coastal enterprises and foreign investors will speed up their move to central and western region.

1.6 Conclusions

In light of the analyses in the foregoing, this chapter reaches the following conclusions.

First, since the adoption of the reform and opening-up, regional economic development in China has come under an imbalanced growth pattern, and regional disparity has been widening continually. This is especially the case with the disparity between eastern and western regions, which has been growing at a higher speed after the advancement of nation's market-oriented reform in response to the remarks made by Deng Xiaoping during his January 1992 South China inspection tour. This indicates that the market force is a major factor leading the growing regional disparity in the current reform years. In other words, the ever-widening regional disparity is an outcome of the nation's transition from central planning to market economy. It should be noted, however, that this phenomenon occurred in the context of a robust economic growth throughout China since the adoption of the reform and opening-up. It is a kind of widening disparity in the midst of high-speed economic growth.

Second, as things stand today, regional economic development in China has entered a pivotal or "watershed" period in recent years. A few major indications are the high growth in investment in central, western, and north-eastern regions; a relative equilibrium that has been on the horizon at a time when regions are drawing closer to each other in terms of economic growth rate; narrowing disparities between the eastern and western regions and among provinces; and the fact that foreign investors and coastal enter-prises are quickening their relocation in western region. These encouraging changes are closely related to changes in the stage of, and environment for, the Chinese economic development. They are also a result of supportive

---

[7]Both indicators are calculated according to the arithmetic mean value of the index values of the provinces concerned. See Wei and Zhang (2008).

government policies. If this watershed period can bring about a smooth strategic transition, it can further promote sustained and stable high-speed growth of the Chinese economy. The robust Chinese economy will maintain its high speed of growth at least for 15 to 20 years.

Third, with coastal enterprises and foreign investors headed north and west, and with the central, western, and northeastern regions tapping into their inherent growth potentials, the regional economies in China will enter an age of a diversified competitive pattern marked by the emergence of a host of competing economic dynamos. Since the adoption of the reform and opening-up, China's high-speed economic growth has been sustained by the PRD, YRD, and a few other regions, which have emerged as the second generation of economic pace-setters for China in the wake of old industrial bases such as Shanghai and Liaoning. Judging from the future pattern of development, a number of "latecomers" — such as Beijing–Tianjin–Hebei metropolitan area, Shandong Peninsula urban agglomeration, Harbin–Dalian industrial belt in northeastern region, Zhongyuan urban agglomeration, Wuhan urban circle, Changsha–Zhuzhou–Xiangtan urban agglomeration; Chengdu–Chongqing metropolitan area, and Guanzhong urban agglomeration — are likely to become new economic pace-setters and growth poles for China, thereby bringing about a diversified competitive pattern marked by the emergence of a host of competing economic dynamos.

References

Li, D. (2004). Reflections on GDP. *Economic Research Journal*, (4), 26–28.

Liu, S. *et al.* (1994). Calculation and Analysis of Regional Income Disparity in China, and Policy Proposals. In S. Liu, Q. Li and T. Xue (Eds.), *A Study of Regional Economic Development in China*. Beijing: China Statistics Press.

Mao, T.-t. (1999). *Collected Works of Mao Tse-tung*. Vol. 7. Beijing: People's Publishing House.

Western Development Office of the State Council (2007). *Step up the Interactions between the East and West Region, and Further Promote Development of the Western Region: A Summary of Relevant Issues*, November 23.

Wang, Y. and H. Wei (2006). Characteristics of Industries, Competition for Space and the Geographic Concentration in Manufacture. *Management World*, (4), 68–77; 171–172.

Wei, H. (2004). Industrial Agglomeration in China: Characteristics, Problems and Countermeasures, *Economic Perspectives*, (9), 58–61.

Wei, H. (2007). Regional Economic Disparity in China's Transition to Market Economy: Social Impact and Policy Adjustment. *Research on Development*, (4), 1–8.

Wei, H. and D. Zhang (2008). Development of China's Western Region: Status Quo and Major Issues. *Review of Economic Research*, (5), 14–18.

Wei, H., K. Liu, M. Zhou, D. Yang and W. Hu (1997). *The Development of Regions in China — Economic Growth, Changes of the System, Regional Disparity.* Beijing: Economy & Management Publishing House.

Wei, H. *et al.* (2005). *A Study of Readjustment of Industrial Location in China.* Internal research report. Beijing: Institute of Industrial Economics, Chinese Academy of Social Sciences.

Chapter 2

Theoretical Issues in the Current Regional Economic Development

Wei Houkai

Since the reform and opening-up of China's economy, its regional economic development has advanced by leaps and bounds, which has lead to a great demand for the study of the regional economic theory. In the face of huge demand from economic practice, the academia has strengthened research on some of the major theoretical issues in the regional economic development. Different scholars have proposed a variety of views from different angles and have launched a fierce debate on this topic, which have played an important role for the prosperity and development of China's regional economics. However, so far, the academia has not come to a consensus on certain theoretical issues in the current regional economic development, and many issues still need to be further studied. This chapter aims to focus on a number of major theoretical issues in regional economic development and express my own opinions so as to arouse contention in the academia and inspire in-depth exploration.

2.1 The Selection of Central Regional Policy Goals

The contention that the Chinese central government's regional policy should pay more attention to efficiency or fairness has been the source of a long-standing debate. In general, there are three main perspectives. The first one prioritizes efficiency, which emphasizes that the central government's regional policy goal should focus on efficiency and give priority to supporting regions with its own advantages and favorable conditions, particularly the developed regions, to accelerate development. The second one prioritizes fairness, which stresses that the central government's regional policy goal should focus on fairness. They advocate that priorities should be given to support key problem areas, especially the backward and declining areas, to accelerate development. The third one advocates proper consideration of both efficiency and fairness, that is to say, the central government should simultaneously achieve the twin goals of efficiency and fairness. In addition to the above opinions, some scholars propose to emphasize the coexistence of fairness and efficiency (Lan, 2006), while others propose to pursue the unity of fairness and efficiency (Zhang and Zhao, 2000). In fact, this point of view is almost the same as the third one mentioned above, just differing in expression. In the priority theory, the academia used to highlight "the priority to efficiency with due consideration to fairness", but in recent years, "prioritizing fairness and taking into account of efficiency" has been put forward (Wang and Yang, 2001). These two views can be seen as the modification and improvement of the priority theory.

Due to the different beliefs in theory since the foundation of New China, the Chinese central government has been indecisive over the goal of regional policy for a long time, leading to several major changes of the objectives regarding efficiency and fairness. As far as the relationship between Eastern and Western China is concerned, when the central government focuses on efficiency, the more developed eastern region can enjoy more preferential treatment; however, when focus is shifted to fairness, the relatively backward Western regions, or "third-line" regions can receive more attention. As a result, the central region located in the middle ground has long been "squeezed". In the longer period after the reform and opening-up, the central government's regional policy attached more importance to efficiency, and the eastern part of China, with its more advantageous position, benefited greatly in investment and policy. This kind of situation did not change until the recent couple of years. Under the impact of such preferential policy, the average industrial tax bearing of the Western region is much higher than that of the eastern region. In 2004, suppose the proportion of taxes of the industrial products sales revenue in the eastern region is 100, then that of the central region is 172,218 for the western region, 160 for northeast region (Institute of Industrial Economics of the CASS, 2006).

Table 2-1   Average Tax Bearing of Industrial Enterprises Above Designated Size in Various Parts of China.

| Regions | The percentage of taxes in the sales revenue (%) | | | Relative level | | | | | |
| | | | | Take the whole country as 100 | | | Take the East as 100 | | |
	2000	2004	2008	2000	2004	2008	2000	2004	2008
Whole country	6.1	4.7	4.8	100	100	100	125	127	120
East	4.9	3.7	4.0	80	79	83	100	100	100
Northeast	7.8	6.0	4.8	127	126	100	160	160	120
Central	7.4	6.4	6.4	122	135	133	153	172	160
West	10.1	8.1	7.1	166	172	148	208	218	178

Note: The industrial enterprises total taxes are the sum of product sales taxes plus extra charges and VAT.

Source: Institute of Industrial Economics of the CASS, 2006; Wei and Yuan (2010).

The average industrial tax bearing of the western region is 2.18 times that of the eastern region (see Table 2-1). In 2008, the average industrial tax bearing of the western region is still 77.5% higher than that of the eastern part (Wei and Yuan, 2010).

There are three main factors attributed to the comparatively higher average industrial tax bearing in the central and western regions in the recent years. The structural factors come first. The energy and raw materials industries occupy a large share in the central and western regions. In terms of light industries, the alcohol and tobacco industries enjoy obvious advantages, most of which belong to the high-tax industries. Second, the state's preferential policies matter. In recent years, although China has implemented the strategy of western development and central rise, policies and measures with real value are rare. Up to now, the various "special economic areas" that enjoy more preferential treatment given by the central government, such as special economic zones, economic and technological development zones, export processing zones, bonded zones, bonded port area, and the Pudong New Area and the Binhai New Area, are still mainly concentrated in the eastern region. A vast majority of the various preferential policies implemented by the central government to attract FDI and encourage exports have benefited the eastern region. Third, due to the weak economic strength and the severe shortage of the financial resources in the central and western regions, tight policy is adopted during tax collection in order to fill the ever-growing fiscal gap. In contrast, the developed eastern regions have abundant financial resources, implementing a loose policy to "turn on the water pisciculture". Under such circumstances, the enterprises in the central and western regions, compared with those in the east, are mostly faced with a "tight" taxation environment.

In terms of the rural–urban relations, due to overemphasis on efficiency, extensive government resources have been invested in the central cities, especially in large- and medium-sized cities with more advantages, whereas the small towns and rural areas have long been ignored. The "city governs county" system implemented a couple of years ago further exacerbates this trend of "centralization". As a result, under the joint efforts of government policies and market forces, the central city simply became the carrier absorbing the resources and factors from the countryside, which produced an extremely negative impact on the rural and county's economic development. At the same time, because of the administrative allocation of resources and the domination by the principle of "efficiency first", government resources are asymmetrically deployed in the administrative centers at all levels throughout the country, especially in the provincial capitals. Under such circumstances, the vast majority of the provincial capital cities have become the largest cities in terms of local population and economic scale. This phenomenon has become a major feature of the current Chinese economy.

When evaluating the objectives of the central government's regional policy, one must take the institutional background and stage of development into account. In the planned economy system, because the government owns and controls most of the resources, the central government's regional policy is more of a policy about production allocation. Therefore, in the distribution of resources, the central government has to take both the efficiency and fairness objectives into consideration. Since the reform and opening-up, China has transferred from a planned economy to a market economy. In the early stages of this transition, the market mechanism is far from perfect, so the central government still controls a considerable part of the resources, coupled with the low level of economic development, it is understandable the central government's regional policy focuses more on efficiency goal in order to accelerate national economic development and narrow the gap with the developed countries. However, after over 30 years' practice of reform and opening-up, China has initially put in place a basic framework of the socialist market economy. Studies have shown that the degree of marketization of China's economy has reached 73.8% in 2003 (Institute of Economic and Resources Management, Beijing Normal University, 2005). However, there is still controversy in the academia over the ability to accurately measure the degree of marketization. What is certain, however, is that the degree of marketization of the Chinese economy has been greatly improved. Moreover, China's comprehensive national strength is markedly enhanced and the level of economic development is significantly improved. In such a situation, the efficiency and fairness issue, which requires overall consideration by the government in the past planned economy era, will be handled by the market and government together. The market mechanisms can play the basic role of spatial configuration of resources, while the government leads a role of regulation, supervision, and positive guidance.

As we all know, efficiency or interest is the basic principle when market distributes resources. Thus, under the conditions of market economy, the market mechanisms will be mainly relied on to achieve the goal of efficiency in resource allocation. However, international experiences prove that market forces alone will normally be expanding rather than narrowing the regional gap (Myrdal, 1957). This is because, under the market's benefit-driven principle, capital, talent, and other factors will flow from the slowly growing backward regions to the prosperous developed regions, thus exacerbating the widening of regional disparities. As a matter of fact, since the reform and opening-up, and with the expansion of market forces, factors such as the capital and human resources are pouring out of the backward central and western regions into the eastern developed regions, and out of the rural areas into urban areas, especially into the large and medium-sized cities. Such large-scale mobility has already become an indisputable fact. In particular, the market-oriented reforms initiated in the state-owned commercial banks during the recent years have enhanced the intermediary function of absorbing funds from the central and western regions to invest into the east, i.e., investment from the rural areas into the cities. Brain drain is also very prominent in the central and western backward region and in the old industrial base of the northeast; for instance, the initial "Peacocks Fly to the Southeast" later evolved to "Sparrows Fly to the Southeast". The assembly of production factors as well as the mobility trend will inevitably intensify the widening of the gap of urban and rural areas, further exacerbating the degree of social disharmony. Thus, for the central government, the regional policy should put more or major emphasis on fairness objectives. For example, for the key problem areas, which are too serious to be solved by themselves, and which are indeed in need of government's aid and support, the government must offer timely help rather than perfecting the already developed and prosperous regions. These key problem areas include the underdeveloped, poverty-stricken areas, the old industrial bases in the recession, the resource-based cities in difficult transformation, the major grain-producing areas with a heavy financial burden, and the border areas blending of various problems (Wei, 2006).

Hence, it can be learned, from a macro-strategic level, that efficiency and fairness are the different principles followed by the market and government intervention, respectively. The former is the principle followed by the market mechanism which only functions to despise the poor and curry favor with the rich, while the latter is the principle followed by government intervention, which pays attention to offering timely help and ensuring justice and harmony. From the perspective of the income distribution process, the former can be seen as the initial distribution of national income while the latter is the re-distribution of national income. Therefore, in the socialist market economy, the central government's regional policy should first give full play to the basic role of market mechanisms on this basis, and then highlight and emphasize the fairness objectives, execute "inverse-market regulation" to remedy market failure, provide more aid and support to all kinds of key problem areas rather than simply focus on efficiency goals as before by implementing the "pro-market adjustment," and give strong support to the prosperous and developed regions. With the market mechanism marching to perfection, it is redundant and unnecessary for the central government to implement the "pro-market adjustment" regional policy anymore, because the improvement of market mechanisms can serve the same purpose. More importantly, this approach will ceaselessly enlarge a trend of regional disparities and increase social disharmony factors. It does not conform to the scientific outlook on development and the requirement of building a socialist harmonious society, which may even cause distortions of the market mechanism and prevent the market mechanism from functioning. From the experience of developed countries, almost no country would set the goal of regional policy as expanding the gap between regions.

It needs to be pointed out what I have emphasized is that the central government's regional policy should focus more on fairness objectives from the national macro-strategic level, and the central government should concentrate on providing regional aid and support to the key problem areas which are truly in need of state support. This is not to say that the central government does not need to take efficiency issues into consideration when choosing the specific assistance program. In fact, during the enforcement of the policies, the central government has to give consideration to both fairness and efficiency when providing aid and support to the key problem areas. Especially in the early stages of development, appropriate emphasis on the principle of efficiency is highly necessary. This means, on one hand, the central government ought to focus on fairness goals by supporting the poverty-stricken and most needy group of people in the problem areas; on the other hand, the government needs to place appropriate emphasis on efficiency goals by assisting the group of people with the highest potential in these areas. From the nature of central assistance, the former is equivalent to a donation while the latter can be regarded as a kind of investment. This sort of assistance, which is like an investment or can stimulate investment, will not only enhance self-development capability of the problem areas but also improve their sustained competitiveness.

2.2 The Gradient Theory and the Gradient-Transfer Strategy

The gradient theory and the gradient-transfer strategy have been disputed for more than two decades in the Chinese academic circles. The reason for such a long-running debate is that the various kinds of perspectives in the background imply or represent the interests of different regions. As a result, the theoretical argument in the academia has become a battle of interests among various regions. The concept of "gradient theory" was first put forward by Xia and Feng (1982) from the eastern part of China. Later, He (1983) further summarized the theory as "gradient-transfer law of domestic technology transfer". They argue the imbalanced development of economy in China has formed a technology gradient in the country; for example, some areas possess "advanced technology", some areas have "intermediate technology," while other areas only have "traditional technology". Therefore, we should give full play to the technology gradient, and let the regions, where conditions permit first master the world's advanced technology, and then gradually shift to the "intermediate technology" zone, and finally to the "traditional technology" zone. With the development of the economy, the acceleration of technology transfer will gradually narrow the gap between different regions. Obviously, what is referred here is a technological gradient-transfer strategy. However, in the use of the notion, a very broad concept — "gradient theory" is adopted. Thus the groundwork has been laid for confusing gradient theory with the gradient-transfer strategy in the academia, as well as the long-term dispute between the two theories.

In fact, the gradient theory and the gradient-transfer strategy are two totally different concepts. In any country and region, both economic and technological gradients exist objectively. The economic and technological gradient transfer also occurs widely, such as industry and technology transfer from developed regions to the backward regions, or movement to the suburbs and rural areas from urban centers. Therefore, in a broad sense, we can collectively name all the theories and perspectives applied to reveal and explain the formation and change of the economic and technological gradient as "the gradient theory". Gradient-transfer strategy is a strategic concept, which originally advocates that the developed eastern regions first master the world's leading technology, after digestion and absorption, and then gradually transfer and spread to the central and western regions. Afterward, some other scholars extended the strategic thought of technical gradient transfer to state investment allocation, key developing areas, and opening-up, arguing that the focus should be first placed on opening-up and developing the eastern region, after the conditions are ripe, and then gradually be shifted to development to the western region. This strategic thinking involves the interests of various regions, causing widespread controversy in the academic and political circles. The most distinctive views are from the central and western scholars and politicians; these views, including "anti-gradient theory" (Guo, 1986), leaping strategy theory (Gu, 1985), combination of east and west theory (Lin, 1985), "center flowering" or central rise theory,[1] etc. In fact, the conflict of these development strategies is no longer a purely academic dispute, but a fight for development privileges and national key support for their own regions; therefore, it is also a battle of economic interests.

Apparently, the gradient-transfer strategy is brought forward mainly for national strategic decision of introduction of technology, opening-up to the outside world, institutional reform, and investment distribution, advocating the allocation of state resources that should follow the gradient and launch gradually. This is a typical planned economy mindset, with its implicit theoretical premises as follows: (1) The economic and technological gradient is objective and reasonable; (2) efficiency is prioritized when the central government gives out aid and support to regions; and (3) there is less stickiness or resistance of the gradient transfer. It now appears that these preconditions are not fully established. First of all, economic and technological gradients among China's eastern, central, and western regions, though being an objective reality, is not entirely reasonable. We cannot use unreasonable objective existence as the basis for the government's future strategic decisions. In fact, the current striking disparity between the east and west in China has become a major obstacle to building a moderately prosperous society and a harmonious socialist society. Second, in the initial stage of the reform and opening-up, the central authorities focused more on efficiency goals for the purpose of accelerating economic growth since market forces were relatively weak. However, with the socialist market economic system gradually becoming established and perfected, the central government's regional policy should divert and place emphasis on equality objectives rather than giving priority to efficiency. Third, the domestic and international experiences indicate that the economic and technological gradient transfer has strong stickiness or resistance, requiring the government to guide actively through policy. Even so, sometimes this cannot produce preferable results. Japan's development of Hokkaido is a typical example. In the case of China, although the central government in recent years has encouraged foreign capital to invest in central and western regions, the actual effect is not obvious. Especially in 2005, foreign direct investment

---

[1]Also known as "Cow Belly Theory". See Zhang (1997).

(FDI) in China further concentrated in the east, and the proportion of actual utilization of FDI by the 10 eastern provinces and municipalities among the total of all regions increased 6.5 percentage points over the previous year, an increase of 3.0 percentage points compared to 2001.

In addition, the initial gradient-transfer strategy also has the following shortcomings (Wei, 1990). First of all, this strategy divides the three regions in terms of geographical units and regards the comprehensive technical level as indicators to mark out the technology gradient. Obviously, this method of division is very rough. In fact, many major cities in central and western regions, such as Xi'an, Wuhan, Chongqing, and Chengdu, boast of strong scientific and educational strengths, which is far from comparison with the eastern cities. Second, the transfer of technology gradient is just one form of spatial technology transfer (diffusion), rather than a common law. Spatial technology transfer has multiple forms. In terms of technical gradient, there are vertical gradient transfer and counter-gradient transfer, or cross-gradient transfer as well as horizontal transfer. From the perspective of spatial pattern of the technical transfer (diffusion), the main forms include hierarchical diffusion, radiative diffusion, and neighborhood diffusion. Third, the gradient-transfer strategy regards the technology gradient as the only criterion to determine a country's investment preference and key development regions. As a matter of fact, in all countries, whether developed or developing, the choice of regions to be selected as the first key development areas is influenced and restricted by many factors. In the outline of China's the Eleventh Five-Year Plan, it is clearly put forward that "the region's resources and environmental-carrying capacity, the current development density and development potential must be taken into account when considering and coordinating China's future population distribution, economic allocation, spatial use, and urbanization patterns, dividing the country's territory into four main functional areas of optimized development, key development, restricted development, and prohibited development".[2] This suggests that China's future key development areas will be determined by three criteria, namely resources and environmental-carrying capacity, existing development density, and development potential,

---

[2]See the "Eleventh Five-Year Plan for National Economic and Social Development of People's Republic of China", March 16, 2006.

rather than technical gradient alone. Fourth, the gradient-transfer strategy envisages narrowing down the regional disparities through the acceleration of technology transfer. However, this argument lacks solid evidence both in theory and in practice. A large number of empirical studies have shown that, with the economic development, technology transfer does speed up, but this shift is more of a horizontal one, which means to transfer technology to the regions on the similar level, rather than the vertical gradient transfer.

Thus, if without careful analysis, the initial technology-gradient transfer is applied to the state investment allocation, reform and opening-up, and even institutional reform simply by analogy, which will inevitably bring about a series of problems. In fact, since the reform and opening-up, some gradient-transfer approaches taken by the government in state investment allocation, the practice of opening-up, institutional reform, etc., has become one important reason for aggravating regional disparities, especially the gap between the east and the west, and triggering social disharmony. Take the effects of opening-up for example, between 1979 and 2005, 81.2% of the actual use of FDI all round China was concentrated in the 10 eastern provinces and municipalities, while the 6 central provinces, the 12 western provinces and municipality, as well as the 3 northeastern provinces, respectively, accounted for only 7.6%, 4.5%, and 6.7% (Wei and Liu, 2006). In 2005, the eastern provinces and municipalities made up 88.5% of China's total export, while the 6 central provinces, the 12 western provinces and municipality, as well as the 3 northeastern provinces held only 3.6%, 3.5%, and 4.4%, respectively. It is obvious that FDI and foreign trade exports are highly concentrated in a few coastal regions, significantly deepened the regional disparities. At present, since the government favors foreign investment enterprises with "super-national treatment" and since most foreign business in China cluster in the coastal region, it becomes another crucial factor contributing to the high average industrial tax bearing in the central and western regions. Therefore, it can be assumed that the reform and opening-up has accelerated the process of China's economic globalization, but this globalization is mainly accomplished in a small number of coastal regions, while the vast areas of the Central and Western China were unable to enjoy many benefits during the globalization tide (Wei, 2005).

Of course, to examine from a historical aspect, in the initial stage of reform and opening-up, considering the imbalance of economic and technological development in China, the gradient-transfer strategy advocates to gradually narrow the gap between regions, which has, back then, played a vital role in transforming the concept of China's regional development and gradually deepening the research of strategic theory. In particular, under the then historical conditions, due to the low level of economic development, limited comprehensive national strength, the central command of major resources, and the strong colors of planned economy, the government took the lead to support the coastal regions with better conditions to develop first, which is believed to be a last-resort option. Given the historical conditions at that time, market forces were very weak, and the central government's regional policy needed to consider not only the efficiency goal but also the equality objective. With the gradual transition of Chinese economy from a planned economy to a market economy, the strategy of giving priority to supporting coastal development becomes obsolete, for it will just further widening the regional disparities and inciting social disharmony. As mentioned earlier, in a socialist market economy, the central government's regional policy should focus more on equality objective, and make contributions to promote social harmony, not the other way around. Therefore, under the new historical circumstances, there is no such a thing as "gradient-transfer strategy". Strategy, here referring to a method adopted by the government, should not be confused with technological and industrial gradient transfer in a market economy. It can be said that this technological and industrial gradient transfer is an objective existence, a result of market forces, which the government should actively guide.

2.3 The Migration of Labor and Movement of Jobs

During the process of promoting coordinated development of regional economy, the dilemma "should jobs move to people, or people to jobs" (Hoover, 1990) has long been a controversial issue for the government policy-makers. From the perspective of spatial configuration of resources, the former is to let the assembly of the labor force attract capital to create jobs, which I call "moving capital by labor" strategy; the latter is to let the accumulation of capital or jobs attract migrant labor to come, which I call "moving labor by capital" strategy. The migration of jobs between regions can be understood as essentially the relocation of capital. Here, the capital refers to a complex compound of funds, technology, marketing experience and brand, etc.

The two regional development strategies are not entirely opposite. They have their own advantages and disadvantages and can complement each other. For government policy makers, whether to put more weight on "moving capital by labor" strategy or "moving labor by capital" strategy, the main consideration should be given to three aspects. First, compare the cost of movement of capital with migration of labor. Generally speaking, the movement of capital is much easier, and comprehensive cost is much lower, especially considering the long distance and many restrictions posed to international labor migration. Past experience has indicated that the large-scale population or labor migration tend to be very costly and highly unstable because these immigrants have to face a new environment, bear tremendous psychological stress, and endure a lifestyle change. Second, it depends on the orientation of the policy objectives adopted by the government. If the government pursues efficiency and focus on GDP growth, it will follow the "moving labor by capital" strategy to create more jobs in those capital-gathering centers; whereas if the government pursues fairness with emphasis on balanced regional development, it would turn to "moving capital by labor" strategy to produce more jobs in the relatively labor-concentrating areas. Third, different strategies should be adopted during different stages of development. In the early stages of economic development, due to the low level of development and limited economic strength, capital agglomeration tendency is more evident, and thus more efforts should be paid to "moving labor by capital" strategy. In the mid- and late stages of economic development, with increased level of development and economic strength, there is a growing trend of capital diffusion and thus the strategy of "moving capital by labor" should be adopted by a gradual transition to capital-moving mainly.

From the perspective of national macro strategy, since the reform and opening-up, China has mainly taken a "moving labor by capital" strategy, namely to create more employment opportunities in the eastern region, to attract the large amount of labor force from the central and western regions. It is undeniable that this strategy historically has some rationality because it can take advantage of the superior geographic location and the relative abundance of capital, talent, and technical factors of the eastern region so as to give full play to the agglomeration economies and reduce uncertainty. However, the implementation of this strategy also has many drawbacks.

First, it intensifies the tendency for production factors and economic activities to concentrate in the east. Between 1980 and 2005, the GRP of the 10 eastern provinces and municipalities accounted for 55.5% of nation's total, an increase of 11.9 percentage points from 43.6%, while the 3 northeastern provinces; 6 central provinces; and 12 western provinces, autonomous regions, and municipality decreased by 5.0, 3.5 and 3.4 percentage points, respectively. According to our research, from 1985 to 2003, the production capacity for manufacturing industries, such as steel, petrochemical, electronic information, and textiles all switched to the east, except the tobacco industry. After analyzing 28 manufacturing industries, it is discovered that there are 18, 13, and 7 industries in the PRD (Guangdong) and the YRD (Jiangsu, Zhejiang, and Shanghai) and the BSR (Beijing, Tianjin, Hebei, and Shangdong) which witnessed a growth of over 5 percentage points of the proportion of industry output value of the nation's total (Wang and Wei, 2006). In fact, since the reform and opening-up, some manufacturing industries in the central and western regions, such as consumer durables, textiles, and garments, have started to show signs of decline. Obviously, if this phenomenon cannot be effectively curbed, some of the backward central and western regions will face the danger of being "marginalized".

Second, it fuels the mismatch between population distribution and the economic activities. In 2005, the population of 10 provinces and municipalities in eastern China (excluding Liaoning and Guangxi) occupied only 36.1% of the country's total, but accounted for 55.6% of the country's GRP, 59.8% of industrial added value, 89% of total exports, and 85% of the actual use of FDI. In view of its development trend, the uncoordinated coefficient of the distribution of population and GRP is 14.6 percentage points in average from 1980 to 1990; the number increased to 18.1 percentage points from 1991 to 2000, and further rose to 20.3 percentage points from 2001 to 2005.[3] Obviously, the high degree of uncoordinated distribution of

---

[3]The uncoordinated coefficient of the distribution of population and GRP $= \frac{1}{2} \sum |GRP - P|$. *GRP* and *P*, respectively, refers to the proportion of regional GRP and population to the country's total GRP and population. It reflects deviation of economic activity distribution to the population distribution.

population and economic activity is closely related to the current migration policy, which makes it extremely difficult for the labor force to settle down, but to "floating". The result is to further deepen the gap between regions, especially East and West.

Third, there is a profound discrepancy among the origin of resources, processing locations, and consumption areas, resulting in the large mobilization of various resources all over the country. China's resources, energy, and population are mainly located in the central and western regions, while the processing and manufacturing industries are highly concentrated in the eastern part, and this trend will be further strengthened. Thus there is a nationwide labor flow and a huge mobilization of resources, including the large-scale "migrant workers tide," "South-to-North water diversion project," "West-to-East natural gas transmission project," and "West-to-East electricity transmission project", which not only worsens the transportation system but also adds to unnecessary waste of resources.

Fourth, the household registration reform lags far behind. Although a large number of labor forces from the central and western regions are long employed in the PRD, YRD, etc., it is difficult for them to settle down and enjoy the fruits of reform and opening-up with the local people. Workers from central and western regions, while having made tremendous contributions to the prosperity of the eastern region, are labeled only as "migrant workers" and are regarded as "marginalized" at present.

At present, there are a variety of job opportunities in the PRD, YRD, and other coastal regions, but the labor supply has already become very tight or even experienced a shortage. In contrast, the central–western and northeastern regions maintain a large surplus labor, but the jobs are very limited. Therefore, to address the serious imbalance between the distribution of the labor force and jobs and promote coordinated development of the regional economy, we must appropriately deal with the relationship between "moving capital" (moving jobs) and "moving labor". At present, on the national macro level, China has entered a new stage, shifting its emphasis from the past "moving labor by capital" to "moving capital by labor". In other words, we have to adjust the national strategy on industrial location in a timely manner and make great efforts to create more jobs in the central–western and northeastern regions to advance their industrialization and urbanization, achieve coordination of the regional jobs opportunities and labor distribution, to promote its economic development compatible with resources and environmental-carrying capacity, and stimulate the harmonious development between man with nature. Meanwhile, the reform of household registration system should be advanced to allow people from other parts of the country who have fixed jobs to settle down in the east so that these migrant workers can share their interests while contributing to the eastern prosperity. Of course, from the medium and micro view, in a certain area, more focus should be placed on "moving labor by capital" strategy through creating more jobs in the area with enormous development potential, especially the urban areas, and guiding people in the rural and ecological-fragile areas to gather here.

In fact, in recent years, one of the important tasks of carrying out the western development, the northeast revitalization, and the central rise is to create more jobs in the central–western and northeastern regions. Up until now, some still hold a negative attitude toward developing the western region. They propose large-scale population migration or the central government's transfer payments to alleviate poverty. It cannot be denied that population migration and transfer payments do play an important role in narrowing the gap, but to rely solely on these measures cannot solve the problem once and for all. First of all, as we all know, China's western regions occupy more than 70% of the country's territory, with a population of 360 million. Even without considering the limit of resources and environmental-carrying capacity in the east, it is unrealistic to trigger the emigration of hundreds of millions of people from the west. Not to mention as a socialist country, China should not allow only a few regions get wealthy and prosperous first, while leaving two-thirds of the total land areas to wane. That is to say, across the country, we should not only pursue the prosperity of the people, gradually closing the gap in per capita income and living standards between different regions, but also take into account the prosperity of the territories, achieving the coordinated regional development. Besides, since the resources and environmental-carrying capacity in the eastern regions is limited, it is impossible to absorb all the surplus labor who have emigrated from other regions. In fact, there is a trend of weakening the carrying capacity of metropolitan areas in the PRD and YRD over the recent years. In the near future, the key task is to push ahead industrial restructuring and upgrading, rather than constantly promoting the large-scale population and industrial agglomeration. This requires the timely transfer and dissolution of industries that do not have or are about to lose comparative advantages. As for the transformation of processing trade in the PRD and other regions, a combination of local upgrading and industrial transfer should be adopted.

Generally speaking, there are two ways to create abundant jobs in the central–western and northeastern regions: one is to activate the local capital, especially private investment, and encourage all people to innovate and venture; the other is to actively guide foreign investment and coastal enterprises to "moving up north and going west". In recent years, there is an emerging trend of the foreign investment and coastal enterprises shifting to the central and western region, as long as the central government would actively guide them through policy, the tendency of industrial transfer will be dramatically accelerated. At present, there are three main obstacles which hinder the foreign investment and coastal enterprises from "going west". First, compared to the east, the soft environment for investment in the west still lags far behind. Second, the low industrial supporting capacity in the west cannot meet the demand of large-scale development of manufacturing industries. Third, the companies in the western region bear a heavy tax, which is much higher than the average level of the eastern region. Therefore, the central government should guide the industrial transfer and expansion in the PRD, YRD with "carrot and stick" approach. The so-called "stick" is to set higher industry access standards, including technical content, the independent innovation capacity, energy consumption per unit of output, the "three wastes" emissions, output per unit of land, and other indicators, to encourage the coastal economic core area to speed up industrial upgrading. The so-called "carrot" is to give policy support to foreign capital and coastal enterprises investing in the central-western and northeastern regions, such as land supply, the government-funded interest discount, and tax preferences. Obviously, the large-scale entry of private capital at home and abroad will be a strong impetus to advance the process of developing the western region and revitalizing the northeast old industrial base.

2.4 Spatial Agglomeration of Economic Activities

It is a long-standing controversial issue in the academic circles as to whether the human economic activity should be centralized or decentralized from the aspect of spatial distribution. The Southern Jiangsu model is a typical representative of township enterprises development in the 1980s. At that time, people were willing to embrace the mode of "leaving the land but not the countryside, entering the factory but not the city". The development pattern turns out to be "every village lights a fire" and "every household belches smoke". In fact, this is an advocate of industrial decentralization, ruralization, or non-urbanization model of development. Southern Jiangsu's experience has proved that the early industrial decentralized model is unsuccessful, which is not consistent with today's general economic and social development trends. Beginning in the 1990s, Southern Jiangsu devoted significant efforts to launch the campaign of "constructing cities" and "setting up parks". They aimed to use the all sorts of industrial parks and cities and towns as the carrier, actively guide the economic activities to cluster in urban areas and industrial parks, and take a road of industrial centralization, realizing the interaction of industrialization and urbanization. Clearly, in today's information era, industrialization must take the road of centralization and urbanization, rather than decentralization and ruralization.

At present, both the central government and the local governments at various levels have attached great importance to promote and guide the concentration of industrial activities to the advantageous regions. In the recent couple of years, governments at all levels have promulgated and implemented numerous policies, among which, the proposition to promote industrial agglomeration appears frequently. Compared with the past decentralized industrial allocation ideas, it is undoubtedly an important step forward to promote and guide the practice of industrial clustering, because it can give full play to regional advantages and improve the efficiency of spatial allocation of resources. However, industrial agglomeration, as a neutral concept, has a dual character, that is to say, it may have both positive and negative effects. In government planning and policy-making, simply advocating to enhance and guide the industrial agglomeration is not entirely correct. What we are pursuing is a reasonable industry concentration compatible with the resources and environmental-carrying capacity, rather than placing undue emphasis on the promotion of industrial clustering.

Industrial agglomeration, being an important economic phenomenon in life, has both reasonable and unreasonable clustering. Generally speaking, unreasonable industrial agglomeration is mainly reflected in two aspects: one is the excessive agglomeration. A large number of the population and industries accumulate in a small geographical space, beyond the carrying capacity of the regional resources and the environment, resulting in non-coordination of the population, economy, as well as the resources and environment, and produce serious problems of diseconomy of agglomeration, such as traffic congestion, environmental degradation, energy shortage, and tight supply of resources. The other is ineffective or uncorrelated agglomeration. This refers to a kind of gathering that is inefficient or lack of industrial correlation. For example, when attracting investment, some industrial parks are indiscriminate toward all the companies. The corporations introduced lack of industrial association, moreover, the industrial allocation of parks lack specialization and functional division. It is like "a large sack filled with a lot of potatoes". Therefore, the phenomenon of "only companies but no industries" appeared, leading to the inefficient or unassociated agglomeration.

Therefore, for any region, we must proceed from the realities, conduct reasonable and orderly development in accordance with its resources and environmental-carrying capacity, and promote and guide the industries to cluster reasonably, instead of engaging in over-development or "over-exploitation," which exceeds the carrying capacity of resources and environment and accumulates excessive population and industries. The key here is to grasp the "degree" of land development, based on the carrying capacity of resources and the environment. At present, overexploitation has emerged in some cities of China's PRD and YRD regions. According to data provided by the NDRC, the land development intensity in Shenzhen has reached up to 40%, 38% in Dongguan, 30% in Foshan, and 29% in Shanghai, all much higher than that of the foreign metropolitan areas. For instance, the figures for the three major metropolitan areas in Japan are 15.6%, 19% for Hong Kong, 20% for Stuttgart in Germany, 21% for Paris (Yang, 2008). Therefore, for urban areas, "two lines" must be reasonably determined, i.e., the upper limit of the intensity of land development and the lower limit of eco-space so as to grasp the intensity of territorial development scientifically and promote the formation of a reasonable spatial structure. As for the state-level optimized development areas and key development areas, the overall development intensity is recommended to be less than 25%; furthermore, as for cities in the two types of main functional areas, the development intensity should not surpass 30% (Wei, 2008).

From a national perspective, whether the phenomenon of overconcentration has appeared in the PRD, YRD, and Beijing–Tianjin–Hebei Metropolitan areas remains a controversial issue. Particularly, in the past several years, some scholars believe that the carrying capacity of the three major coastal metropolitan areas is still large and therefore require further enhance the industrial agglomeration among the three areas. For example, in the special study for National Medium- and Long-term Science and Technology Planning, it argues that Japan's three major metropolitan areas (Greater Tokyo, Hanshin, and Nagoya) account for 70% of the country's total GDP, while China's three major metropolitan areas account for only 35% of the total GDP. So, there is still a large gap between China's three major metropolitan areas and the world-renowned metropolitan areas. In other words, they still possess significant potential and space to further gather more industries in the future. Obviously, there is no comparison between the two. The Greater Tokyo area in Japan occupies 9.8% of the country's territory and owns 32.6% of the total population, while China's three major metropolitan areas account for only 3.62% of the country's territory and 15.11% of the whole population but contribute to 32.18% of the total GRP in 2008 (Wei, 2010). Meanwhile, referring to the cases from abroad, the proportion of total economic output of the major metropolitan areas is relatively high, and its proportion of the population is also high, and the two are basically coordinated. However, China's PRD, YRD, and Beijing–Tianjin–Hebei metropolitan areas show a different picture. The large-scale gathering of industries in the past did not bring about corresponding large-scale gathering of population, resulting in serious non-coordination between the distribution of population and economic activities. In 2008, the ratio of population share to output (GRP) share in China's three coastal major metropolitan areas went up to 1:2.13. Compared with other countries, in 2000 the ratio in the core developed regions of the US was 1:1.21, 1:1.36 in Japan's Tokyo, Osaka Prefecture, and Kanagawa Prefecture, and 1:1.24 in Britain's Greater London, Greater Manchester, and West Midlands region (Li and Fan, 2003).

In fact, since the reform and opening-up, with the large-scale clustering of various kinds of industries, nowadays there have been signs of the so-called "city disease", such as traffic congestion, energy, and power shortage; tight industry land use; rising cost of production factors; and environmental degradation in the PRD, YRD, and other metropolitan areas, whose resources and environment-carrying capacity is declining day by day. Therefore, to some extent, over-exploitation or over-density of the economy has already appeared in the three major metropolitan areas. Under this circumstance, in order to enhance the coordinated development of regional economy, the central government, on one hand, ought to promote and guide the industry to reasonably cluster, and on the other hand, it ought to actively guide the decentralization of the industries and prevent "city disease" in certain areas caused by "overconcentration" as well as the economic marginalization in some remote areas, resulting in the issues of "overdensity" and "oversparseness" of economy. From the national level, the focus should be placed on reasonably guiding the enterprises and industries of the PRD, YRD, and other coastal regions to expand to the central–western and northeastern regions. At present, we can learn from the experience of regions such as Greater London and Greater Paris, and adopt the approach of "carrot and stick" when dealing with the industrial diffusion in the PRD, YRD, and other coastal regions. On one hand, the central government should provide the corresponding policy support to the industries transferred from the coastal regions to the central–western and northeastern regions, such as land supply, investment and employment subsidies, subsidized loans, tax preference, and accelerated depreciation. On the other hand, the governments at all levels should gradually raise the access threshold of the industries in the PRD, YRD, and other coastal regions, vigorously guide and accelerate industrial upgrading, raise the level of participation in the international labor division and economic globalization, and enhance the international competitiveness of industry.

References

Gu, Z. (1985). Rethinking the New Technological Revolution and the "Leaping Strategy". *Economic Problems*, (10), 47–49.

Guo, F. (1986). The Definition and the Real Meaning of "Anti-Gradient Theory". *Research on Development*, (3), 39–40.

He, Z. (1983). On the Domestic Technology Gradient Process. *Science Research Management*, (1), 18–21.

Hoover, E. M. (1990). *An Introduction to Regional Economics (Chinese Edition)*. Beijing: The Commercial Press.

Institute of Economic and Resources Management, Beijing Normal University. (2005). *A Report on the Development of China's Market Economy 2005*. Beijing: China Commerce and Trade Press.

Institute of Industrial Economics of the CASS (2006). *China's Industrial Development Report 2006*. Beijing: Economic & Management Publishing House.

Lan, Q. (2006). On Fairness and Efficiency in the Coordination of Regional Economic Growth. *Probe*, (2), 121–124.

Li, G. and H. Fan (2003). The Distribution of Production, Population and Regional Inequality. *Economic Research Journal*, (11), 79–86.

Lin, L. (1985). East-West Combination in China's Strategic Layout. *People's Daily*, December 9.

Myrdal, G. (1957). *Economic Theory and Underdeveloped Regions*. London: Duckworth.

Wang, Yan and Xiuchang Yang (2001). Giving Priority to Fairness with Due Consideration to Efficiency — Fairness and Efficiency in the Operation of Regional Finance. *Journal of Shanxi Finance and Economics University*, 23(S2), 59.

Wei, H. (1990). Comments on China's Macro Regional Development Theory. *China Industrial Economics*, (1), 76–80.

Wei, H. (2005). Globalization, National Strategies and Regional Difference of China. *Journal of Jiaxing College*, (1), 91–95.

Wei, H. (2006). Directional Adjustment of China's Regional Policy during the "Eleventh Five-Year" Period. *Study & Exploration*, (1), 15–24.

Wei, H. (2008). Achieving Development and Affluence but not through Exploitation, *People's Tribune*, (3), 18–19.

Wei, H. (2010). Accelerating the Transformation of China's Urbanization and Urban Development. In Jiahua Pan and Houkai Wei (Eds.), *China Urban Development Report No.3*. Beijing: Social Sciences Academic Press.

Wei, H. and C. Liu (2006). Negative Effects of Foreign Funds Utilization in China and the Direction of Strategic Adjustment. *Henan Social Sciences*, 14(5), 21–25.

Wei, H. and X. Yuan (2010). On the Evaluation and Directional Adjustment of Tax Policies of Western Development in China. *Taxation Research*, (2), 3–8.

Xia, Y. and Z. Feng (1982). *Gradient Theory and the Regional Econom: Research and Suggestions.* Vol. 8. Shanghai: Shanghai Science Research Institute.

Yang, W. (2008). Promote the Establishment of Main Functional Area, Optimize the Pattern of Spatial Exploitation. *Economic Review*, (5), 17–21.

Zhang, P. (1997). Cow Belly Theory. *The Economic Izvestia.* May 16.

Zhang, S. and N. Zhao (2000). Seek the Unity of Fairness and Efficiency: Assessment of Western Development Strategy. *Management World*, (6), 25–33.

Chapter 3

A Critical Review of Theoretical Research on Firm Relocation

Bai Mei

Today, due to the increasing globalization, regional integration, and urbanization, international and domestic markets are experiencing increasingly intense competition. Both international companies and domestic small and medium enterprises (SMEs) have accelerated their progress of firm relocation, in order to obtain and maintain the competition advantage, to occupy the leading position, and to find better location for production and management. As a result, many actions have been made, such as (1) changing the headquarters (HQs) location, (2) establishing new research and development (R&D) branches in other places, and (3) moving the manufacturing factories to those countries or regions with lower manufacturing costs. As firm relocation is of increasing concern to enterprises and local government, it has been adopted as one of their business strategies; for example, an important strategy of the government of many regions is to improve local development by attracting international enterprises. With the increasing number of firm relocations, scholars worldwide have started to pay attention to this trend.

Foreign countries started the research of firm relocation from 1950 onward,[1] and the researches were mainly to discuss the firm relocation condition of British enterprises, with some about Dutch, German, French, and Italian companies. Most of the foreign firm relocation studies were based on

---

[1]There is another viewpoint, the firm relocation research started from Webber's industrial location theory. Weber's location theory involves firm location and location factors, but these studies are not aimed at the firm relocation.

empirical and case studies, while some were pure theoretical researches; the established firm relocation models were mainly empirical models, within which the main topic was to study the motivation of firm relocation and the policy influence. China started the firm relocation research from the beginning of this century. According to the literatures, the studies were concentrated on the aspects, including influencing factors of firm relocation, the ways of firm relocation, and firm relocation of private enterprises.

3.1 Factors Influencing Firm Relocation

From the review of Chinese and foreign literatures, it has been found that large numbers of literatures have researched the influencing factors of firm relocation, including internal and external factors, regional policies, and location factors.

3.1.1 *External Factors*

The first book that studied firm relocation motivation was *Why Industry Moves South: A Study of Factors Influencing the Recent Location of Manufacturing Plants in the South*, by McLaughlin and Robock (1949). This book obtained support from Planning and Development Committee, Tennessee, USA. In this book, McLaughlin and Robock described the condition of American manufacturing, during the mid-20th century, moving from the Northeast America, which was initially manufacturing hub, toward the southeast regions. They also pointed out that the reason leading to this relocation event is the constant high cost of labor force in Northeast America and the enormously fierce competition between enterprises, alongside the fact that Southeast America is a region with a high number of low-cost labor force, less local trade association, and less fierce competition. Stressed in their research was the effect of company external factors. According to a paper published by Garwood (1953) in the journal *Economic Geography*, from his research on the firm relocation of Utah and Colorado, market and raw material are also factors that affect companies to move to Utah and Colorado. By using the data analysis method, Scott and Rooth (2002), from the Department of Economics, University of Portsmouth, UK, collected the historical data of enterprises that moved to UK during the WWII, and obtained the following conclusion: temporary tariff was a main reason causing enterprises to move to UK. With an increasing number of companies moving from the central district of the cities to the suburbs, people began to realize that the main reasons for this phenomenon are (1) lack of room in urban areas, (2) increasing land price, (3) traffic and parking problems, and (4) labor market issues. Overall, during the period from WWII to 1970s, academics were concerned about the external condition that influences firm relocation, i.e., the external force that pushes enterprises to leave the current location and the external force that pulls enterprises to move to new places.

3.1.2 *Internal Factors*

From a further-step research about the firm relocation reasons, academics found that the decision of a firm to relocate can be influenced by its internal dynamic adjustment, rather than traditional external factors. Cameron and Clark (1966), Keeble (1976), and Townroe (1972) all proved that the company's internal factors — such as firm expansion — could be an important reason for firm relocation. As one of the forms of firm expansion, firm spatial expansion has three types: spatial centralization, spatial integration, and spatial diversification. Spatial concentration is an expansion that the enterprise's production and business activities concentrate in the same space. Spatial integration means that the activities of the company's business (one single business) are expanded within different spaces, which include horizontal and vertical integration. Spatial diversification is the expansion activity in which the operation of different businesses of the company is distributed toward different spaces. In addition, horizontal integration refers to the condition that the same production line is distributed in different spaces, whereas vertical integration refers to the condition in which different sections of one same production line are distributed on different spaces. A common trend of firm spatial expansion is from single plant of a region to multiple plants of a region; then to the inter-regional expansion within a country, i.e., multiple plants of a country; subsequently to multiple countries and finally numerous plants within many countries in the global (Chapman and Walker, 1987). This trend can be perfectly explained by the expansion process of Haier.

3.1.3 *Regional Policy as an Influencing Factor for Firm Relocation*

Since the 1950s, many countries have provided different types of subsidies for firms that moved to developing or recession regions, in order to reduce the inequality of inter-regional income and job opportunities. For example, the industrial decentralization and industrial suburbanization policies implemented by the Dutch government relocated the industry from the core areas to other areas and moved the industrial zones from cities (such as Amsterdam, Rotterdam, Hague, and Utrecht) to suburbs. Similar policies have also been adopted by the French government to avoid the concentration of industry within Paris, and these policies have obtained sound results. Today, academics are studying the policy influence on firm relocation and assessing the firm relocation policies. For example, Ortona and Santagata (1983) described the effect of local land-use policies on firm relocation in Turin, Italy. Keeble (1976) believes that regional policy is an important reason that caused the inter-regional industry relocation phenomenon in the UK during 1966 to 1971, and he concluded that all the policies, including regional policies, could have a certain effect on the firm relocation. During the 1970s, people held forth the view that firm relocation is an effective way to balance the regional development. On one hand, firm relocation solves problems like congestion, labor force, and space capacity of the core areas; on the other hand, it encourages companies to relocate from the core areas to the outskirts in order to effectively improve the development of backward areas, thereby solving the inequality problems of regional development. However, this conclusion was disagreed by Cameron and Clark (1966) with their research on the same question during the same period. They raised the point that the result of the regional policy, as expected by the government, was mostly inconsistent with the result of firm relocation, and normally they can be quite contradictory. Especially during the 1990s, as learned from the experience in 1980s, people believed that using firm relocation to develop regional economy may not be a good idea, and the key to regional development is to have more energetic economic condition by establishing regional innovation environment. If a region lacks resources required for innovation, then the effective subsidy for this region should be the improvement of the construction of necessary infrastructures and knowledge center.

3.1.4 *Location Factors on Firm Relocation*

Recently, as regional integration became an important feature of current regional economies, academics have tried to analyze the effect of regional integration on firm relocation. Barbier and Hultberg (2001), University of Wyoming, USA, discussed firm relocation under the condition of regional integration. They believe that, in addition to the size of the market, the degree of regional integration is one of the factors that influence firm relocation. They have also established a model with two countries and two firms.

Some studies focus on changes at the macro-level of the population, as a result of processes of birth, death, migration, as well as growth/decline and ageing of existing firms. An example of such a macro-level study based on a micro-simulation model can be found in Van Wissen (2000).

3.2 Dynamic Mechanism of Firm Relocation

The main theories behind the explanation of motivational mechanism of firm relocation include the neo-classical theory, the behavioral theory, and the new institutional theory.

3.2.1 *The Neo-classical Theory*

The neo-classical theory of firm relocation studies assume that rational firms would choose those locations that have highest profit potential. When a firm is no longer in its marginal profit space, it will lead this firm to relocate to a different place (pushing force), which can be a region with the potential of profit (pulling force). The main factor that promotes the firm to relocate is the cost of transportation and labor force. In fact, there are two key implied assumptions within the neo-classical firm relocation theory: (1) the manager has reasonable knowledge and decision-making ability, and (2) the manager tries to obtain the maximum profit.

The neo-classical theory of firm relocation, which is derived from standard classical economic theory, focuses on cost-minimization or profit-maximization theories. The general principle of classical location theory was proposed by Isard (1956) based on the theory of Adam Smith (Porter, 1998), which has then been named as least-cost theory. The principle of the theory is that enterprises choose the best production location based on the point with lowest production cost. According to the theory of agricultural location by Johann Heinrich von Thünen, the cost of agricultural production is considered as the most important factor, but this theory only discusses the transportation cost of the product from the production place to the market, without taking into account the costs in fuel, raw materials, and labor. However, the German scholars Launhardt (1882) and Weber (1929), who were the earliest representative of least-cost theory, promoted this school into a systematic theory. Alfred Weber's theory of the location of industries points out that an industry shall be located where the transportation costs of raw materials and final product is a minimum; whereas for other location factors, such as labor or external economies, the consideration shall be similar for the least-cost analysis. Apparently, the total cost can be obtained by calculating the costs of all the location factors, and similarly the location profit can be calculated as well. The profit of the firm in a location is equal to the total income within this location minus the total cost, thereby determining whether a location is profitable This method can be used to define the spatial margins to profitability. The spatial margins to profitability refer that the firm can only be profitable within certain areas, exceeding which, even a little, could lead to financial loss. Supporters for the spatial margins to profitability theory include the British economic geographer E. M. Rawstron (1958) and the American economist D. M. Smith (1966, 1971).

Following the neo-classical location theory, Nakosteen and Zimmer (1987), from the University of Evansville in Indiana, USA, proposed a decision model which explains the behavior of firm relocation by measuring the profit. Anderson *et al.* (1992) studied the spatial equilibrium of firms and established two types of location equilibrium: the first is a simultaneous price and location game; whereas the second is a two-stage game — i.e., location-then-price game. The equilibrium locations under the second are further apart, since firms internalize the harmful price competition effect of moving close to each other.

The model of Nakosteen and Zimmer is as follows and based on the assumptions that (1) the aim of the firm is to reach profit-maximization and (2) individual firms, in the aspects of products and factor markets, are price takers. Under this circumstance, the decision of firm relocation is made among many factors that influence the profit margins. Therefore, for a firm i, which is to maximize its profit margin and is located within the region of

j, the profit function is:

$$E_{ij} = E(X_i, Z_j, \varepsilon_{ij}) \tag{3-1}$$

where X_i is the observed firm- or market-specific factor; Z_j is the observed regional-specific factor; and ε_{ij} is the unobserved firm-region specific factor, which is normally presumed to follow a random distribution for different industries. For a specific industry k, firms would check their profitability regularly to compare with the expected profit threshold. This profit threshold is determined by the competition standard of different industry. Due to the change of the external environment and internal condition of the firm, the profit margin of some companies may decrease, or even be lower than the expected profit level of the industry as a whole, i.e.,

$$E_{ijk}(X_i, Z_j, \varepsilon_{ij}) < E_k \tag{3-2}$$

According to the standard economic theory and from the point of long-term development, if the average variable cost cannot be compensated by the output price, then these marginal firms would be shut down. In the economic reality, however, not all the marginal firms would be shut down, as some firms might consider relocation to the regions with lower costs, increasing the profitability to the expected profit level E_k. Clearly, if a firm expects to obtain higher profitability from another place, relocation could be a good solution. It is important to compare the cost and profit between two places so as to make the decision whether the firm should relocate some of its activities. As a result, with the relocation being taken as a capital investment project, the increase of profit from this project during the period of t is:

$$PV_i(t) = \int_t^\infty (E_{ij'} - E_{ij})^{-rt} dt - C_{ij'} \tag{3-3}$$

in which, j' is the competition region; r is the discount rate of shareholders; and $C_{ij'}$ is the relocation cost of the present value. Apparently, the presumption whether the firm should practice relocation is the discount value of the profit difference between the expected region and the current region, which value shall be higher than the relocation cost of this firm, i.e., $PV_i(t) > 0$.

3.2.2 *The Behavioral Theory of Firm Relocation*

Not satisfied with the explanations — such as pushing, pulling, and maintaining factors — of the decision-making behavior, some academics believe that these above-mentioned explanations could not be an in-depth understanding of firm relocation, and, in fact, some unknown reasons are the key for making the decision of firm relocation. Under the assumption that the firm is rational and the information is complete, the neo-classical firm relocation theory can be viewed as ideal and valuable for using professional terms of economics to explain the optimal space behavior of the firms; whereas when the information is not complete or with other uncertainties — e.g., the firm's ultimate aim is not to maximize the profit — it is very difficult to understand the internal motivation of the firm's relocation decision under a certain condition. More essential and in-depth factors, therefore, shall be identified to better study the process about how the decision makers consider the firm relocation decision, and during this process what the limits could be. The earliest study of the decision making process is the behavior school; Neo-classical and behavioral schools of thought have proposed different theories to explain such location decisions (Hayter, 1997; Pred, 1969). During the 1970s, Townroe (1972) described this method and proposed five successive stages of the decision process: (1) stimulus, (2) problem definition, (3) search, (4) formulation and comparison of alternatives, and (5) choice and action. The choice-stage was further divided into eight subsequent steps. Later, Lloyd and Dicken (1977) produced even more complicated models of the location decision-making process. It is very scarce to see the application of their schemes and models in empirical research. Therefore, the understanding of regional decision-making process is still standardized and descriptive, rather than empirical. In the 1990s, the interest in studying firm relocation decision-making process was aroused once again. Louw (1996) gave an example of a practical application of decision stage models in his PhD thesis about location choice behavior of (migrating) large offices in The Netherlands. Louw divided the decision-making process into three phases, *viz.*, an orientation phase, a selection phase, and a negotiation phase. This roughly corresponds to the phases 3, 4, and 5 of Townroe (1972). It turns out then, that spatial factors (these are geographical position, accessibility, parking possibilities, proximity of facilities and public transport, and quality of the spatial surroundings) play an important role in the first two phases. However, financial and contractual factors are getting more important in the third phase, as the result of negotiation. The spatial factors in the decision process is most important when firms want to own their site and building, and relatively less important in case of a firm renting its premises. For the theory study, people have high interest in the decision-making process during firm relocation. But currently, there are still a lot of uncertainties about the firm decision-making process, especially the process during the firm's relocation. In addition, the method for studying firm relocation decision-making process is still limited as very descriptive. Even for case study of the relatively more rigorous statistical model about the Dutch firm, (Van Dijk and Pellenbarg, 2000) the drawback is that it overly relied on questionnaire survey and empirical researches, obtaining conclusions with high amount of description and exploratory, thereby lacking of explanation model, which has higher applicability. Meanwhile, similar to the neo-classical firm relocation theory, this theory gave too much concern to the location factors, while insufficient attention to questions like the production, investment, and expansion process of the company. Another drawback is that the behavior theory overly considered about the *soft* variables such as social and psychological issues, while ignoring the economic variables (Scott, 2000). Therefore, it might be more applicable to use the combination of firm relocation behavior theory with the neo-classical theory.

3.2.3 *New Institutional Theory of Firm Relocation*

Till the 1980s, the neo-classical and behavior theory of firm relocation have received quite a lot of criticism, because both are under static conditions to study how firms make the choice from a group of options, and both study the decision-making mechanism of firm relocation under static conditions. The firm needs to make the decision from several locations. As a result, some researchers believe that the spatial economic process is mainly determined by the cultural institutions and value systems of society. In other words, to study the firm relocation, what shall be considered is not only firm behavior but also the social and cultural connotations embedded the behavior.

The assumption of the new institutional theory is that the spatial economic process is formed by social and cultural institutions and value systems, rather than the firm's location behavior. The environment is either the interface of location factors that have been filtered by the enterprises or the information carrier; the firm's location behavior can be viewed as the result of the negotiation — about price, wages, taxes, subsidies, and infrastructure — with the suppliers, government, trade unions, and other organizations. As the firm has to negotiate with its distributors, suppliers, local government, trade unions, and other organizations for the key issues about the production, such as price, wages, taxes, subsidies, and infrastructure, the location behavior of the firm is the result of the negotiations. The research method can be well applied for large firms, because the large firms have better negotiation skills and ability, bringing more influence toward the surrounding environments. It is clearly useful to use the institutional theory to understand the firm's spatial dynamic behavior. However, there still exists criticism for the institutional theory. If the combination of economic and non-economic factors was considered, then the firm relocation decision-maker is either "*homo economicus*" or "satisficer man" (Pellenbarg *et al.*, 2002; Pellenbarg, 1985).

3.2.4 *Motivation of HQs Relocation and R&D Relocation*

The firm relocation has also been studied from the aspects of value chain, which includes the relocation of production, HQs, and R&D. It is also believed that their motivation may be different, and the firm relocation of each industry has its own dynamic mechanism, which shall be separately studied.

(1) Change and dynamic mechanism of HQs relocation. The HQs relocation is always closely related to the economic development level of a country (Wei, 2006). With the change of economic development and external environment, the location of the firm's HQs will experience a process from decentralization to centralization, and then relative decentralization. Based on the change of economic development level, Semple and Phipps (1982) proposed a four-stage model for the firm HQs relocation. At the early stage, limited by the infrastructure, especially by transport and communications conditions, the HQs of large firms are normally located at the national control centers, which are always the capitals or the primary cities. At the second stage, besides the capitals or primary cities, some regional control

centers will be formed with the development of national economy and the improvement of the transportation. At the third stage, the major regions will be full-blown, and there will be no real control centers. The location of the firm HQs will show the tendency of decentralization. Currently, the US is stepping into this stage. A feature of the fourth stage is a more mature country. During this time, there would be no national or regional control centers, and the HQs would be, to the largest extent, decentralized around the country. The studies of the Chinese academics indicate that the HQs of large companies and the research organizations are centralizing toward the major cities of China; while in some advanced economies, the HQs are decentralizing, due to the rapid development of transport and communication technologies. According to relevant research, during the 1980s, the number of top-500 companies in the US which set up their HQs in cities like Atlanta, Boston, Washington, Philadelphia, Richmond, and Dallas was increasing, whereas that in big cities like New York, Chicago, Los Angeles, and Detroit was decreasing. Holloway and Wheeler (1991) base their time-series analysis on data for Forture 500 companies. Both studies find evidence of redistribution among the head quarters cities away from New York to mostly mid-size metropolitan areas. This locational change was mainly caused by the relocation of firm HQs and mergers between companies.

(2) R&D change feature and policy study. The main reasons why multinational firms set up the R&D activities within the home countries are: (1) to locate the main R&D activities within the home country that could have better control of the development of new technologies, reducing the potential risk of technical innovation leakage; (2) R&D activities of enterprises have apparent advantage of centralization: therefore, the R&D carried out in home countries could make full use of scale economies effect, reducing the potential of high costs caused by the decentralization; (3) the HQs in home countries can have better financial control, making the best use of all kinds of academic instruments and equipment and reducing cost; (4) the centralization of R&D organization can also avoid the repeated researches or high communication expense due to the spatial distance and language barrier, all of which are likely to be caused by the decentralized condition; and (5) to prevent the industrial hollowing-out, the home country government, e.g., Japan, may ask the firm to complete the research and manufacturing of core techniques or products.

3.3 Research on Firm Relocation in China

Since the end of the 20th century, a phenomenon began to appear wherein those firms from Zhejiang province, China — especially from Wenzhou city — relocated outward. Limited by the resources and environment and room for development, some private enterprises in Zhejiang began to relocate to those regions with less resource limit and cheaper land price. In March 2005, the local government of Guangdong province published *Opinions on Joint-promoting Industrial Transfer between Mountain Area, East and West Wings, and Pearl River Delta (for Trial Implementation)*. The aim is to promote the relocation of labor-intensive industries from the PRD region to the East and West Wings, and achieving a coordinated economic development of Guangdong province. This firm relocation phenomenon soon attracted the interest of many academics; for example, Liu's paper (2001) can be viewed as the earliest research about the Chinese firm relocation condition; Wei (2004, 2006) was the first academic who discussed the firm relocation issues within the textbook *Industrial Economics and Regional Economics*, arousing people's concern about firm relocation; Bai (2003a, 2003b, 2005) began researching firm relocation for her doctoral thesis. She introduced foreign firm relocation theories to China, together with a detailed and systematic theoretical research. From the questionnaire and analysis conducted by Enterprise Investigation Team of NBSC and Zhejiang Enterprise Investigation Team (2005) about the Zhejiang firm relocation issues, Chen (2002), Zhao (2003), Qian and Wu (2003), Wen (2004), Xiang (2004), Yi (2005), and other researchers have provided valuable researches about the Chinese firm relocation phenomena.

On the other hand, Wei (2003) analyzed the relationship of firm relocation with the company competitiveness and regional competitiveness. He believes that firm relocation can be viewed as a dynamic game between the firm and the government — in not only the moving-out areas but also the moving-in areas — as well as an environmental competition between different local governments. From the point of view of spatial expansion, the first stage of the relocation of firm economic activities is the relocation of the sales department, followed by the manufacturing factories, and finally the relocation of R&D department alongside the HQs. The firm relocation could have positive or negative influences on the competitiveness of the firm, the moving-in area, and the moving-out area. Therefore, viewed from the point of government intervention, it is necessary to have some guide and regulation to avoid all kinds of unnecessary adverse effects, thereby achieving a win-win-win result.

Based on the analysis of several case studies, Bai (2003a) summarized the patterns of firm relocation; established a firm relocation dynamic model under the analysis framework of Neo-classical theory; analyzed the internal, external, and location factors of firm relocation from many perspectives such as firms, regions, and cities; summarized some basic laws involved in the firm relocation, raising the point that relocation possibility of the manufacturing firms is higher than that of other industries, and compared with SMEs, those big companies may have more frequent relocation activities; and discussed the governmental subsidy involved in firm relocation. Bai (2007) also studied the relocation of Chinese listed firms' HQs and the related policies.

Liu (2001) believes that the firm relocation is becoming very active, which not only affects the enterprise's own business activities but also has great external effect, changing the pattern of regional economic development and improving the competitiveness of a country as a whole. Therefore, the government shall encourage the firm relocation and try to reduce the relocation cost, improving the management structure of the competition between regions.

Living in YRD region, Zhao (2003), of Fudan University, has relatively more direct and clear observation of the Chinese private firms' relocation phenomena. He believes that the main reason is the change of factors required by the enterprise development and the competition between local governments. Yi (2005) conducted a research about the private firm relocation in the Southeast regions of Fujian, proposing that the increasing prominent finance "bottlenecks" problems of the Fujian local private companies caused the firms to move out.

Current China's empirical researches are mainly about Zhejiang province. Taking Haining — a more economically developed city in Zhejiang — Qian (2003) used the questionnaire survey of 200 companies to study the opinion of rural enterprises about relocation. He mentioned two main factors that affect the concentration of rural firms: the degree of life satisfaction of the entrepreneurs at different regions; and the relocation cost.

Wen (2004), by focusing on third-line enterprises, studied the effect of relocation on firms. He thinks that the firm can get rid of the geographic limit by relocating, and start resource integration within new business places, thereby improving the productivity level of various factors and the competitiveness of the company.

Close attention has been paid to the firm relocation from the perspective of government in Zhejiang province. Based on the survey of about 600 companies, the Enterprise Investigation Team of NBSC and Zhejiang Enterprise Investigation Team (2005) studied the firm relocation within Zhejiang and among Jiangsu, Zhejiang, and Shanghai. Some important conclusions have been obtained: (1) the quantity of firm relocation in Zhejiang — both moving in and moving out — is increasing, and the level of relocation within the YRD region is higher than that cross the YRD region. (2) Most of the moving-out firms are labor-intensive companies and the relocation is mainly for company expansion. The percentage of Zhejiang companies moving to other provinces was extremely high — as much as 83.7%, 34.4 percentage points higher than that of companies moving into Zhejiang province (49.3%). Shanghai, Jiangsu, Jiangxi, etc., are the main destinations for the moving-out Zhejiang firms. Shanghai presents advantage for central management, which holds great attraction to HQs relocation; whereas Jiangsu, Jiangxi, etc., show advantages in the production side, which can be seen as factor attraction. The moving-out firms in Zhejiang are concerned more about (1) land resource (agreed by 55.6% of respondents of the questionnaire), (2) power supply (45.4%), (3) raw materials and energy supply (42.9%), and (4) available policies of tax reduction or exemption (41.8%). The concerns of the moving-in firms were: (1) land resource (46%), (2) improvement of corporate image (42.7%), (3) available policies of tax reduction or exemption (40.7%), (4) awareness of government services (35.3%), and (5) supporting industry and market size (33.3%). In addition, the percentage of companies that moved in with the entire company as a whole was 15.3%, which was higher than the figure of moving-out companies by 10.2%.

3.4 Conclusion

In this research, we noticed that the foreign firm relocation services, compared with that in China, are also very striking. In the US, there are many consultancy companies who provide firms with relocation services and provide the governments with the price that can attract firms from different places. GMAC Global Relocation Services is the largest global relocation management company, with HQs located in the US. GMAC Global Relocation Services provides international companies with individualized relocation and human resource management services (Bai, 2003a). Later, organized by GMAC Global Relocation Services, National Foreign Trade Council (NFTC), and SHRM Global Forum, the annual report — Global Relocation Trends Survey Report — has been published since 1993. This survey is mainly about the human resource problems within global firm relocation. Some international accounting companies, such as Ernst & Young, Deloitte and Touche, also provide consultancy services, including information like government policies, taxation, infrastructure, labor force, plant equipment, and living conditions.

The firm relocation theories have opened new horizon of microscopic study of regional economics. Domestic and foreign scholars have conducted huge amounts of research on the influencing factors, formation mechanisms, regional effects, and related policies of firm relocation. These studies can help us understand the basic laws and trend of the firm relocation activities. Meanwhile, the high amount of firm relocation activities provides us with excellent research background and prospects for future policies application. However, from the quantity and content of relevant literatures, both Chinese and foreign studies still lag behind the real practice of firm relocation. In addition, research on firm relocation is yet to become a main branch of regional economics study, leaving considerable room for further development. Combining with the Chinese firm relocation reality and the feature of regional economic development, the future directions of this research should be: (1) to research the firm relocation by combining with the problems of regional development, and to discuss the effect of firm relocation on improving regional development, i.e., how to make relevant policies, from the central government point of view, based on the common pattern of firm relocation, encouraging the firms and industries to relocate on a proper and reasonable way; (2) to discuss the basic features and patterns of relocation of enterprise HQs and R&D etc., effectively; and (3) to study the common pattern of Chinese firms relocation to a further depth, connecting the domestic study with our foreign peers.

References

Anderson, S. P., A. De Palma and G. S. Hong (1992). Firm mobility and location equilibrium. *Canadian Journal of Economics*, 25, 76–88.

Bai, M. (2003a). *Research on Firm Relocation*. Doctoral Dissertation, Nankai University, Tianjin.

Bai, M. (2003b). Research on the Strategies of the MNCs' International Relocation. *Journal of Henan Normal University (Philosophy and Social Sciences Edition)*, (2), 34–35.

Bai, M. (2005). Review of Three Theories of Firm Relocation and their Development. *Economic Perspectives*, 8, 83–88.

Bai, M. (2007). *Research on Headquarter Relocation of Chinese Companies and the Policy*, Post-doctoral graduation thesis, Chinese Academy of Social Sciences.

Barbier, E. B. and P. T. Hultberg (2001). *Economic Integration, Environmental Harmonization and Firm Relocation*, Working Paper, Department of Economics and Finance, University of Wyoming.

Cameron, G. C. and B. D. Clark (1996). *Industrial Movement and the Regional Problem*, University of Glasgow Social and Economic Studies, Occasional Paper No.5. Edinburgh: Oliver & Boyd.

Chapman, K. and D. Walker (1987). *Industrial Location: Principle and Policies*. Oxford, UK: Basil Blackwell.

Chen, J. (2002). Empirical Research of Current Chinese Firms Relocation — Based on Analysis of Questionnaire Report of 105 Companies from Zhejiang Province. *Management World*, (6), 64–74.

Enterprise Investigation Team of NBSC and Zhejiang Enterprise Investigation Team. (2005). Why Zhejiang Companies are Moving out. *China National Conditions and Strength*, (3), 16–17.

Garwood, J. D. (1953). An Analysis of Postwar Industrial Migration To Utah and Colorado. *Economic Geography*, 29(1), 79–88.

Hayter, R. (1997). *The Dynamics of Industrial Location: the Factory, the Firm and the Production System*. New York: Wiley Chichester.

Holloway, S. R. and J. O. Wheeler (1991). Corporate Headquarters Relocation and Changes in Metropolitan Corporate Dominance, 1980–1987. *Economic Geography*, 67(1), 54–74.

Isard, W. (1956). *Location and Space-Economy*. Cambridge, MA: MIT Press.

Keeble, D. (1976). *Industrial Location and Planning in the United Kingdom.* London: Methuen & Co.

Launhardt, W. (1882). Die Bestimmung des zweckmäßigsten Standortes Einer Gewerblichen Anlage. *Zeitschrift des Vereins Deutscher Ingenieure,* 26, 106–115 (in German).

Liu, H. (2001). Firm Relocation within Economic Development. *The Theory and Practice of Finance and Economics,* 22(3), 114–116.

Lloyd, P. E. and P. Dicken (1977). *Location in Space* (2nd Edition). New York: Harper & Row.

Louw, E. (1996). Kantoorgebouw En Vestigingsplaats. *Stedelijke En Regionale Verkenningen. Regional Science. Delft, Technical University Delft.*

McLaughlin, G. E. and S. H. Robock (1949). *Why Industry Moves South: A Study of Factors Influencing the Recent Location of Manufacturing Plants in the South.* Kingsport Tennessee: Committee of the South, National Planning Association, Kingsport Press.

Nakosteen, R. A. and M. A. Zimmer (1987). Determinants of regional migration by manufacturing firms. *Economic Inquiry,* 25(2), 351–362.

Ortona, G. and W. Santagata (1983). Industrial Mobility in the Turin Metropolitan Area, 1961–77. *Urban Studies,* 20(1), 59–71.

Pellenbarg, P. H. (1985). *Firm Relocation and Spatial Cognition.* Ph.D. Thesis, University of Groningen, Holland.

Pellenbarg, P. H. *et al.* (2002). *Firm Relocation: State of the Art and Research Prospects.* Research Report No. 02D31, Research Institute SOM, University of Groningen, Holland.

Porter, M. E. (1998). The Adam Smith Address: Location, Clusters, and the "New" Microeconomics of Competition. *Business Economics,* 33(1), 7–13.

Pred, A. (1969). *Behavior and Location: Foundations For A Geographic and Dynamic Location theory:* Part 2, University of Lund. Lund Studies in Geography.

Qian, W. and J. Wu (2003). Empirical Research of the Willingness of Relocation of Rural Firms during Urbanization. *Zhejiang Social Sciences,* (1), 191–193.

Rawstron, E. M. (1958). Three principles of industrial location. *Transactions and Papers (Institute of British Geographers),* (25), 135–142.

Scott, P. and T. Rooth (2002). *Firm Migration to Britain in the Aftermath of the 1931 Emergency Tariff.* Colchester, Essex: UK Data Archive (distributor) SN: 4337, http://dx.doi.org/10.5255/UKDA-SN-4337-1.

Scott, A. J. (2000). Economic geography: the great half-century. *Cambridge Journal of Economics*, 24(4), 483–504.

Semple, R. K. and A. G. Phipps (1982). The Spatial Evolution of Corporate Headquarters within an Urban System. Urban Geography. *Urban Geography*, 3(3), 258–279.

Smith, D. M. (1966). A Theoretical Framework for Geographical Studies of Industrial Location. *Economic Geography*, (42), 95–113.

Smith, D. M. (1971). *Industrial Location: An Economic Geographical Analysis*. New York: Wiley.

Townroe, P. M. (1972). Some behavioural considerations in the industrial location decision. *Regional Studies*, 6(3), 261–272.

Van Dijk, J. and P. H. Pellenbarg (2000). Demography of Firms: Spatial Dynamics of Firm Behavior. *Netherlands Geographical Studies*, (262), 98–99.

Van Wissen, L. (2000). A Microsimulation Model of Firms: Applications of Concepts of the Demography of the Firm. *Papers in Regional Science*, 79(2), 111–134.

Weber, A. (1929). *Theory of the Location of Industries*. Chicago: University of Chicago Press.

Wei, H. (2003). Development trend and effect towards competitiveness of firm relocation, *Fujian Tribune (The Humanities & Social Sciences Monthly)*, (4), 11–15.

Wei, H. (2004). Industrial Transfer and Firm Relocation, In JIN Pei (Eds.), *Industrial Economics* (new edition). Beijing: Economics & Management Publishing House.

Wei, H. (2006). *Modern Regional Economics*. Beijing: Economics & Management Publishing House.

Wen, S. (2004). Thoughts Concerning the Firm Relocation of the Third Front Companies. *Aerospace Industry Management*, (8), 18–21.

Xiang, H. (2004). Research on the Migration and Rooted Issues of Foreign-funded Enterprises — Taking Taiwan-funded Enterprises for Example. *Zhejiang Social Sciences*, (3), 66–71.

Yi, C. (2005). Research of Relocation and the Investment and Financing Environment of Private Enterprises in Southeast regions of Fujian. *Journal of Harbin University*, 26(11), 87–92.

Zhao, F. (2003). Economic analysis of private firms relocation. *China Business Times*, April 15.

Chapter 4

Characteristics and Tendency of Enterprise Relocation in China

Wei Houkai and Bai Mei

Although enterprise relocation in China has a long history, it did not begin to accelerate until a decade or two ago. As domestic enterprise relocation accelerates, the issue of enterprise relocation has garnered increasingly high attention and become one of important studies in regional economics since the 1990s. This chapter will place emphasis on the history of enterprise relocation in China, its present characteristics, future development, determining factors, and policy suggestions concerned.

4.1 The Concept and Classification of Enterprise Relocation

Enterprise relocation, a special form of enterprise location adjustment, is a change of enterprises' spatial activities in value chain (Bai, 2003). It can be a complete relocation, namely to close business at an enterprise's current location and relocate it to another. It can also be a partial relocation, namely to relocate one part of business, such as establishing branch factories or relocating the general headquarters or the R&D department. Enterprise relocation can be simply seen as a change in an enterprise's location. Therefore, relocation, actually, is a new choice for an enterprise's location. Naturally, there are scholars who see subcontract as a main form of enterprise relocation in an extended way (Bianchi and Mariotti, 2003). However, the view is not widely accepted in academia.

Enterprise relocation has a variety of forms. Generally, it is classified in the following aspects.

4.1.1 *Classification According to Driving Force*

Based on the driving force, enterprise relocation can be classified as government-driven and market-driven. The former, which is also called forced removal of enterprises, is a passive relocation in which an enterprise has to move to another place generally due to major project construction or policy adjustment by the government, such as third-line enterprises, submerged enterprises within the Three Gorges reservoir area, chemical plants, industrial enterprises within central district of metropolis being forced to relocation due to policy limitation, etc. The latter refers to an enterprise that spontaneously moves to a more favorable investment location under market forces because of a change in external conditions. Most of enterprise relocations in recent years belong to the latter.

4.1.2 *Classified According to Administrative Division*

In terms of administrative division, there are two types of relocation: international relocation and domestic relocation of enterprises.

First, international relocation can be subdivided into transnational out-migration and in-migration. In a transnational out-migration, an enterprise moves from its home country to a target foreign location, and transnational in-migration indicates *vice versa*. Most transnational enterprise relocations took place between two closely developed countries in the past. However, there has been an increase in relocation from developed countries to developing ones in recent years.

Second, domestic relocation can be subdivided into intra-regional relocation and inter-regional relocation in accordance with whether the original location and the target location are within the same region. The "region" can be a city, a metropolitan area, a province, or even larger domestic area such as Northeast China. Intra-regional relocation takes place within a certain region, while inter-regional relocation involves two regions.

4.1.3 *Classified According to Relocation Direction*

Based on the economic level of the two regions involved, enterprise relocation can be classified into three forms. They are upward, parallel, and downward relocations. First, upward relocation means an enterprise moving from an underdeveloped to a developed area, namely, a West-to-East removal. The "West" indicates underdeveloped areas, while the "East" stands for developed areas. Downward relocation is just opposite to upward relocation. Parallel relocation refers to an enterprise moving between two areas with similar economic development level. For instance, an enterprise moving from Zhengzhou to Shanghai is classified as upward relocation. Conversely, the relocation is downward. But if it moves from Changsha to Zhengzhou, it is parallel relocation. The way in which relocation is classified is mainly used to study relocation direction.

4.1.4 *Classified According to Relocation Distance*

There are three types of relocation in terms of distance: short-distance relocation, long-distance relocation, and remote relocation. The way relocation is classified is mainly used to observe if the enterprise relocation is distance-decaying. Usually, it is short-distance relocation if it happens within 1,000 km, long-distance relocation if it is between 1,000 and 3,000 km, and remote relocation if beyond 3,000 km.

4.1.5 *Classified According to Determining Factors*

According to the determining factors, relocation is classified into three types. They are: market-expansion relocation, cost-pushing relocation, and industry-upgrading relocation. Among the three, the first also means space expansion, when an enterprise is relocated in want of a larger market share and more market opportunities. For instance, Haier Group[1] mainly produced refrigerators in Qingdao, Shandong Province, during its initial years. Then it began to plan and establish inter-regional production and selling bases as it developed. Haier Group illustrates an example of market-expansion relocation. Market-expansion relocation can be further subdivided into production-expansion relocation, R&D expansion relocation, and administration relocation. Production-expansion relocation indicates that an enterprise adjusts its production and operation in accordance with its strategic

---

[1] Haier is the No. 1 worldwide white household appliance manufacturing group, established in Qingdao, Shandong Province, in 1984.

planning of development and expands its productivity via relocation. For example, some garment factories in Wenzhou, Zhejiang Province, were relocated in neighboring counties or cities or in the central and western region like Chongqing Municipality, Sichuan Province, which illustrates an example of production-expansion relocation. R&D expansion relocation means the R&D department of an enterprise is relocated in other places, such as Sant'Angelo Group[2] setting up a fashion design center in Shanghai and Judger Group[3] setting up its R&D centers in Shanghai and Milan, Italy.

Cost-pushing relocation indicates that an enterprise, at a loss of cost advantage in the previous location due to changes in factor supply and demand, is resettled to a lower-cost location to maintain its advantage in competition. Take Dongguan of Guangdong Province as an example. As its urban economy grew rapidly and economic aggregate reached a certain scale, there was an essential change of economic environment. Accordingly, comprehensive business costs rose, which caused a loss of comparative advantage to some enterprises in the city. But these enterprises succeeded in keeping their competitive position in the market by moving to other areas. Transnational enterprises usually relocate their factories into developing countries such as China, most of which belong to cost-pushing relocation.

Industry-upgrading relocation means that an enterprise relocates its low-end and high-pollution manufacturing links because of an urgent shortage of land resources, a rise in labor cost, and stricter environmental protection system in areas of high development. For instance, the Kangnai Group,[4] with its headquarters in Wenzhou, Zhejiang Province, mainly aims at designing and developing high-end products; it has relocated the low-end manufacturing in Chongzhou, Sichuan Province, because there is an abundant supply of labor and land resources. In another case, in response to land and energy shortage as well as environmental pollution, Dongguan has put forward the strategy "socio-economic dual transformation", and other cities

---

[2]Founded in 1996, a shares-controlled group that combines industrial management and capital management, involving designing, producing and selling high-grade garment.
[3]A non-territorial garment enterprise group established in 1996, in possession of 12 member enterprises and more than 2,000 employees.
[4]One of the representative leather product groups in China, founded in 1980, with more than 20,000 employees.

of Guangdong like Shenzhen, Guangzhou, and Foshan have brought about a policy "to empty the cage for the new birds", which all essentially aim at promoting industry-upgrading. This policy symbolizes that the existing enterprises (that is "birds") are moved out to make room for upgraded industries and higher-end manufacturing links. It is the regional upgrading of industrial structure that has resulted in enterprise relocation.

4.2 Course of Enterprise Relocation in China

Since 1949, with the further development of economy and society, as well as introduction of institutional reform, especially with gradual improvement of socialist market economy, the patterns and dynamic mechanisms of enterprise relocation in China have been radically transformed: the commanded relocation arranged by governments has been gradually replaced by voluntary relocation of the enterprises, and relocation patterns have become diversified. Based on the features and dynamic mechanism, the course of enterprise relocation in China can be divided into four stages since the founding of the People's Republic of China in 1949.

4.2.1 *Government-Driving Relocation Dominated between 1949 and 1978*

After the founding of PRC in 1949, a highly centralized planning economy was implemented in China, and industrial enterprises serving as the state's manufacturing shop could not decide independently with regard to investment and operation. Under the traditional planning economy, enterprises had to turn over revenues to the governments from whom they received appropriation for investing, and underwent *in situ* expansion. As a result, there was no voluntary relocation of the enterprises. In this period, among the few cases of enterprise relocation, most were forced removal by government drive, e.g., relocations of the third-line enterprises, and relocations of enterprises for important engineering construction. In 1964, in order to facilitate the construction of the strategic rear area, the central government decided to remove significant facilities (usually the only enterprise in its industry nationwide) in the first-line area and those needed for the sake of strategic rear construction to the third-line areas (Bo, 1993). In 1965, the

National Construction Committee held the National Relocation Work Conference, where such proposals were made: relocation projects should be widely distributed across the nation but comparatively concentrated at the local level, and some of the advanced defense projects should be "scattered in mountainous areas, well-concealed, or even reestablished in the caves". Based on the statistics in 1971, a total number of 380 enterprises had been relocated to inland regions, including 145,000 workers and 38,000 pieces of equipment since 1964 (Wang, 1986).

4.2.2 *Overseas Enterprise Relocations to China Played a Major Role from 1979 to 1991*

Ever since 1979, with the purpose of speeding up the pace of opening-up, the Chinese government has carried out "special policies and flexible measures" in Guangdong and Fujian Provinces, established special economic zones, and open port cities, economic open areas in coastal region as well as Fujian Taiwanese investment zones, and Pudong New Area in Shanghai, thus forming a coastal open-economic belt stretching from south to north. During this period, overseas enterprise relocation to China played a major role, and most were channeled to the coastal region, especially the Pearl River Delta (PRD) region. From 1983 to 1991, foreign direct investment (FDI) and investment of other forms into coastal region came to US$ 18.81 billion, taking up 90.6% of the total investment in China. From 1983 to 1984, the PRD region actually absorbed 71.8% of total investment (including FDI and investment of other forms) in China, and the percentage reduced to 43.3% during 1985 to 1991, whereas the proportion Yangtze River Delta (YRD) region (including Jiangsu, Zhejiang, and Shanghai) attracted increased, from 6.3% to 13.1%, and that of Bohai Sea Rim (BSR) region (including Beijing, Tianjin, Hebei, Shandong, and Liaoning) increased from 10.5% to 22.0%. These figures show that as the opening-up starting from South China has gradually moved up north since 1984, foreign investment, for the first time, tended to move up north. Meanwhile, inland-based business also set up branches in coastal region. Besides, at the end of 1983, the central government set out to adjust the distribution of those third-line enterprises which were improperly distributed. Amid this, the number of removals from the original sites to other areas approximately took up 40% (Lin and Li, 1992).

From 1985, metropolises like Beijing began to explore ways to remove the facilities located in the city center.

4.2.3 *Relocations of Overseas and Domestic Enterprises were Laid Equal Stress from 1992 to 2000*

Ever since Deng Xiaoping's South Tour Speeches in 1992, China had carried out a market economic reform nationwide. And in October 1992, the 14th National Congress of CPC defined the goal of economic system reform as the establishment of a socialist market economy. With the progress of marketization reform, inter-regional flow of production factors and inter-regional business investment increased. As a whole, bulk of the foreign investment was concentrated in the coastal region, but the investing tendency gradually moved up north. From 1992 to 2000, FDI and investment of other forms in the coastal region came to US$ 287.13 billion, accounting for 87.7% of the total foreign investment in China. The proportion PRD region attracted in the period reduced from 33.6% to 30.5% of the total FDI and investment of other forms into China, whereas that of YRD region increased from 20.0% to 26.6%, and that of BSR region fluctuated around 20%. Driven by the market forces, the domestic capitals, talents, and industries began to move into the coastal region, yet enterprises in the coastal region, especially in Zhejiang Province, and some other places, gradually started to expand to other regions. By the first half of 2000, Zhejiang businesses had invested over RMB 90 billion in the central and western region, and a total of RMB 50 billion in Shanghai. About 65% of the businesses regarded larger market share as their main motive and goal of outward expansion and industrial transfer (Chen, 2002). In addition to the market-driving relocations, the number of relocations that were government-driven also went up. For supporting the Three Gorges Project, the state has initiated the program to relocate the enterprises to be submerged in the Three Gorges reservoir since 1993. In 1995, Shanghai transferred the production capacity of 500,000 spindles to Xinjiang Uygur Autonomous Region to answer the call of transferring cotton textile industry from east to west launched by the State Council. Moreover, with the rapid progress of suburbanization, metropolises like Beijing, Wuhan, Dalian, Harbin, Chongqing, and Shenyang sped up the pace of removing those enterprises located in the city center (see Table 4-1).

Table 4-1   Summary of Metropolises' Enterprise Relocation.

Cities	Relocation plans
Wuhan	In 1994, *Decisions of Relocating and Reconstructing Some Enterprises in the City Center* was issued. In 1996, *Regulations of Accelerating Relocation and Reconstruction of Polluting Industrial Enterprises Located in the City Center* was launched. In 2008, *Implementation Opinions of Promoting Relocation and Renovation of Chemical Enterprises Located within the Third Ring Road* was published. By now, 147 industrial enterprises have been relocated and re-established.
Beijing	In 1995, *Solutions to Polluting and Daily Life-Disturbing Enterprises Relocation of Beijing* was launched. In 2000, *Executive Solutions to Industrial Enterprise Relocation within Third and Fourth Ring Roads of Beijing* was issued. In 2002, *Beijing Olympic Action Planning* was published, aimed at relocating and renovating the chemical industrial zones in the southeast suburb and 200 polluting enterprises within the 4th ring road by 2008.
Dalian	In 1995, *Implementation Plan of Development-oriented Relocation and Reconstruction of Enterprises in Dalian City Center* was issued, and successively published 33 relocation plans concerning 289 enterprises. Presently, 205 projects of enterprise relocation and reconstructing have been completed.
Harbin	In 2001, Harbin set out to relocate the enterprises from the city center to the suburbs, paying much attention to the 177 key enterprises located downtown. A total of 64 enterprises moved out before 2005 and 93 before 2010. In 2004, *The Tentative Approaches to the Relocation of State-owned Enterprises in Harbin* was published, defining five types of state-owned enterprises that should move out of the city center.
Chongqing	In 2002, environmental protection projects of relocating polluting enterprises were launched. In recent years, the municipal government has approved 138 enterprises to conduct relocation. A total of 63 enterprises have completed relocation by the end of 2008, and the rest 75 enterprises will have finished by the end of 2011.

(Continued)

Table 4-1 (*Continued*)

Cities	Relocation plans
Shenyang	Since 2002, 214 enterprises in the old Tiexi District have been moved to the development zones. In 2007, *Work Plan of Intensifying Energy Conservation and Emission Reduction* was launched, aimed at finishing relocation and renovation of the first group of 56 enterprises in 2008, and relocating and renovating all the high-pollution enterprises in the urban area in 2009.
Shijiazhuang	During the 10th Five-year Plan, Shijiazhuang plans to complete the relocation of 120 polluting enterprises. In 2008, *Implementation Plan of Accelerating the Enterprise Relocation and Industrial Upgrading in the City Center* was issued, intending to relocate and re-establish the 49 city-center enterprises particularly supervised by the government, or to order them to change the line of production or close by 2010.
Hefei	In 2005, the project of relocating the chemical industrial enterprises was launched, planning to move the whole chemical industry out of the city center to the newly-built industrial park in the county of Feidong. The allocated investment of this project, which will be completed by 2015 in three stages, reaches RMB 21.1 billion.
Nanjing	In 2006, Nanjing decided to move 10 enterprises out of the urban area, including Nanjing Chemical Fiber, Nanjing Chemical, Nanjing Taining Iron Foundry, Nanjing Jinfurun Food, Nanjing Jinsanli Rubber & Plastic, Nanjing No.2 Machine Tool Works, Nanjing Textile and Pyro electricity, Nanjing Dyeing and Finishing & Decoration Factory, Nanjing Titanium Dioxide Chemical, and Nanjing Chemical Plant under Sinopec, and to move another 20 enterprises between 2008 and 2010.
Qingdao	In 2008, *Work Plan of Promoting the Enterprise Relocation and Renovation in the Old City Center* was published, and *Plan of Relocating, Retaining and Shutting the Old City Center Enterprises in Pairs of Three* and *Plan of Relocating and Re-establishing the Old City Center* were issued, planning to relocate 110 enterprises. Amid, 20 enterprises are to be relocated at the first stage and another 10 in 2009.

Source: Related government documents mentioned in the table.

4.2.4 *Enterprise Relocation Accelerates Since* **2001**

In order to facilitate a coordinated development of all regions, in recent years, the central government has successively initiated the strategies of development of Western China, revitalizing Northeast China and other old industrial bases and rising of central region. It also encourages foreign investment and coastal businesses to move to central and western region and Northeast China. In 2006, the Ministry of Commerce launched a project to facilitate thousands of enterprises to start business in the central and western region (also known as *"Wan Shang Xi Jin"*), inspiring the central and western region to take over industry transfer and processing trade transfer from the coastal region, and supporting the coastal businesses and economic and technical development zones going west. In August 2007, NDRC and some other five ministries jointly announced the *Proposals on Stepping up Interaction between Eastern and Western Region and Thoroughly Promoting Development of the Western Region*. Meanwhile, because of the rapid progress of industrialization, urbanization, and large-scale aggregation of industries, many problems concerning energy and land shortages, increasing cost, and aggravating pollution have emerged in the coastal region in recent years. This has led to heavier pressure in upgrading industries and rising environmental protection standard. Against such a backdrop, China's businesses, especially those in coastal region, have accelerated to relocate to the central and western region.

Ever since 2000, many Zhejiang enterprises (and the number is increasing year by year), especially labor-intensive ones, have set about investing outside of Zhejiang Province. According to the data revealed by Zhejiang Economic and Technological Cooperation Office and *Zheshang* (*Zhejiang Businessmen*) Periodical Office in 2006, Zhejiang businessmen invested over RMB 1 trillion across China, equal to the GDP of Zhejiang Province in 2005. Shanghai, Beijing, and Guangdong received RMB 200 billion or more; Gansu Province got RMB 100 billion; the provinces Anhui, Jiangsu, Jiangxi, Tianjin, Hubei, Heilongjiang, and Yunnan attracted RMB 50 billion or more; the provinces Sichuan, Guangxi, Liaoning, Hunan, Shandong, Guizhou, Henan, and Shaanxi got RMB 20 billion or more; and Chongqing, along with the provinces Shanxi, Jilin, Hainan, Fujian, and Xinjiang getting more than RMB 10 billion (Shen and Hu, 2006). Accordingly, Zhejiang businessmen poured 49.4% of their total investment into the eastern region of China, 20.9% into the central region, 22.7% into the western region, and 7.0% into Northeast China. Up to now, more than 1,000 enterprises have retreated from Wenzhou, 250 of which conducted the integral moving, and the estimated outflow of capital surpassed RMB 10 billion (Yang, 2009). In the large- and medium-sized cities, with continuing expansion of the city center, facilities located in the urban areas have improved, resulting in relocation. Projects involving retreating from the secondary industry and engaging in the service sector as well as retreating from housing programs and engaging in business have been launched in many cities to further optimize urban spatial structure. During the period, more foreign investment has gone to western region at a quicker tempo.

4.3 Characteristics of Enterprise Relocation in China

In recent years, enterprise relocation has become common with the development of market economy. Nowadays, enterprise relocation in China presents following features.

4.3.1 *Downward is the Dominant Enterprise Relocation Direction*

Spatially, enterprise relocation in China is of gradient type, that is, businesses remove from more developed regions to less developed ones. The downward relocation is the main trend in China now. First of all, the overseas enterprises relocated into China are mostly from more developed countries and regions, such as the US, Japan, South Korea, Hong Kong, and Taiwan. In particular, PRD region took over most businesses relocated from Hong Kong and Taiwan in the early days when the policies of reform and opening-up were being implemented. The GDP per capita of China and Guangdong were US\$ 313 and US\$ 321, respectively, in 1980, and that of Hong Kong and Taiwan were US\$ 5,649 and US\$ 2,367, respectively. So it is obvious that enterprises relocated from Hong Kong and Taiwan to PRD region is typically downward.

Second, with regard to the domestic enterprise relocation, both the coastal enterprise relocation to central and western region and city center enterprise relocation to the suburb are downward, and these two forms of relocation are quite common recently. For the past few years, Zhejiang enterprises have quickly expanded and relocated to the central and western region. For instance, RMB 2.3 billion was invested in Sichuan Province in 2002, RMB 2.8 billion in 2003, RMB 5.1 billion in 2004, RMB 7.9 billion in 2005, RMB 14.9 billion in 2006, RMB 27.3 billion in 2007, and RMB 36.2 billion in 2008 — a growth rate of about 1500% in six years (He, 2009). In 2008, Zhejiang enterprises invested nearly RMB 10 billion in Chongqing, RMB 9.582 billion in Yunnan province, RMB 6.57 billion in Xinjiang Uygur Autonomous Region, and over RMB 4 billion in Guizhou Province (Gong, 2009). Ever since 2005, under pressure from increasing cost and upgrading industries, some traditional labor-intensive nterprises in PRD region have moved outside, mainly toward the east and west parts of Guangdong Province, northern mountainous areas in Guangdong, and the central and western region of China. Having launched in succession the projects of retreating from the secondary industry and engaging in the service sector as well as retreating from housing programs and engaging in business, some of the large- and medium-sized cities relocate enterprises in the city center to the suburb industrial park. For example, Shenyang set out to rebuild Tiexi District in 2002, relocating its 214 facilities to the development zones.

Third, as to the manufacturing industry in PRD region being relocated abroad, most have chosen Southeast Asia, where the cost is lower. Due to the increasing cost, some labor-intensive enterprises have recently started to move their production bases to Southeast Asia. Humen Town in Dongguan alone has relocated over 300 IT enterprises to Vietnam (Zhen, 2008). Textile enterprises have also undergone a similar experience. At present, nearly 1,000 textile enterprises have invested and established new facilities in the Southeast Asian countries and regions such as Vietnam, Cambodia, and Bangladesh. According to the Textile Association of Vietnam, there are more than 2,000 textile enterprises in Vietnam, among which 500 are foreign-owned, over 200 are funded by mainland China, and about 150 by Taiwan (Ye, 2008).

4.3.2 *Most Chinese Enterprises Relocate to Realize Outward Expansion*

Currently, Chinese enterprises mainly adopt the manner of expanding themselves by investing and establishing new facilities in other places.

The Zhejiang Enterprise Investigation Team has conducted a survey to investigate the actual or intended relocation of 596 enterprises and found that, among the 346 enterprises undergoing transprovincial relocation, 68.8% have chosen to invest and set up new facilities in other provinces, only 17.1% aim to relocate the production base, 9.5% aim to conduct integral moving, and 4.3% are transferring the headquarters. Among the 196 enterprises of Zhejiang Province that are moving to other provinces, 83.6% invest and set up new facilities in the destination, only 9.7% transfer the production base, and 7.1% move the R&D base; Among the enterprises which relocate within Zhejiang Province, 62.5% choose to invest and establish new facilities in other areas, only 20.3% move the production base, and 18% conduct the integral moving (Enterprise Investigation Team of NBSC and Zhejiang Enterprise Investigation Team, 2005). Among the private enterprises of Leqing, Zhejiang Province, which expanded, 75% choose to expand by transferring to other areas, only 25% conduct *in situ* expansion (Li *et al.*, 2004). In PRD region, only 9.8% of the enterprises conduct integral moving, whereas 83.7% undergo expansion of production capability and production links transfer, or multiply investing manners (Liu and Zhang, 2008). Most enterprises in Shenzhen also choose to expand by transferring to other areas, and the output value of such enterprises accounts for about 75% of the total output value of the enterprises which transfer to other areas (Shen, 2008).

4.3.3 *Relocation has the Effect of Distance-Decaying*

Since the reform and opening-up in China, the relocation of enterprises has had an obvious effect in reducing the distance. First of all, most overseas enterprises which move to China are from the neighboring countries and regions. By 2007, China has attracted 632,300 FDI projects, in which 77.1% are from Hong Kong (45.2%), Taiwan (11.9%), Macao (1.8%), and seven neighboring Asian countries and regions, including South Korea (7.4%), Japan (6.3%), and Singapore (2.6%). Second, the main form of domestic enterprise relocation is to transfer to the surrounding areas. Enterprises in the city centers of metropolises such as Beijing and Shanghai usually move to the suburbs and the surrounding areas. A considerable part of Zhejiang businesses transfer to nearby Shanghai, Jiangsu, and Jiangxi, and enterprises in PRD region tend to move to other places in Guangdong Province as well as adjacent Jiangxi, Hunan, and Guangxi. According to the survey, 37.8% of the enterprises in PRD region choose to transfer or expand within the Delta, and 47.8% choose the outside of the Delta. In the latter case, 14.6% choose the eastern and western parts and the northern mountainous areas of Guangdong Province, 20.3% move to pan-PRD region (mostly to Guangxi, Fujian, Hunan, and Jiangxi), and only 12.9% to other regions Liu and Zhang (2008). About 85% of Shenzhen enterprises transfer to other places of Guangdong Province such as Dongguan, Huizhou, and Zhongshan, which are within Shenzhen radial area. Among the 224 Bao'an enterprises which transfer to the outside of Bao'an, 43.3% choose Dongguan and 18.3% choose Huizhou (Shen, 2008). Third, most of the outward investment of China's enterprises flows to Asian countries and regions, and most are short-distance relocations. By the end of 2007, the outward direct net investment of China's enterprises has come to US$ 117.911 billion, 67.2% of which flows to Asian countries and regions (Hong Kong alone takes in 58.3%). Among those shoemaking enterprises transferred outside of PRD region, about 25% move to neighboring countries such as Vietnam and India, and 50% to central and western region of China.

4.3.4 *Features of Industrial Distribution of Enterprise Relocation*

In terms of industrial distribution, enterprise relocation in China is diversified. First, an increasing number of overseas enterprises in different industries relocate to China, and the development level and technical content is improving. At the early stage of the reform and opening-up, most overseas enterprises that relocated into China were in the labor-intensive processing sector, mainly in the lower links of the industrial chain. It was particularly true of Hong Kong- and Taiwan-funded enterprises, as many as 65% of which were in the processing sector in 2006. However, as a whole, recent overseas enterprise that have relocated into China have been diversified in terms of industrial distribution, and the proportions of high and new technological industries and modern service industry are rising. What's more, overseas enterprise relocation has shifted from the once mono transfer of manufacturing industry into transfer of the whole industrial chain, and the transnational corporations have been establishing more and more headquarters, R&D institutions, design centers, operation centers, and purchasing centers in China.

Second, the domestic enterprises which conduct relocations are mainly labor-intensive and high-pollution industries. Among the labor-intensive industries are textile, jewelry, watches, calculators, or telecommunication products; printed matter or packing materials; standard machinery; hardware, etc. High-pollution industries include leather, ceramics, cement, chemical industry, etc. For example, most enterprises that relocated from the PRD region in 2007 are labor-intensive industries such as hardware, toys, clothes, shoe-making, and plastics, and 90% of them are medium- and small-scale enterprises funded by Hong Kong and Taiwan businessmen. Most enterprises moved from Shenzhen are engaged in the low-end links of labor-intensive industries such as electronics, machinery, toys, instruments, and plastics. About 69% of them are the enterprises engaged in "three-processing and one compensation"[5] and foreign-funded enterprises. Besides, some of them are key targets of environmental protection organizations because they produce a high level of pollution (Shen, 2008). Among the 1,124 Zhejiang enterprises which moved out of Zhejiang Province, 68.1% are engaged in manufacturing industries of clothes processing, low-voltage apparatus, etc.; 14.9% are in wholesale and retail business and catering service; 11.1% are in the real estate industry; 3.5% in the high-efficiency agriculture; and 2.4% in tourism (Research Group of Zhejiang Provincial Administration for Industry & Commerce, 2004). The enterprises that moved out of Wenzhou mainly are producers of valves, water pumps, motors, plastics, leather, automobile accessories and clothes, and printing industries; and the enterprises that moved from Taizhou mainly belong to the pharmaceutical industry and other industries like plastics, food, textile, mold, water pump, handiwork, and automobile accessories (Yu *et al.*, 2006).

Besides, domestic enterprises that moved overseas are widely distributed in marketing network, shipping and physical distribution, resource development, manufacturing, wholesale and retail business, public goods, design and R&D, particularly in mining industry, manufacturing industry, and wholesale and retail business. By 2007, 25.9% of China's net direct investment to the outside world has been poured into lease and commercial

---

[5]"Three-processing and one compensation" is that process raw materials on clients' demands, assemble parts for the clients and process according to the clients' samples, or engage in compensation trade.

services, 17.2% to wholesale and retail business, 14.2% to financial sector, 12.7% to mining industry, 10.2% to storage and mail service, and only 8.1% to manufacturing industry. In contrast, among the accumulated FDIs into China, 69.9% of the projects and 62.3% of the contract foreign investments gravitate toward the manufacturing industry.

4.3.5 *Features of Target Areas of Enterprise Relocation*

In view of target areas of enterprise relocation, there are two features. One is that the popular destinations of overseas enterprise relocation are the coastal regions of China. Even in recent years, the situation has not changed at all. By the end of 2006, among the registered foreign-funded enterprises across China, 79.9% concentrate in the eastern region, merely 7.7% in northeast China, 6.4% in the central region, and 6.0% in the western region. Amongst the coastal regions, the PRD region is the most popular destination of overseas enterprise relocation at the beginning, gradually the YRD region and BSR region got more and more attention later. In 2006, FDI into YRD region was as much as US$ 27.238 billion, taking up 43.2% of the total FDI into China, whereas PRD region and BSR region received 20.9% and 22.6%, respectively.

The other feature is that overseas manufacturing industry gradually moves from the first-tier and the second-tier cities to the third-tier and fourth-tier cities. Conventionally, the first-tier cities include Beijing, Shanghai, Guangzhou, and Shenzhen; the second-tier cities include Tianjin, the capital cities of some developed provinces, and some open coastal cities; the third-tier cities are prefecture-level cities and the capital cities of those less developed provinces; and the fourth-tier cities are county-level cities and county towns (Wang, 2008). In the past few years, with the development of the reform and opening-up in China, the destinations of overseas enterprise relocation spread by degree to the third-tier and the fourth-tier cities from several first-tier and second-tier cities, which are the most wanted at the beginning stage. Meanwhile, with the improvement of people's living standards, the first-tier and some of the large second-tier cities have attracted more overseas service businesses, and manufacturing industry is gradually transferring to the smaller cities with less affluence (American Chamber of Commerce in the People's Republic of China, 2009).

Third, the destinations of domestic enterprise relocation are differentiated. At present, the destinations of relocation of the coastal enterprises are mainly a small number of regions with better conditions in the following provinces: Jiangxi, Anhui, Guangxi, Hunan, Henan, Chongqing, and Sichuan. But the destinations of enterprises in different regions and in different industrial chains are different. For instance, Shanghai, Jiangsu, and Jiangxi are the popular destinations for enterprises situated in Zhejiang Province, which would like to move out of Zhejiang. The survey reveals that among the 196 enterprises which have conducted transprovincial relocation, half choose Shanghai; in particular, when it comes to headquarter relocation and R&D department relocation, the selection rate of Shanghai reaches 88.9% and 71.4%, respectively; 14.3% of them choose Jiangsu, mainly to invest in a new factory or relocate the production department; and 12.8% of them choose Jiangxi, mainly to relocate the production department (Xu, 2004). Nearly half of Wenzhou enterprises which expand themselves by removing outside of their original sites to establish new factories choose Shanghai, whereas popular destinations for the integral moving are in central and western region (Yang, 2009). According to another investigation, 77% of the enterprises of Cixi in Zhejiang Province relocate outside Zhejiang, and most of them choose Shanghai and Jiangsu as their destination (Zhang, 2009); whereas in Leqing, 80% of enterprise relocations are within Zhejiang province, transprovincial relocation is mainly between the developed coastal regions, especially the PRD and YRD regions (Li *et al.*, 2004).

Fourth, enterprise relocation among the metropolises is increasingly active. In the PRD region, YRD region, and BSR economic circle, mutual enterprise relocation is increasingly becoming active. Based on the survey of Zhejiang Province, among the 346 enterprises which conduct transprovincial relocation, 41.3% of them are transprovincial relocation in Jiangsu Province, Zhejiang Province, and Shanghai. Among the 196 enterprises which remove to the outside of Zhejiang Province, the most popular destinations are Shanghai and Jiangsu Province: 40.3% of them relocate to Shanghai and 13.3% to Jiangsu Province; whereas among the 150 enterprises which relocate to Zhejiang Province from elsewhere, 16.7% of them are from Shanghai, and 10.7% from Jiangsu (Research Group of Zhejiang Enterprise Investigation Team, 2004).

4.4 Determinants of Enterprise Relocation in China

Enterprise relocation is common for the development of regional economy, and it is affected by the nature of the enterprise, type of industry, geographical features, and government policies. Generally speaking, enterprises of different nature or in different industries should have different determinants for relocation. For example, private and state-owned enterprises should consider different factors when it comes to relocation. So should large-scale enterprises and medium- and small-scale enterprises, high and new tech enterprises, and the traditional labor-intensive enterprises. The different links of the industrial chain, like headquarters, R&D, design, manufacturing, and sales, will also consider different relocation factors. Therefore, it is safe to conclude that the factors affecting enterprise relocation in China are manifold. Based on the survey of the relocation of Zhejiang and Guangdong enterprises, these factors tend to be diversified (see Table 4-2). As a whole, the major factors of the current enterprise relocation in China are as follows.

4.4.1 *Demands for Enterprise Development*

The demand for endogenous development is the internal impetus of enterprise relocation. The process of an enterprise's growth is that of its spatial expansion. When it is of relatively small scale, it tends to adopt *in situ* expansion. However, as the scale grows, it will ask for more ways to expand itself in other places, such as setting up sales outlets and production bases, so as to gradually transform into a national, transnational, or even global enterprise. Relocation by means of investment expansion makes it possible for an enterprise to take advantage of new investing opportunities to broaden and seize new markets. It is also good for optimizing the distribution of an enterprise's production and sales outlets, shaping a nationally or even internationally unified industrial chain. In fact, most of the recent enterprise relocation in China, especially Zhejiang enterprise relocation, is realized by means of investment expansion. The survey shows that the most important motive behind Zhejiang enterprise relocation is to increase sales and export as well as to facilitate overseas expansion (Chen, 2002). As to the relocation policies of PRD region enterprise, factors affecting endogenous development accounts for 43.8% (Liu *et al.*, 2008). Obviously,

Table 4-2 Factors Affecting Enterprise Relocation in China.

Source	Investigator	Investigated regions	Sample number	Major factors
Chen (2002)	Chen Jianjun	Zhejiang province	105 enterprises above designated size	To increase sales volume (selection rate: 65.71%); To increase export (38.10%); To promote corporate recognition (20.95%); To make use of better social infrastructure and soft and hard infrastructure (18.10%); To introduce technology (16.19%); and to facilitate overseas expansion (16.19%).
Xu (2004)	Zhejiang Enterprise Investigation Team	Zhejiang province	196 enterprises relocate out of Zhejiang	Land resources (identification rate: 55.6%); Power supply (45.4%); Supplies of raw materials and energy (42.9%); To be granted with tax reliefs in the destination city (41.8%); To alter geographical conditions and promote corporate image (34.2%).
Liu *et al.* (2008)	Liu Li and Zhang Jian	Pearl River Delta	418 enterprises	Enterprise endogenous development demand (43.8%); Increase of production cost (34.0%); Less local preferential policies (17.9%); Guidance of macro policies and industry transfer policies (11.2%).
Shen (2008)	Shenzhen Trade Development Council	Shenzhen	Not clear	Too much facilities rent (57.8%); High labor cost including salary, welfare and social security fees (53.3%); Unsatisfied land requires (45.6%).

Source: Referring to relevant data.

this sort of relocation is the normal voluntary relocation under the influence of market economy; therefore, the government should not interfere too often.

4.4.2 *To Exploit and Utilize Local Resources*

A major reason for enterprises to relocate, or to expand investment elsewhere, is to avoid resource cap on land, energy, raw material, and human resources, for example, of the current location, and to fully exploit and utilize local resources. For example, in Zhejiang and PRD regions, high concentration of industries has resulted in a shortage of industrial land, energy (electricity in particular), and labor forces, thereby containing the potential development of local enterprises. In order to play the abundant resources of the target area into their full use, enterprises in coastal regions have accelerated their pace to migrate to its neighboring areas, and the central and western region. Among these, migrating firms in Zhejiang Province have paid increasingly more attention to the supply of land, electricity, and raw material. As researches revealed, land resource, electricity capacity, and power supplies are considered the most important factors by migrating firms from Zhejiang Province (Xu, 2004). In recent years, many large- and medium-sized cities have relocated their industrial enterprises to the city center, mainly out of considerations for space, land efficiency, and environment. On top of that, a couple of private enterprises in Zhejiang, like Youngor and Zhengtai, have moved their headquarters to Shanghai, so as to strengthen connections between the headquarters and its branches, by employing top-notch technologies, education, human resources, information, commercial service, market networking, and relationships in Shanghai, with an aim to boost their corporate image and brand value. For similar reasons, enterprises at home and abroad are establishing or relocating their R & D centers in Beijing.

4.4.3 *To Cope with Escalating Costs*

Regional cost difference plays a vital part in the decision-making of enterprise relocation. Such difference constitute an essential appeal to enterprises from outside mainland China, particularly those in Hong Kong and Taiwan, to set foot on mainland China, and also pushed coastal enterprises in PRD region and YRD region to move from east to central and west region. In addition, since 2000, in Zhejiang and PRD region, due to the mounting costs of energy, raw materials, land, and salary, and the appreciation of RMB and adjustments in trading policies, operating costs have been escalating on an average scale. It was estimated that, in 2007, the average salary in the YRD region (Jiangsu, Zhejiang, Shanghai) and in the PRD region (Guangdong) was 58% and 42% higher than that of central region of China, respectively, and 49.3% and 34.1% higher than that of Western China, respectively. From 2000 to 2007, land price in key cities of YRD region increased by 162.8% and by 97.5% in PRD region, which were much higher than that of the central and western region. In 2007, the average land price in major cities of YRD region and PRD region were 2.95 and 2.01 times that in the south-central region respectively, 2.39 and 1.62 times as high as the price in southwest region respectively, and even more, 4.43 and 3.01 times as high as the price in northwest region respectively (see Table 4-3). Those labor-intensive firms at the low- or medium-end of the industry chain are heavily struck by the increasing costs, for their tight budgets are extremely subject to costs of land price, rent, salaries, and electricity bills. Once the cost has gone beyond their reach, they would easily relocate elsewhere so they can survive within the budget. According to a survey released by Shenzhen Trade & Development Bureau, the top three causes for enterprise relocations are, "high rent", "high cost for labor force including salaries, welfares, and social security fees", and "unfulfilled land requirements" (Shen, 2008). Obviously, increasing cost is driving local enterprises away, and henceforth gathers new momentum for them to find a new place to thrive (Klimenko, 2003).

4.4.4 *To Reduce Pressure from Industrial Upgrading and Environment Protection*

Enterprise relocations have always concurred with regional industrial upgrading. More often than not, in order to speed up industrial upgrading, some governments in developed countries and regions have set up more strict entry standards, including technology advancement, efficient resource utilization, and environmental awareness, and therefore forced some medium- and low-end businesses, along with some high-pollution enterprises, to migrate to developing countries. Since the 1960s, Japan has moved over

Table 4-3 2007–2008 Comprehensive Land Price.

Region	Provinces involved	2000 Comprehensive land price (Yuan /m²)	2000 Relative level	2007 Comprehensive land price (Yuan /m²)	2007 Relative level	2000–2007 Overall increase (%)	2000–2007 Comparable change
Countrywide		998	100	1751	100	75.5	
YRD region	Jiangsu, Zhejiang, Shanghai	1485	149	3903	223	162.8	+74
Beijing and Tianjin	Beijing, Tianjin	1727	173	3172	181	83.7	+8
PRD region	Guangdong	1344	135	2655	152	97.5	+17
South-central region	Hunan, Hubei, Jiangxi, Anhui, Chongqing	879	88	1324	76	50.6	–12
Southwest region	Sichuan, Yunnan, Guizhou, Guangxi, Shaanxi	981	98	1635	93	66.7	–5
Northwest region	Inner Mongolia, Shanxi, Gansu, Ningxia, Qinghai, Xinjiang, Tibet	684	69	881	50	28.8	–19

Source: Referring to relevant data in dynamic monitoring system of city land price of Ministry of Land and Resources.

60% of their high-pollution industries out to the Southeast Asia and Latin America, while the US has moved more than 39% of their high-pollution, high energy consumption industries out (Zhao, 2001). In terms of China, during past few years, accelerating development of major cities propelled coastal economical and urban transformations. In 2009, per capita GRP in Guangzhou, Wuxi, Foshan, Suzhou, Shanghai, Ningbo, Zhuhai, and Beijing exceeded US$ 10,000, and that of Shenzhen was over US$ 13,000. To meet the demands for industry upgrading, local governments in the PRD and YRD regions intensified structural readjustment and raised technology and environment protection standards as a sign of their resolution to eliminate outdated equipment. In addition, they screened for high consumption, high emission, and low-end enterprises and readjusted them accordingly. With quicker industry upgrading in the developed coastal region and large- and medium-sized cities, high-consumption, high-emission, low-end enterprises have been forced to transfer to the less developed surrounding areas, central and western region, or rural areas. Also, it should be noted that, as the developed areas shut down a large number of environment-destruction firms, some government agencies in the less developed areas would rush to attract investment. In these cases, what they have actually "attracted" is pollution instead of investment, and in such sense, enterprise migration changes to pollution transfer.

4.4.5 *Policies Encouragement*

With an aim to maintaining a coordinated development among regions and optimizing their spatial structures, governments at various levels have formulated a series of policies and measures to encourage proper relocation of enterprises. On a national scale, since 1999, China has launched strategies of Development of Western China, Revitalizing Northeast China, and Rising of Central Region, along with a set of policies and measures, so as to attract foreign funds and coastal enterprises to enter the central and western region and northeast China. In 2006, the Ministry of Commerce initiated the "*Wan Shang Xi Jin*" Project to appeal overseas enterprises, coastal processing trade business, and development zones going west. Meanwhile, they established some industry transfer promotion center in the coastal region and set up a good number of national bases and demonstration parks for in-migrating enterprises in the central and west region. To facilitate relocation and reconstruction of enterprises in the city center, the Ministry of Finance and State Administration of Taxation promulgated *Notice on Relevant Issues Concerning the Enterprise Income Tax on Incomes from Policy-based Relocation* in 2007, which clarified the handling of income tax for policy-based relocating enterprises. On a regional scale, governments at various levels in the central and western region employed multiple measures to attract investments, providing a favorable environment for international and coastal enterprises. To address the issue of imbalanced development, the coastal provinces Guangdong, Zhejiang, and Jiangsu, for example, also adopted policies to encourage enterprises to migrate to less developed cities. In March 2005, the Guangdong Province introduced *Opinions on Joint-promoting Industrial Transfer between Mountain Area, East and West Wings, and Pearl River Delta (for Trial Implementation)*. With co-built industrial parks, the policy aims to balance the overall economy by encouraging labor-intensive industries to move from PRD region to the northern mountainous area, and the east and west parts of Guangdong Province, where the economies are relatively weak. The Jiangsu Provincial Party Committee called for "Promoting Common Development through South-North Industrial Transfer", and later implemented *Opinions on Accelerating South-North Industrial Transfer*, to actively lead enterprises in the south to move to the north. Those above-mentioned policies and measures have played an important role in guiding the process of domestic enterprise relocation.

4.4.6 *Cluster Effects of Enterprise Relocation*

The essence of enterprise relocation is the change of its investment location. Where a company chooses to invest affects other companies' decisions, and therefore cluster effects emerge during the process of enterprise relocation. Cluster effect means the migration of an enterprise will have the effect of inducing a group of related enterprises to shift their locations. It has three embodiments. The first is the demonstration effect. Generally, a successful case of relocation will bring in more followers. The second is the linkage effect. A key enterprise will normally induce a myriad of related companies to move in the neighborhood. Volkswagen and Hyundai started up a branch in Shanghai and Beijing, respectively, and consequently attracted a bunch of vehicle component manufacturers. In June 2004, when Ningbo AUX Group moved into Nanchang Economic and Technological Development Zone, more than 140 related companies followed. The third is the congregation effect. Like human beings, companies tend to congregate. Related companies move together to reduce risks and uncertainties. This particularly applies to medium- and small-scale private enterprises in Zhejiang Province, which are highly motivated to relocate.

4.5 The Future for Chinese Enterprise Relocation

At present, Chinese enterprises have entered the era of massive relocation. Relocations have been frequent both internationally and domestically. Looking into the future, against the background of deepening reform and opening-up, the relocation of Chinese enterprises will be accelerated and diversified.

4.5.1 *Coastal Region will Become the First Choice of Oversea In-Migration*

Since the reform and opening-up, the scale of FDI has been expanding. By 2008, it has reached US$ 92.4 billion equaling 2.1% of GDP in China that year. In terms of target areas, however, 88% of FDI concentrate on coastal region (including Liaoning and Guangxi). From the viewpoint of development tendency, they will continue to be the most favored choice for the following three reasons. First, coastal region have high densities of population, cities and towns, and industries. The region also serves as a key economic region in China. In 2008, 43% of Chinese population resided here and it produced 60.6% of GDP in China. Such situation can hardly change in short terms. Besides, the coastal region has undergone a new round of development and opening-up (see Table 4-4), like the construction of Tianjin Binhai new area and two centers in Shanghai, and the planning of Haixi (Western Taiwan Straits) economic region in Fujian province, Beibu Gulf economic region in Guangxi Province, the YRD region, the PRD region, coastal economic belt in Liaoning province, coast area in Hebei province, Yellow River Delta in Shandong Province, and coastal area in Jiangsu

Table 4-4   Recent Region Planning and Related Policies Approved by the State Council.

Region	Time	Region planning and related policies
Coastal region	Jan 2006	The State Council officially approved *Overall Plan for Trial Comprehensive Supporting Reform in Pudong New Area*
	May 2006	The State Council released *Opinions on Relevant Issues Concerning Development and Opening-up of Tianjin Binhai New Area*
	Feb 2008	The State Council approved and promulgated *Development Plan for the Guangxi Beibu Gulf Economic Region*
	Mar 2008	The State Council approved *Overall Plan for Trial Comprehensive Supporting Reform in Tianjin Binhai New Area*
	Sep 2008	The State Council released *The Guiding Opinions on Further Promoting the Reform, Opening-up and Social-Economic Development of the Yangtze River Delta Region*
	Dec 2008	The State Council reviewed in executive meetings and approved in principle *the Outline of Pearl River Delta Regional Plan on Reform and Development*
	Mar 2009	The State Council approved Zhongguancun Science Park to build the national demonstration zone for independent innovation
	Apr 2009	The State Council released *Opinions on Promoting the Development of Modern Service Industry and Advanced Manufacturing of Shanghai into an International Financial Center and International Shipping Center*
	May 2009	The State Council approved *Overall Plan for Comprehensive Supporting Reform in Shenzhen*

(*Continued*)

Table 4-4 (*Continued*)

Region	Time	Region planning and related policies
	May 2009	The State Council released *Several Opinions on Facilitating Fujian in Accelerating the Construction of Western Taiwan Straits Economic Region*
	Jun 2009	The State Council discussed in executive meetings and approved in principle *Coastal Development Plan of Jiangsu Province*
	Jul 2009	The State Council discussed in executive meetings and approved in principle *Development Plan of Liaoning Coastal Economic Belt*
	Aug 2009	The State Council promulgated *Overall Development Plan for Hengqin Island*
	Dec 2009	The State Council officially approved *Development Plan for Highly-effective Ecological Economic Region in Yellow River Delta*
	Jan 2010	The State Council promulgated *Several Opinions on Promoting the Construction and Development of the Hainan International Tourism Island*
	May 2010	The State Council promulgated *Regional Plan for the Yangtze River Delta*
	Jan 2011	The State Council promulgated the *Development Planning of Blue Economic Region in Shandong Peninsula*
	Feb 2011	The State Council promulgated the *Planning of Zhejiang Demonstration Area for Marine Economic Development*
	Jun 2011	The State Council approved to set up Zhoushan Islands New Area in Zhejiang province
	Aug 2011	The State Council promulgated the *Development Planning of Guangdong Comprehensive Experimental Area for Marine Economy*

(*Continued*)

Table 4-4 (*Continued*)

Region	Time	Region planning and related policies
	Nov 2011	The State Council officially approved *Development Planning of Hebei Coastal Area*
	Sep 2012	The State Council promulgated the *Development Planning of Nansha New Area in Guangzhou*
Inland region	Apr 2006	Central Committee of Communist Party of China (CCCPC) and the State Council promulgated *Several Opinions on Boosting the Rise of Central Region*
	Jun 2007	The State Council authorized Chongqin and Chengdu to establish national urban and rural comprehensive supporting reform pilot area
	Aug 2007	The State Council approved *the Plan of Revitalizing Northeast China*
	Sep 2007	The State Council released *Opinions on Further Boosting the Economic and Social Development of Xinjiang*
	Dec 2007	The State Council accredited Wuhan and Changsha-Zhuzhou-Xiangtan urban agglomerations as resource-conserving and environmental-friendly society comprehensive supporting reform pilot area
	Jul 2008	The State Council released *Opinions on Supporting Social and Economic Development of Tibet in Recent Period*
	Sep 2008	The State Council released *Several Opinions on Further Promoting Social and Economic Development in Ningxia*
	Sep 2008	The State Council approved *Overall Plan for Comprehensive Supporting Reform in Establishing a Resource-conserving and Environmental-friendly Society in Wuhan Urban Agglomeration*

(*Continued*)

Table 4-4 (*Continued*)

Region	Time	Region planning and related policies
	Nov 2008	The State Council released *Several Opinions on Supporting Economic and Social Development of Tibetan Region in Qinghai, etc.*
	Dec 2008	The State Council approved *Overall Plan for Comprehensive Supporting Reform in Establishing a Resource-conserving and Environmental-friendly Society in Changsha-Zhuzhou-Xiangtan Urban Agglomeration*
	Jan 2009	The State Council released *Several Opinions on Promoting Overall Urban-rural Reform and Development in Chongqin Municipality*
	Apr 2009	The State Council approved *Overall Plan for Trial Comprehensive Supporting Reform in Chongqing Municipality*
	May 2009	The State Council approved *Overall Plan for Trial Comprehensive Supporting Reform in Chengdu City*
	Jun 2009	The State Council officially approved *Development Plan for Guanzhong-Tianshui Economic Region*
	Nov 2009	The State Council approved *Outline of Cooperative Development Plan in China's Tumen River Region*
	Dec 2009	The State Council approved *Plan for Ecological Economic Region in the Poyang Lake*
	Dec 2009	The State Council approved Wuhan East Lake New Technology Development Zone to build the national demonstration zone for independent innovation
	May 2010	General Office of the State Council released *Several Opinion on Further Supporting Economic and Social Development of Gansu*
	May 2010	The State Council agreed to set up Liangjiang New Area in Chongqing Municipality

(*Continued*)

Table 4-4 (*Continued*)

Region	Time	Region planning and related policies
	Jun 2011	The State Council released *Several Opinion on Further Promoting Good and Fast Development for Inner Mongolia Economy and Society*
	Sep 2011	The State Council released the *Guidance Opinion on Supporting Henan Province for Accelerating Construction of Zhongyuan Economic Region*
	Sep 2011	The State Council released *Several Opinion on Supporting the Construction of Kashgar and Korgas Economic Development Zone*
	Jan 2012	The State Council released *Several Opinion on Further Promoting Good and Fast Development for Guizhou Economy and Society*
	Apr 2012	The State Council released the *Planning for Revitalization of Old Revolutionary Base Area in Shaanxi, Gansu and Ningxia*
	Jun 2012	The State Council released *Several Opinion on Supporting Revitalization and Development of Original Central Soviet Areas such as South Jiangxi, etc*
	Aug 2012	The State Council released *Several Opinion on Vigorously implementing Strategy for the Rise of Central Region*
	Aug 2012	The State Council agreed to set up Lanzhou New Area in Gansu province

Source: Referring to relevant data.

Province, all of which constitute tremendous attractions to the overseas investors. Last but not the least, to tackle the consequences of financial depression, coastal provinces, such as Shanghai, Zhejiang, Guangdong, Jiangsu, and Shandong, waste no time to volume up economic transformation and upgrading, and strive to reshape and optimize industries. Such actions bring supreme advantages to the region. In the foreseeable future, with a quickened and comprehensive opening-up, overseas companies will establish the PRD region and YRD region as their bases, and spread to

BSR economic circle in the north and to Beibu Gulf economic region (Nanning, Beihai, Qinzhou and Fangchenggang in Guangxi, and Zhanjiang in Guangdong) in the south.

4.5.2 *More Coastal Enterprises will Going West*

With the mounting cost of all factors in the coastal region and quickening economic reform, coastal enterprises and processing trade accelerate their pace to migrate to the central and western region. And an increasing number of enterprises in the east is going west. It is predicted that such migration will continue to accelerate in the next 5 to 10 years. First of all, the central and western region has the potential for industries to locate. In 2008, the per capita GRP in the eastern region reached US$ 5,331, with cities like Shenzhen, Shanghai, Ningbo, and Suzhou surpassing US$ 10,000. The eastern region of China is already at the final stage of industrialization, while the central and west region has just embarked its process of industrialization, with a GRP of US$ 2,565 and US$ 2,297 per capita, respectively. Such considerable potential has created favorable conditions for enterprise migration. Second, the central and western region has an abundant resource of energy, minerals, agricultural products, and biology and cultural tourism, and is considered to be the most important base for energy and raw material. Moreover, the central and western region is comparatively rich in industry land resource and has a lower cost of land and labor force, etc. With a huge market potential, the central and western region has become an ideal option for possible investors home and abroad. Third, during the past few years, infrastructure building in railways, roads, airports, waterways, and communications has constantly improved, so does its industrial supporting capabilities. Especially, regions like Wanjiang Urban Belt, Changsha–Zhuzhou–Xiangtan Urban Agglomeration, Nanchang–Jiujiang–Jingdezhen Economic Region, Zhongyuan Urban Agglomeration, Guanzhong Economic Region, Chengdu–Chongqing Economic Region, and Beibu Gulf Economic region, have formed favorable conditions for massive enterprise relocation. With freeways connecting the coastal cities, nearby coastal regions like Jiangxi and Anhui Provinces and cities like Ganzhou, Yingtan, Shangrao, and Ma'anshan have gradually become an important gathering place for relocation of coastal enterprises.

4.5.3 *Continued Differentiation in Domestic Enterprise Relocation*

During recent years, with an accelerated globalization of China's economy, some major enterprises started to establish its systems of R&D, design, manufacturing, marketing, transportation, and purchasing at home and abroad. Different functions are separated spatially, and such situations substantially promote differentiation in enterprise relocation. In a foreseeable future, headquarters, R&D institutes, design centers, and operation and purchasing centers will agglomerate in the heart of major cities like Shanghai and Beijing. On the other hand, manufacturing industries, especially general manufacturers, will gradually migrate to the suburbs of metropolises, medium- or small-sized cities, or even small towns. As a result, different links in the industry chain will be redistributed and a new pattern of regional division will emerge during the course. Regional diversity even exists in manufacturing sector, the high-, medium- and low-end links of it differentiate among cities and towns of various sizes. As headquarters, R&D, design and operation centers concentrate in few major cities, a group of management control centers will be formed. These centers can be categorized into three levels: international management control centers, including Hong Kong, Shanghai, and Beijing; national management control centers, including Shenzhen, Guangzhou, Qingdao, Dalian, Wuhan, Chongqing, Chengdu, Xi'an, etc., and regional management control centers, including other key cities and capital cities of some provinces.

4.5.4 *More and More Chinese Enterprises Relocate Overseas*

Since the adoption of "Going-out Strategy", an increasing number of Chinese enterprises are migrating overseas, with rapid growth in Outward Foreign Direct Investment (OFDI), which amounted to US$ 6,144 million (non-financial investment) in 2008. In terms of the developmental stage, despite the fact that China has not been ready for massive "going-out", overseas migration of Chinese enterprises is bound to accelerate, with surging investment, as the open economy evolves. It should be noted that some labor-intensive processing trade enterprises in PRD region tend to move to Southeast Asia under the pressure of economic downturn. On a large scale, however, the present conditions are not favorable for the concerned companies to shift to countries like Vietnam, Bangladesh, and

Pakistan. Compared to these Southeast Asian countries, the central and western region welcomes the coastal processing trade business, promising greater potential and more favorable conditions. First, the social and economic environment is not conducive in these countries. As a result of the 2010 economic crisis, the economic and social trends remain uncertain. The livelihoods of local workers have been affected, which leads to frequent strikes. Such circumstances present extra management problems and corresponding costs. Second, incomplete supporting facilities also add up the cost. Take the shoemaking business for example: raw material and accessories are imported to factories in Southeast Asia, while accessories are constantly in short supply. With an incomplete and immature supply chain, the preparation period for production is prolonged and thus decreases production efficiency, which could be detrimental to firms dependent on small-scale order. Third, language and culture gap translate into increased communication cost. Chinese enterprises often encounter communication problems in their daily operations. Fourth, human resources, especially high-skilled workers, in countries like Vietnam and Laos are limited, indicating that a massive transplantation will face a lack of labor forces.

4.6 Policy Suggestions on Promoting Enterprise Relocation

Apart from a few government-driven relocations, most enterprises initiated the process voluntarily. Self-motivated enterprise relocation on a large scale can serve as an effective way to optimize the spatial structure and at the same time possibly exercise negative influence on the regional economy, such as causing economic recession and "hollowing out" of industries in original regions and transferring pollution to the target regions. Therefore, under the conditions of market economy, it is of vital importance that governments frame related policies and measures to guide and regulate enterprise relocation, especially "East Enterprises Going West", so as to boost a coordinated, balanced, and sustainable regional economy.

4.6.1 *Initiate Interactions between the West and the East*

Both the original and targeted regions must gear up when the transplantation of coastal enterprises and processing business to the central and western region is evident, in which case both parties should create a win-win situation through interactions and cooperation. The coastal region should seek economic transformation and upgrading through multiple means, such as closing, upgrading, transferring, and introducing, etc. As with those promising enterprises that are contained by land and labor costs, the government should encourage and facilitate them to relocate to neighboring areas and central and western region. For the target regions in central and western region, it is advisable to provide favorable conditions to further improve investment environment and industry supporting system, thereby ensuring a smooth transfer. Under the current circumstances, some pair-up demonstration projects between the East and the West can be have positive effects. Namely, under the support of the government, coastal cities and the central and western region cities could pair up in the spirit of voluntary cooperation and mutual benefit and jointly promote the relocation of land-limited enterprises and misfits firms in the coastal region. Such actions will push coastal processing trade and development zone to going west and encourage both parties to co-build industrial park (Wei, 2009).

4.6.2 *Improve Investment Environment in Central and West Region*

Although the investment environment in the central and western region has greatly improved, problems such as incomplete supporting system, relatively high transportation costs, and tax burden still persist. Especially in medium- and small-scale processing business located in the coastal region, transportation cost is a major factor in the decision to relocate, since its raw material and market mainly come from overseas countries. If they migrate to the central and western region, which is distant from seaports, the transportation costs will increase. The costs include added transportation fees from the extra traveling miles, freeway fees, as well as intermediary service fees. For this reason, it is necessary to strengthen transportation capacity between the central and western region and main ports, to gradually cancel or reduce toll fees along freeways from the central and western region to coastal ports, and to set up a group of "dry ports" in major inland cities and bonded logistic parks. Such measures aim to establish an efficient transportation network between the East and the West and effectively reduce transportation costs for the processing enterprises in central and western region. Meanwhile, we can also take full advantage of the industry chain in the investment attracting process, to guide in-migrated companies to concentrate in well-equipped industrial parks and gather a momentum for the development of industrial clustering. Such patterns will in turn compensate for the current deficiency in the supporting system. In addition, we should reinforce construction of social networks and connecting systems through building some public platforms for product promotion, technology exchange, training and counseling, and information and technological support.

4.6.3 *Further Improve National Policies*

To begin with, the government should further improve policies for the processing trade business going west. Currently in related new national policies, there are preferential measures for coastal processing trade enterprises that relocated to central and western region, including being exempted 50% of the deposit. Also, some processing trade enterprises dealing with 1,853 products, such as plastic raw materials and products, textile yarns, clothes, and furniture, have been restricted in the east. The main task at present is to advance the development of processing trade business in the central and western region with constant policies, clarify the time limitations on the policies, build up confidence in those in-migrated firms, and maintain them this way. Next, central finance should set up a special fund in service of migrating enterprises into the central and western region. This fund provides discount loans, investments, and employment subsidies, and in such a way reduces risks and costs for the concerned enterprises and prevents them from escaping to some Southeast Asian counties like Vietnam and Cambodia. Specifically, it helps them in the following three aspects. First, it provides loans with a financial discount interest for in-migrated enterprises that intend to add fixed asset in form of technology upgrading. Second, it compensates some of sunk cost from the relocation. Last, it also gives employment subsidy to those enterprises that offer jobs to out-migrant workers in central and western region. Moreover, for enterprises that relocate or invest to expand in the central and western region, there are corresponding support structures in land, tax, railway transportation, etc.

4.6.4 *Prevent Pollution Transfer*

In the process of relocation to the central and western region, some high-pollution industries are poised to spread alongside. For example, the lead-acid battery industry would emit a large amount of smoke, dusts, and wastewater containing Pb as byproducts, and the industry is classified as a high-pollution industry. Since 2004, Changxing County in Zhejiang Province, the production base for the lead-acid battery in China, has begun to regulate local lead-acid battery enterprises on a large scale, after which, only 50 out of its original 175 factories survived. During the period, interested parties from Jiangxi, Hubei, Anhui, Yunnan, etc., came here to attract investment. With the relocation of these factories, some high-pollution enterprises spread over to broader area. For this reason, central and western region must set up industry entry standards and select with certain principles. Even in receiving some labor-intensive medium- and low-end industries, the local governments should urge companies to constantly improve technology, added value, and wellbeing of their employees by investing in equipment, following national environment protection standards, and protecting labor force. The local governments should ensure enterprise relocation without any pollution transfer.

References

American Chamber of Commerce in the People's Republic of China (Amcham China, 2009). *American Business in China: 2009 White Paper*. Available at: http://web.resource.amchamchina.org/Podcasts/WhitePaper2009.pdf

Bai, M. (2003). *Research on Firm Relocation*. Doctoral Dissertation, Nankai University, Tianjin.

Bianchi, L. and I. Mariotti (2003). Mezzogiorno and SEEC: Do They Compete in the Attraction of Italian Relocating SMEs? Draft paper for *RSA International Conference*, April 12–15, Pisa.

Bo, Yibo (1993). *In Reflection of Certain Critical Decisions and Events*. Beijing: Party School of Central Committee of CPC Press.

Chen, J. (2002). Empirical Research of Current Chinese Firms Relocation — Based on Analysis of Questionnaire Report of 105 Companies from Zhejiang

Province. *Management World*, (6), 64–74.

Enterprise Investigation Team of NBSC and Zhejiang Enterprise Investigation Team. (2005). Why Zhejiang Companies are Moving out. *China National Conditions and Strength*, (3), 16–17.

Gong, Y. (2009). Seize the Opportunity: Investment Report during 2008–2009 for Zhejiang Entrepreneurs. *Zhejiang Entrepreneurs*, (12), 52–56.

He, X. (2009). In Accordance with National Strategy: Outward Investment Focus of Zhejiang Entrepreneurs during 2008–2009. *Zhejiang Entrepreneurs*, (12), 57–60.

Klimenko, M. (2003). *Strategic Interoperability Standards and Trade Policies for Industries with Network Externalities*. San Diego, Mimeo: University of California.

Li, W., S. Zhu and C. Wang (2004). A Survey of Private Enterprises' Relocation and Expansion Phenomenon: Evidence from Leqing City in Zhejiang Province. *On Economic Problems*, (9), 30–32.

Lin, L. and S. Li (Eds.) (1992). *Production Distribution of China Three-tier Cities*. Chengdu. China: Sichuan Publishing House of Science & Technology.

Liu, L. and J. Zhang (2008). Investigation on Enterprises Relocation in the Pearl River Delta and its Regional Transfer Effects. *International Economics and Trade Research*, 24(10), 74–77.

Research Group of Zhejiang Provincial Administration for Industry & Commerce. (2004). Private Enterprises in Zhejiang under the Context of Firm Relocation. *Zhejiang Economy*, (16), 20–22.

Research Group of Zhejiang Enterprise Investigation Team. (2004). Investment Difference of Zhejiang, Shanghai and Suzhou under the Context of Firm Relocation. *Zhejiang Economy*, (24), 38–40.

Shen, H. and Z. Hu (2006). Unveiling Investment Patterns of Zhejiang Businessmen. *Economy Information*, June 12.

Shen, Y. (2008). Exploring Firm Relocation in Shenzhen and its Policy Readjustment. *Contemporary Economy*, (6), 96–97.

Wang, H. (Ed.), (1986). *The History of Industry Economy of China*. Beijing: Economy & Management Publishing House.

Wang, W. (Ed.), (2008). *Scientific Development on Regional Central Cities in China*. Beijing: Social Sciences Academic Press.

Wei, H. (2009). Problems and Solution of Coastal Economy. *China Development Observation*, (7), 12.

Xu, H. (2004). Firm Relocation in Zhejiang and Its Influence. *Zhejiang Economy,* (21), 30–32.

Yang, W. (2009). Reflections on Wenzhou Pattern: from Firm Relocation. *Northern Economy,* (9), 81-83.

Ye, Y. (2008). Vietnam Crisis will Postpone Firm Relocation in Textile. *Shanghai Securities News,* June 16.

Yu, L., Y. Chen, and J. Feng (2006). Analysis of Firm Relocation in Zhejiang. *Review of Economic Research,* (56), 37–44.

Zhang, C. (2009). Reflections on firm relocation in Cixi. *Zhejiang Statistics,* (4), 19.

Zhao, H. (2001). High-Pollution Firm Relocation in Developed Countries and Our Solution. *Academic Journal of Zhongzhou,* (5), 30–31.

Zhen, J. (2008). Dongguan Industry Transfering. *South Reviews,* (14), 30–32.

Chapter 5

Dynamics and Determinants of Manufacturing Location in China

Wang Yeqiang and Wei Houkai

The world economic development at present provides an interesting interpretation of spatial patterns. On one hand, the benefits of rapid development of information technology and transportation systems facilitate cross-border flows of capital, goods, information, and technology in an unprecedented way, and economic globalization has promoted the industrial economic activities to reallocate resources in the global context. On the other hand, the role of spatial factors in world economic growth has been strengthened rather than weakened in the past, which has been illustrated by the vigorous development of the industrial agglomeration. A world economic map dominated by industrial agglomeration is easy to be observed just by looking around. These gathering areas are similar to "the viscous points in the smooth space", absorbing the condensed economic energy and then nurturing a large number of world-class industries and enterprises.

The industrial location changes are a complex spatial economic phenomenon, which involves many aspects of the regional economic development. The most striking phenomenon is the industrial location movement and spatial agglomeration. What has caused an industry to shift from one location to another? How does an industrial transfer affect regional industrial structure? What is the spatial allocation of the transferred industry? Why the clustering phenomenon occurred in some areas? What kind of economic laws hide behind the common economic development phenomenon? These are the main issues that will be discussed in this chapter.

5.1 Literature Review

The present studies on industrial location changes are mainly advancing in the following two directions: analyzing the relationship between industrial shift and regional economic development from the perspective of regional industrial structure, and analyzing the industry's spatial agglomeration phenomenon from the perspective of the regional industries' competitiveness.

The researches on industrial transfer are numerous and unorganized, but its basic logic is guided by the analyses of industrial activities of developed countries or regions. These analyses study the industrial transfer problems within the framework of the Neo-Classical economics, which ignored the effects of spatial agglomeration in the process of industrial location shift and its impacts on the regional competitiveness. These two inter-related concepts were separated. The American economist Lewis (1984) deems that the rising labor cost in developed countries will lead the shift of labor-intensive industries from developed countries to the developing countries, which will upgrade the former country's domestic industrial structure to a higher level. Prebisch (1990) believes that the import substitution industrialization strategy employed by some developing countries due to the development pressure indirectly leads to the international industry transfer. Vernon (1966) thinks that inter-regional industry transfer is the result of the industry cycle evolution at a certain stage. The Japanese scholar Kiyoshi Kojima (1987) believes that the cost ratio of goods is the basis of foreign direct investment and industry transfer.

Chinese scholars have also carried out many researches on the relationship between regional industry structure and industry transfer. Chen (2002) believes that industry transfer is a spatial motion which aims at expanding the industrial market share, restructuring the industrial structure, maximizing the marginal benefit of management resources, and satisfying the growth needs of the enterprise. Zheng *et al.* (2004) considers that the main reasons for international manufacturing capital diverting to the eastern China are the low investment costs and the enormous potential of Chinese market. Zhao and Wang (2005) believe that the international industry transfer includes the industry space's concentration and diffusion linked by the value chain, and the production systems reorganized by the multinationals on a global scale. Shi (2004) believes that industry transfer is a way to achieve market integration. Chen and Chen (2001) argues that the changes of regional industries competition which leads to the relocation of industries will result in the industry transfer. It is the expression of industrial development process, namely of the spatial morphology. Wei (2003) believes that industry transfer has different influences on the transferred-out and transferred-into districts. Many of those transferred-out industries are forced by the regional industry structure adjustment and upgrade. In return, those transferred-into districts will usually improve their industry competitiveness, increase employment opportunities and industrial supporting capabilities, and thus form industrial agglomeration.

The current researches on industrial agglomeration usually start with studying increasing returns, which systematically elaborate the viscous effects of those industrial accumulations on economic resources, but ignore the influence of the industrial location change on industry structure changes in both districts and industry agglomeration. Ellison and Glaeser (1999) believe that the location of industry is influenced by a variety of natural advantages. Traistaru and Martincus (2003) emphasize that demand and comparative advantage are the main driving forces of the relatively geographic concentration of the manufacturing industry. Traistaru *et al.* (2002) find that factor endowments and the geographical closeness to the European core determined the manufacturing industry location of those joining countries. Helpman and Krugman (1985) point out that, due to the increasing returns, a larger market scale area will occupy a larger share of production. Subsequent agglomeration economy theory, which is based on development economics, states that the enterprises' agglomeration in turn promotes the further expansion of the market size, which puts the area into a self-reinforcing process. Krugman (1991) thinks that the agglomeration of labor force is an important driving force for the industrial cluster. Venables (1996) claims that, under the circumstances of incomplete competition, the industrial linkages internally determine the market scale of different areas. This effect will promote regional industry specialization, making the manufacturing industry or a certain industries concentrated in a limited number of areas; Wen (2004) argues that China's industrial agglomeration which based on the effect of increasing returns to scale is determined by trade and production accumulation. The decrease of trading and transportation costs could further promote the regional agglomeration of manufacturing industry. Brülhart and Torstensson (1996) consider that those industries which have increasing returns tend to move to the central countries that have better accesses to the market. Midelfart-Knarvik *et al.* (2000) find that comparative advantage and forward and backward linkages are important to the manufacturing industry concentration. In recent years, domestic scholars have gradually started to pay attention to this issue. He and Xie (2006) argue that economic globalization, comparative advantage, and economy of scale are the reasons for the industry's spatial concentration. Wang and Wei (2007) claim that the main determinants of geographic concentration of industries are the industry's technology preferences and the market size.

Industry location change is a relatively comprehensive idea, which includes industrial diffusion and concentration. These two aspects are interdependent and mutually influenced. Whether industrial structure or regional competitiveness is the consequence of industrial location changes? Research on industrial location is a process of change. In this process, industry diffusion and concentration are the two opposing forces, which are always difficult to distinguish. Factors that contribute to the concentration of industries in the targeted area may be the exact reason for industry diffusion in the other area. Therefore, we should treat those two aspects as a whole when researching the issue of industrial location change. Section 5.2 analyzes the concept of industry location change and then presents a theoretical framework for a comprehensive analysis of this theory. Section 5.3 applies statistics to describe the share change of China's manufacturing industry area. Section 5.4 is about model and variable selection. Section 5.5 conducts an empirical analysis to identify the factors which affect the manufacturing industry's location change under the former theoretical framework. Section 5.6 is the conclusion of this chapter and provides a further discussion about the effect of regional endowment and industrial characteristics on manufacturing location change.

5.2 Agglomeration and Diffusion: A Comprehensive Theoretical Framework

5.2.1 *Definitions and Related Conceptions of Industrial Location Change*

Industry location change is actually a process in which one industry transfers from the initial location to the destination location. Industry diffusion refers to the transfer process from the perspective of the initial location, while the industry agglomeration is studied from the perspective of the destination area. Thus, industry agglomeration and diffusion constitute to the main contents of industrial location change.

The formation and development of industrial agglomeration are inseparable from industry transfer, so the factors of industry transfer are contained in industry agglomeration. Industry transfer is the beginning of the industrial agglomeration, while industrial agglomeration is the result of industry transfer. Due to increasingly fierce industrial competition, on one hand, low-technology and labor-intensive industries have developed to a certain extent in early gathering areas. But, as a consequence of demand and supply structure change and high costs, low economic efficient phenomenon ensued in the above areas. Regional industry structure optimization and upgrading will inevitably lead to slow development of some relatively backward industry in the gathering area, and to some extent this had hindered the overall economic development. Therefore, these industries shift to other less developed regions. On the other hand, due to the advantages of regional resources and labor, these similar enterprises that scattered in the area then clustered to achieve the external economies of scale. Based on the region's comparative advantage, local government attracted foreign investments, so that foreign or other domestic industries transferred to this area, which resulted in the formation of industry agglomeration. As the industry continues to cluster, the agglomeration area's economy grows rapidly. Thus, industry transfer and industry agglomeration has increasingly become a phenomenon of symbiosis. They explain the industrial location change together. Here, we define industrial location changes as the relative change in the regional industry share. It includes the meaning of "change" and "move". On one hand, a change in the local productivity will lead to economic growth, which will in turn lead to changes in the share of regional industry. On the other hand, industry transfer between the regions will also cause the share change.

5.2.2 *The Dynamic Mechanism of Industrial Location Change*

The Core and Periphery theory suggests that a relatively complete regional economic system usually has one or a few core areas, which are the vertex of a multi-layer spatial structure. When focused on a specific area, we can find that the long-term economic development is actually a process of "growth" and "recession" with the alternating phenomenon of "clustering" and "diffusing". In industrial development, it represents as the recession of a certain industry or industry groups, or the replacement by a new industry with higher production efficiency. Under the analysis of new spatial economics framework, industrial transfer (or diffusion) and agglomeration is actually different segments of the industrial location change. When the transportation costs change, an increase in the land price and labor costs in the clustering center would cause these lower transportation costs production to cluster in the surrounding areas. Once the transportation fees declines, those production activities will transfer from the core area to the surrounding areas in a "flying geese state".

International trade and investments optimize the global resources allocation, which have promoted the spread of international industries and the development of productivity. In parallel with this phenomenon, rapid rises of specialized industrial clusters in different regions with distinct features are observed. Diffusion and agglomeration are two paralleled dynamic processes in the global industrial space's integration and restructuring (Liu, 2005). On one hand, the development of information network technology, as well as modern transportation and logistics promote the world's industrial diffusion which driven by foreign direct investments. Due to the development of rapid transit, remote IT, and computing network technology, the world is increasingly becoming a "zero distance" assembly. Industries are being relocated and restructured under the global context, which has largely promoted the pace of industrial restructuring and the convergence of real factor prices. On the other hand, the increasing returns to scale, spillover effects, and resources sharing have accelerated the local industries to cluster in the center. At the same time, the informal system, such as culture and customs, has maintained and strengthened this trend. The industry's network agglomeration effect in the local space also increases. Especially, the cluster of traditional manufacturing industries and burgeoning industries make its competitive advantage increasingly prominent.

Dramatic changes happened in knowledge and technology creation, dissemination, and sharing, which give rise to the re-integration of industry value chain and the labor division system. In this process, the multinational corporations have spread their businesses in the global context, which forms a global division of labor force. At the same time, the characteristics of regional industry agglomeration has become increasingly prominent in those factors such as "learning effect", "knowledge spillover effect", and "increasing returns to scale". From the perspective of globalization, the development of multinational corporations will promote the global economic integration and will eventually eliminate the regional differences to form the convergence of the global economy. But a large number of characteristic facts in the process of globalization state that industrial globalization and regional "stickiness" are never two different isolated processes. With the widely spread foreign direct investments to the whole world, the innovation networks in those host countries have been stimulated and strengthened outside. In other words, the globalization of proliferation and local agglomeration of industry are two aspects of the parallel process of international industrial space integration. The declining costs in the modern transportation and information transmission have led to two effects. On one hand, it encourages the production activities to move to the place that has the lowest cost or the most obvious learning effects, such as resource-directed location and market-directed location. On the other hand, the increasing returns to scale will stimulate these production activities to accumulate to some nodes, where the nodes can be technology-directed locations or they may simply be formed due to the initial state and path dependence. Once established, these industrial agglomerations will continuously develop and maintain themselves in the long term.

5.2.3 *Determinants of Industrial Transfer (or Diffusion)*

5.2.3.1 *Global Strategy, Economies of Scale and Industrial Transfer (or Diffusion)*

Cross-border investment and international trade are different forms of industrial transfer. The incentives and motivations of the industrial transfer first depend on a country's comparative advantages and resource endowments. In order to obtain long-term stable global competitive advantages, these multinational corporations has employed a global point of view, taking the regional comparative advantages of different countries and regions to disperse and then re-configure all aspects and functions on the value chain in order to make them organically combined to implement the operational integration. Thus, they can make use of low-cost synergies in different global locations, which will in return reduce the total cost of the production and maximize the global operational efficiency. The global strategy focuses on maintaining the innovative advantages of the corporation headquarter or the industry cluster base, and meanwhile other activities spreads to different places in order to secure low factor costs and opportunities of the foreign markets (Porter, 1998). Second, increasing returns to scale also contributed to the transfer of industry. Krugman (2000) believes that the reasons why economies of scale has led to the international division of labor and the transfer of industries are the specific local market requirements, the specific location, or even a "historical event" effect, which inducing an industry to gather to a particular country. Those gatherings would lead to increasing returns and economies of scale. Therefore, international division of labor can be formed even under situations where two countries involved have the same factor endowments. Factors concentration that resulted in economies of scale will inevitably further promote the trade expansion. Thus, we can explain the underlying reasons for the long-term existing trades and mutual investments between the developed countries and newly industrialized countries which are under the same stage of economic development and have the same factor endowments.

5.2.3.2 *Regional Endowments, Competition and Industrial Transfer (or Diffusion)*

An Enterprise's competitiveness will be significantly affected by the local industrial environment. The degree of openness, cultural background, information infrastructure, research institutes, industrial policies, legal system, and existing capital stock and the degree of specialization will all have some impact on industry's development. The degree of environmental stability, homogeneous or heterogeneous, centralized or decentralized, simple or complex, the degree of turbulence, and the available amount of resources will comprise the uncertainty part in enterprise development. These uncertainties will increase the risk of failure of organization's action, increase decision-making costs, and decrease the probability of success. To cope with the environmental change, and improve economic performance, multinational corporations will adjust its industrial chain and spatial layout. In general, the greater the environmental differences, the more obvious restriction on the company's space activities will be. The more complex and volatile an environment is, the higher cost of accession to the information will be. At the same time, the uncertainty of management decisions will also increase significantly. Therefore, flexible, diversification or horizontal integrated industrial structure will able to cope with the uncertainty of risk. On the contrary, facing with a more certain environment, corporations will adopt a relatively stable layout structure.

5.2.4 *Determinants of Industry Agglomeration*

5.2.4.1 *Industrial Agglomeration, Cost and Domestic Supporting Capacities*

If the production costs decreases with the increase of industry's total output, there will be agglomeration economies. The advantages of agglomeration economies are economies of scale and externalities of the intermediate input goods production, labor market sharing, and knowledge outflow. Demand effects, cost factors, and the supporting capacities of the investor together constitute major decision variables for site selection of the cross-border investment activities. Generally speaking, as long as there are transportation costs, the market externalities are bound to inspire the upstream industry, downstream industries, or different industries to clustering in order to reduce the opportunism and transportation costs of "space isolation" in the decentralized market. Agglomeration stability not only depends on the world market's final demand of products and trade costs but also depends on supporting capacity and associated effects within the cluster's internal industries. Developing countries lack the high level of intermediate products and related service providers. Then the multinational corporations will guide, encourage, and support their overseas supporting enterprises to invest in the developing countries, which will in turn form a foreign-pulled industry agglomeration. In the industry transfers among industrialized countries, the cluster effect of the investment location choice is obvious too.

5.2.4.2 *Industry Characteristics, Spatial Competition, and Industrial Agglomeration*

Industrial agglomeration is an expression of fierce spatial competition between different industries, which is a change in the industrial organization form in response to the competition for space. It is an important source and concentrated expression of the modern industry's competitiveness. Porter (2002) believes that the nature of the economic concentration is a process that is affected by the economies of scale, scope, and external economies. Economies of scale have resulted in the industrial agglomeration point, coupled with the industrial agglomeration districts, together leading to a core economic concentration area. Increasing returns of a single manufacturer may be endogenous, but not all of the economies of scale exist within firms, and increasing returns may be entirely external to the manufacturer. Some industries have decreased their production costs by agglomeration. However, the scale of companies in these industries would probably be small, and then economies of scale should exist in industry rather than in a single company. The interaction of decision-making by manufacturers will lead to the external economy. When technology is becoming increasingly important, the external economy will become more important, and then exogenous increasing returns will also become increasingly common. In fact, no matter whether it is endogenous or exogenous, as long as there are increasing returns, those companies will have the incentive to agglomerate.

Therefore, the analysis of industrial location change should be carried out from two aspects, that is, regional endowments and industrial characteristics. On one hand industrial transfer and agglomeration are affected by the initial location and resource endowments of the target area while on the other, they are determined by their own characteristics. Therefore, in this chapter, it is intended to build a comprehensive decision mechanism of the industrial location change mainly from the perspective of the interaction of regional endowments and industrial characteristics.

5.3 Statistical Description of Manufacturing Location Change in China

5.3.1 *The Spatial Characteristics and Trends of Manufacturing Location Change*

Looking at the manufacturing sector changes between the four regions from 1980 to 2003, it is obvious that China's manufacturing industries had increasingly concentrated to the east, while in the northeast, central,

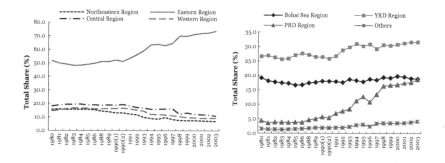

Figure 5-1   Trend of China's Manufacturing Spatial Change.

Note: 1990 (1) and 1990 (2) are manufacturing output share calculated respectively with constant prices of 1980 and 1990.

Source: Wang and Wei (2007).

and western parts of the country, the share of manufacturing has declined annually. From the perspective of changes in amplitude, the eastern region has the largest increase, while the northeast, central, and western regions have decreased a little. This shows that China's manufacturing agglomeration is geographically presented by an incremental change, rather than stock change (see Figure 5-1).

When viewing the industrial location changes within the eastern part, it is easy to observe that the growth of manufacturing share varies significantly in different regions. The Pearl River Delta (PRD) region has the largest increase of manufacturing share, followed by the Yangtze River Delta (YRD) region, while the increase of the Bohai Sea Rim (BSR) region was not so significant. However, viewing from the current share of manufacturing total output, the YRD region accounted for more than 25%, ranked the first, followed by the BSR region. However, after a rapid expansion, the PRD region's manufacturing share in 2003 reached 18.71%, which has gradually caught up with the share of the BSR region.

5.3.2   The Characteristics of Industrial Structure and the Trends of Manufacturing Location Change

Manufacturing location changes are closely linked to the escalation of regional industry. In accordance with different standards, the manufacturing industries can be divided into different categories, and thus characteristics of industrial structure and its developing trend can be determined. According to the criteria for the classification of high-tech industries published by the NBSC, the 28 manufacturing industries can be divided into three categories of high technology, medium technology, and low technology (Wang, 2007). The results (Table 5-1) showed that, between 1985 and 2005, the manufacturing share of the eastern part of the three types of technology have shown different degrees of expansion. Among these, the eastern part's share of low technology output has an increase of 15.2 percentage points; medium technical share of manufacturing output has an increase of 14.41 percentage points; and high-tech share of manufacturing output has an increase of 23.52 percentage points. This shows that the manufacturing industry of the eastern part is gradually upgraded with the increase of its total output. Over the same period, the central and western region's high-tech manufacturing output share have dropped by 8.51% and 6.84%, respectively, and the Northeastern region has fell by 8.17 %. This further shows that since the reform and opening-up, along with the clustering of manufacturing industries to the eastern region, the technical differences between the Northeastern, Midwestern, and the Eastern region of China are also gradually expanding.

5.4 Model and Variables Selection

5.4.1 *Model*

Manufacturing location change includes two interacting processes. One is transfer of industrial space, the reason the industry is transferred from one region to another; the other is agglomeration of industry in space, which is why industry gathered to a certain region. Only taking all the effects of the two factors into account, a complete explanation of manufacturing location changes can be obtained. Industrial location change phenomenon is a complex form of industrial space movement, according to the preceding analysis, and the determinants can be decided based on two categories: general factors generated by the market mechanism and external factors caused by the government's balance of payment and foreign trade. In analyzing the impact of each factor, this part applies an econometric model with the interaction of industrial and geographical characteristics to analyze the determinants of industrial location change. Midelfart-Knarvik *et al.* (2000) has studied the issue of the EU countries' industrial concentration from these two levels, that is, the industrial level and the national level.

Table 5-1 Trend of Manufacturing Output Share in Different Regions (%).

Regions		Low-tech			Mid-tech			High-tech		
		1985	1995	2005	1985	1995	2005	1985	1995	2005
Northeastern region		9.98	6.80	5.22	15.61	10.17	7.48	15.60	11.34	7.43
Eastern region	Beijing, Tianjin Shandong and Hebei region	18.93	17.88	23.94	16.27	17.20	22.19	18.36	19.60	20.76
	YRD region	30.73	27.29	30.37	28.49	29.08	29.21	27.48	27.81	32.93
	PRD region	4.88	12.14	11.98	6.74	11.27	13.10	4.49	12.38	18.79
	Other regions	1.91	4.36	5.37	1.54	2.51	2.93	1.56	2.37	2.93
	Total	56.46	61.67	71.66	53.03	60.08	67.44	51.89	62.17	75.41
Central region		19.37	17.57	12.88	17.04	16.99	14.60	17.74	14.98	9.23
Western region	Northwestern region	5.27	3.95	3.27	5.77	4.24	3.52	5.44	4.43	3.73
	Southwestern region	8.82	10.02	6.97	8.56	8.52	6.96	9.33	7.09	4.20
	Total	14.08	13.96	10.24	14.32	12.76	10.49	14.77	11.52	7.93

Source: Based on the 1985, 1995 National Industrial Census Materials and *Industrial Statistics Yearbook* (2005).

Also, they have surveyed the effects on industrial agglomeration from following two aspects: factor endowment and economic and geographical factors. Wolf (2004) believes that the most important mechanism in industrial agglomeration is the interaction between technology-intensive industries and skilled labor in those regions. Brülhart and Torstensson (1996) have researched the EU industrial concentration from the national level, which has shown that industries with increasing returns are more likely to be concentrated in the central countries which have a better market access. Therefore, we propose the following econometric model (Table 5-2)[1]:

$$\ln(r_i^k) = \alpha + \sum_j \beta[j](x_i[j] - \bar{x}[j])(y^k[j] - \bar{y}[j]) + \varepsilon_i^k, \qquad (5\text{-}1)$$

which can be expanded as:

$$\ln(r_i^k) = \alpha + \sum_j (\beta[j]x_i[j]y^k[j] - \beta[j]\bar{y}[j]x_i[j] - \beta[j]\bar{x}[j]y^k[j])$$

$$+ \sum_i \mu_i + \sum_k v^k + \varepsilon_i^k. \qquad (5\text{-}2)$$

In above formula, r_i^k is industry k's share in region I; μ_i is the fixed effect of regional endowment; v^k is the fixed effect of industry characteristic; α is a constant; $\beta[j]$ is the interaction coefficient of j; $x_i[j]$ represents the regional endowment; $y^k[j]$ represents the industry characteristics; $\bar{x}[j]$ represents the average regional endowments; and $\bar{y}[j]$ represents the average industry characteristics.

5.4.2 *Variables Selection*

(i) Location Gini coefficient that put forward by Krugman (1993) can be used to reflect the degree of unevenness of the economic activities in the geographical distribution. According to the actual situation, the employment condition can be replaced by indicators such as the incremental output or trade volume. Different scholars use different methods to calculate this

---

[1]Midelfart-Knarvik *et al.* (2000) had constructed a perfect competition model which contains the factors involved in the new classic theory and new economic geography theory.

Table 5-2 The Interaction Table of Variables in The Model.

Category	Serial No.	Regional characteristic $x_i[j]$	Industrial characteristic $y_k[j]$
Market factor	$J = 1$	Regional total population (*PEO*)	Labor intensity (*LAB*)
	$J = 2$	Human capital (*HUM*)	Technology intensity (*TECH*)
	$J = 3$	Fixed assets investment (*FIX*)	Economies of scale (*SCAL*)
	$J = 4$	Railway resource (*RAIL*)	Industrial scale (*MARK*)
	$J = 5$	Market potential (*MP*)	Intra-industry linkage (*LINK*)
	$J = 6$	Market potential (*MP*)	Inter-industry linkage (*OTHER*)
Government influence	$J = 7$	Regional fiscal value added tax revenue (*VA*)	Value added tax payable (*TEX*)
	$J = 8$	Subsidy expenditure (*SID*)	Subsidy income (*TIE*)
	$J = 9$	Local fiscal deficit (*DEF*)	Operational profit (*REV*)
Opening-up factor	$J = 10$	Foreign direct investment (*FDI*)	Foreign trader's capital (*FOR*)
	$J = 11$	Total export (*EX*)	Total export delivery (*OUT*)

Source: Based on the data collected by the author.

coefficient. Here, we have adopted Wen (2004)'s method to calculate it. The formula can be expressed as follows:

$$G_i = \frac{1}{2N^2 \bar{x}^k} \sum_{i_1}^{N} \sum_{i_2}^{N} |x_{i_1}^k - x_{i_2}^k|, \qquad (5\text{-}3)$$

where G_i is the location Gini coefficient; $\bar{x}_i$ is the average share of industry k in the regions, which equals to $1/N$; i_1, i_2 refer to two different regions; and N represents the number of regions. The Gini coefficient is between zero and one. Zero indicates a completely equal distribution of production activities between regions, while one represents that all of the production activities have clustered in only one region. Location Gini coefficient is a commonly used indicator that measures the unevenness of industrial location distribution.

(ii) Labor intensity (*LAB*). According to the HOV model, the differences in factor endowments between trading partners will lead to differences in relative cost, while a larger cost difference will lead to the concentration of the relatively larger industries. And labor resource is the main factor affecting the costs of these industries, so we apply labor intensities of industry to illustrate the impact of comparative advantage on the industrial location change. The absolute deviation of industrial unit output to the sample's average level can be used as labor intensity, which can be expressed by following formula (Traistaru and Martincus, 2003).

$$LAB_k = \left| \frac{\sum_{i=1}^{N} L_{ik}}{\sum_{i=1}^{N} VA_{ik}} - \frac{\sum_{i=1}^{N} \sum_{k=1}^{M} L_{ik}}{\sum_{i=1}^{N} \sum_{k=1}^{M} VA_{ik}} \right|, \tag{5-4}$$

where LAB_k indicates the labor intensity of industry k, which measures the characteristics of industry k's labor input and L_{ik} and VA_{ik}, respectively, denotes the proportion of the region i industry k's employment and added value.

(iii) Technology intensity (*TECH*). Industry competition, in the final analysis, is technology competition. Different industries have varied production technical requirements and factors inputs demand. According to the factor inputs demand, industries can be classified into labor-intensive, capital-intensive, and technology-intensive industries. Then it is concluded that technology is an important factor which will affect the industrial location change. It can be calculated as follows (Traistaru and Martincus, 2003):

$$TECH_k = \sqrt{\frac{1}{N} \sum_{i=1}^{N} \left[\frac{VA_{ik}/L_{ik}}{(1/N) \sum_{i=1}^{N} VA_{ik}/L_{ik}} - \frac{\sum_{k=1}^{M} VA_{ik}/L_{ik}}{(1/N) \sum_{i=1}^{N} \sum_{k=1}^{M} VA_{ik}/L_{ik}} \right]^2}, \tag{5-5}$$

where $TECH_k$ is the technology intensity of industry k, which represents the technological characteristics of industry k; L_{ik} and VA_{ik} bear the same meaning as above, and N is the number of regions.

(iv) Economies of scale ($SCAL$). Krugman (1993) analyzed the formation of industrial districts and stated that industry's economies of scale is the main factor that causes industrial agglomeration, which further leads to the formation of new industrial districts. The new trade theory suggests that economy of scale and absolute industrial agglomeration has a relatively strong correlation. There are many methods to calculate the economies of scale. Based on the availabilities of the data, we choose the following calculation method (Traistaru and Martincus, 2003).

$$SCAL_k = \frac{L_k}{EST_k} \qquad (5\text{-}6)$$

Here, $SCAL_k$ denotes industry k's characteristics in economy of scale, L_k represents the employment proportion of industry k, and EST_k indicates the number of infrastructure in industry k and is substituted by the proportion of fixed asset balance in industry k.

(v) Industrial scale ($MARK$). The use of this indicator is to measure the impact of the economic range factors on industrial concentration. We believe that the diversity of the market demand has posed new requirements of production, which is transforming from large-scale replication of production to a flexible, diversified production and making the production organization flattened to accommodate market demand at the same time. Therefore, we use market size to measure the effects of economies of scope, using the formula expressed here (Traistaru and Martincus, 2003):

$$MARK_k = \sqrt{\frac{1}{N} \sum_{i=1}^{N} \left(\frac{E_{ik}}{\sum_{i=1}^{N} E_{ik}} - \frac{\sum_{k=1}^{K} E_{ik}}{\sum_{i=1}^{N} \sum_{k=1}^{K} E_{ik}} \right)^2} \,. \qquad (5\text{-}7)$$

In the formula, $MARK_k$ represents the market characteristics of industry k; here we use it to measure the impact of economies of scope on industrial location change E_{ik} indicates the demand of product k, which is substituted by product sales revenue here.

(vi) Intra-industry linkage (*LINK*) and inter-industry linkage (*OTHER*): the investment share of intermediate goods in total output value. New economic geography theory (NEG Theory) believes that the linkage between input and output will affect the industry's location concentration. Faced with a lower cost market and a bigger product market, the input–output linkages will lead to industry concentration. The input–output data between industries are not available, and the input–output table published in *the China Statistical Yearbook* only for every five years with limited industries. Here, we use the 2002 input–output table for calculation. Intermediate inputs in objective industry divided by the total industrial output in the same year, represents the intra-industry linkage, while the intermediate inputs divided by the total industry output represents inter-industry linkage. The formula is as follows:

$$LINK_k(OTHER_k) = \frac{\sum_{i=1}^{N} M_{ik}}{\sum_{i=1}^{N} X_{ik}} \qquad (5\text{-}8)$$

$LINK_k(OTHER_k)$ indicates the intra-industry linkage (or inter-industry linkage), M_{ik} indicates the intermediate inputs to industry k that comes from industry i (or from other industries), and X_{ik} represents the total industrial output of industry k.

(vii) Market potential (*MP*). Harris (1954) came up with a formula, which assumes that market potential is proportional to the region's purchasing power and inversely proportional to the distance of the current region to other regions.

$$MP_j(Harris) = \sum_i \frac{PP_j}{DIST_{ij}} \qquad (5\text{-}9)$$

(viii) Industry value added tax (*TEX*), subsidy income (*TIE*), operating profit (*REV*), foreign capital (*FOR*) and export delivery value (*OUT*) describes the external characteristics of the industry, and those data are sourced from the China Statistical Applications decision support system database.

(ix) The region's total population (*PEO*), human capital (*HUM*), fixed assets investment (*FIX*), railway resources (*RAIL*), regional VALUE-ADDED TAX (*VA*), financial subsidies and expenditures (*SID*), local budget deficit (*DEF*), foreign direct investment (*FDI*), and region's total exports (*EX*) describe the geographical characteristics of the region, and all of these data are sourced from CEI database.

5.5 Empirical Results Analysis

The empirical analysis using data from *the Industrial Statistics Yearbook* from 1997 to 2005, and the statistical applications decision support system database from 2002 to 2005. The analysis of geographical concentration of general factors on manufacturing based on the former set of data, and the government and opening-up factor analysis used the latter set of data. Though different data sources, these two sets of data have been processed in a constant way. With respect to the estimation method, the estimation models applied on these two cases are different. When estimating the interaction effect of industry characteristics and geographical characteristics, we use the OLS model, which has a double fixed effect, aiming to distinguish this two sources that bring about heteroscedasticity — the differences between different industries and different regions. To estimate the regional differences of different industries, we have applied the Hausman test in different industries to decide which model should be used of fixed effects model or random effects model. In the fixed effects model, we use the estimation methods within the group; in the random effects model, we use the GLS model to estimate.

5.5.1 *Market Factor Analysis*

To test the interaction effect of industrial and geographical characteristics, we have estimated the data of every year, respectively. By the coefficients comparison, we then obtained the changes of every variable. As we have applied two kinds of cross-sectional data, the OLS estimates are likely to generate the problem of heteroscedasticity. Moreover, we cannot determine which kind of heteroscedasticity is more important; therefore, we tested all the assumptions with the White test.

5.5.1.1 *Not Taking the Regional and Industrial Fixed Effects into Account*

First, we have combined nine years of data, and the results are shown in Table 5-3, column 2. The equation's R^2 and F-statistics are satisfactory. The interaction between industrial economies of scale factors and investment in fixed assets factors plays a leading role in the industrial location change,

Table 5-3 Market Factors Regression Results (a).

	Pool	1997	1999	2001	2003	2005
C	1.127793	1.3174	1.2049	1.1439	1.2634	1.3132
	(15.3373***)	(7.1755***)	(5.1834***)	(5.8924***)	(6.1420***)	(6.3616***)
PEO*LAB	1.1305	6.0674	8.6625	-13.9942	-32.8462	-31.9246
	(0.1037)	(0.5496)	(0.4341)	(-0.4837)	(-1.2492)	(-1.0314)
HUM*TECH	-5.5642	-11.7860	-12.1222	-6.0016	-5.3354	-7.6874
	(-1.1419)	(-1.8348)	(-1.9965**)	(-1.0734)	(-0.8910)	(-1.2062)
FIX*SCAL	17.1462	17.9135	26.8371	32.0125	26.8909	26.7531
	(4.1188***)	(3.9306***)	(5.1231***)	(4.5778***)	(4.0425***)	(2.9719***)
RAIL*MARK	-48.5729	-5.2852	-26.6680	-46.6297	0.8275	50.3671
	(-0.8689)	(-0.0415)	(-0.4405)	(-0.4135)	(0.0078)	(0.4162)
MP*LINK	3.111519	1.1964	2.6063	4.6741	6.8150	5.7096
	(1.3958)	(0.3148)	(0.8164)	(1.3736)	(1.6877*)	(0.8297)
MP*OTHER	-1.3322	-1.4583	-1.3215	-2.2755	-2.9662	-4.3898
	(-3.1152***)	(-2.0130***)	(-2.1058***)	(-3.6186***)	(-4.1337***)	(-4.1293***)
Adjusted R^2	0.2680	0.2970	0.2720	0.2622	0.2453	0.2062
F-statistic	164.1809	20.6545	18.2703	17.3752	15.8908	12.6980
R^2	0.0369	0.0227	0.0392	0.0306	0.0388	0.0480
Observed Value	8091	899	899	899	899	899

Note: The sample interval of the table is from 1997 to 2005, estimated by Eviews. The digits in the brackets are the t-statistics of the estimated coefficients of the explanatory variables. ***, **, * indicate, respectively, that the t-statistic is significant at the level of 1%, 5%, and 10%. Due to space constraints, the test values of 1998, 2000, 2002, and 2004 have been deleted from the table.

and the results is statistically significant at the 1% level; the interaction of the labor intensity and regional demographic factors as well as the mutual impact of market potential and intra-industrial linkage effects are positively correlated to industrial location change, but their statistical results did not pass the significance test. The interaction of the technology intensities and regional demographic factors as well as the mutual impact of market potential and industrial linkage effects are negatively correlated to the industrial location change, but the statistical result is not significance either. The mixed data estimation is actually based on the assumption that parameter values do not change over time, however, regional endowments and industrial characteristics will change over time, thus the parameter values should change. So, we separate the data and carry out the test for each year, the results are as follows:

First, the interaction of economies of scale and investment in fixed assets is the main force that promotes the industrial location change. Irrespective of estimating it with the mixed data, or separately with each year's data, the coefficient of economies of scale is always positive and significant at 1% statistical level. This shows that the main factors which affect the industrial location change originated from two aspects — the industry's scale and the region's industrial environment. To view the industrial transfer within international experience, it is easy to find that the level of local supporting capabilities is crucial to the international industry transfer. Actually, this rule has already dominated the industrial transfer between the eastern and the western China.

Second, the market size of industry negatively correlated with geographic concentration. In accordance with international experience, the factors that affect industrial location change are mainly the market factors, transportation costs, and administrative factors. In other words, the market factor should have an obvious impact on industrial location change, but our empirical test results are inconsistent with this assumption, which needs a further analysis.

Third, the traditional comparative advantage factors have negatively impacted on the industrial location change. Checking the results from the mixed data, we may find that both labor intensity and technology intensity have negative impact on the industry's agglomeration. According to the data, we may find that labor intensity had positively impacted on the industrial location change before 2000; while after the year 2000, the impact has turned into negative. This shows that the industrial agglomeration regions have been gradually losing their labor cost advantages. The technology-intensity interaction coefficient has always been negative, indicating that the poor level of industrial technology as well as the technical endowment has restricted the spatial concentration of the industry. The statistical result of the equation was not significant, needing further tests in the future.

Fourth, the new economic geography theory has emphasized industrial-related factors, but it is contrary to China's manufacturing industry statistics. Here, we divided the industry linkage into intra-industry linkage and inter-industry linkage. Our empirical results is that the mutual effect of the intra-industry linkage and market potential has promoted industrial transfer, but its statistical results are not very significant; while the mutual effect of the inter-industry linkage and market potential has a negative impact on the industrial location change with its statistical results significant at the 1% level. In our view, China's market economy has born out of the planned economy, for which the industrial fragmentation phenomenon are quite serious. Though after the reform and opening-up, the marketization degree of the Chinese economy has been improved, the vertical linkages of industry are much stronger than the horizontal linkages. From the regional level, the administrative division has also imposed an obvious constraint on China's market integration level.

5.5.1.2 *Taking the Regional and Industrial Fixed Effects into Account*

In the above estimation, we have ignored the existence of heteroscedasticity caused by the different regions and industries. For a longer period, the regional endowments and industrial characteristics tend to have great impact on the industrial layout. Therefore, in the estimated equation, we must consider the industrial fixed effects and regional fixed effects. Amended with those effects, the stability of the equation has been greatly improved (Table 5-4).

First, the explanatory ability of the equation has been greatly improved. The value of R^2 increases from about 0.24 to 0.30. Meanwhile, a variety of interactions that affect the industrial location have not changed very much. The DW-statistic of the equations is around 2, which indicates that the equation does not have the autocorrelation problem. The F-statistics are significant at 95% level, which also shows that the equation has strong explanatory ability.

From the dual fixed effects regression model we conclude that the interaction of fixed assets scale and industrial economies of scale has a positive influence on the industrial location change with a strong statistical significance, which is consistent with the statistical result of the non-fixed effect model. With respect to the other five interactions, they are all negatively correlated to the industrial location change except the interaction between market potential and intra-industry linkage. In these five interactions, only the interaction of regional population and labor has a significant impact on industrial location change, the other four were not statistically significant. This is consistent with the former findings in statistics.

Second, the original equation is relatively stable in explaining the industrial location change. In the estimated equation of 2005, we have removed every interaction in the equation in turn, and then compared those results with the former ones; the results show that the coefficient has not changed much. Judging from the statistical results, we find that those coefficients have limited explanation ability over the equation.

In the dual fixed effects model, we categorize all the market factors which affect the industrial location change into three aspects, that is, interaction effect, industrial characteristics effect, and regional endowment effect. With respect to the interaction effect, the regional fixed assets factor and the industrial economies of scale have a relatively strong positive impact on the industrial location change, while the regional population and labor interaction has a negative impact. With respect to the industrial characteristics effect, only inter-industry linkage has significant positive impacts on the industrial location. With respect to the regional endowment, the market potential is positive and significant.

When removing those interactions in turn, we find that the interaction of regional population and labor force and the interaction of regional fixed assets investment and industrial economies to scale have always been significant, and the former is positive, while the latter is negative. In the industrial characteristics effect, the inter-industry effect is more obvious; in the regional endowment effect, the market potential is more significant.

Table 5-4　Market Factors Regression Results (b).

		ALL		-PEO*LAB		-HUM*TECH	
	C	131.3513	(1.1162)	126.5693	(0.977)	0.7427	(2.5641**)
Interaction	PEO*LAB	−92.3888	(−2.4322**)			−86.725	(−2.6077***)
	HUM*TECH	−5211.5	(−1.4076)	−4783.13	(−1.1568)		
	FIX*SCAL	81.7123	(4.6531***)	64.2452	(4.6282***)	70.5072	(4.3855***)
	RAIL*MARK	−120.69	(−0.5132)	−182.997	(−0.8744)	−96.2867	(−0.4148)
	MP*LINK	9.7727	(0.6599)	11.6046	(0.7218)	4.5613	(0.3187)
	MP*OTHER	0.1527	(0.0435)	0.7017	(0.2002)	−0.7860	(−0.2413)
Industrial	PEO*LAB1	−52.3734	(−1.1850)			−47.7225	(−1.1666)
characteristics	HUM*TECH1	−5291.88	(−0.8999)	−5631.95	(−0.9004)		
	FIX*SCAL1	−2.3506	(−0.2636)	2.8213	(0.4508)	−4.3635	(−0.4936)
	RAIL*MARK1	−81.0619	(−0.3245)	−67.619	(−0.2695)	−76.9483	(−0.3015)
	MP*LINK1	−12.6462	(−1.4484)	−12.7897	(−1.4973)	−15.5599	(−2.1426**)
	MP*OTHER1	17.9091	(11.4596***)	17.8821	(12.5694***)	17.3629	(10.2346***)
Regional	PEO*LAB2	−57.9905	(−0.8263)			−32.4215	(−0.3927)
endowment	HUM*TECH2	−4370.13	(−0.6588)	−2725.24	(−0.3649)		
	FIX*SCAL2	57.6933	(1.1709)	26.6231	(1.0990)	29.3393	(0.4798)
	RAIL*MARK2	−9.4463	(−0.0465)	12.7204	(0.0640)	−3.7833	(−0.0181)
	MP*LINK2MP	30.5850	(1.0688)	31.0234	(1.0457)	22.5894	(0.9484)
	MP*OTHER2	9.9496	(2.3210**)	10.6333	(2.4151**)	8.3742	(2.3557**)
Industrial/Regional fixed effect		Y	Y	Y	Y	Y	Y
Adjusted R^2/F-statistic		0.3095	4.8484	0.3088	5.050	0.3082	5.0345
R^2/Observed value		0.1647	899	0.1608	899	0.1621	899

Note: The sample is the statistic of 2005, estimated by Eviews. The digits in the brackets are the t-statistics of the estimated coefficients of the explanatory variables. ***, **, * indicate, respectively, that the t-statistic is significant at the level of 1%, 5%, and 10%.

These results suggest that under the double fixed effects model, the market factors have not affected the industrial location change so much.

5.5.2 *Fiscal Revenue and Expenditure Factors Analysis*

The interaction of industrial value added tax and local government value added tax revenues (VA * TEX) measures the tax relationship between industries and regions. The tax revenue has an opposite correlation with the industrial location change, that is to say, the taxation revenue of one region is negatively correlated with the degree of region's industrial geographical concentration. The interaction of local financial subsidies and industrial subsidies (SID * TIE) measures the support provided by local government to industry, which is an important index that positively correlated with the industrial location change. The local government's fiscal position

-FIX*SCAL		-RAIL*MARK		-MP*LINK		-MP*OTHER	
34.1038	(0.2897)	124.9605	(1.0373)	133.6908	(1.1788)	116.6088	(0.8557)
38.0370	(1.1576)	−97.5683	(−2.8035***)	−93.8081	(−2.4507**)	−87.3582	(−2.38**)
642.4708	(0.1692)	−4992.97	(−1.3662)	−4913.71	(−1.3915)	−5164.31	(−1.4132)
		82.1125	(4.7118***)	81.1976	(4.7337***)	81.206	(4.620***)
−150.844	(−0.6946)			−122.695	(−0.5222)	−118.144	(−0.5053)
4.5224	(0.2813)	9.8223	(0.6665)			10.7803	(0.767)
1.7624	(0.3718)	0.1009	(0.0288)	0.8571	(0.2619)		
24.6815	(0.5942)	−58.7053	(−1.2955)	−50.3342	(−1.1179)	−75.2984	(−1.3715)
−3140.27	(−0.5436)	−4952.24	(−0.8084)	−5893.96	(−1.0011)	−4182.49	(−0.5563)
		−1.5444	(−0.1707)	−1.4186	(−0.1608)	13.45431	(1.0397)
−117.945	(−0.4647)			−65.2307	(−0.2793)	−99.8922	(−0.4498)
−13.6653	(−1.4292)	−12.7516	(−1.4760)			3.1267	(0.1639)
18.7341	(11.9573***)	17.4470	(11.3663***)	17.0967	(10.2811***)		
7.9459	(0.2390)	−66.6674	(−0.9526)	−59.0997	(−0.8307)	−64.467	(−0.8616)
−740.79	(−0.1054)	−4462.7	(−0.6643)	−3638.62	(−0.5662)	−3961.19	(−0.6171)
		62.2453	(1.2800)	55.1003	(1.1067)	65.745	(1.2505)
7.4600	(0.0377)			−13.7459	(−0.069)	−54.1349	(−0.2932)
26.1301	(0.8683)	30.9093	(1.1372)			40.6963	(1.3709)
10.8360	(2.1771**)	10.0976	(2.3888**)	12.0633	(2.7364***)		
Y	Y	Y	Y	Y	Y	Y	Y
0.2841	4.4841	0.3125	5.1366	0.3094	5.0622	0.2982	4.8027
0.1413	899	0.1661	899	0.1638	899	0.1558	899

has a great influence on the industrial location change. Usually, regions with better financial conditions will pay greater attention to improving local investment environment and providing better matching policies to facilitate corresponding investment project. Therefore, we believe that the revenue and expenditure of local governments will affect geographic concentration of industry. Based on the indicators selected to carry out the statistical analysis (Table 5-5), we can come up with the following judgments:

Firstly, the interaction of industrial value added tax and local government value added tax revenues negatively affect the degree of industrial location change. What the indicator shows is consistent with the experience judgments, but it did not pass the significance test. To observe the overall test results of the equation, we find that the adjusted R^2 has maintained around 0.29, the F-statistics have also passed the significance test. In the comprehensive judgment of all the factors, the index has passed the significance test at 5% or 10%. This suggests that the taxation level has a relatively big impact on the industrial location change, while obvious regional differences exist.

Table 5-5 Financial Factors Regression Results.

Variable	2002			2005		
	(1)	(2)	(3)	(4)	(5)	(6)
C	64.2417 (1.5882)	45.5323 (1.1041)	56.2207 (1.4827)	53.7108 (1.8880*)	49.0392 (1.6876*)	51.1131 (1.9571*)
PEO*LAB	-45.3141 (-1.6307)	-48.2869 (-1.6861*)	-51.0179 (-1.8634*)	-53.3204 (-1.7250*)	-67.2184 (-1.9972**)	-67.5263 (-2.2340**)
HUM*TECH	-5875.252 (-1.5654)	-4141.539 (-1.0826)	-5144.851 (-1.4620)	-5001.375 (-1.8549*)	-4553.551 (-1.6536*)	-4768.245 (-1.9239*)
FIX*SCAL	66.2781 (3.6819***)	72.5397 (3.8653***)	77.8319 (4.6172***)	67.3997 (3.6809***)	70.8041 (3.6736***)	77.3486 (4.2055***)
RAIL*MARK	-171.0412 (-0.9738)	-183.6540 (-0.9561)	-185.7556 (-1.0805)	-124.8834 (-0.7540)	-156.6762 (-0.8152)	-123.8523 (-0.7726)
MP*LINK	6.0601 (0.8217)	7.5228 (0.8042)	8.9585 (1.1622)	5.8747 (0.4269)	7.8497 (0.5287)	10.6554 (0.7577)
MP*OTHER	-0.6873 (-0.3821)	-1.2256 (-0.6820)	0.0925 (0.0471)	0.0559 (0.0167)	-0.8425 (-0.2616)	1.0585 (0.2799)
VA*TEX	-117.4943 (-2.4730**)	-54.1561 (-1.1565)		-112.3719 (-1.8661*)	-61.7858 (-1.2603)	

(Continued)

Table 5-5 (*Continued*)

Variable	2002			2005		
	(1)	(2)	(3)	(4)	(5)	(6)
SID*TIE	36.9809	30.9083		8.9843	6.4271	
	(1.0830)	(0.8957)		(0.6778)	(0.4209)	
DEF*REV	−3.2090	29.8319		11.6708	5.8064	
	(−0.0311)	(0.2820)		(0.1705)	(0.0762)	
FDI*FOR	52.5167		24.1686	20.5150		2.2467
	(2.0960**)		(0.7906)	(0.9588)		(0.0990)
EX*OUT	23.3181		27.3778	22.7460		27.7775
	(2.7634***)		(2.6911***)	(2.6119***)		(2.7456***)
Regional effect	Y	Y	Y	Y	Y	Y
Industrial effect	Y	Y	Y	Y	Y	Y
Adjusted R^2	0.3466	0.3243	0.3347	0.3145	0.2998	0.3154
F-statistic	6.3742	5.9514	6.3421	5.5131	5.3113	5.8084
R^2	0.1479	0.1369	0.1451	0.1651	0.1531	0.1615
Observed value	899	899	899	899	899	899

Note: The sample interval of the table is from 2002 to 2005, estimated by Eviews. The digits in the brackets are the t-statistics of the estimated coefficients of the explanatory variables, ***, **, * indicate respectively that the t-statistic is significant at the level of 1%, 5%, and 10%. Due to space constraints, the test values of 1998, 2000, 2002, and 2004 have been deleted from the table.

Secondly, the subsidy expenditure of government and subsidy income of industries have prompted industrial location change. However, the statistical results are not significant. This suggests that fiscal policies have played a certain role in pushing forward the industrial location change, but the location change has mainly been dominated by the effect of scale economies and intra-industry linkage. The fiscal subsidy's function is limited.

Thirdly, the interaction of the local government fiscal balances and industry's revenue has an ambiguous impact on industrial location change. When holding the industrial characteristics as constant, we find that the fiscal income and expenditure factors have a positive impact on industrial location change. But, under the comprehensive test, the influence turned out to be negative without statistical significance. This contradiction makes us unable to determine the impact that the interaction imposed on industrial location change.

When looking into specific industries, we find that taxation interaction, subsidy interaction, and profit interaction have positive impact on industries' geographic agglomeration (Table 5-6).

First, when the high-tech industries are observed, we may find that, of these seven high-tech manufacturing industries, only three have negative taxation interaction coefficients, of which only subsidy interaction coefficient is significant. Subsidy interaction coefficients are negative in three industries, in which only the Instrumentation and Office Supplies Manufacturing Industry has a significant coefficient. Profit interaction coefficients are negative in three industries, in which only the coefficient of the Electronic and Communications Equipment Manufacturing Industry shows significance.

Second, when the low-tech manufacturing industries are taken into account, we find that among all 11 industries, the taxation interaction coefficients are negative in 8 industries, 6 of which are significant. The subsidies interaction coefficients are negative in six industries, four of them are significant. The profit interaction coefficients are positive in six industries, all of them are significant. Thus, for the low-tech manufacturing industries, tax and subsidy have negative effects, while profit has an obvious positive effect.

Third, when viewing the mid-tech manufacturing industries, we find that among these 10 industries, the taxation interaction coefficients are

Table 5-6 High-Tech Industry Regression Results.

Industry	Oil processing and coking industry	Chemical materials and chemical products manufacturing industry	Pharmaceutical manufacturing industry	Machinery manufacturing industry	Special equipment manufacturing industry	Electronic and communication equipment manufacturing industry	Instruments and office machinery manufacturing industry
Code	25	26	27	35	36	40	41
C	0.9025 (2.4124**)	1.1813 (5.9791***)	3.3123 (5.898***)	0.3354 (3.0231***)	1.3281 (7.661***)	0.5561 (4.4861***)	0.6002 (2.2914**)
PEO*LAB	−315.914 (−2.0061**)	127.7938 (0.4519)	−694.411 (−0.8621)	121.2543 (5.4744***)	145.2583 (6.1732***)	23.5965 (2.011**)	123.4851 (2.2438**)
HUM*TECH	32.9075 (0.6259)	−33.6217 (−1.6113)	−49.0158 (−1.4709)	11.1825 (1.8518*)	−26.2196 (−14.3668***)	−6.4299 (−0.8824)	18.473 (1.0228)
FIX*SCAL	−1290.63 (−1.1669)	13.9982 (0.1704)	91.6252 (0.6686)	−35.9949 (−5.2292***)	22.5164 (1.9481*)	−0.464 (−0.0147)	−8.1368 (−0.8526)
RAIL*MARK	1333.082 (2.0984**)	−252.044 (−0.6297)	−2662.85 (−1.3792)	76.945 (0.5297)	−480.149 (−3.3926***)	−67.803 (−1.3591)	−106.58 (−0.9309)
MP*LINK	3018235 (1.0874)	−104502 (−3.5780***)	−437762 (−0.6654)	−44763.2 (−1.0946)	1030868 (22.7275***)	−119753 (−1.2968)	173442.2 (0.8573)
MP*OTHER	−157115 (−1.0874)	21768.11 (3.5787***)	178799.5 (0.6655)	10347.63 (1.0944)	−105382 (−22.7334***)	22350.75 (1.2971)	−15157.6 (−0.85765)
VA*TEX	574.6226 (1.2867)	−44.8659 (−1.1132)	−1163.19 (−1.5794)	344.4714 (9.6257***)	−294.767 (−7.4679***)	51.5145 (2.0286**)	465.0878 (1.0317)
SID*TIE	−38.9843 (−0.9461)	13.5648 (0.468)	833.1542 (2.0656**)	−99.9753 (−1.0349)	30.6526 (0.4287)	7.1998 (1.2875)	−223.379 (−2.3715**)

(Continued)

Table 5-6 (*Continued*)

Industry	Oil processing and coking industry	Chemical materials and chemical products manufacturing industry	Pharmaceutical manufacturing industry	Machinery manufacturing industry	Special equipment manufacturing industry	Electronic and communication equipment manufacturing industry	Instruments and office machinery manufacturing industry
DEF*REV	-83.3939 (-0.6868)	55.8044 (0.5164)	1247.402 (1.0652)	14.2229 (0.675)	57.175 (0.8468)	-99.0888 (-4.0924***)	-196.867 (-0.6874)
FDI*FOR	156.1707 (0.411)	35.2598 (1.7862*)	147.1805 (0.9251)	64.6594 (18.8607***)	-78.6969 (-3.6845***)	6.9956 (2.1471**)	-107.861 (-3.0011***)
EX*OUT	-509.842 (-1.9901**)	-69.1563 (-1.6545*)	302.762 (1.3581)	-205.763 (-19.1634***)	311.5264 (2.2936***)	14.2214 (10.2981***)	141.4862 (4.6065***)
R^2	0.2504	0.0859	0.2544	0.2204	0.9928	0.3617	0.1997
F-statistic	3.4013	0.9565	3.4741	2.878	274.998	5.7694	2.5411
Hausman	5.18	7.36	5.53	10.87	33.43	5.03	8.68
p-value	0.8792	0.6908	0.8529	0.3675	0.0002	0.6565	0.5629
Model	RE	RE	RE	RE	FE	RE	RE
Observed value	124	124	124	124	124	124	124

Note: 1. The sample interval of the table is from 2002 to 2005, estimated by Eviews. The digits in the brackets are the t-statistics of the estimated coefficients of the explanatory variables. ***, **, and * indicate, respectively, that the t-statistic is significant at the level of 1%, 5%, and 10%.

negative in six industries, in which only the coefficients of Colored Metal Smelting and Processing Industry and Electrical Machinery and Equipment Manufacturing Industry are significant. The subsidy interaction coefficient are positive in seven industries, of which four are significant. The profit interaction coefficients are positive in three industries, the rest seven are negative. Thus, for mid-tech manufacturing industries, taxation and profit have negative effects, while the subsidy has a positive effect.

5.5.3 *Opening-up Factors Analysis*

To estimate the impact of foreign trade on industrial location change, we have built up two indicators. One is the interaction of attracted foreign investment and the proportion that foreign investment occupies in the industry (*FDI* * *FOR*); the other is the interaction of export level of the region and the industry's export proportion (*EX* * *OUT*). These two indicators have measured the opening-up's influence on domestic industry's spatial layout in both input aspect and output aspect. In this design, these two interactions have a positive relationship with the industrial location change, that is, foreign investment and trade will prompt the agglomeration of domestic industries. Judging from the statistical results, we can draw the following conclusions:

First, foreign trade interaction is a main factor that gives impetus to the industrial location changes. Since the reform and opening-up, the eastern part of China has utilized the regional advantages to vigorously develop the export processing trade, the foreign markets' demand promotes a continuously cluster of the domestic production factors to the coastal region. Development of processing trade also brings capital and technology to the eastern region that facilitate industry upgrading, which further prompt geographic agglomeration of manufacturing industries in the east. It can be drawn from the foreign trade equation that from 2002 to 2005 the coefficient is positive with significance at 1% level. In the combined effects equation, this indicator still maintains the 1% level statistical significance, which further confirmed the conclusion.

Second, foreign investment also contributed to industrial location changes. Since the reform and opening-up, the southeast coastal regions as the forefront of opening-up have attracted a large number of foreign direct investments. These foreign investments have further induced the labor and capital of the central and western regions to gather to the eastern regions, which sharply raised the manufacturing share of the southeastern coastal region. The statistical results in Table 5-6 also prove this. Between 2002 and 2005, the interaction of the region's total exports and the industry's export has positively impacted the industrial location change, but it did not pass the significance test. With the deepening of the opening-up, the eastern part's production factors such as labor, land costs have continued to rise. At the same time, the central and western regions have gradually accelerated their opening-up steps. As a result, the foreign investments tend to be decentralized, and thus the impact of foreign investment has been weakened.

In different types of industries, export factors and foreign investment factors have positive impact on most of the manufacturing sectors' geographic agglomeration. In other words, these two interactions are conducive to manufacturing geographic concentration, though showed great differences in specific industries.

First, the majority of the high-tech manufacturing industries have utilized the interaction of attracted foreign investments and the regional occupied foreign investment, and that of export level of the region and the industry's export proportion, which has a significant effect on the industry's geographical agglomeration. But these interactions have negative effects in a few industries. Foreign investment interaction has negative impact on the Special Equipment Manufacturing Industry and Instruments and Office Machinery Manufacturing Industry. Export factors have negative impact on Oil Processing and Coking Industry, Chemical Materials and Chemical Products Manufacturing Industry, and Ordinary Machinery Manufacturing Industry in their geographic agglomeration with statistical significance.

Second, for the traditional low-tech manufacturing industries, foreign investment interaction and export interaction are positively impacted on its location. Among the 11 low-technology manufacturing industries, 5 have positive foreign interaction coefficients. The rest six industries have negative coefficients. In which only the Coefficient of Clothing and Other Fiber Products Industry is significant but the other 5 industries do not pass through the significant test. As to the export interaction, 11 are positive, while 4 are negative. In these positive coefficients, five of them have passed the significance test. Therefore, we can conclude in general that foreign investment interaction and foreign trade interaction are conducive to spatial agglomeration of low-tech manufacturing industries.

Third, for mid-tech manufacturing industries, foreign investment interaction has a positive impact on the manufacturing industry's geographic agglomeration, while the export interaction has a negative impact. In the 10 mid-technology manufacturing industries, merely three have negative foreign investment interaction coefficients, but only the coefficient of the Ferrous Metal Smelting and Rolling Processing Industry has passed the significance test. Seven industries have negative export interaction coefficients, in which three of them have passed the significance test, indicating that the negative effects of export factors is not very obvious.

5.6 Conclusions

This chapter considers the issue of industrial location change from a relatively macro level. The industrial location change here is treated as an integrated problem of industrial transfer and industrial agglomeration. The industrial transfer and industrial agglomeration are two sides of a coin, which is like a paralleled dynamic process. So we need to analyze this problem comprehensively with "push" and "pull" factors. In terms of the industrial transfer, cross-border investment and international trade are two forms of an industry's global spread. The factors that affect industrial transfer should contain, but not be limited to, the comparative advantage, resource endowments, global strategy and increasing returns to scale, and regional comparative advantages in the degree of openness, cultural background, infrastructure, etc. In terms of industrial agglomeration, economies of scale in the intermediate inputs production, externality, labor market sharing and knowledge spillovers, demand effects, cost factors, and supporting capacities together determine the industrial agglomeration. Through empirical analysis, this chapter proposes the following conclusions.

First, China's manufacturing industry had increasingly concentrated to the east, when viewing the growth of manufacturing share within the eastern part. It is easy to observe that the growth rate varies significantly. The YRD region occupies the biggest share, while the PRD region has a faster growth rate. Meanwhile, the manufacturing location change has always been linked to the region structural upgrading. The eastern region's manufacturing industries have not only expanded themselves in scale but also upgraded its industrial structure, enjoying a fast grow in its high-tech industries. The central and western regions have developed relatively slower in the high-tech area with an increasingly wider technology gap when comparing with the eastern part. Above conclusions are consistent with the facts since China's reform and opening-up. More than 30 years of reform and opening-up, on the one hand, China has stimulated the growth of national economy, turning China into a world factory; on the other hand, with the gradual widening regional urban–rural gap, all the regions compete with each other fiercely to seize more resources, investments, and talents, and to take the lead in the market. Regional friction and competition becomes increasingly fierce, and the regional coordination and industrial layout adjustment will become the main theme of macroeconomic regulation and control.

Second, from the market perspective, the interaction of scale economies and fixed assets investment has played the most important role in promoting industrial location change. Market factors should be the most important factor in industrial location change, but the poor level of industrial technology as well as technical endowment has restricted industry spatial agglomeration. The industry-related factors are contrary to China's manufacturing industry statistics. This shows that the main factors affecting industrial location change come from two aspects: one is the industry's scale and the other is region's industrial development environment. The impact of product sales on the industrial location change needs a further study. The industrial agglomeration areas have gradually lost their labor cost advantages, at the same time, the industrial technology level and technology endowment differences between regions have hampered the clustering of industries; the industrial fragmentation phenomenon are quite serious; the vertical linkages of the industry are much stronger than the horizontal linkages. The administrative division has also imposed an obvious constraint on China's market integration level.

Third, from the fiscal revenue and expenditure perspective, the financial subsidy expenditure and industrial subsidy income have played an obvious role in prompting industrial location change, while the regional government's value added tax and industrial value added tax have hampered the change of industrial location, still the fiscal condition of the local government and industrial profit level have an ambiguous effect on industrial location change. This shows that the financial transfer payment has played a more significant role in promoting industrial location changes. But, the industrial location change is mainly determined by scale economies and intra-industry linkage effects, where financial subsidies have a limited impact. The taxation level has a relatively great impact on industrial location change, and it varied significantly in all the regions. In industries with different technology levels, the taxation factor will hamper the agglomeration of low-tech and mid-tech industries, but its impact on the high-tech industry is limited; the subsidy factor is unfavorable to the low-tech industry's agglomeration, while favors the high-tech industry.

Fourth, from the opening-up perspective, foreign trade is the main force that prompt China's industrial location change, at the same time, foreign investment also contributed to it. Since the reform and opening-up, the eastern part has fully utilized its regional advantages to vigorously develop the export processing trade. The foreign markets' demand promotes the continuously cluster of domestic production factors to the coastal region, which in turn prompting manufacturing industries to agglomerate in the eastern region. The pouring foreign investments have also led labor and capital clustering to the eastern region from the central and western regions. Thus, the manufacturing share of the southeast coastal regions has sharply risen. In industries with different technology levels, we find that the export factor and foreign investment factor have obvious pushing effects on the majority of manufacturing industries, though it varied in different regions when comes to specific industries.

References

Brülhart, M. and J. Torstensson (1996). *Regional Integration, Scale Economies and Industry Location*. Discussion Paper No. 1435, Centre for Economic Policy Research.

Chen, G. and H. Chen (2001). Inter-district Industrial Transfer Theories. *Social Sciences in Guizhou*, (4), 2–6.

Chen, J. (2002). Empirical Research of Current Chinese Firms Relocation — Based on Analysis of Questionnaire Report of 105 Companies from Zhejiang Province. *Management World*, (6), 64–74.

Ellison, G. and E. L. Glaeser (1999). The Geographic Concentration of Industry: Does Natural Advantage Explain Agglomeration? *The American Economic Review*, 89(2), 311–316.

Harris, C. (1954). The market as a factor in the localization of industry in the United States. *Annals of the Association of American Geographers*, 64, 315–348.

He, C. and X. Xie (2006). Geographic Concentration and Provincial Specialization of Chinese Manufacturing Industry. *Acta Geographica Sinica, 61*(2), 212–222.

Helpman, E. and P. Krugman (1985). *Market Structure and Foreign Trade.* Cambridge: MIT Press.

Kojima, K. (1987). *Foreign Trade Theory (Chinese Version)*. Tianjin: Nankai University Press.

Krugman, P. M. (1991). Increasing Returns and Economic Geography. *Journal of Political Economy*, 99(3), 483–499.

Krugman, P. M. (1993). First Nature, Second Nature, and Metropolitan Location. *Journal of Regional Science*, 33(2), 129–144.

Krugman, P. M. (2000). *Geography and Trade (Chinese Version)*. Beijing: Peking University Press, China Renmin University Press.

Lewis, W. A. (1984). *The Evolution of the International Economic Order (Chinese Version)*. Beijing: The Commercial Press.

Liu, J. (2005). The Global Industrial Space Integration's New Trend-Diffusion and Agglomeration. *Research on Development*, (2), 23–26.

Midelfart-Knarvik, K. H., H. G. Overman, S. J. Redding and A. J. Venables (2000). *Comparative Advantage and Economic Geography: Estimating the Location of Production in the EU.* CEPR Discussion Paper No. 2618, London.

Porter, M. E. (1998). Clusters and the new economics of competition. *Harvard Business Review*, 76(6), 77–90.

Porter, M. E. (2002). *Competitive Advantage (Chinese Version)*. Beijing: Huaxia Publishing House.

Prebisch, R. (1990). *Peripheral Capitalism: Crisis and Transformation* (Chinese version). Beijing: The Commercial Press.

Shi, Qi (2004). Economic Integration Principles and Industrial Transfer. *China Industrial Economics*, (10), 5–12.

Traistaru, I. and C. V. Martincus (2003). *Determinants of manufacturing concentration patterns in Mercosur.* Paper presented at the *ERSA Conference '03*, p. 191. European Regional Science Association.

Traistaru, I., P. Nijkamp and S. Longhi (2002). Regional Specialization and Concentration of Industrial Activity in Accession Countries, *ZEI Working Paper.*

Venables, A. J. (1996). Equilibrium Locations of Vertically Linked Industries. *International Economic Review*, 37(2), 341–359.

Vernon, R. (1966). International Investment and International Trade in the Product Cycle, The *Quarterly Journal of Economics*, 80, 190–207.

Wang, Yeqiang and Houkai Wei (2007), Characteristics of Industries, Competition for Space and the Geographic Concentration in Manufacture. *Management World*, (4), 68–77; 171–172.

Wang, Yeqiang (2007). *Formation Mechanism and Determinants Analysis of Geographic Concentration.* PhD. Dissertation, Graduate School of the Chinese Academy of Social Sciences, Beijing.

Wei, Houkai (2003). Development Trend and Effect Towards Competitiveness of Firm Relocation. *Fujian Tribune (The Humanities & Social Sciences Monthly)*, (4), 11–15.

Wen, Mei (2004). Regional Repositioning and Aggregation of Chinese Industries. *Economic Research Journal*, (2), 84–94.

Wolf, N (2004). *Endowments, Market Potential, and Industrial Location: Evidence from Interwar Poland (1918–1939).* Working Paper.

Zhao, Zhangyao and Bin Wang (2005). International Industrial Transfer Mode Study. *China Industrial Economics*, (10), 12–19.

Zheng, Jianghuan, Chunliang Gao, Zongqing Zhang and Jian Liu (2004). International Manufacturing Transfer: Motive, Technological Learning, and Policy-oriented. *Management World*, (11), 29–38.

Chapter 6

Manufacturing Location Change in China: Structural Effects and Spatial Effects: A Test of the "Krugman Hypothesis"

Wang Yeqiang and Wei Houkai

6.1 Literature Review: The Development of "Krugman Hypothesis"

In recent years, the impact of economic integration on the spatial structure of economic activity has aroused broad interest of the economists; consequently, all kinds of trade theories, economic geography theory, and growth models have been used to explain the spatial structure of economic activity. The spatial structure effect on the local economic activity caused by European economic integration has become a typical example of this issue (Krugman, 1991a, 1991b, 1993). Krugman puts forward a hypothesis based on this: regions become more specialized and economic activity will become more geographically concentrated. This well-known hypothesis becomes the starting point of the analysis of spatial economic structure.

From the perspective of theoretical research development, trade theory and location theory are very close and even accepted as "two sides of the same coin" (Isard, 1956), however, for a long time, they are seen as the two branches of economics. It was not until the 1990s did the economists began to study the spatial dimensions of trade theory. In particular, Krugman's study combined international economic and regional economic theory, which formed an industrial location theory framework incorporating trade theory, economic geography theory, and urban economic theory (Krugman, 1991a, 1991b). In term of current research development, the impact of the economic integration on regional specialization and industrial activity location can be divided into three types of models. The traditional trade theory uses the comparative advantage of production costs formed by productivity (or technical) difference (Ricardo, 1817) and the factor endowment differences between countries (or regions) (Heckscher, 1919; Ohlin, 1933) to explain the pattern of specialization. The new trade theory focuses on the role of the interaction between enterprises in the formation of the increasing returns on the product market, as well as the accessibility of national (or regional) commodity markets to explain the pattern of specialization and location of industrial activities (Krugman, 1979, 1980, 1981; Helpman and Krugman, 1985; Krugman and Venables, 1990). According to the new economic geography model, market advantage is endogenous, and the pattern of specialization is the spatial concentration of economic activity (Krugman, 1991a, 1991b; Krugman and Venables, 1995; Venables, 1996). Among the different interpretations of the spatial structure of the industry, these three theoretical approaches all regard the raising level of specialization as a result of trade liberalization and economic integration. The difference is that the traditional trade theory is based on productivity and regional endowment differences to explain regional specialization, while new trade theory and new economic geography model emphasize increasing returns, agglomeration economies, and cumulative processes to explain the concentration of economic activity in a particular country or region.

Compared to the progress in theoretical research, the empirical interpretation is very limited. The existing studies mostly come from Europe. Brülhart (1996) and Brülhart and Torstensson (1996) research the evolution of the pattern of specialization of the 11 EU countries, to support U-curved relationship between regional integration and spatial agglomeration. Amiti (1999) found that the specialization levels of Belgium, Denmark, Germany, Greece, and New Zealand noticeably improved in the period of 1968–1990. On the contrary, the specialization level of France, Spain, and the Britain during 1980–1990 is significantly lowered. In addition, some studies suggest that the European specialization level has increased between 1980 and 1990 (Hine, 1990; Greenaway and Hine, 1991; Aiginger *et al.*, 1999; Midelfart-Knarvik *et al.*, 2000).

However, according to the empirical analysis of trade data, the EU Member States have a diverse rather than specialized manufacturing export model (Sapir, 1996; Brülhart, 2001). Amiti (1999) discovered that the degree of industrial geographical agglomeration varies, it increased in 17 regions whereas decrease was observed in 6. Brülhart and Torstensson (1996) found that from 1980 to 1990, the EU industrial economies of scale and industrial concentration were positively correlated with the central area. Brülhart (1998) found that the industries highly concentrated in the countries at the center of Europe are considerably influenced by the economies of scale. Midelfart-Knarvik *et al.* (2000) found that in the years of 1970–1997, the EU industrial location had experienced stark changes, the slowly increasing and unskilled labor-intensive industries become more concentrated in the peripheral low-wage countries, while at the same time some high-tech industries become more diffused. Other scholars have done some research on the spatial structure of US manufacturing sector. Hanson (1996) found that aggregation is related to increasing returns. The integration of the US economy leads the Mexico industries to concentrate in the accessible areas of the US market. Ellison and Glaeser (1997)'s studies of the geographic concentration of US manufacturing sector showed that all industries have a tendency to be localized; however, the degree of most industrial concentration is not obvious; and the concentration of industry and natural advantages are correlated.

Empirical evidence from the EU countries' level tends to assume that the EU is at a more concentrated and specialized stage, and thus proves the Krugman hypothesis (Aiginger and Leitner, 2002). Some studies have described the EU's internal specialization and geographic concentration. However, due to the availability and quality of the data, many researchers have used the national-level data (Aiginer and Pfaffermayr 2004; Brülhart, 2001; Midelfahrt-Knarvik *et al.*, 2000, 2002; Amiti, 1999; Haaland *et al.*, 1999), and the researches targeted at the regional level within the EU are very limited. The existing literature researches on the EU all support the argument of that the EU countries have become more specialized after 1970. However, there are two sides regarding regional specialization and industrial geographical concentration: on one hand, it is the rise of the level of specialization and geographic concentration, on the other hand, it is the emergence of non-specialization and industrial decentralization. For instance, Aiginger and Leitner (2002) have pointed out that the EU's regional economic activities are going through a decentralized process. Therefore, Combes and Overman (2004) and Krieger-Boden

(2000) advocate that the researchers must be careful when observing the regional level.

At present, the domestic researches are mainly carried out from three aspects: First is the study of regional specialization. Cai *et al.* (2002) examined the trend of regional specialization of the Chinese economy as a whole, as an industrial economy, and as an agricultural economy, respectively. Fan (2007) found that the level of regional specialization of the Chinese industry has witnessed a great improvement since the late 1980s. Second is the study of geographic concentration. Gao (2002) explored the reasons for industrial geographic agglomeration, and pointed out that the natural advantage agglomeration forces, spillovers agglomeration forces, and cultural cohesion are the fundamental driving forces of industrial geographic concentration; Wang and Wei (2007) analyzed the factors influencing manufacturing sector's geographical concentration. Third is taking these two aspects into account. Fan (2004) advocated that China was still in the phase of "high industrial agglomeration, low regional specialization; Xian and Wen (2006) found that, since 1985, both the Chinese industrial localization and regional specialization had deepened; Chen and Yang (2006) maintained that the specialization level of different provinces in China had presented a notably increasing trend from 1993 to 2003; the degree of concentration in most manufacturing sectors was up dramatically and the agglomeration level of the entire manufacturing industry also increased. In terms of research methodology, the existing researches all follow the path of Krugman (1991b). However, all the above studies of regional specialization and industrial geographic concentration fail to clearly identify the difference between the two and distinguish these two kinds of effects.

This chapter attempts to start from the differences of geographic concentration and regional specialization in statistics, give them different economic implications, then use the Chinese industrial economic data to analyze the different effects of economic integration of big country on the industrial economic activity, thus explaining the transformation of manufacturing industry's location. Section 6.2 will systematically introduce the development and application of the Shift-Share Model; Section 6.3 is devoted to the preliminary analysis of the manufacturing activities in China; Section 6.4

adopts the spatial dependence and spatial filtering model to further analyze the spatial effect; and Section 6.5 is the conclusion.

6.2 Analyzing Methods and Models

Regional specialization of an industry and an industry concentrated in a certain area are two interrelated economic phenomena. In general, the specialization of the regional industrial structure means a few industries contributing to most of the output value of the region, showing a strong structural effect, resulting in areas of high level of specialization and areas of low level of specialization. Therefore, we define regional specialization as the structural effects of economic integration; the industrial geographic concentration means most of the industrial outputs are concentrated in a few areas, which indicates this industry possesses the agglomeration effects in space, thus forming the central region and peripheral region. We define geographic concentration as the spatial effect of economic integration. There are many formulas estimating the regional specialization and industrial geographic concentration, but in the existing empirical literature, it is in fact different calculation methods of the same industrial activity matrix (rows of the matrix representing region and the column representing industry). Index calculated from a regional perspective is to measure the specialization level while the index calculated from the industry point of view is to indicate the degree of geographical concentration (Krugman, 1991; Midelfahrt-Knarvik *et al.*, 2000; Amiti, 1999; Brülhart, 2001; Glaeser *et al.*, 1992).

In addition to the above two statistical methods, some scholars use the shift-share analysis to decompose the industrial activity matrix, and reach some new conclusions (Dunn, 2005; Hewings, 1976; Nazara and Hewings, 2004; Mayor and López, 2008). Shift-share analysis, as a statistical analysis tool, is widely used in the analysis of regional growth. In the shift-share analysis, regional economic growth can be split into three components: the first component refers to the increased amount of a particular industry in accordance with the growth rate of all industries of the country during a base period, which measures the common part of the economic growth. It is the basis for the development of all industries in all regions. The second component refers to the difference between the real increased amount of the industry and increased amount at the average growth rate of all industries of the country, reflecting the economic development divergences brought about by regional industrial structure difference, that is the structural effect, if the growth rate of one industry exceeds the national average economic growth rate, the component is positive. The third component is the difference of increased amount between the actual growth rate of a particular industry in a specific area and that of the country, reflecting competition between overall economies of all regions, which is the spatial effect.

Dunn (2005) believes that the main objective of the classic shift-share analysis is to quantify the geospatial changes; therefore, spatial dependence and spatial differences are rarely considered. The classic shift-share analysis only considers the overall effect of the regional economy in line with the country's economic development, while ignoring the link between the regional units. Hewings (1976) proposed a shift-share model including spatial interactions. If the regional economy starts convergence with the national economy, at the same time, in an economy excluding from external influences, the same industry among different regions will be independent of each other, the spatial interdependent can be separated from the classic formula.

There are usually two alternative methods when introducing spatial dependence factors into the shift-share analysis model. First one is to extend the classical analysis model, define the spatial weight matrix and introduce the shift-share model. The second is based on regression model (random shift-share analysis) and introduces spatial independence and remaining dependent variable, to filter the variable data. Isard (1960) believes that any space units are subject to the influence of adjacent units. Nazara and Hewings (2004) give more weight to the spatial structure. As a result, the regions with similar structure have also been seen as the adjacent areas and would influence economic growth, so the effect of recognition is not independent.

6.2.1 *Classic Shift-Share Model*

In Equation (6-1), X_{ij} is to show the initial value of the economic activities of i-sector in j region, X'_{ij} is used to represent the final value of the same index, then the changes of economic activities of the two periods can be expressed by a formula as follows:

$$X'_{ij} - X_{ij} = \Delta X_{ij} = X_{ij}r + X_{ij}(r_i - r) + X_{ij}(r_{ij} - r_i). \qquad (6\text{-}1)$$

Here,

$$r = \frac{\sum_{i=1}^{s}\sum_{j=1}^{R}(X'_{ij} - X_{ij})}{\sum_{i=1}^{s}\sum_{j=1}^{R}(X_{ij})}; \quad r_i = \frac{\sum_{j=1}^{R}(X'_{ij} - X_{ij})}{\sum_{j=1}^{R}(X_{ij})}; \quad r_{ij} = \frac{X'_{ij} - X_{ij}}{X_{ij}}.$$

Then the right-hand side of Equation (6-1) represents the national component ($NE_{ij} = X_{ij}r$), industrial structural effect ($SE_{ij} = X_{ij}(r_i - r)$), and competition effect ($CE_{ij} = X_{ij}(r_{ij} - r_i)$), respectively. National component reflects the increased amount at the growth rate of all national industries. In addition to the national component, the second component reflects the specialized structural effect on the economic growth when industrial production is above or below the average level. The third reflects the spatial competition effect of one industry in a certain area compared to that industry of the country. Divide both sides of Equation (6-1) by ΔX_{ij},

$$1 = \frac{r}{\Delta X_{ij}/X_{ij}} + \frac{r_i - r}{\Delta X_{ij}/X_{ij}} + \frac{r_{ij} - r_i}{\Delta X_{ij}/X_{ij}}. \qquad (6\text{-}2)$$

The first term on the right side of the above equation represents the contribution rate of the country's overall economy to the economic growth; the second term represents the contribution rate of the industrial structural effect to the economic growth; and the third represents the contribution rate of the industrial competition effect to the economic growth.

However, the shift-share analysis has some flaws. On one hand, the weight selection cannot change with the production structure change; on the other hand, the results of the analysis is related with the overall size of the industries and the effect of economic growth on the industrial structure is not separated from the spatial effect, resulting in the interdependence between the sectors and regions. In addition to these problems, Dinc *et al.* (1998) believe that the spatial dependence between the sectors and regions make the problem even more complex, therefore, the term reflecting the spatial interactions should be added into the model. Esteban-Marquillas (1972) introduces the "homothetic change, X^*_{ij}" into the model. He believes that if the regional sectoral structure is the same as the national sectoral structure, then the "homothetic change" will be able to indicate the industrial scale.

$$X_{ij}^* = \sum_{i=1}^{S} X_{ij} \frac{\sum_{j=1}^{R} X_{ij}}{\sum_{i=1}^{S} \sum_{j=1}^{R} X_{ij}} = \frac{\sum_{i=1}^{R} X_{ij}}{\sum_{i=1}^{S} \sum_{j=1}^{R} X_{ij}} \sum_{j=1}^{R} X_{ij}.$$

The classic shift-share model can be written as:

$$\Delta X_{ij} = X_{ij}r + X_{ij}(r_i - r) + X_{ij}^*(r_{ij} - r_i) + (X_{ij} - X_{ij}^*)(r_{ij} - r_i)$$

$$(6\text{-}3)$$

The third term of the above equation represents the spatial competition effects (SCE), indicting the advantages or disadvantages of each region compared to the overall economy. When $X_{ij} \neq X_{ij}^*$, the fourth term is known as the location effect (LE), used to measure the concentration level of industries in a certain region.

6.2.2 *The Spatial Dependence Model*

Nazara and Hewings (2004) used spatial weight to amend the growth rate. On this basis, Mayor and López (2005) proposes an alternative method to measure the extent of influence of one region by the adjacent areas, this method is similar to the homothetic change (X_{ij}^v) introduced by Esteban-Marquillas (1972) to the model, the difference is that he incorporates the regional environmental impacts into the model. It can be expressed by a formula as follows:

$$X_{ij}^v = \sum_{i=1}^{S} X_{ik} \frac{\sum_{k \in V} X_{ik}}{\sum_{i=1}^{S} \sum_{k \in V} X_{ik}}$$

In this case, economies of scale are defined as the function of adjacent areas' economic activity, therefore the concept of homothetic change is replaced with the concept of spatial effect size. According to the weight of spatial structure, we can effectively calculate the value of economic activity of interaction between regions and sectors. Then the shift-share model can be written as:

$$\Delta X_{ij} = X_{ij}r + X_{ij}(r_i - r) + X_{ij}^{v*}(r_{ij} - r_i) + (X_{ij} - X_{ij}^{v*})(r_{ij} - r_i)$$

$$(6\text{-}4)$$

Here,

$$X_{ij}^{v*} = \sum_{k \in V} w_{jk} X_{ik}$$

Here, V represents a set of adjacent areas of the region j; w_{jk} represents the economic dependence degree between spatial geographic unit j and k; if the two regions are adjacent, then $w_{jk} = 1$, in other cases $w_{jk} = 0$ (Moran, 1948; Geary, 1954). However, an obvious drawback of the above equation is to lead $\sum_{i,j} X_{ij}^{v*} \neq \sum_{i,j} X_{ij}$, in order to solve this problem, the amended concept of sectoral weights can be used, i.e., $\frac{\sum_{j=1}^{R} X_{ij}^{v*}}{\sum_{i=1}^{S} \sum_{j=1}^{R} X_{ij}^{v*}} = \frac{X_i^{v*}}{X^{v*}}$, and thus get a spatial homothetic effect value:

$$X_{ij}^{v**} = X_j \frac{X_i^{v*}}{X^{v*}}$$

The new correction can meet $\sum_{i,j} X_{ij}^{v**} \neq \sum_{i,j} X_{ij}$, therefore, an alternative model can be expressed as:

$$X_{ij}r + X_{ij}(r_i - r) + X_{ij}^{v**}(r_{ij} - r_i) + (X_{ij} - X_{ij}^{v**})(r_{ij} - r_i) \qquad (6\text{-}5)$$

The third term is the space-dependent competition effect (SDCE) and the fourth term is spatial dependence location effect (SDLE).

6.2.3 *Spatial Filtering Model*

The spatial filtering model is an alternative to deal with the autocorrelation in regression process, through the variable filtering to eliminate spatial interaction. As for a region with n sub-region, $G_i(d)$ is the ratio of total economic value of sub-region with the distance d to the region i, and that of the all regions excluding the region i, i.e,

$$G_i(d) = \frac{\sum_{j=1}^{n} w_{ij}(d)x_j}{\sum_{j=1}^{n} x_j}; \quad i \neq j$$

In order to eliminate the spatial dependence effects, filter variable can be used as follows:

$$\tilde{x}_i = \frac{x_i \left(\frac{\sum_{j=1}^{n} w_{ij}(d)}{n-1} \right)}{G_i(d)}$$

The most famous filtering method is put forward by Getis (1990, 1995). Mayor and López (2008) proposes three models for analysis.

Model 1: after variable filtering, one can obtain the traditional shift-share analysis model taking into account both spatial and non-spatial variables. The results obtained are not strictly related to the initial data; this is because different filtering procedures are adopted in the initial period and final period, and growth rate in each case is different. The growth rate of filter variable ($\tilde{X}$) is as follows:

$$\tilde{r} = \frac{\tilde{X}^t - \tilde{X}^{t-k}}{\tilde{X}^{t-k}}, \quad \tilde{r}_i = \frac{\tilde{X}_i^t - \tilde{X}_i^{t-k}}{\tilde{X}_i^{t-k}}, \quad \tilde{r}_{ij} = \frac{\tilde{X}_{ij}^t - \tilde{X}_{ij}^{t-k}}{\tilde{X}_{ij}^{t-k}}$$

Therefore, shift-share can be decomposed as follows:

$$\Delta \tilde{X}_{ij} = \tilde{X}_{ij}\tilde{r} + \tilde{X}_{ij}(\tilde{r}_i - \tilde{r}) + \tilde{X}_{ij}(\tilde{r}_{ij} - \tilde{r}_i) \tag{6-6}$$

Model 2: from this model, one can get two new effects: the filtering space competition effects (FSCE) and non-spatial or filtering location effect (FLE). Like the Esteban-Marquillas' decomposition method, in the model, the homothetic changes are replaced by the expected value of the variable without spatial effect, and the deviation between the expected and the true value is caused by the spatial spillover effects. Therefore, the filtering space competition effects and the filtering location effect are expressed as follows:

$$FSCE_{ij} = \tilde{X}_{ij}(r_{ij} - r_i)$$
$$FLE_{ij} = L_{ij}(r_{ij} - r_i) = (X_{ij} - \tilde{X}_{ij})(r_{ij} - r_i) \tag{6-7}$$

As the above decomposition can be superimposed, and meet CE = FSCE + FLE, the impact of filtering competition and that of the traditional model are strictly comparable.

Model 3: compared the results based on the value of filtered economic activity with the results depend on the spatial shift-share model proposed by Mayor and López (2005), one can reach some new conclusions. In order to define an alternative homothetic change (Esteban-Marquillas, 1972) concept and spatial homothetic effect values (Mayor and López, 2005), sector weight (without space spillover) amended by the filter variable can be adopted. Spatial effect variable is replaced by the following filter value ($\tilde{X}$):

$$\frac{\sum_{j=1}^{R} \tilde{X}_{ij}}{\sum_{i=1}^{S} \sum_{j=1}^{R} \tilde{X}_{ij}} = \frac{\tilde{X}_i}{X}$$

Therefore, the non-spatial filter homothetic activity values can be obtained by the following formula:

$$\tilde{X}_{ij}^{**} = X_j \frac{\tilde{X}_i}{\tilde{X}}$$

Here comes the decomposition:

$$\Delta X_{ij} = X_{ij}r + X_{ij}(r_i - r) + \tilde{X}_{ij}^{**}(r_{ij} - r_i) + (X_{ij} - \tilde{X}_{ij}^{**})(r_{ij} - r_i) \tag{6-8}$$

From the above equation, one can obtain two different effects: one is the filtered net space competition effect (FNSCE), describing the expected change of the national sectoral structure variables without space spillover. The other is the filtered net location effect (FNLE), indicating the difference between the expected value and actual value caused by the regional sectoral specialization and spillovers effects.

6.3 Statistical Analysis of Manufacturing Location Changes in China

In this chapter, all data come from the *Yearbook of Industrial Statistics 1997–2005* (regional version), 1985 and 1995 industrial censuses, *China's Yearbook of Industrial Statistics* as well as the annual *China Statistical Yearbook*. Given the limitations of statistical data, we use the administrative divisions as the regional dimension of the manufacturing location, examining the industrial geographic distribution specifically at the provincial level. We also divide the 31 provinces, municipalities, and autonomous regions into four regions for analysis. The northeastern region includes the 3 provinces of Liaoning, Jilin, and Heilongjiang; the eastern region incorporates 10 provinces and municipalities, which are Beijing, Tianjin, Hebei, Shandong, Shanghai, Jiangsu, Zhejiang, Guangdong, Fujian, and Hainan;

the central region includes Hubei, Hunan, Anhui, Jiangxi, Shanxi, and Henan, all together 6 provinces; the western region includes 12 provinces, namely Shaanxi, Gansu, Ningxia, Inner Mongolia, Qinghai, Xinjiang, Chongqing, Sichuan, Guizhou, Yunnan, Guangxi, and Tibet. Conclusions can be drawn as follows through the decomposition and analysis of the manufacturing sector output:

6.3.1 *Manufacturing Industry in China's Four Regions has risen in Varying Degrees, the Structural Effects and Competition Effects of Location Changes are Consistent in Time*

From 1985 to 2005, manufacturing output of the eastern region increased by 26.37 times, the central and western regions grew by 11.72 times and 11.10 times, respectively, however, the northeastern region only grew by 8.53 times. From the medium-term (1995–2005) and short-term (2000–2005) points, the manufacturing output had various degrees of growth (see Table 6-1). Deconstructed as the above formula, we have found that structural effects and competition effects of the manufacturing location changes are consistent with time. As can be seen from the table, the northeastern and eastern regions always have a positive structural effect, no matter in the short or medium or long term (1985–2005); on the contrary, the central and western regions always have a negative structural effect. The industrial structure of the eastern region has been noticeably optimized, whereas that of the central region is deteriorating. As for the competition effects, only the eastern region demonstrates the positive competition effects, the other three regions show a negative competition effect. The industries from the western region are in a manifestly disadvantageous position during the competition. After further decomposition of the competition effects, it is discovered that changing trends of competition effect and spatial competition effect maintain consistency, but the industrial location effect show different trends, the location effects of the eastern regions are negative in the short and medium term, even for the long run, it only showcase a weak positive effect; the northeastern, central, and western regions have a positive location effect, among which the advantages of the location effects are obvious in the central region.

Table 6-1 Decomposition of Manufacturing Output Growth Effects of China's Four Regions.

Regions	Growth (RMB 100 million)	Growth rate (%)	National effect	Structural effect (SE)	Competition effect (CE)	#Structural competition effect (SCE)	#Location effect (LE)
2000–2005							
Northeastern	8733.4	140.7	132.3	0.3	−32.6	−40.1	7.5
Eastern	103,651.9	206.8	90.0	0.9	9.2	10.4	−1.3
Central	16,381.6	164.3	113.2	−0.2	−13.0	−19.6	6.6
Western	11,406.4	126.1	147.5	−7.7	−39.8	−40.5	0.7
1995–2005							
Northeastern	10,443.6	232.1	151.5	5.7	−57.1	−67.8	10.6
Eastern	124,561.4	426.5	82.4	1.8	15.8	15.8	−0.04
Central	18,433.3	232.8	151.0	−12.5	−38.5	−50.0	11.6
Western	14,347.7	235.2	149.5	−3.7	−45.8	−52.6	6.8
1985–2005							
Northeastern	13,374.0	852.6	219.2	14.6	−133.7	−134.8	1.1
Eastern	148,147.2	2637.3	70.9	0.8	28.4	28.4	0.001
Central	24,279.6	1172.2	159.4	−8.4	−51.0	−60.7	9.7
Western	18,759.8	1110.5	168.3	−5.5	−62.8	−64.5	1.7

Note: The growth and growth rate are calculated at current prices. So are the following tables.
Source: Authors' calculations.

6.3.2 *The Industrial Structure Convergence[1] in Very Prominent in Various Regions and Regional Advantages have not been Reflected in the Spatial Competition*

Between 2000 to 2005, through the decomposition of China's manufacturing output growth, it can be found that in recent years, the fast developing manufacturing industries of all region are concentrated in the Ferrous Metal Smelting and Rolling Processing Industry, Non-Ferrous Metal Smelting and Rolling Processing Industry, General Machinery Manufacturing Industry, Furniture Manufacturing Industry, and other resource-intensive industries, while the high-tech industries generally grow very slowly. From the aspect of growth share, under the influence of imported iron ore and other factors, Ferrous Metal Smelting and Rolling Processing Industry and Non-Ferrous Metal Smelting and Rolling Processing Industry, such high resource-intensive and heavily polluting industries continue to maintain rapid growth in the eastern region. However, the Central and Western regions, which are rich in natural resources and under little environmental pressure, show a negative spatial effect, which will further intensify the contradiction among the resources, the environment and economic development. From 2000 to 2005, the Ferrous Metal Smelting and Rolling Processing Industry and Non-Ferrous Metal Smelting and Rolling Processing Industry in the eastern showed the negative location effect, which proved this point exactly. The favorable industrial development environment in the eastern region ensured its obvious advantages in the industrial spatial competition effects, which significantly offset its own location disadvantage,[2] thereby impeding the spatial transfer of industries.

6.3.3 *There is Significant Structural Effect Difference Among Different Manufacturing Industries, While the Competition Effect is Quite Similar*

After analyzing the different manufacturing industries' output growth from 1985 to 2005 (Table 6-2), we found that the manufacturing industries with

---

[1]Wei (2007) argues that, to some extent, the regional industrial structure convergence is the inevitable trend of economic and social development.

[2]The location disadvantage mainly refers to diseconomy of industrial agglomeration.

Table 6-2 Decomposition of Growth Effects of Top Five Growth of Manufacturing Industries in China's Four Regions 2000–2005.

						Contribution to the growth (%)			
							Competition effect (CE)		
Regions	Industries	Growth (RMB 100 millions)	Growth rate (%)	National effect	Structural effect (SE)		#Structural competition effect (SCE)	#Location effect (LE)
Northeastern	General Machinery Manufacturing Industry	677.3	267.3	69.6	23.3	7.1	7.1	0.1
	Food Processing Industry	823.0	243.0	76.6	−0.4	23.8	21.6	2.2
	Ferrous Metal Smelting and Rolling Processing Industry	1441.2	243.0	76.6	69.0	−45.5	−30.0	−15.6
	Special Equipment Manufacturing Industry	319.8	239.3	77.8	−3.6	25.8	34.9	−9.1
	Furniture Manufacturing Industry	58.8	228.5	81.4	43.5	−25.0	−29.6	4.6
Eastern	Ferrous Metal Smelting and Rolling Processing Industry	10299.2	404.3	46.0	41.4	12.5	15.5	−3.0
	Furniture Manufacturing Industry	918.8	319.8	58.2	31.1	10.7	9.2	1.5
	Non-Ferrous Metal Smelting and Rolling Processing Industry	2717.0	312.0	59.6	25.0	15.4	25.6	−10.2

(*Continued*)

Table 6-2 (*Continued*)

Regions	Industries	Growth (RMB 100 millions)	Growth rate (%)	Contribution to the growth (%)				
				National effect	Structural effect (SE)	Competition effect (CE)	#Structural competition effect (SCE)	#Location effect (LE)
	Electronic and Communication Equipment Manufacturing	18874.6	288.0	64.6	24.8	10.6	8.1	2.5
	General Machinery Manufacturing Industry	5760.1	262.3	70.9	23.7	5.3	4.9	0.4
Central	Ferrous Metal Smelting and Rolling Processing Industry	2939.9	338.0	55.1	49.6	−4.6	−3.3	−1.3
	Non-Ferrous Metal Smelting and Rolling Processing Industry	1591.5	281.9	66.0	27.7	6.3	3.2	3.1
	Food Processing Industry	460.6	222.1	83.8	−10.8	27.0	24.9	2.2
	Timber Processing, Bamboo, Rattan, Palm and Straw Manufacturing Industry	180.2	210.2	88.5	−3.7	15.2	15.4	−0.2
	General Machinery Manufacturing Industry	693.2	200.4	92.9	31.0	−23.9	−27.8	4.0

(*Continued*)

Table 6-2 (*Continued*)

Regions	Industries	Growth (RMB 100 millions)	Growth rate (%)	National effect	Structural effect (SE)	Competition effect (CE)	#Structural competition effect (SCE)	#Location effect (LE)
Western	Food Processing Industry	415.6	300.1	62.0	−8.0	46.0	57.5	−11.5
	Ferrous Metal Smelting and Rolling Processing Industry	2057.8	284.7	65.3	58.9	−24.2	−19.0	−5.2
	Special Equipment Manufacturing Industry	445.0	283.1	65.7	−3.0	37.3	62.5	−25.2
	Leather, fur and down Manufacturing Industry	92.9	244.3	76.2	−11.7	35.6	151.0	−115.5
	Non-Ferrous Metal Smelting and Rolling Processing Industry	1264.8	213.9	87.0	36.5	−23.5	−10.4	−13.1

Source: Authors' calculations.

great increase also have larger structural effect of location change, the negative structural effect often occurs to the manufacturing sectors ranked after 20. For example, the output value of top 3 growth industries: Electronics and Communications Equipment Manufacturing, Petroleum Processing and Coking industry, and Transportation Equipment Manufacturing Industry, increased by 109.7 times, 41.6 times, and 40.3 times, respectively; its structural effects contribution rate are 83.1%, 55.1%, and 53.7%, respectively, but the competition effects are almost the same, the contribution rate is about zero, which is inconsistent with the objective facts of the uneven distribution of China's manufacturing space. Decomposition of the competition effects shows that the manufacturing sectors with large increase have a strong spatial competition effect and a negative location effect. On the contrary, the manufacturing sectors ranked behind in the increased amount have a strong negative structure effects, such as General Machinery Manufacturing, Food Manufacturing, and Special Equipment Manufacturing Industry, whose contribution rate of the structural effects are −329.9% −275.9%, and −239.4%.

6.3.4 *Recently, Manufacturing Industries have Undergone a Large Scale of Fluctuation in Various Regions, and Industrial Location has Entered a Period of Substantial Adjustment*

The decomposition and analysis of the manufacturing output in 1985, 1995, and 1997–2005 has shown that, since the mid-1990s, China's manufacturing industrial location has entered a period of substantial adjustment. During this period, while the increase in manufacturing output changes greatly, the structural effect and the competition effects of industrial location change also experienced large magnitude of change. Take the long-term top three for example, the location of Electronics and Communications Equipment Manufacturing Industry changes dramatically in years between 2000 and 2005, the location of Oil Processing and Coking industry changes greatly between 1998 and 2002, and the Transportation Equipment Manufacturing industry went through severe adjustment between 2001 and 2005 (see Figure 6-1); as for the bottom three: General machinery Manufacturing industry, Food Manufacturing industry, and Special Equipment Manufacturing industry,

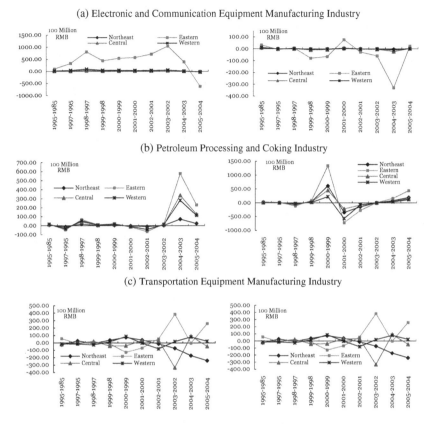

Figure 6-1   Trend of Structural Effect and the Competition of the Top 3 Industrial Output Value Growth 1985–2005.

Note: in Figures 6-1 (a–c), the left side denotes are the competition effects; and on the right are the structural effects The differential values of 1985–1995 is the 10-year arithmetic mean; and that of 1995–1997 is the 2-year arithmetic mean.

the structural effect and spatial effect of the location change between 2001 and 2005 all confronted with greater adjustment than ever.

6.4   Further Decomposition of the Competition Effect

In Table 6-3, which is the decomposition of manufacturing growth in a longer period, we have found an interesting phenomenon, that is, the competition effect of all manufacturing industries is close to zero, this means

Table 6-3 Decomposition of Growth Effects of Chinese Manufacturing Output 1985–2005.

| | | | | | | | Contribution to the increased amount (%) | | |
| | | | | | | | | Competition effect (CE) | |
Code	Industry	Growth (RMB 100 millions)	Growth rate (%)	Ranking	National effect (NE)	Structural effect (SE)	Spatial competition effect (SCE)	Location effect (LE)
C13	Food Processing Industry	9629.9	977.6	24	192.54	−91.2	6.8	−6.8
C14	Food Manufacturing Industry	3146.5	497.1	27	378.60	−275.9	3.9	−3.9
C15	Beverage Manufacturing Industry	2939.4	1960.8	19	95.99	4.7	2.9	−2.9
C16	Tobacco Industry	2638.5	1304.5	22	144.28	−43.2	−3.1	3.1
C17	Textile Industry	11615.3	1099.5	23	171.19	−70.0	−14.1	14.1
C18	Clothing and other Fiber Products Manufacturing Industry	4210.3	550.8	25	341.72	−239.3	−13.5	13.5
C19	Leather, Fur and Down Products Manufacturing Industry	3378.7	4018.1	4	46.15	54.2	−1.7	1.7
C20	Timber Processing, Bamboo, Rattan, Palm and Straw Manufacturing Industry	1771.0	3121.5	13	60.30	40.1	20.5	−20.5

(Continued)

Table 6-3 (*Continued*)

Code	Industry	Growth (RMB 100 millions)	Growth rate (%)	Ranking	National effect (NE)	Structural effect (SE)	Spatial competition effect (SCE)	Location effect (LE)
							Competition effect (CE)	
							Contribution to the increased amount (%)	
C21	Furniture Manufacturing Industry	1379.9	2914.5	14	64.58	35.9	−3.3	3.3
C22	Papermaking and Paper-Products Manufacturing Industry	4007.5	2604.6	17	72.26	28.3	6.1	−6.1
C23	Printing Industry Medium Reproduction	1358.9	1616.9	20	116.41	−15.6	−1.6	1.6
C24	Educational and Sports Goods Manufacturing Industry	1444.9	3837.2	8	49.05	51.3	−30.4	30.4
C29	Petroleum Processing and Coking Industry	11,719.1	4164.3	2	45.20	55.1	17.9	−17.9
C30	Chemical Materials and Chemical Products Manufacturing Industry	15,794.8	2796.3	15	67.31	33.2	0.3	−0.3
C34	Pharmaceutical Manufacturing Industry	4123.2	3239.5	11	58.10	42.3	0.3	−0.3

(*Continued*)

Table 6-3 (*Continued*)

Code	Industry	Growth (RMB 100 millions)	Growth rate (%)	Ranking	National effect (NE)	Structural effect (SE)	Competition effect (CE)	
							Spatial competition effect (SCE)	Location effect (LE)
C35	Chemical Fibers Manufacturing Industry	2529.1	3189.4	12	59.01	41.4	-10.9	10.9
C39	Rubber Products Manufacturing Industry	2058.6	1490.3	21	126.29	-25.4	-2.1	2.1
C25	Plastic Products Manufacturing Industry	4926.7	3489.4	10	53.94	46.4	-11.4	11.4
C26	Non-metallic Mineral Products Manufacturing Industry	8772.5	2075.4	18	90.69	10.0	1.8	-1.8
C28	Ferrous Metal Smelting and Rolling Processing Industry	20,928.4	3857.4	7	48.80	51.6	11.3	-11.3
C31	Non-ferrous Metal Smelting and Rolling Processing Industry	7741.3	3937.0	5	47.81	52.5	4.7	-4.7
C32	Metal processing Industry	6323.1	2706.5	16	69.30	31.2	-6.3	6.3
C33	General Machinery Manufacturing Industry	8626.3	434.8	28	433.01	-329.9	-1.2	1.2

(*Continued*)

Table 6-3 (*Continued*)

Code	Industry	Growth (RMB 100 millions)	Growth rate (%)	Ranking	National effect (NE)	Structural effect (SE)	Spatial competition effect (SCE)	Location effect (LE)
							Competition effect (CE)	
C27	Specific Machinery Manufacturing Industry	5150.2	550.7	26	341.80	−239.4	1.3	−1.3
C36	Transportation Equipment Manufacturing Industry	15,334.8	4034.3	3	46.65	53.7	11.2	−11.2
C37	Electrical Machinery and Equipment Manufacturing Industry	13,546.0	3812.8	9	49.37	51.0	−7.5	7.5
C40	Electronic and Communication Equipment Manufacturing Industry	26,750.5	10967.4	1	17.00	83.1	−21.1	21.1
C41	Instrument and Cultural, Office Supplies Manufacturing Industry	2711.5	3898.1	6	48.29	52.1	−7.9	7.9

The header "Contribution to the increased amount (%)" spans the National effect through Location effect columns.

Source: Authors' calculations.

that China's manufacturing spatial distribution is relatively even, which is clearly contradictory to the fact that manufacturing industries are over-concentrated in the east (Wang and Wei, 2007). Using homothetic change variables excluding interaction between industry and space, one can get a variable which reflects the spatial effect. The spatial dependence model and the spatial filter model decompose the competition effects into two parts by introducing a new variable, reflecting the growing importance of the role of spatial externalities in the new economic geography theory and endogenous growth theory, which further explains the impact of regional interaction and space spillover on regional economic development. Based on different model decomposition formula, we decompose 28 manufacturing output value growth values from 1997 to 2005 and obtain the following results:

First, under the condition of mutual influence between regions, the structural effect of the overall manufacturing sectors has been strengthened. In Table 6-4, among the 28 manufacturing sectors, the structural and location effect of 25 industries is greater than 1, so the structural effect has obvious advantages. But only 10 industries change in the same direction of the structural and location effect; moreover, only 3 have positive structural and location effects, they are: Electrical Machinery and Equipment Manufacturing industry (C39), Electronic and Communication Equipment Manufacturing industry (C40), and Instrument and Cultural Office Machinery industry (C41), the ratio of structural effect to location effect is 1.31, 5.46, and 2.98, respectively, indicating that the Krugman hypothesis is not universal in China. As can be seen from Table 6-4, only 9 industries have positive structure effect, while 15 industries demonstrate a positive regional effect, indicating that most of the manufacturing growth is driven by the regional effect, and the low level of industrial structure significantly restricts the increase of manufacturing. Moreover, the sum of the structural and location effects is negative, further indicating that both the structure and space of our manufacturing industry are distributed unreasonably. In addition to the 3 industries whose structural and location effects are both positive, in the other 25 industries, 6 of them have a positive structure effect, such as Ferrous Metal Smelting and Rolling Processing industry (C32) and Nonferrous Metal Smelting and Rolling Processing industry (C33), the contribution rate of structure effect on economic growth is 41.66% and 40.45%, respectively. A total of 12 industries enjoy positive location effect, such as

Table 6-4   Further Decomposition of the Spatial Dependence Model.

Code	Growth (RMB 100 millions)	National effect (NE) contribution rate (%)	Structural effect (SE) contribution rate (%)	Competition effect (CE)		Structure/ Space
				Spatial dependence competition effect (SDCE) contribution rate (%)	Spatial dependence location effect (SDLE) contribution rate (%)	
C13	6822.45	148.13	−48.13	−7.10	7.1	−6.78
C14	2476.85	140.14	−40.14	−1.43	1.43	−28.1
C15	1469.65	293.67	−193.67	2.10	−2.1	92.08
C16	1544.69	223.58	−123.58	63.70	−63.7	1.94
C17	7911.32	160.34	−60.34	−20.46	20.46	−2.95
C18	3129.36	157.13	−57.13	−18.06	18.06	−3.16
C19	2276.45	138.87	−38.87	−24.47	24.47	−1.59
C20	1201.36	138.94	−38.94	27.87	−27.87	1.4
C21	1107.08	77.07	22.93	0.72	−0.72	−31.65
C22	2916.88	113.69	−13.69	−1.67	1.67	−8.19
C23	868.55	176.23	−76.23	−0.76	0.76	−99.79
C24	992.29	131.65	−31.65	−24.45	24.45	−1.29
C25	9431.49	72.59	27.41	28.79	−29.11	−0.94
C26	11,637.31	108.14	−8.14	5.46	−5.46	1.49
C27	2988.25	112.56	−12.56	4.31	−4.31	2.92
C28	1746.44	131.53	−31.53	−20.48	20.47	−1.54
C29	1415	147.22	−47.22	−7.07	7.07	−6.68
C30	3625.42	106.03	−6.03	−8.11	8.12	−0.74
C31	5367.72	190.02	−90.02	8.02	−8.02	11.23
C32	17,614.67	58.34	41.66	20.60	−20.6	−2.02
C33	6488	59.55	40.45	10.03	−10.03	−4.03
C34	4478.67	123.65	−23.65	−6.71	6.71	−3.53
C35	7797.02	96.15	3.85	0.66	−0.66	−5.85
C36	4014.43	137.48	−37.48	20.99	−20.99	1.79
C37	11591.8	94.78	5.22	9.13	−9.13	−0.57
C39	10535.17	85.14	14.86	−11.38	11.38	1.31
C40	23073.39	45.28	54.71	−10.02	10.02	5.46
C41	2181.1	73.30	26.7	−8.95	8.95	2.98

Source: Calculated based on the Yearbook of Industrial Statistics 1997–2005.

Leather, Fur and Down Products industry (C19), and Educational and Sports Goods Manufacturing industry (C24), and the contribution rate of location effects to the economic growth rates is 24.47% and 24.45% (see Table 6-4).

Second, after the spatial filtering of the economic variables, the manufacturing structural effect has been further enhanced and the spatial effect is significantly reduced (see Table 6-5). In 28 industries, only 7 have positive structure effect, but the location effect of all manufacturing industries has been further weakened, demonstrating a strong structure effect. The structural and location effects of 11 industries change in the same direction, moreover, 3 have positive structural and location effects simultaneously. Therefore, the applicability of the Krugman hypothesis does not change significantly. The manufacturing industries with strong structural effects are Electronic and Communication Equipment Manufacturing industry (C40), Educational and Sports Goods Manufacturing industry (C24), Rubber Manufacturing industry (C29), and Furniture Manufacturing industry (C21), and their structural effect contribution rate is 71.00%, 65.78%, 66.26%, and 73.96%, respectively. In fact, the negative structural effect is more obvious, such as Drinks Manufacturing industry (C15), Special Equipment Manufacturing industry (C36), Non-Metallic Mineral Products industry (C31), and their structural effect contribution rate is −952.94%, −310.55%, and −272.29%, respectively. However, before the filtering, the competition effect contribution rate is generally close to zero, and its impact on economic growth can be almost ignored, therefore, it needs further decomposition.

Third, in Table 6-5 model 2, there are 10 industries whose structural and location effects change in the same direction, 7 out of which are positive. Compared with model 1, applicability of Krugman hypothesis has improved noticeably. Model 2 further decomposes the competition effects. It is discovered that, after filtering, the spatial competition effect of 25 industries are positive, but there are only two industries whose absolute value of structural effect to spatial effect ratio is less than 1, the contribution of location effect to economic growth is universal, but the number is not great. In the industries with an obvious filtered location effect, the tobacco industry (C16) has the largest positive effect, and its contribution rate is 68.14%; however, its negative structural effect is also the largest (−1243.80%). This indicates that though it occupies a lower level in structural hierarchy, the tobacco industry

Table 6-5 Further Decomposition of Spatial Filtering Model.

Code	Growth (RMB 100 millions)	National effect (NE) contribution rate (%)	Structural effect (SE) contribution rate (%)	Model 1 Competition effect (CE) contribution rate (%)	Model 2 Filtered spatial location effect (FSLE) contribution rate (%)	Model 2 Structure/ Space	Model 3 Filtered Net location effect (FNLE) contribution rate (%)	Model 3 Structure/ Space
C13	764,371	384.97	−285.59	0.000195	20.73	−13.78	5.53	−8.7
C14	303,537	295.08	−195	−0.00057	13.25	−14.72	1.01	−39.68
C15	94,116	1052.95	−952.94	−0.00073	−17.23	55.29	−1.31	147.82
C16	70,616	1343.80	−1243.8	0.000717	68.14	−18.25	−54.7	2.26
C17	4,161,786	142.58	−42.6	1.05E−05	11.82	−3.6	24.15	−2.5
C18	5,454,169	72.76	27.18	−0.00066	11.07	2.46	42.15	−1.36
C19	1,174,057	135.80	−35.81	0.001514	22.88	−1.57	35.56	−1.09
C20	1,050,494	77.51	22.48	−0.00336	20	1.12	−41.68	0.93
C21	1,010,914	26.04	73.96	0.001395	7.7	9.61	−0.63	−36.12
C22	795,179	136.18	−36.19	−0.00011	26.35	−1.37	1.48	−9.24
C23	154,413	250.09	−150.18	−0.00036	32.64	−4.6	0.54	−140.3
C24	5,404,337	34.23	65.78	0.000872	10.5	6.27	107.05	−0.3
C25	604,252	351.37	−251.43	0.001698	−606.92	0.41	−24.67	−1.11
C26	1,246,173	208.00	−108.03	0.000732	2.77	−39.03	−3.01	2.7
C27	216,873	369.80	−269.73	0.002805	−105.98	2.55	−2.82	4.46

(Continued)

Table 6-5 (*Continued*)

Code	Growth (RMB 100 millions)	National effect (NE) contribution rate (%)	Structural effect (SE) contribution rate (%)	Model 1 Competition effect (CE) contribution rate (%)	Model 2 Filtered spatial location effect (FSLE) contribution rate (%)	Model 2 Structure/Space	Model 3 Filtered Net location effect (FNLE) contribution rate (%)	Model 3 Structure/Space
C28	653,807	240.24	−140.2	0.001835	26.93	−5.21	39.34	−0.8
C29	3,518,007	33.81	66.26	−0.00108	8.54	7.76	10.61	−4.45
C30	924,578	164.11	−64.11	0.000429	29.91	−2.14	9.28	−0.65
C31	665,897	372.37	−272.29	−0.00091	11.36	−23.98	−5.07	17.74
C32	1,696,470	157.64	−57.62	0.000216	14.51	−3.97	−14.02	−2.97
C33	332,806	146.38	−46.38	−0.00108	12.9	−3.6	−3.59	−11.28
C34	1,456,849	119.28	−19.32	0.001431	17.23	−1.12	5.81	−4.07
C35	1,625,735	157.14	−57.33	−0.00076	31.63	−1.81	−0.57	−6.74
C36	425,113	410.48	−310.55	0.001487	14.65	−21.2	−15.98	2.34
C37	3,994,632	138.14	−38.08	0.000379	30.26	−1.26	−13.34	−0.39
C39	1,963,173	157.64	−57.64	−0.00023	19.99	−2.88	10.88	1.37
C40	16,825,055	29.14	71.00	−0.00217	18.06	3.93	14.61	3.75
C41	686,218	91.70	8.30	0.001231	20.32	0.41	10.91	2.45

Note: The increases and the contribution rate of the national growth effect is the same as in Table 6-4.

Source: Calculated based on the *Yearbook of Industrial Statistics 1997–2005*.

possesses a strong competitive edge in the space layout. The largest negative location effect belongs to Petroleum Processing and Coking industry (C25) (−606.92%), but its structural effect contribution rate is also negative (−251.44%), indicating that, no matter in terms of structure and space, it is not a competitive industry.

Fourth, in model 3, the filtered net location effect is significantly weakened while the structure effect is significantly enhanced. In Table 6-5, 15 out of the 28 manufacturing industries have a positive net location effect but the net location effect is considerably weaker compared to the structural effect of these industries, and the absolute value of structural effect to spatial effect ratio of only 5 industries is less than 1. The number of industries whose structural and net location effects change in the same direction is 10, among which only 3 are positive, still unable to justify that the "Krugman hypothesis" has universal applicability in China. The largest net location effect goes to Educational and Sports Goods Manufacturing industry (C24); its contribution to economic growth rate is 107.05%, while the structural effect contribution rate is negative, indicating that the industry needs to increase investment in science and technology as well as upgrade the industrial structure level; and the largest negative net location effect is the tobacco industry, which is obviously contrary to model 2 and requires further analysis, but the lower level of its industrial structure is an indisputable fact.

6.5 Conclusion

The chapters analyzes the manufacturing output growth according to shift-share model, investigates into the structural effect and spatial effect in our manufacturing location changes, and tests the applicability of "Krugman hypothesis" in China with the Chinese manufacturing data. Based on the above analysis, we can draw the following conclusions:

First, the manufacturing location changes are consistent in terms of structure and space. To take an overall look of the manufacturing industries, both structural and spatial effects exist simultaneously, but the structural effect is greater than the spatial effect. As can be seen from the decomposition results, in the regional level, the eastern region has a higher level of economic development and a positive effect on the structure and space, while the central and western regions have both negative structural effects and spatial effects. It can prove that, to a certain extent, the "Krugman hypothesis" has applicability in China.

Second, manufacturing sectors showcase a significant "over-mismatch" in space. Some of the high energy-intensive resource industries are overly concentrated in the eastern region. Consequently, although these industries enjoy larger structural effect, they also result in larger negative spatial effects, which partially offset the advantages of structural effects. On the contrary, some light processing industries in the eastern region have a large spatial effect, but there is a strong negative structural effect.

Third, the structural effect of China's manufacturing industries is strong and the spatial effect is universal. After the introduction of spatial externalities to the model, we can observe that there is a strong structural effect in the manufacturing industries, and generally positive. "Krugman hypothesis" is established only in some industries. This shows that since the reform and opening-up, China's manufacturing growth effect mainly comes from the reconfiguration in space. Most of the manufacturing industries show significant negative structural effects in spite of the overall economic growth in the region, so the industrial structure needs to be further optimized.

References

Aiginger, K. *et al.* (1999). Specialisation and (Geographic) Concentration of European Manufacturing. Enterprise DG Working Paper No 1, Background Paper for the Competitiveness of European Industry: 1999 Report, Brussels.

Aiginger, K. and W. Leitner (2002). Regional concentration in the United States and Europe: Who follows whom? *Review of World Economics*, 138(4), 652–679.

Aiginger, K. and M. Pfaffermayr (2004). The Single Market and Geographic Concentration in Europe. *Review of international economics*, 12(1), 1–11.

Amiti, M. (1999). New Trade Theories and Industrial Location in the EU: A Survey of Evidence. *Oxford Review of Economic Policy*, 14(2), 45–53.

Brülhart, M. (1996). *Commerce et spécialisation géographique dans l'Union européenne. Economie Internationale*, 65(1), 169–202 (in French).

Brülhart, M. (1998). Economic Geography, Industry Location and Trade: The Evidence. *The World Economy*, 21(6), 775–801.

Brülhart, M. (2001). Evolving Geographical Concentration of European Manufacturing Industries. *Review of World Economics*, 137(2), 215–243.

Brülhart, M. and J. Torstensson, (1996). *Regional Integration, Scale Economies and Industry Location*. Discussion Paper No.1435, Centre for Economic Policy Research.

Cai, F., D. Wang and M. Wang (2002). China's Regional Specialization in the Course of Gradual Reform. *Economic Research Journal*, (9), 24–30, 93.

Chen, L. and K. Yang (2006). Specialization, Concentration and Agglomeration Evidence from China's Manufacturing Industries. *Economic Geography*, 26(S1), 72–75.

Combes, P. P. and H. G. Overman (2004). The Spatial Distribution of Economic Activities in the European Union. *Handbook of Regional and Urban Economics*, 4, 2845–2909.

Dinc, M., K. E. Haynes and L. Qiangsheng (1998). A Comparative Evaluation of Shift-Share Models and their Extensions. *Australasian Journal of Regional Studies*, 4(2), 275–302.

Dunn, E. S. (2005). A Statistical and Analytical Technique for Regional Analysis. *Papers in Regional Science*, 6(1), 97–112.

Ellison, G. and E. L. Glaeser (1997). Geographic Concentration in U.S. Manufacturing Industries: A Dartboard Approach, *Journal of Political Economy*, 105(5): 889–927.

Esteban-Marquillas, J. M. (1972). A Reinterpretation of Shift and Share Analysis. *Regional and Urban Economics*, 2(3), 249–255.

Fan, F. (2007). The Measurement of Regional Specialization. *Economic Research Journal*, (9), 71–83.

Fan, J. (2004). Market Integration, Regional Specialization and Tendency of Industrial Agglomeration: An Implication for Regional Disparity. *Social Sciences in China*, (6), 39–51.

Gao, F. (2002). Theoretical Analysis and Application of Industrial Geographic Concentration. *Social Sciences in Nanjing*, (1), 15–18.

Geary, R. C. (1954). The Contiguity Ratio and Statistical Mapping. *The Incorporated Statistician*, 5(3), 115–146.

Getis, A. (1990). Screening for Spatial Dependence in Regression Analysis. *Papers in Regional Science*, 69(1), 69–81.

Getis, A. (1995). Spatial filtering in a regression framework experiments on regional inequality government expenditures and urban time. In Anselin, L., and Florax, R. (eds.), *New Directions in Spatial Econometrics*. Berlin: Springer, pp. 172–188.

Glaeser, E. L., H. D. Kallal, J. A. Scheinkman and A. Shleifer (1992). Growth in Cities. *Journal of Political Economy*, 100(6), 1126–1152.

Greenaway, D. and R. C. Hine (1991). Intra — Industry Specialization, Trade Expansion and Adjustment in the European Economic Space. *Journal of Common Market Studies*, 29(6), 603–622.

Haaland, J. I., H. J. Kind, K. H. Midelfart-Knarvik and J. Torstensson (1999). *What Determines the Economic Geography of Europe?* CEPR Discussion Paper, No. 2072.

Hanson, G. H. (1996). Economic Integration, Intra-industry Trade, and Frontier Regions. *European Economic Review*, 40(3), 941–949.

Heckscher, E. F. (1919). The Effect of Foreign Trade on Distribution of Income, *Economisk Tidskrift*, pp. 497–512, Reprinted in Ellis, H.S. and Metzler, L. A. (eds.), (1949). *Readings in the Theory of International Trade*. Philadelphia: Blakiston Company, pp. 272–300.

Helpman, E. and P. R. Krugman (1985). *Market Structure and Foreign Trade: Increasing Returns, Imperfect Competition, and the International Economy*. Cambridge, MA: MIT Press.

Hewings, G. J. D. (1976). On the Accuracy of Alternative Models for Stepping-down Multi-county Employment Projections to Counties. *Economic Geography*, 52, 206–217.

Hine, R. C. (1990). *Economic Integration and Inter-Industry Specialization*. CREDIT Research Paper 89/6, University of Nottingham.

Isard, W. (1956). *Location and Space-Economy*. Cambridge, MA: MIT Press.

Isard, W. (1960). *Methods of Regional Analysis: An Introduction to Regional Science*. Cambridge, MA: MIT Press.

Krieger-Boden, C. (2000). *Globalization, Integration and Regional Specialization*. Kiel Institute of World Economics Working Paper, No. 1009, Kiel.

Krugman, P. R. (1979). Increasing Returns, Monopolistic Competition, and International Trade. *Journal of International Economics*, 9(4), 469–479.

Krugman, P. R. (1980). Scale Economies, Product Differentiation, and the Pattern of Trade. *American Economic Review*, 70(5), 950–959.

Krugman, P. R. (1981). Intraindustry Specialization and the Gains from Trade. *The Journal of Political Economy*, 89(5), 959–973.

Krugman, P. R. (1991a). *Geography and Trade*. Cambridge, MA: MIT Press.

Krugman, P. R. (1991b). Increasing Returns and Economic Geography. *The Journal of Political Economy*, 99(3), 483–499.

Krugman, P. R. (1993). First Nature, Second Nature, and Metropolitan Location. *Journal of Regional Science*, 33(2), 129–144.

Krugman, P. R. and A. Venables, (1990). Intergration and the Competitiveness of Peripheral Industry. In C. Bliss and J. B. De Macedo (eds.), (1990). *Unity with Diversity in the European Economy: The Community's Southern Frontier*. New York: Cambridge University Press.

Krugman, P. R. and A. Venables (1995). Globalization and the Inequality of Nations. NBER Working Paper No. 5098.

Mayor, M. and A. J. López (2005). The Spatial Shift-share Analysis New Developments and Some Findings for the Spanish Case. In *Proceedings of the European Regional Science Association ERSA 2005*, Amsterdam.

Mayor, M. and A. J. López (2008). Spatial Shift-share Analysis versus Spatial Filtering: an Application to Spanish Employment Data. *Empirical Economics*, 34(1), 123–142.

Midelfart-Knarvik, K. H., H. G. Overman, S. J. Redding and A. J. Venables (2000). *Comparative Advantage and Economic Geography: Estimating the Location of Production in the EU*. CEPR Discussion Paper No. 2618, London.

Midelfart-Knarvik, K. H., H. G. Overman, S. Redding and A. J. Venables (2002). Integration and Industrial Specialisation in the European Union. *Revue économique*, 53(3), 469–481.

Moran, P. A. P. (1948). The Interpretation of Statistical Maps. *Journal of the Royal Statistical Society. Series B (Methodological)*, 10(2), 243–251.

Nazara, S., and G. J. D. Hewings (2004). Spatial Structure and Taxonomy of Decomposition in Shift — Share Analysis. *Growth and Change*, 35(4), 476–490.

Ohlin, B. (1933). *Interregional and International Trade*. Cambridge, MA: Harvard University Press.

Ricardo, D. (1817). *On the Principles of Political Economy and Taxation*. First published by Cambridge University Press in 1951. 1951, 1952, 1955, 1973 by the Royal Economic Society Typographical design 2004 by Liberty Fund, Inc., London.

Sapir, A. (1996). The Effects of Europe's Internal Market Program on Production and Trade: A First Assessment. *Review of World Economics*, 132(3), 457–475.

Venables, A. J. (1996). Equilibrium Locations of Vertically Linked Industries. *International Economic Review*, 37(2), 341–359.

Wang, Y. and H. Wei (2007). Industry Characteristics, Space Competition and Manufacturing Geographical Concentration — the Empirical Evidence from China. *Management World*, (4), 68–77.

Wei, H. (2007). The New Industrial Division and Conflict Management in Metropolitan Region — Based on the Perspective of Industrial-chain Division. *China Industrial Economics*, (2), 28–34.

Xian, G. and D. Wen (2006). FDI, Regional Specialization and Industrial Agglomeration. *Management World*, (12), 18–31.

Chapter 7

Manufacturing Firm Relocation in East China: Tendency and Mechanism

Jiang Yuanyuan

Nowadays, the transnational and regional relocation activities of international manufacturing business are growing on a daily basis. Relocation is not only an important way of firm expansion but also a significant means to interregional balance development in developed countries' regional policies. In recent years, against the backdrop of international manufacturing industry's considerable relocation to China, there is a gradual tendency of enterprises relocation from East China into West China. According to the data provided by Western Development Office of the State Council (2007), from 2000 to the first half of 2007, the number of enterprises in eastern region, which have invested a business in the western region reaches 200,000, the amount of which totals RMB 1,500 billion. Moreover, the volume of investment from nearly Shanghai amounts to more than RMB 170 billion. Accordingly, the sum of investment from Zhejiang and Fujian reach 130 billion separately. In the first half of 2007, the number of domestic regional cooperation projects implemented by Hunan Province totals 2937, the contract funds being RMB 293.9 billion; the actual funds in place is RMB 58.6 billion which increases by 26.1% year-on-year; besides, the sum of funds from the YRD region amounts to 11.68 billion, taking up 19.9% of the total amount and increasing by 23.5% year-on-year. The investment from Beijing, Guangdong, Zhejiang, Jiangsu, Fujian, and Shanghai in Hunan province accounts for 74.4% of the whole.[1] However, the relocation of enterprises from the eastern region to western region serves as a double-edged sword to the regional development of China. On one hand, it mitigates the ever-growing factor prices and aggravating pressure for the resource- and environment-bearing capacity, which is rooted in the agglomeration economy in eastern region, thereby making room for the upgrade of industry in this region. On the other hand, the westward relocation of business goes hand in hand with the inflow of advanced production factors, which contributes to the economic development of the central and western regions. This chapter focuses on the inter-regional relocation of business, that is, the specific inter-provincial relocation behavior of the manufacturing business from the developed eastern region to surrounding areas, i.e., the central and western regions. By analyzing the industry characteristics, tendency, and influence factors of such relocation, the author further explores the initiative mechanism of the relocation. This chapter is arranged as follows: Section 7.1 briefly discusses the theoretical explanation of firm relocation, Section 7.2 probes into the research methods and data sources of firm relocation, and Section 7.3 particularly analyzes the sectional characteristics and the relocation tendency of manufacturing firms from the eastern developed region, and Section 7.4 specifically explores the mechanism of the firm relocation of the developed eastern China. Finally, the author discusses the relevant policies of firm relocation.

7.1 Theoretical Explanation of Firm Relocation

Location theory is an important basis for modern firm relocation theory. The neo-classical school, behavioral school, and institutional school explain the determining factors of firm relocation from different perspectives, constituting the main content of the firm relocation theory (Brouwer *et al.*, 2004; Pellenbarg *et al.*, 2002). Hayter (1997) analyzes the industrial location theory from the perspective of firm theory (see Table 7-1), and there are also scholars who incorporate the evolution theory into the scope of firm relocation theory (Mariotti, 2005) (see Table 7-2). Mariotti (2005) and Van

---

[1]Yu, Wenjie (2007). Domestic Regional Cooperation and Investment Introduction on Full Bloom, *Hunan Daily*, July 17.

Table 7-1   Enterprise Theory and Industrial Location Theory.

Characteristic	Neo-classical theory	Behavioral theory	Institutional theory
Decision type	Economic man	Satisficer Person	Technique architecture
Decision ability	Perfect rationality, complete information	Imperfect rationality, incomplete information	Strategy, structure, power
Target(s)	Minimization of cost/maximization of profit	Satisfaction of psychological desire	Increase, safety and profit
Competition theory	Pure (and 'fair')	Perfect competition	Monopolistic competition
Economic character-istics	Cost and profit	Information action/ action space	Big enterprise, big production and big government
The nature of economic relationship	Fair transaction	Information flows	Bargain, bribery and encouragement
Location decision	Automatic and immediate	Learning process	Bargain process
Location change	Adjustment according to economic power	Leaning adjusts according to economic power	Political economy and technology

Source: Hayter (1997, p. 80).

Dijk and Pellenbarg (2000) state that three factors influence firm relocation: namely, the internal factor of firm, the location factor, and the external factor of firm. The internal factor of firm includes the choice of industry's expansion pattern of organization structure, the management factor, the goal of business development, the economy in finance, capital inertia, or sunk cost. The location factor consists of the usable land scale, the ownership characteristics, the feasibility of space expansion, the convenience of transportation, quality of public space, distance to the suppliers and the market, and the land usage policy. The external factor of business is made up of the number and the construction of suppliers and demanders, changes of region, labor market, government policy, the number of subjects suitable for relocation, location and quality, as well as the overall economical conditions.

Table 7-2   Determining Factors of Relocation.

Theoretical structure	Key factors of determining relocation	Relocation cost considered
Neo-classical school	Location factor (market position, drop of cost)	No
Behavioral school	Internal factors of business (information/entrepreneur's capability/expectation/location image)	Yes
Institutional school	Institutional factor (network, trust and social capital)	Yes
Evolutional school	External factor of business (route dependence, creativity, competition, localized knowledge, convention)	Yes

Source: Mariotti (2005).

7.2   Research Methods and Data Source

Generally, the research of relocation of business starts basically from macro and micro perspectives. The macro research mainly uses the region's aggregate data. It focuses on the relocation issues in the process of a business's development, for example, the relocated departments, relocation timing, and spatial distribution. And the micro research's main target is to explain the determinants of firm relocation. Researchers obtain the required data through visiting or conducting questionnaires with the decision-maker of business, and then they establish the disaggregated choice model and finally reach relevant conclusions. Some European countries have made some steps in terms of database. For example, the Mutation Balance project of the Dutch Chambers of Commerce gathered the relevant data about the foundation, relocation, and closure of Holland's businesses. In Britain, Consultant Company Prism Research owns a database named "CREDO" (Company Relocation and Economic Development Observatory), which records the relocation data of single location enterprises, enterprise headquarters, and holding companies. Although Italy does not have a professional database, its business relocation data could be found from the firm demography (Registro Imprese) of the Italian Chamber of Commerce and the ASIA database of National Institute of Statistics (ISTAT). It's mainly about the distribution of enterprises' subsidiaries and headquarters (Mariotti, 2005).

Since there no statistics specific to firm relocation in China is available, conducting micro research is fairly difficult. Only a few scholars probe into this field at present (Chen, J. 2002; Li *et al.*, 2004; Chen, W. 2005; Liu *et al.*, 2005; Chen *et al.*, 2006). This chapter takes advantage of the manufacturing industry data obtained from the applied supporting system of China statistics and data and judges the characteristics and tendency of firm relocation in Chinese eastern region by calculating and comparing the relative changes of regional manufacturing industry's market share. Since business relocation activities occur frequently in the most economically developed eastern coastal region, this chapter will in particular analyze the business relocation phenomenon of eastern developed region. Here, the eastern developed regions particularly refer to the seven provinces and municipalities, including Beijing, Tianjin, Shanghai, Jiangsu, Zhejiang, Guangdong, and Fujian. It differs from the eastern region divided in the familiar four regions (eastern region, northeastern region, central region, and western region).

7.3 Industrial Characteristics and Tendency of Firm Relocation of Eastern Manufacturing Industry

As an important symbol of industrial transfer, the ever-changing market share of the same industry in different regions reflects the regional distribution of industry and showcases the relocation tendency of eastern enterprises. By using the two-digit code SIC manufacturing industry data, we first calculate different factor-intensive manufacturing industries' market share from 1980–2007 (see Table 7-3).[2] The result shows that, the market

---

[2]As Chinese academic cycle has not reached a consensus on the industrial classification based on factor intensity, in this chapter, the authors sort 2-digital manufacturing industries by factor intensity and classify them into 3 types: there are 13 labor-intensive manufactures (from No. 13 to 24, and No. 42), 10 raw-material-intensive manufactures (No. 25 to 34) and 6 capital and technology-intensive manufacturing industries (from No. 35 to 41).

Table 7-3 Market Share Change of Manufacturing Industry in Different Regions (%).

Year	Eastern developed region			Central and western regions		
	Labor-intensive	Raw-material-intensive	Capital and technology-intensive	Labor-intensive	Raw-material-intensive	Capital and technology-intensive
1980	43.54	39.80	44.04	33.86	31.38	31.24
1985	40.83	39.25	45.55	36.38	33.54	31.48
1995	49.12	43.96	57.18	30.64	31.61	23.77
2000	52.60	45.79	63.84	26.05	27.82	18.03
2001	54.48	46.77	64.87	24.50	27.60	17.23
2002	54.59*	46.50	64.39	23.67	27.48	17.30
2003	53.98	46.70*	67.34	22.39	27.05*	15.39
2004	53.77	46.20	69.28*	21.29*	27.09	14.19*
2005	51.10	44.59	68.77	22.16	27.60	14.34
2006	49.73	44.17	68.02	22.85	28.32	14.63
2007	48.26	42.88	66.04	24.54	29.89	15.72

Year	Shandong and Hebei			Northeastern region		
1980	11.81	9.46	8.00	10.84	19.77	16.71
1985	12.23	9.20	7.85	10.51	18.00	15.12
1995	13.19	12.28	9.25	6.73	12.00	9.62
2000	16.14	14.43	9.57	4.87	11.72	8.44
2001	16.30	14.48	9.43	4.39	10.94	8.30
2002	17.05	15.72	9.90	4.37*	10.08	8.21
2003	18.15	16.49	9.85	4.53	9.50	7.20
2004	19.52	17.51	9.83	4.61	9.02	6.52
2005	21.01	18.93	10.62	4.95	8.74	6.11*
2006	21.35	18.68	10.96	5.31	8.61	6.27
2007	21.30	18.82	11.30	5.65	8.05	6.82

*Signifies an inflection point.
Note: The eastern developed region includes Beijing, Tianjin, Shanghai, Jiangsu, Zhejiang, Guangdong, Fujian; the central and western region includes Shanxi, Henan, Anhui, Jiangxi, Hubei, Hunan from central region, and Guangxi, Chongqing, Sichuan, Guizhou, Yunnan, Tibet, Inner Mongolia, Shaanxi, Gansu, Ningxia, Qinghai, Xinjiang; the northeastern region includes Liaoning, Jilin, and Heilongjiang.
Source: According to *the 1985 Industrial Census Material of People's Republic of China*, *The Third National Industrial Census Material Anthology of People's Republic of China* in 1995 as well as relevant data from the applied supporting system of China's statistics and data (2000–2007), the following is the same.

share of manufacturing industry of the eastern developed region begins to drop gradually after 2002; in particular, the labor-intensive manufacturing industry initiated transfer from the eastern developed region. The relocated manufacturing industry share is absorbed partially by the central and western regions, and partially by Shandong and Hebei province.

In 1980, differences in the market shares of three types of manufacturing industry are small between the eastern developed region and the central and western regions. After 1985, the manufacturing industry began to concentrate toward the eastern region, among which the capital- and technology-intensive manufacturing industry is the most significant. In 1995, the market share of capital- and technology-intensive manufacturing industry in the eastern developed region reached 50% of the whole nation, and climbed to the summit in 2004, taking up 68.29%. The market share of labor-intensive and raw-material–intensive manufacturing industries in the eastern developed region reached the summit in 2002 and 2003, being 54.59% and 46.70%, respectively. The market shares of the three different types of manufacturing industries in the central and western regions reached the top in 1985, taking up about one-third of the national total, respectively. Afterward, the market share began to drop and then rebounded after respectively reaching one's nadir in 2004, 2003, and 2006.

All the market shares of the raw-material–intensive, capital- and technology-intensive manufacturing industries in the central and western regions increased while they decreased in the eastern developed region, and these opposite turning points took place basically at the same time. However, the inflection point of share-increasing of the labor-intensive manufacturing industry in the central and western regions occurred two year later than the inflection point of share-decreasing in eastern developed region. On one hand, this is because that the relocated firms from East China to the central and western regions required certain period to put into production after founding factories. The relocation effect would not show until this course ends. On the other hand, it reflects the competitive relations between central and western regions and Shandong and Hebei in their process of receiving industrial transfer. A part of the transferred market share from the eastern developed region has been absorbed by Shandong and Hebei. Since 1985, the market shares of Shandong and Hebei in those three different types of manufacturing industries have maintained a relatively stable growth. Yet in northeastern region, there was a shrinking state, which improved a little

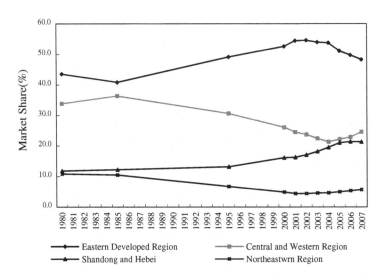

Figure 7-1   Market Share Change of Labor-Intensive Manufacturing Industry in Different Regions.
Source: According to the 1985 Industrial Census Material of People's Republic of China. The Third National Industrial Census Material Anthology of People's Republic of China in 1995, Support system for China's Statistics and Application (http://info.acmr.cn/).

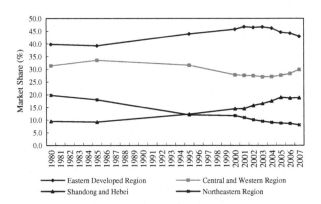

Figure 7-2   Market Share Change of Raw-Material–Intensive Manufacturing Industry in Different Regions.
Source: Same as Figure 7-1.

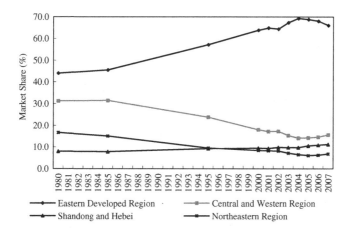

Figure 7-3   Market Share Change of Capital and Technology-Intensive Manufacturing Industry in Different Regions.

Source: Same as Figure 7-1.

only till 2002–2005. The decrease in the share of the raw-material-intensive manufacturing industry has slowed down, and the other two types of manufacturing industries' market shares have been on the rebound.

This discovery has proved the predicted westward relocation tendency of business in the eastern region by Chinese academia. To better describe the tendency, we conduct a comparison and analysis of the two digits code manufacturing industry's market share between the eastern developed region and central and western regions from 2004 to 2007. The result shows that, during this period, the market share of most manufacturing industry in the eastern developed region declined; 26 industries have shown a significant tendency of relocating to the central and (or) western regions except 3 industries.[3] That is, the decrease in market share in the eastern developed region went hand in hand with the increase of market share in the central and (or) western regions (see Table 7-4). Besides, in the eastern developed region, the decrease in the extent of the market share of the relocated labor-intensive and raw-material–intensive manufacturing industries is higher than that of capital- and technology-intensive manufacturing industry.

---

[3]Including one labor-intensive manufactures (No. 16), one raw-material-intensive manufactures (No. 28) and one capital and technology-intensive manufacturing industries (No. 37).

Table 7-4 The Characteristics and Tendency of Westward Relocated Manufacturing Industry from the Eastern Developed Region.

Classification	Name of industry	Market share in 2004 (%)			Change from 2004 to 2007 (percentage point)		
		Eastern developed region	Central region	Western region	Eastern developed region	Central region	Western region
Labor-intensive	13 Agricultural and sideline products processing industry	28.29	15.47	13.95	-5.50	3.89	0.59
	14 Food manufacturing industry	40.48	16.86	14.14	-9.49	3.54	0.61
	15 Beverage manufacturing industry	39.05	15.56	19.76	-6.55	4.05	4.18
	16 Tobacco manufacturing industry	21.95	24.08	35.14	8.01	2.57	-1.56
	17 Textile industry	66.07	8.74	4.64	-6.26	1.68	0.70
	18 Textile, clothing, shoes and caps manufacturing industry	80.40	5.04	0.84	-5.22	1.75	0.46
	19 Leather, fur, feather (down) and its products manufacturing industry	71.47	6.18	3.45	-3.81	2.88	1.00
	20 Wood processing and wood, bamboo, vine, palm fiber and herb products manufacturing industry	52.93	13.49	6.29	-10.16	4.05	1.27
	21 Furniture manufacturing industry	73.57	4.75	3.96	-8.27	2.64	1.37
	22 Paper-making and paper products industry	51.90	12.94	7.06	-3.55	3.14	-0.59
	23 Printing and copy of printing medium	66.66	11.54	10.92	-6.46	2.13	0.29
	24 Education and PE products manufacturing industry	84.20	2.47	0.13	-1.24	1.41	0.20
	42 Handicrafts and other manufacturing industry	66.46	8.06	5.32	-0.02	2.14	-1.69
Raw-material-intensive	25 Oil processing, coking and nuclear fuel processing industry	34.20	16.82	13.04	-2.19	-1.55	2.51
	26 Chemical raw material and chemical products manufacturing industry	52.49	12.11	10.86	-4.76	1.55	0.29
	27 Medical manufacturing industry	43.84	14.88	16.22	-6.19	3.34	-0.86

(Continued)

Table 7-4 (*Continued*)

Classification	Name of industry	Market share in 2004 (%)			Change from 2004 to 2007 (percentage point)		
		Eastern developed region	Central region	Western region	Eastern developed region	Central region	Western region
	28 Chemical fiber manufacturing industry	74.36	8.51	2.02	6.56	-1.37	1.06
	29 Rubber products industry	47.04	10.02	5.30	-2.31	2.48	0.05
	30 Plastic products industry	72.98	7.46	5.04	-5.04	1.69	-0.44
	31 Non-metal mineral products industry	42.39	18.19	11.12	-6.13	4.38	-0.17
	32 Black metal refinery and rolling processing industry	35.63	17.98	13.07	-0.07	0.71	-0.15
	33 Colored metal refinery and rolling processing industry	36.02	25.73	23.36	-4.02	3.70	1.22
	34 Metal products industry	72.71	6.56	3.67	-5.07	1.59	0.33
Capital and technology-intensive	35 Communication equipment manufacturing industry	60.46	9.17	6.67	-6.27	1.13	0.22
	36 Special equipment manufacturing industry	47.33	14.82	9.67	-3.75	2.55	0.41
	37 Transportation equipment manufacturing industry	45.63	14.79	13.31	0.80	-0.57	0.10
	39 Electrical mechanics and equipment manufacturing industry	71.04	7.56	4.35	-2.87	2.03	0.72
	40 Communication equipment, computer and other electronic equipment manufacturing	89.92	1.93	2.32	-1.60	0.36	0.28
	41 Instruments and apparatuses, culture and office mechanics manufacturing industry	83.99	4.42	4.55	-4.71	2.01	-0.30

7.4 Mechanism of Manufacturing Industry's Westward Relocation from East China

Since 2002, the industrial factors and regional factors in the eastern developed region have changed, pushing the eastern manufacturing business to make location decisions again and to start to relocate to the central and western region gradually. Furthermore, the industrial factors mainly include the products' life cycle, cost factor, as well as influence from the new labor division of industries; whereas the regional factors include the regional differences of factor cost, the ever-narrowing regional differences of return on investment, the foreign trade policy, as well as the function of local government, etc.

7.4.1 *Industrial Factors Influencing the Westward Relocation of Eastern Manufacturing Business*

7.4.1.1 *The relocation of labor and raw-material-intensive manufacturing industries from the eastern region is jointly determined by product life cycle and cost factor*

The relocation of labor-intensive and raw-material–intensive manufacturing industries from the eastern developed region could be attributable to mainly two reasons. First, different factor-intensive manufacturing industries are in different development stages. Vernon's product life cycle theory explains the phenomena of industry relocation from the developed countries to developing countries, disclosing the relations between the manufacturing industry's development trend and the change in market, location, and technology. The theory was afterward widely used in the study of developed countries' product life cycle and site selection dynamics (Krumme and Hayter, 1975; Healy and Clark, 1985; quoted from Hayter, 1997, p. 101). And it was also used to explain the industrialization of the agricultural region in the US. In the stage of product standardization, the most definitive influence factor of location is the labor cost, which caused the industry to filter down from the US metropolises to the low-income rural regions instead of transnational transfer. (Erickson, 1976; Erickson and Leinbach, 1979; Norton and Rees, 1979; Rees, 1979; Markusen, 1985; quoted from Hayter, 1997, p. 101) This has provided the basis for us to use the product life cycle theory to explain the westward relocation of industry in the eastern developed region.

The industrial export-oriented development pattern in the eastern developed region enables us to judge the alternation of leading industry from the evolution of its export structure. From the evolution pattern of the export structure, namely "textile products-electronics-hi-tech products", we could conclude that the leading industries in the eastern developed region have evolved from the low value-added, labor-intensive, and raw-material–intensive industries to capital- and technology-intensive processing manufacturing industry with high value addition. Since the labor-intensive and raw-material–intensive industries reached the maturity stage earlier than the capital- and technology-intensive industry, the earliest industry relocation took place in these two types of sectors. For the newly increased capacity of the labor- and raw-material–intensive sectors, the eastern developed region has lost its relative comparative advantage. In the meantime, the product life cycles of different types of capital- and technology-intensive industries differ from each other, and the processing equipment manufacturing industry is a relative labor-intensive industry. Therefore, when the labor- and raw-material-intensive industries relocate from the eastern developed region to the west, there are also relocations happening in the processing equipment manufacturing industries, such as communication equipment manufacturing, instruments and apparatuses, culture and office mechanics manufacturing, and other industries alike.

Moreover, different factor-intensive manufacturing industries differ in their bearing ability to the price fluctuation. Puga and Venables (1996) founded a simple model of two countries and two sectors, describing the process of industry transferring from one country to another under exogenous growth. They explored the industries of different labor intensity, upstream and downstream, and of different industrial linkages, and discovered that, with the growth of regional relative wage, the labor-intensive industries, downstream industries and weakly linked industries would transfer earlier. If other conditions maintained, facing the same degree of factor supply change, the labor-intensive and raw-material–intensive manufacturing industries will bear bigger pressure from higher costs because of the high percentage taken up by labor and raw materials cost and lower added value. Therefore, these types of manufacturing industries will move out part of the original and new production capacity to take better advantage of the cheap labor and big potential market in the central and western regions. In contrast, the capital- and technology-intensive industry has relatively higher value addition, and its bearing capacity to the rising price of factors is stronger, suffering not so much from the impact of factor market.

7.4.1.2 *The westward relocation of eastern manufacturing industry is the result of the new labor division of industries*

The westward relocation of manufacturing industry from the eastern developed region is not only the consequence of disintegration of enterprise organization but also stands for the deepening of China's new regional labor division. In the different stages of industrial development, different types of agglomeration economies play a part. The localization economy occupies an important place in mature industry development, whereas the urbanization economy exerts great influence in the high-tech industry development (Henderson *et al.*, 1995). Therefore, there is an intimate relation between city specialization and product's life cycle, namely, the new industry usually rises from diversified metropolitan area while the mature industry is distributed in small specialized cities. Duranton and Puga (2005) developed the view of Henderson by combining the evolution of city's labor division and the disintegration of enterprise organization for further analysis. And they discovered that, the distance cost, which results from the separation of manufacturing sector from corporate headquarters, had been greatly cut down by the development of transportation and communication technology, and an integrated enterprise could relocate its manufacturing sectors from its headquarters to a location which possessed similar specialized sectors and could provide intermediate products, then shift its headquarters to the location with excellent commercial service, and finally achieve the minimization of the costs of the above two sectors at the same time. The enterprise's vertical disintegration could push the cities to transfer from sector specialization to functional specialization, thereby forming independent big commercial center and small manufacturing cities. Afterward, this transregional functional labor division of industry is named as new industrial division by Wei (2007).

The rise of various factors' price and the heated competition of usable land in the eastern developed region pushed the enterprises' cost to go up. However, urbanization economies produced by the diversified production, rich and convenient commercial services, and face-to-face informal communication externality together decrease enterprises' headquarter operating cost. Moreover, the contact cost drops day by day, which encourages the organizational disintegration of enterprises in a mature stage, transferring the original and newly increased manufacturing sectors to the central and western region, taking advantage of their industrial foundation to produce intermediate products. This is no doubt the optimum location choice and form of organizational disintegration for the labor-intensive and raw-material–intensive enterprises in the eastern developed region. The high-end products are developed in the eastern developed region, and the standardized production is operated in the central and western regions, which is one of the major forms of China's new regional labor division and gradually developing into a tendency. Our analysis further proves this judgment.

The analysis shows that the ever-evident localization economy in the central and western regions is the major pulling force of the relocation of eastern manufacturing enterprises. Since the regional specialization level is one measurement of the localization economy, we have calculated the location quotient of 26 two-digit code manufacturing industries which relocated in 2007 (see Table 7-5). The result reflects that the central region has relatively higher specialization level among 11 industries, including 5 labor-intensive manufacturing industries, 5 raw-material-intensive manufacturing industries, and one capital- and technology-intensive manufacturing industry; the western region comparatively deeply specialized in 7 industries, including 3 labor-intensive manufacturing industries and 4 raw-material–intensive manufacturing industries. Yet, the eastern developed region proves high specialization level in 7 labor-intensive manufacturing industries, 2 raw-material-intensive manufacturing industries, and 4 capital- and technology-intensive manufacturing industries, forming staggered development with the central and western regions. All of these indicate the pattern of China's new industrial division of labor. We maintain that, to pursue economic profit, enterprises in the eastern developed region usually choose the central and western regions as the target location, which are able to provide relatively cheaper intermediate products. It means that the central

Table 7-5 Manufacturing Industry Location Quotient of Three Regions in 2007.

Factor intensity	Sector	Eastern developed region	Central region	Western region
Labor-intensive	13 Agricultural and sideline products processing industry	0.46	1.30	1.26
	14 Food manufacturing industry	0.63	1.37	1.28
	15 Beverage manufacturing industry	0.66	1.31	2.08
	17 Textile industry	1.22	0.70	0.47
	18 Textile, clothing, shoes and cap manufacturing industry	1.53	0.45	0.11
	19 Leather, fur, feather(down) and its products manufacturing industry	1.38	0.61	0.39
	20 Wood processing and wood, bamboo, vine, palm fiber and herb products manufacturing industry	0.87	1.17	0.66
	21 Furniture manufacturing industry	1.33	0.50	0.46
	22 Paper-making and paper products industry	0.98	1.08	0.56
	23 Printing and copy of printing medium	1.22	0.91	0.98
	24 Education and PE products manufacturing industry	1.69	0.26	0.03
	42 Handicrafts and other manufacturing industry	1.35	0.68	0.32
Raw-material-intensive	25 Oil processing, coking and nuclear fuel processing industry	0.65	1.02	1.35
	26 Chemical raw material and chemical products manufacturing industry	0.97	0.91	0.97

(*Continued*)

Table 7-5 (*Continued*)

Factor intensity	Sector	Eastern developed region	Central region	Western region
	27 Medical manufacturing industry	0.77	1.22	1.34
	29 Rubber products industry	0.91	0.84	0.47
	30 Plastic products industry	1.38	0.61	0.40
	31 Non-metal mineral products industry	0.74	1.51	0.95
	32 Black metal refinery and rolling processing industry	0.72	1.25	1.12
	33 Colored metal refinery and rolling processing industry	0.65	1.97	2.14
	34 Metal products industry	1.38	0.55	0.35
Capital- and-technology-intensive	35 Communication equipment manufacturing industry	1.10	0.69	0.60
	36 Special equipment manufacturing industry	0.89	1.16	0.88
	39 Electrical mechanics and equipment manufacturing industry	1.39	0.64	0.44
	40 Communication equipment, computer and other electronic equipment manufacturing	1.80	0.15	0.23
	41 Instruments and apparatuses, culture and office mechanics manufacturing industry	1.61	0.43	0.37

and western regions must possess good industry foundation, or industry-supporting capability, which could enormously decrease the relocation cost of enterprises from the eastern developed region. Therefore, the diminished effect of localization economy in the eastern developed region will make some manufacturing industries change their intermediate products suppliers, thus speeding up the relocation process toward the central and western regions. For those 13 manufacturing industries which possess specialization advantage in the eastern developed region while having relatively lower specialization level in the central and western regions, the shifted market share is slightly lower than the other 13 manufacturing industries. The latter have lost specialization advantage in the eastern developed region and in the meantime they still possess high specialization level in the central and western regions.

7.4.2 The Change of Regional Factor is the Deeper Reason for Westward Relocation

7.4.2.1 *The regional factor cost differences are significant, and manufacturing industry's relative production cost in the eastern developed region soars*

We have compared the labor price and industrial land price between the eastern developed region and the central and western regions. In the first place, let us look at the labor price. In the mature stage of products, the enterprises usually replace the skilled labor with unskilled labor to decrease cost. We employ the efficiency wage,[4] namely the wage cost by per production, to measure the labor cost. The higher the efficiency wage is, the higher the actual paid wage is for producing the same output. The congestion effect caused by agglomeration economy in the eastern region augments living cost, thereby pushing the wage level up. The labor cost advantage in the eastern developed region is losing continuously since 2002 (see Table 7-6). In 2002, 14 two-digit code manufacturing industries' efficiency wage levels in the eastern developed region are lower than central and (or) western regions, including four labor-intensive industries (C16 Tobacco Manufacturing Industry; C17 Textile Industry; C20 Wood Processing and Wood, Bamboo, Vine, Palm Fiber and Herb Products Manufacturing Industry; C22 Paper-manufacturing and Paper Products Industry), 5 raw-material-intensive industries (C25 Oil Processing, Coping and Nuclear Fuel Processing Industry; C26 Chemical Raw Material and Chemical Products Manufacturing Industry; C28 Chemical Fiber Manufacturing Industry; C32 Black

---

[4]The efficiency wage = current year payable gross payroll/value added of industrial output × 100%.

Table 7-6 Comparison of Efficiency Wage of Manufacturing Industry between Eastern Developed Region and Central and Western Regions.

Industry code	2002			2007		
	Eastern developed region (%)	Central region minus eastern region (percentage points)	Western region minus eastern region (percentage points)	Eastern developed region (%)	Central region minus eastern region (percentage points)	Western region minus eastern region (percentage points)
13	13.98	−4.70	0.90	12.21	−5.01	−2.25
14	24.21	−8.52	−7.39	20.88	−10.82	−9.10
15	13.58	−0.38	−1.42	15.75	−6.09	−6.87
16	3.75	1.95	0.92	3.01	1.70	1.40
17	24.50	2.41	10.14	24.15	−8.13	−4.85
18	35.75	−14.92	0.61	36.80	−16.44	−9.56
19	34.50	−21.57	−16.00	41.15	−28.88	−23.66
20	17.95	−1.58	7.66	20.40	−7.73	−3.44
21	26.14	−12.04	3.02	36.42	−21.24	−21.12
22	14.49	1.62	8.29	19.46	−9.87	−1.91
23	26.37	−9.50	−2.46	28.92	−15.10	−12.80
24	40.88	−15.76	−17.18	44.52	−19.12	−20.90
25	10.86	1.13	−1.86	9.21	−0.24	2.12
26	17.51	2.36	5.25	13.52	−0.73	2.78
27	19.09	−3.66	−3.56	17.75	−6.42	−6.12
28	15.25	11.63	13.78	9.02	7.83	6.09
29	23.65	−4.85	0.38	25.22	−15.85	−6.27
30	21.29	−5.49	−3.72	25.91	−14.79	−8.97
31	23.03	−0.49	6.81	21.00	−8.96	−1.83
32	16.10	6.87	8.86	7.95	4.50	4.31
33	14.77	6.57	9.63	9.54	−1.77	1.58
34	21.76	−5.06	3.07	22.90	−10.15	−4.28
35	25.18	1.91	6.39	21.33	−5.63	−1.73
36	24.13	−2.12	11.55	24.61	−8.45	−0.76
37	16.84	5.34	5.44	16.79	−0.68	0.22
39	21.33	−3.10	4.34	21.92	−11.39	−9.17
40	14.03	2.31	−0.45	24.62	−11.40	−9.26
41	42.22	−19.17	−7.68	27.82	−13.39	−4.55
42	30.89	−8.11	−13.12	32.49	−20.46	−2.81

Note: efficiency wage = gross payroll/industrial added value × 100%.

Source: According to relevant data from the applied supporting system of China's statistics and data (2002, 2007).

Metal Refinery and Rolling Processing Industry; C33 Colored Metal Refinery and Rolling Processing), and five capital and technology-intensive industries (C35 Communication Equipment Manufacturing Industry; C36 Special Equipment Manufacturing Industry; C37 Transportation Equipment Manufacturing Industry; C39 Electrical Mechanics and Equipment Manufacturing Industry; C40 Communication Equipment, Computer and Other Electronic Equipment Manufacturing). However, in 2007, the number declined to only 3 (C16, C28 and C32). Black Metal Refinery and Rolling Processing Industry), which means that, with the rise of labor cost in the eastern developed region, the labor cost advantage of manufacturing industry in the central and western regions is more and more obvious. The shifting advantages in labor cost encourage the mature manufacturing industries in the eastern developed region to relocate towards the central and western regions.

Besides, since land supply is inelastic, the large-scale agglomeration of population and industries in the eastern developed region give rise to the price increase of the industrial land. In 2002–2005, the average price of the industrial land in the southeastern cities was higher than that of other regions; following it was the price of industrial land in cities of North China, which stood second of the whole country, and first in the 2006–2007 time period. However, the prices of the industrial land in the central-south, southwestern, northwestern, and northeastern cities have been lower than the average level of the country since (see Table 7-7). The average price of the industrial land in the southwestern cities reached RMB 544/m^2 in 2002, which was RMB 165 higher than that of the central-south region, RMB 121 higher than that of the southwestern region, and RMB 113 higher than that of northwestern region. In 2007, the average price of industrial land in the southwestern and North China cities have reached to RMB 575/m^2 and RMB 650/m^2, which were RMB 118 and RMB 193 higher than that of the central–south region, RMB 111 and RMB 186 higher than that of the southwestern region, and RMB 118 and RMB 193 higher than that of the northwestern region. Judging from above data, we could conclude that the gap of price for industrial land in the eastern developed region and the central and western regions is widening. The higher factor price narrows the profit space of manufacturing industries in the eastern developed region, particularly of the low value-added, labor-intensive, and raw-material–intensive

Table 7-7 Comparison of Average Price for Industrial Land in Each Region (Yuan/m^2).

Year	South-eastern region	Central-south region	South-western region	North-western region	North China	North-eastern region	Average price of the country
2002	544	379	423	431	517	349	456
2003	527	425	427	442	526	357	463
2004	544	446	389	475	543	363	495
2005	589	462	447	453	538	373	481
2006	527	429	452	442	622	387	485
2007	575	457	464	457	650	399	507

Note: The southeastern region includes Shanghai, Jiangsu, Zhejiang, Guangdong, Hainan, the central-south region includes Anhui, Hubei, Hunan, Jiangxi, Chongqing, the southwestern region includes Shaanxi, Sichuan, Guizhou, Yunnan, Guangxi, the northwestern region includes Shanxi, Inner Mongolia, Gansu, Ningxia, Qinghai, Xinjiang, Tibet, the North China includes Beijing, Tianjin, Hebei, Henan, Shandong, the Northeastern region includes Liaoning, Jilin, and Heilongjiang.
Source: Arranged according to the Dynamic Monitoring System of Urban Land Price of China.

manufacturing industries. These manufacturing enterprises are pushed to realize the minimization of cost by readjusting spatial distribution of production.

7.4.2.2 *The gradually narrowing gap of return on investment
between eastern developed region and central
and western regions. The increase of production
efficiency of central and western regions as well as
the change of Chinese foreign trade policy push
eastern manufacturing industry to relocate toward
central and western regions*

As is known, economic activity pursues profit; thus the regional return on investment is an important factor influencing the westward relocation of the eastern enterprises. And the regional production efficiency is the key to the realization of profit for the eastern enterprises which move to the west. The gap of average profit rate and overall labour productivity between the eastern developed region and the central and western regions is narrowing from 2002–2007. Compared with 2002, in 2007, there were 24 two-digit manufacturing industries in the central region whose profit rate exceeded that of the eastern region, and 21 in western area. To be specific, in 2002, the gap of manufacturing industry's profit rate between the eastern developed region and the central and western regions was evident, and there were only 7 among the 29 two-digit manufacturing industries, whose profit rates were higher than those of the eastern developed region; by contrast, in 2007, there were 18 already (see Table 7-8). In the aspect of regional labor productivity differences, from 2002 to 2007, the overall labour productivity gap between the eastern developed region and the central and western regions is obviously shrinking. In 2002, apart from one manufacturing industry (19), the overall labour productivity of the other 28 manufacturing industries in the central and western regions were much lower than that of the eastern developed region. There has been outstanding growth till 2007, with 17 two-digit manufacturing industries' labor productivity higher than that of the eastern developed region. The other 12 industries' labor productivity's gap between the two regions is also narrowing (see Table 7-9). When comes to the policy in China, the newly issued *Catalogue for Restricted Commodities in Processing Trade* (Announcement No. 44) in 2007,[5] which aims at the small- and medium-sized enterprises in the eastern coastal region that pursuing profit by consuming high amounts of energy, causing serious pollution, and wasting resources, imposes double pressures on these enterprises in terms of investment and policy. However, the central and western enterprises can still enjoy the preferential policies of processing trade. Thereby, the national policy has accelerated the intra-regional industrial transfer by pushing a large number of eastern SMEs to relocate toward the west from the eastern region.

---

[5]There are 2,247 customs commodity codes listed on the table of processing trade restricted goods, including some labor-intensive products, such as plastic raw materials and products, textile yarns, cloths and furniture, etc.

Table 7-8 Comparison of Average Profit Rate of Manufacturing Industry between the Eastern Developed Region and Central and Western Regions.

Industry code	Average profit rate in 2002			Profit rate change from 2002 to 2007 (percentage points)		
	Eastern developed region (%)	Central region minus eastern region (percentage points)	Western region minus eastern region (percentage points)	Eastern developed region (%)	Central region	Western region
13	2.09	−0.19	−0.97	2.22	3.42	5.23
14	2.45	1.29	−2.12	3.84	2.42	7.48
15	6.82	−3.89	2.54	0.93	7.20	10.21
16	34.55	−24.00	−27.23	19.80	16.60	10.99
17	3.06	−2.74	−6.29	0.57	2.73	5.41
18	4.22	−1.75	−2.77	0.43	3.41	2.00
19	2.62	−2.61	−7.85	1.88	6.28	10.18
20	2.29	0.06	−0.69	2.47	7.22	12.91
21	3.83	1.51	1.49	0.35	3.05	−1.05
22	7.10	−3.18	−9.93	−0.61	2.65	4.84
23	8.86	−0.60	−3.91	−1.36	0.32	4.85
24	4.60	−1.12	−1.36	−1.15	2.68	−2.53
25	3.06	−3.09	−1.27	−0.71	1.70	0.53
26	4.93	−3.26	−3.28	2.06	5.06	10.14
27	9.47	−3.57	−0.19	1.81	3.04	4.37
28	−0.32	0.95	2.05	5.08	8.23	4.03
29	5.93	−3.30	−8.70	−1.65	2.65	5.67
30	5.65	−0.49	−5.49	−0.76	1.01	3.45
31	4.47	−2.29	0.73	1.24	5.12	1.12
32	5.14	−0.75	0.52	−0.08	2.32	−1.81
33	2.17	−0.06	1.49	2.72	5.43	6.88
34	4.09	−0.67	0.44	0.76	2.31	0.10
35	5.25	−4.12	−5.72	2.60	5.58	6.93
36	7.64	−2.46	−9.71	1.31	3.19	6.20
37	5.55	0.29	−4.79	2.12	−0.54	2.83
39	7.47	−4.52	−5.88	−0.82	2.83	4.07
40	5.44	−1.37	−2.22	−1.26	−1.10	1.34
41	6.55	2.77	−8.04	1.60	1.92	9.56
42	3.91	0.65	2.51	2.30	1.06	1.60

Note: This diagram's average profit rate means the arithmetic average value of ratio of profits to cost in manufacturing enterprises of each province and municipality.

Table 7-9 Comparison of Per Capita Productivity of Manufacturing Industry between the Developed Eastern Region and Central and Western Regions.

Industry code	2002 year			2007 year		
	Eastern developed region (1000 Yuan/ person)	Central region/ eastern region	Western region/ eastern region	Eastern developed region (1000 Yuan/ person)	Central region/ eastern region	Western region/ eastern region
13	64.71	0.92	0.70	165.68	1.03	0.86
14	55.67	0.58	0.75	123.50	0.99	1.05
15	117.14	0.44	0.57	217.34	0.70	0.88
16	1262.29	0.30	0.27	3408.02	0.34	0.27
17	38.29	0.49	0.62	70.73	0.84	1.07
18	27.36	0.74	0.67	51.12	1.14	0.80
19	28.94	1.10	1.01	51.73	1.57	2.22
20	50.41	0.69	0.48	87.26	1.07	0.93
21	46.32	0.91	0.44	63.20	1.36	1.18
22	81.00	0.47	0.33	117.08	1.04	0.54
23	63.92	0.74	0.54	90.55	1.28	0.99
24	31.94	0.85	0.48	49.20	1.45	1.31
25	268.65	0.60	0.37	563.41	0.54	0.45
26	92.39	0.41	0.43	234.35	0.57	0.58
27	101.66	0.44	0.57	183.53	0.69	0.96
28	66.02	0.51	1.35	207.52	0.59	0.80
29	47.28	0.77	0.62	80.78	1.48	1.00
30	55.42	0.69	0.56	87.76	1.32	0.90
31	49.90	0.53	0.58	109.04	0.91	0.71
32	121.01	0.53	0.41	442.89	0.61	0.42
33	81.73	0.68	0.73	232.09	1.39	1.10
34	54.76	0.65	0.45	102.81	1.23	0.76
35	54.59	0.49	0.45	131.70	0.81	0.61
36	64.57	0.56	0.33	118.57	0.98	0.68
37	104.25	0.54	0.31	186.35	0.75	0.55
39	69.37	0.63	0.51	140.20	1.15	1.29
40	209.84	0.40	0.44	182.61	0.78	0.68
41	58.58	0.65	0.42	129.50	1.07	0.68
42	38.67	0.67	0.83	86.17	1.10	1.12

7.4.2.3 *The local governments of the central and western regions have played an important role in attracting domestic investment inflow*

Under the evaluation system for the local government of China, the economic growth is still an important goal. The activities of attracting investment of every level of government in the central and western regions have vigorously pushed the eastern manufacturing enterprises to move westward. In recent years, those local governments have frequently carried out promotion activities in the eastern developed provinces and municipalities, communicating face to face with the entrepreneurs from the southeastern coastal region, comprehensively introducing the local economic conditions, including the local situation, location advantage, resource condition, industry characteristic and preferential policies, etc. They have also come up with a series of key investment projects to attract domestic investment. From 2005 to present, the central and western regions have achieved good results in terms of attracting domestic investment, and the major expositions of the central and western regions in 2007 were more successful than the former years, such as the 11th East-West China Cooperation & Investment Trade Fair (EWCCI Trade Fair). In the fair, 158 foreign investment contracts and agreements were signed, the total amount of investment reaching US$ 4.458 billion; the number of inter-regional collaboration contracts and agreements was 1554, with the total investment reaching RMB 237.782 billion. The total amount of the contracts and agreements for internal trade reaches RMB 184.1 billion among which the eastern industry transfer took up 75% of the total. In the second Central China Investment and Trade Expo, Shanxi province signed 212 projects, attracting domestic investment RMB 64.9 billion and coming second to the host Henan province. Jiangxi province introduced domestic investment RMB 7.008 billion and 84 domestic investment projects. With these transferred projects of the eastern industries putting into production, the effect of the westward relocation will present itself.

In a word, the change of the industry factor and the regional factor cause a part of the manufacturing industry to move to the central and western regions from the east. Since the different factor-intensive manufacturing industries stay in different stages of the products' life cycle and the bearing capacity to the change of factor prices are different, the labor-intensive and raw-material–intensive manufacturing industries relocate from the eastern developed region earlier than the capital- and technology-intensive manufacturing industry. The weakening effect of localization economy in the eastern developed region and the accentuation of the localization economy in the central and western regions have together pushed the deepening of the new industrial division. The new labor division makes some manufacturing enterprises accelerate the westward relocation to obtain production profit by transferring the intermediate products supply. The obvious factor cost differences between the eastern region and the central and western regions, the narrowing gap of regional return on investment and the improving production efficiency of the manufacturing industry in the central and western regions, and the change of national foreign trade policy and the role the local governments played in attracting domestic investment have greatly improved the investment environment of the central and western regions, and have pushed the manufacturing enterprises in the eastern developed region to move westward.

7.5 National Policy for Guiding the Eastern Manufacturing Industry to Move West

The tendency for the eastern manufacturing enterprises to relocate westward has appeared and is accelerating. At the same time, the central and western local governments have formulated a series of policies and measures in recent years to encourage and attract the investment and industry transfer from the eastern developed provinces, which is beginning to take effect. With the industrial agglomeration in the eastern developed region stepping into the senior stage and factor prices soaring, the pushing force from the eastern region, the motivation of the enterprise's expansion and the pulling force from the central and western regions will surely stimulate a large number of labor-intensive and raw-material-intensive enterprises to relocate to the west by all means. Thereby, the new situation calls for a higher requirement of the nation's regional policy.

In the first place, the central government should further issue and improve the industrial policy in the eastern developed region and the stimulus policy for encouraging the eastern funds to flow into the central and eastern regions, and raise the market access threshold of the eastern developed region to provide effective incentive for the westward relocation of the eastern enterprises. EU countries had used restricting policy aiming at the prosperous region (Mariotti, 2005). For example, Britain implemented relocation permit policy in the 1960s, and the permit systems restricted the enterprises' swarming into the jammed prosperous region (Twomey and Taylor, 1985). The present industry-restricting policy in China takes the environmental protection as the major criteria. And there are no policies aiming at particular industries in prosperous region, which is very unfavorable to the industrial upgrade of the eastern developed region. To promote the economic transformation and upgrade in the eastern developed region, it is necessary to set up and implement industry-restricting policies in east China. Moreover, the central government should issue encouraging policy to push the eastern enterprises to invest in the western region, providing necessary financial support and tax preference etc. Given the life cycles of different industries and differential regional requirements, the policy should highlight flexibility and differentiation. It is never a solution for all problems. For the hi-tech industry whose development is relatively weaker in the central and western regions, the government should step up the efforts and in the meantime offer corresponding support for the relocation of the labor-intensive and land-consuming enterprises straggled in the eastern region.

Second, the central government should further clarify the regional policy goals and explore the pattern of close cooperation with an appropriate division of labour and benign interaction between the eastern region and central and western regions. That is because it serves not only as a wonderful opportunity of developing for the central and west areas but also as the key for China' coordinated development among regions. At present, the gradient development of the eastern developed region and the central and western regions has shown the embryonic form of "core–periphery" pattern. A "core–periphery" pattern can lead to two possible results: develop new secondary centers or form expanding periphery areas, so it is incomprehensive for the government to just lead westward industry relocation. To promote balanced development of regions and narrow the regional development gap, the local government should actively cultivate new pillar industries in the central and western regions instead of simply accepting the industry relocation as the motivation for development. Furthermore, the government should promote reasonable industrial agglomeration, improve local supporting capacity of industries, cultivate brands, and encourage innovation to nurture endogenous self-development ability of the central and western regions. To reach this goal, it is necessary to make more national policies for supporting the development of central and west regions: for example, decreasing the industrial tax burden, developing characteristic hi-tech parks, stepping up efforts in supporting the service industry, and implementing the plan of talent rejuvenation of central and western regions. Apart from the above, the government needs to further open up the inner land, add bonded port area, cut down logistic cost, and encourage establishment of sourcing network of transnational enterprises in the central and western region, all of which would push the relocation of coastal processing trade of the manufacturing industry to the central and western regions.

In the third place, there is the coordination problem between the local policy and central regional policy. So far, among the developed provinces in East China, there are still some developing areas, such as the north of Jiangsu, the west of Zhejiang, and the mountain area and east and west sides of Guangdong, etc. In March 2005, the Guangdong government issued the *Opinions on Joint-promoting Industrial Transfer between Mountain Area, East and West Wings, and Pearl River Delta (for Trial Implementation)*, and then Guangdong started to set up industrial transfer parks in the backward areas. Some scholars have earlier proposed the industrial transfer to the developing areas in Zhejiang Province (Chen and Ye, 2002). Obviously, the local interest of the developing areas in the eastern developed provinces will contradict with that of the central and western provinces in terms of industrial transfer. Therefore, the central government's relevant policies promoting westward relocation will come across some hurdles in implementation. Measures to strengthen the coordination on enterprise relocation between the local policy and the central regional policy should be highlighted.

References

Brouwer, A. E., I. Mariotti and J. N. Van Ommeren (2004). The Firm Relocation Decision: An Empirical Investigation. *The Annals of Regional Science*, 38(2), 335–347.

Chen, J. (2002). Empirical Research of Current Chinese Firms Relocation — Based on Analysis of Questionnaire Report of 105 Companies from Zhejiang Province. *Management World*, (6), 64–74.

Chen, J. J. and W. Y. Ye (2002). A Study on the Industrial Transference from Developed Areas to Developing Areas in Zhejiang Province. *Business Economics and Administration*, (4), 28–31.

Chen, W. (2005). Analysis of Private Enterprises' Regional Relocation and its Strategy. *Academic Exchanges*, (10), 85–88.

Chen, Z., H. Jiang and J. Xiong (2006). Analysis of Big Enterprises Relocated in Jiangxi and Countermeasures Suggestions. *Enterprise Economy*, (4), 111–113.

Duranton, G. and D. Puga (2005). From Sectoral to Functional Urban Specialization. *Journal of Urban Economics*, 57(2), 343–370.

Erickson, R. A. (1976). The Filtering-down Process: Industrial Location in a Non-Metropolitan Area. *The Professional Geographer*, 28(3), 254–260.

Erickson, R. A. and T. R. Leinbach (1979). Characteristics of branch plants attracted to nonmetropoliton areas. In Lonsdale, R. E. and H. L. Seyler, *Nonmetropoliton Industrialization*, Washington, D.C.: V.H. Winston, pp. 57–78.

Hayter, R. (1997). *The Dynamics of Industrial Location: The Factory, the Firm and the Production System*. New York: Wiley Chichester.

Healy. M. J. and D. Clark (1985). Industrial decline in a local economy the case of country 1974–1982, Environment and Planning, A(17), 1351–1367.

Henderson, V., A. Kuncoro and M. Turner (1995). Industrial Development in Cities. *Journal of Political Economy*, 103(5), 1067–1090.

Krumme, G. and R. Hayter (1975). Implications of corporate strategies and product cycle adjustments for regional employment changes. In Collins, L. and D. F. Walker (eds.) Locational Dynamics of Manufacturing Activity. New York: Wiley, pp. 325–356.

Li, W., S. Zhu and C. Wang (2004). A Survey of Private Enterprises' Relocation and Expansion Phenomenon: Evidence from Leqing City in Zhejiang Province. *On Economic Problems*, (9), 30–32.

Liu, H. and B. Ai (2005). Research of Motives for Enterprise Relocation. *Journal of Changsha University of Science & Technology (Social Sciences)*, (4), 50–53.

Mariotti, I. (2005). *Firm Relocation and Regional Policy: A Focus on Italy, the Netherlands and the United Kingdom*. Amsterdam, Netherlands: Royal Dutch Geographical Society.

Markusen, A. R. (1985). *Profit Cycles, Oligopoly and Regional Development.* Cambridge, MA: MIT Press.

Norton, R. H. and J. Rees (1979). The product cycle and the spatial decentralization of American manufacturing. *Regional Studies*, 13, 141–151.

Pellenbarg, P. H. *et al.* (2002). *Firm Relocation: State of the Art and Research Prospects.* Research Report No. 02D31, Research Institute SOM, University of Groningen, Holland.

Puga, D. and A. J. Venables (1996). The Spread of Industry: Spatial Agglomeration in Economic Development. *Journal of the Japanese and International Economies*, 10(4), 440–464.

Rees, J. (1979). Technological change and regional shifts in American manufacturing. *The Prefessional Geography*, 31, 45–54.

Twomey, J. and J. Taylor (1985). Regional Policy and the Interregional Movement of Manufacturing Industry in Great Britain. *Scottish Journal of Political Economy*, 32(3), 257–277.

Van Dijk, J. and P. H. Pellenbarg (2000). Firm relocation decisions in The Netherlands: An ordered logit approach. *Papers in Regional Science*, 79(2), 191–219.

Wei, H. (2007). The New Industrial Division and Conflict Management in Metropolitan Region — Based on the Perspective of Industrial-chain Division. *China Industrial Economics*, (2), 28–34.

Western Development Office of the State Council (2007). *Step up the Interactions between the East and West Region, and Further Promote Development of the Western Region: A Summary of Relevant Issues*, November 23.

Chapter 8

Changes in the Location of Taiwan-Invested IT Enterprises in Mainland China and Their Relocation Decisions

Wei Houkai and Li Jing

8.1 General Situation of Taiwanese Investment in Mainland China

With the continuous development of the cross-strait economic and trade exchanges between mainland China and Taiwan, the scale of Taiwanese investment in mainland China has been expanding rapidly since the late 1990s, reaching the highest point of US$ 3.97 billion in 2002 (see Figure 8-1). In recent years, both the scale of Taiwanese investment and its proportion to the national total foreign investment actually used have shown a downward trend. In 2007, the Taiwanese direct investment actually utilized by mainland China reached US$ 1.774 billion, accounting for 2.37% of the total foreign investment actually used.[1] Up to the end of 2006, the enterprises that Taiwan had invested in mainland China reached 71,847, with the actual foreign capital amounting to US$ 43.893 billion, accounting for 12.08% of the total foreign-invested enterprises approved and 6.40% of the total foreign capital actually used (Ministry of Commerce of the PRC, 2008).

---

[1] In recent years, there is a sharp decline in Taiwanese direct investment in the mainland, which is closely related to the surge of the Taiwanese investment in mainland through free ports. In 2006, 3752 newly established enterprises were funded by Taiwanese in mainland China, with the actual use of foreign capital reaching US$ 2.136 billion. Besides, Taiwanese also established 1026 enterprises in the mainland through four free ports — Virgin Island, Cayman Island, Samoa and Mauritius, and the actual use of foreign capital was US$ 3.934 billion (Ministry of Commerce, 2008).

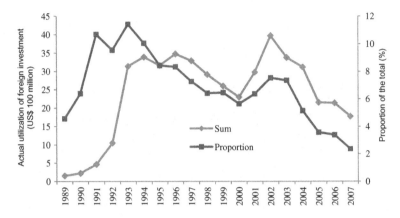

Figure 8-1   Changes of the Actual Utilization of Taiwanese Direct Investment in the Mainland China.

Source: Drawn according to Ministry of Commerce of the PRC (ed.) *China Foreign Investment Report (2007)* and NBSC (ed.), *China Statistical Yearbook (2008)*.

Taiwan's direct investment in mainland China mainly centered at manufacturing. In 2006, Taiwan invested US$ 1.735 billion in manufacturing, mining, and other fields, accounting for 81.23% of its total investment in the mainland, with an increase of 1.82 percentage points compared with that in 2002. At first, Taiwanese investment in the mainland mainly focused on the traditional labor-intensive manufacturing, such as food, plastics, textiles, and clothing. However, the technological content of Taiwan-invested projects has been increasing since the mid-1990s, with the investment focus gradually shifting to capital-intensive and technology-intensive industries. The proportion of electrical industry, electronic industry, precision instruments industry, and other technology-intensive industries are on the rise. In 2006, Taiwanese investment accounts for 10% of the total foreign capital in electronics and telecommunications equipments manufacturing, 9% in integrated circuit manufacturing, and 4% each in computer manufacturing and software industries (Ministry of Commerce of the PRC, 2008).

Taiwan's direct investment in mainland China highly concentrates in the eastern region, especially in Jiangsu, Guangdong, Shanghai, Fujian, and Zhejiang, and these investments altogether took up more than 80% of the total amount. As seen from Figure 8-2, in 1998, 39.8% of Taiwanese investment in the mainland was concentrated in Guangdong province, with

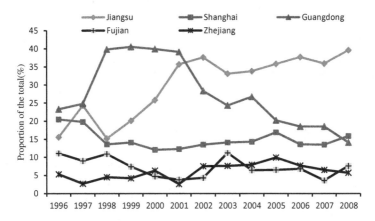

Figure 8-2 Distribution of Taiwanese Investment in Mainland China from 1996 to 2008.

Source: Drawn according to *The Approval of Investment Statistics in the mainland China*, from The Investment Deliberation Commission of the Ministry of Economic Affairs in Taiwan.

the Pearl River Delta (PRD) region as the center, while Jiangsu Province ranked just behind with the proportion was only 15.2%. Later, Taiwanese investment in the mainland gradually shifted from the PRD region to the Yangtze River Delta (YRD) region, especially from Guangdong to Jiangsu. By 2008, the proportion of Taiwanese investment in Guangdong Province had dropped to 14.1%, a decline of 25.7 percentage points compared with that in 1998; while the proportion in Jiangsu surged to 39.6%, an increase of 24.4 percentage points compared with that in 1998. During the same period, the proportion of Taiwanese investment in Fujian and Guangdong combined decreased from 50.7% to 21.7%, while the proportion in Jiangsu, Zhejiang, and Shanghai altogether increased from 33.3% to 61.2%. Therefore, it is obvious that Taiwanese investment in mainland China has been shifting from the PRD region to the YRD region since the late 1990s.

After 20 years of development, a large number of Taiwan-funded enterprises are gradually enlarging their scales and moving toward diversity by deepening their specialization. They "flock together" in the southeast coastal region, forming a number of characteristic industrial clusters inch by inch, and greatly boost the development of local economy. The Taiwan-invested information industry, represented by IT industry, also highly concentrates in the eastern region, and the investment amount increased rapidly each year. According to statistics results, about 75% of the gross output of IT manufacturing in mainland China was from Taiwan-funded enterprises a few years ago (Ren, 2004). The production mode of "order in Taiwan and product in the mainland" not only creates profit for Taiwan-funded enterprises but also promotes the formation of IT industrial chain and boosts the development of local high-tech industries in mainland China.

From the perspective of the geographical distribution of Taiwan-invested IT industries, the coastal areas at present are highly dependent on foreign trade, represented by the PRD, the YRD, and the Bohai Sea Rim (BSR) regions. However, this distribution pattern is not accomplished overnight, but has gone through a long period of relocation showing obvious stage characteristics. Through analyzing the survey data of these enterprises, this chapter aims at discussing whether there are any changes in the investment location or even any relocation law of Taiwan-invested IT enterprises, figuring out what have promoted their relocation decisions. The chapter finally gives specific suggestions on the basis of the actual situation of Taiwan-invested IT enterprises and the regional development strategy.

8.2 Data Source and Research Direction

8.2.1 *Definition of Information Technology Industry*

Information Technology (IT) industry refers to industries related to information communication technology. It is generally believed that there are three kinds of IT industry: networking, software, and integrated circuits; while it can also be divided into two types: IT manufacturing and value-added services. IT manufacturing includes appliance manufacturing such as personal computers and servers, communication network equipment manufacturing, electronic component manufacturing, and IT accessories manufacturing. IT value-added services include three parts — trade in IT service, software, and Internet. However, there is no clear definition of IT industry with regard to research. For the sake of convenience, the chapter defines IT industry as the electronics and telecommunications equipments manufacturing industry (two-digit SIC code, 41) and computer application services (two-digit SIC code, 83) on the basis of the characteristics of IT industry and the Standard Industrial Classification of the National Economy (2002).

8.2.2 *Data Declaration and Research Direction*

The classification and processing of data in this chapter are mainly based on the national directory database for foreign-funded enterprises and *Directory of Taiwan-invested Enterprises in the Mainland*. According to the definition of IT industry mentioned above, there were 2,259 Taiwan-invested IT enterprises in mainland China from February 1986 to February 2006, selected in accordance with the two-digit SIC code.

8.2.2.1 *Selection and Classification Based on Time Period*

It can be seen from the results of initial processing of statistical data that there are three stage characteristics of Taiwan-funded enterprises' investment in the mainland: it is mainly from the mid-1990s that Taiwan businessmen begin to invest in the mainland, and for geographic consideration, the export-oriented production bases were set up in the southeast coast such as Guangdong and Fujian Provinces at first; there had been an investment boom trigged by Taiwan-funded IT enterprises by the end of 1990s as the economy in the mainland continued to open up, especially in the YRD region where investment rose rapidly; in the 21st century, the intention of Taiwan-invested IT enterprises to explore the domestic market becomes increasingly obvious, for the geographical scope of their investment widens gradually and continues to expand towards the north, resulting in a substantial increase in the number of enterprises in the BSR region. Based on the geographical characteristics of the investment of Taiwan-funded enterprises, it can be divided into three time periods: the first period is before and including 1997 (before December 1997); the second period is from 1998 to 2001 (January 1998 to December 2001); the third period starts from 2002 and ends in 2006 (January 2002 to February 2006).

8.2.2.2 *Definition of the Regional Scope*

We use the division of three economic regions (eastern, central, and western regions) here. Taiwanese investment in the mainland is highly concentrated in the eastern region, so the research is mainly set on the eastern region, especially on the three economic core regions: the BSR, YRD, and PRD regions. We further divide the eastern region into three major regions according to the distribution characteristics of Taiwanese businessmen in the mainland: the BSR region, the YRD region, and the PRD and south-eastern coastal region, known as the three core areas. The BSR region includes Beijing, Tianjin and Liaoning, Hebei and Shandong; the YRD region includes Shanghai, Jiangsu, and Zhejiang; while the PRD and south-eastern coastal region include Guangdong, Fujian, and Hainan. However, for the central and western regions, a new division method is adopted. And consequently, the central region includes Jilin, Heilongjiang, Shanxi, Anhui, Jiangxi, Henan, Hubei, and Hunan Provinces, while the western region consists of 12 provinces, autonomous regions and municipality — Guangxi, Inner Mongolia, Chongqing, Sichuan, Guizhou, Yunnan, Tibet, Shaanxi, Gansu, Ningxia, Qinghai, and Xinjiang.

8.3 Distribution Characteristics and Location Changes of Taiwan-Invested IT Enterprises

In accordance with the time periods described earlier, comparison and analysis of the investment of Taiwan-invested IT enterprises in the three economic regions are carried out. The enterprises whose statistical information is incorrect or not detailed in the database are eliminated directly. Another 330 Taiwan-invested enterprises are excluded due to the missing or unclear registration. Therefore, the actual number of sample enterprises in this chapter is 1929.

8.3.1 *The First Period (Before December 1997)*

In the late 1980s, Taiwan-invested IT enterprises began to settle in the mainland. With the investors trying to make money and being afraid of changes in policies at the same time, most of the investments at that time were exploratory. The Taiwanese started to increase their investment in the IT industry in mainland China after the mid-1990s, with the investment proportion of IT industry (mostly manufacturing of electronic and electrical products) increasing constantly. We defined the entering stage as 1997 and before because it was a stage for Taiwan-invested IT enterprises to change from probing at the beginning to gradually developing by the end of 1997 in the mainland. The external environment Taiwanese businessmen faced was relatively stable in this period of time. However, a significant change in the investment motives and tendency of Taiwanese businessmen appeared afterward resulting from the heavy impact of the Asian financial turmoil on Taiwan in 1997.

According to *Directory of Taiwan-Invested Enterprises in the Mainland,* a total of 646 Taiwan-invested IT enterprises had registered in the mainland in and before 1997, with the gross investment reaching US$ 1.37 billion in the first phase, employees amounting to 80,400, and the average investment of each enterprise being about US$ 2.12 million. Most of the Taiwan-invested IT companies in the mainland during this period were small- and medium-sized labor-intensive enterprises, of which there were 394 with single enterprise's investment less than US$ 1 million, accounting for 61.0%; 126 between US$ 1 million and US$ 2 million (including US$ 1 million), and 106 between US$ 2 million and US$ 10 million (including US$ 2 million), accounting for 19.5% and 16.4%, respectively; while only 20 enterprises whose single enterprise's investment amounted to US$10 million, accounting for just 3.1%. Among the 527 Taiwan-invested IT enterprises that had been industrially classified, 183 belonged to electronic components manufacturing and 106 were in the manufacturing of other electronic equipments, 55 in the software development and consulting industry, 40 in computer peripheral equipments manufacturing, 31 in the manufacturing of other communication equipments, and 16 in the semiconductor device manufacturing. There were 431 companies altogether in the six industries, accounting for 81.8% of the total. From the perspective of economics, there were 326 enterprises wholly owned by Taiwanese, accounting for 50.5%; 254 equity joint ventures, accounting for 39.3%; 66 contractual joint ventures, accounting for 10.2%. In the aspect of the aggregate investment, wholly Taiwanese-owned enterprises took up 45.1% of the total, equity joint ventures taking up 48.4% and contractual joint ventures taking up 6.5% (see Table 8-1).

Considering the regional distribution, it was very obvious that most of the Taiwan-invested IT enterprises concentrated in the eastern region. There were 556 enterprises located in the eastern region during this period, with an aggregate investment of US$ 1.228 billion, accounting for 86.07% and 89.67% of the total, respectively (see Table 8-2). The proportions of central and western regions were quite small. The number of enterprises and total investment in the central region accounted for 8.98% and 7.47%, respectively, while in the western region, there were only 4.95% and 2.87%,

Table 8-1   Economic Styles of Taiwan-Funded IT Enterprises in the Mainland (Registered in and Before 1997).

	Number of enterprises		In-service staff		Total investment	
	Number	Proportion (%)	Number	Proportion (%)	Sum (US$ 10 000)	Proportion (%)
Wholly Taiwanese-owned enterprises	326	50.5	45,811	57.0	61,819	45.1
Equity joint ventures	254	39.3	28,720	35.7	66,319	48.4
Contractual joint ventures	66	10.2	5832	7.3	8820	6.5
Total	646	100	80,363	100	136,958	100

Source: According to the foreign-funded enterprises directory database in Ministry of Commerce of the PRC and *Directory of Taiwan-invested Enterprises in the Mainland.*

respectively. In fact, Taiwan-invested IT enterprises mainly concentrated in the PRD and southeast coastal region of the eastern region, with the number of enterprises and total investment accounting for 34.83% and 59.62%, respectively. For the YRD region, the number of enterprises and total investment were 30.19% and 18.86% of the total in China, and the least was the BSR region, the two proportions being 21.05% and 11.19%, respectively. We could learn that there was a gradually decreased trend from south to north in the number, serving staff and total investment amount of Taiwan-invested IT enterprises in view of the three core areas. Not only did the number of enterprises in the PRD and southeast coastal region rank first, but the serving staff and total investment also added up to approximately twice of those in the BSR region and the YRD region in together, with its share accounting for nearly 60% of the nationwide total sum. From 1995 to 1998, the aggregate Taiwanese investment in the mainland reached US$ 9.944 billion, of which IT industry utilized US$ 2.663 billion, accounting for 26.79%. More than half of these Taiwanese IT companies preferred to

Table 8-2 Distribution of Taiwan-Funded IT Enterprises in the Mainland (Registered in and Before 1997).

Region	Number of enterprises		In-service staff		Total investment	
	Number	Proportion (%)	Number	Proportion (%)	Sum (US$ 10 000)	Proportion (%)
Eastern region	556	86.07	72,733	90.50	122,796	89.67
BSR region	136	21.05	7166	8.92	15,322	11.19
YRD region	195	30.19	19,057	23.71	25,825	18.86
PRD and southeast coastal region	225	34.83	46,510	57.87	81,649	59.62
Central region	58	8.98	5757	7.16	10,231	7.47
Western region	32	4.95	1873	2.33	3931	2.87
Total	646	100	80,363	100	136,958	100

Source: According to the foreign-funded enterprises directory database in Ministry of Commerce of the PRC and *Directory of Taiwan—invested Enterprises in the Mainland.*

locate in the PRD region (Yang and Feng, 2002), thus forming a vertical division of labor as "to order in Taiwan, to produce in mainland China and to export in Hong Kong".

From the perspective of distribution at province level, the top five in the number of Taiwan-invested IT enterprises were Guangdong, Fujian, Jiangsu, Zhejiang, and Shanghai, a total of 418 enterprises in and before 1997, accounting for 64.7% of the total in the mainland (see Table 8-3). If sequenced by the aggregate investment, the top five were Guangdong, Fujian, Jiangsu, Zhejiang, and Shandong, and the investment added up to US$ 1.095 billion, accounting for 79.9% of the total. Therefore, it was quite obvious that during this period Taiwan-invested IT companies were highly concentrated in a few coastal provinces and municipalities in the mainland. In the central and western regions, Taiwanese investment in IT industry

Table 8-3   State of Taiwan-Invested IT Enterprises in the Major Provinces (Registered in and Before 1997).

Province	The number of enterprises		In-service staff		Total investment	
	Number	Proportion of the total (%)	Number	Proportion of the total (%)	Sum (US$ 10000)	Proportion of the total (%)
Guangdong	140	21.67	23,783	29.59	49,294	35.99
Fujian	83	12.85	22,519	28.02	32,015	23.38
Jiangsu	80	12.38	8782	10.93	10,923	7.98
Zhejiang	60	9.29	7345	9.14	9422	6.88
Shandong	39	6.04	3666	4.56	7834	5.72
Shanghai	55	8.51	2930	3.65	5480	4.00
Hubei	11	1.70	874	1.09	3954	2.89
Beijing	48	7.43	1353	1.68	3122	2.28
Hunan	10	1.55	1635	2.03	2563	1.87
Tianjin	28	4.33	1601	1.99	2271	1.66
Jiangxi	9	1.39	813	1.01	1685	1.23
Chongqing	7	1.08	1027	1.28	1460	1.07
Anhui	18	2.79	1823	2.27	1420	1.04
Total	588	91.01	78,151	97.24	131,443	95.99

Source: According to the foreign-funded enterprises directory database in Ministry of Commerce of the PRC and *Directory of Taiwan-invested Enterprises in the Mainland*.

was also relatively concentrated in Hubei, Hunan, Jiangxi, Chongqing, and Anhui, with the total investment accounting for 8.1% of the total.

From the perspective of distribution in cities, Taiwan-invested IT companies in mainland mainly located in Shenzhen, Shanghai, Beijing, Xiamen, Suzhou, Fuzhou, Tianjin, Ningbo, Nanjing, and Hangzhou, with 342 companies occupying the 10 cities and accounting for 52.9% of the total in and before 1997 (see Table 8-4). Among them, there were 195 companies in Shenzhen, Shanghai, Beijing, and Xiamen, accounting for 30.2% of the total. However, the scale of Taiwan-invested IT companies in Shanghai and Beijing was not large, with quite a significant amount of investment in software, consulting services, and investment companies. As to the investment amount, the in Shenzhen, it was up to US$ 346 million

Table 8-4 State of Taiwan-Invested IT Enterprises in the Major Cities (Registered in and Before 1997).

City	Number of enterprises		Total investment		City	Number of enterprises		Total investment	
	Number	Proportion (%)	Sum (US$10000)	Proportion (%)		Number	Proportion (%)	Sum (US$10000)	Proportion (%)
Shenzhen	59	9.1	34,627	25.3	Wuxi	10	1.5	1472	1.1
Shanghai	55	8.5	5480	4.0	Quanzhou	9	1.4	2608	1.9
Beijing	48	7.4	3122	2.3	Jinan	9	1.4	1805	1.3
Xiamen	33	5.1	20,507	15.0	Wenzhou	9	1.4	754	0.6
Suzhou	29	4.5	6274	4.6	Zhangzhou	8	1.2	5104	3.7
Fuzhou	29	4.5	3664	2.7	Wuhan	8	1.2	3415	2.5
Tianjin	28	4.3	2271	1.7	Huizhou	8	1.2	3014	2.2
Ningbo	24	3.7	2260	1.7	Shenyang	8	1.2	763	0.6
Nanjing	20	3.1	1195	0.9	Zhaoqing	7	1.1	1821	1.3
Hangzhou	17	2.6	3049	2.2	Chongqing	7	1.1	1460	1.1
Canton	16	2.5	1901	1.4	Yantai	7	1.1	832	0.6
Qingdao	15	2.3	2977	2.2	Zhuhai	7	1.1	782	0.6
Dongguan	14	2.2	2116	1.5	Changzhou	6	0.9	483	0.4
Xi'an	12	1.9	490	0.4	Subtotal	502	77.7	114,246	83.4

Source: According to the foreign-funded enterprises directory database in Ministry of Commerce of the PRC and *Directory of Taiwan-invested Enterprises in the Mainland.*

accounting for 25.3% of the total, which in Xiamen was US$ 205 million accounting for 15.0%, while those in Suzhou and Shanghai were 4.6% and 4.0%, respectively, and there was only 1.5% in Dongguan.

In short, the investment of Taiwan-invested IT enterprises in mainland China was characterized by small number and scale and relative dispersion. In addition, the investors were mostly small- and medium-sized enterprises at this stage. As a whole, Taiwan-invested IT enterprises were still in the downstream manufacturing sectors of the international IT industrial chain and suffered strong restriction exerted by the Taiwan authorities over their scale and technological level in the mainland. Therefore, most of the Taiwan-funded IT companies concentrating in the PRD and southeast coast region were labor-intensive and export-oriented, their role of driving the local economy being relatively limited.

8.3.2 *Rapidly Expanding Stage (January 1998–December 2001)*

Heavily struck by the Asian financial crisis in 1997, Taiwan's industry felt more pressure due to the shrinking profit margins in the global electronic information industry, and that's why Taiwan's IT manufacturing industry began to speed up production relocation to the mainland, coupled with some new features in the investment scale, ways, industries, and geographical distribution. From January 1998 to December 2001, 339 Taiwan-invested IT companies were established in mainland China, with the initial investment up to US$ 648 million, employees amounting to 28,100, and average investment being US$ 1.911 million. The majority of Taiwan-invested IT companies in the mainland during this period were still labor-intensive small- and medium-sized enterprises. Among them, there were 235 enterprises whose investment was less than US$ 1 million, accounting for 69.3%, an increase of 8.3 percentage points compared with that in the previous stage; 50 companies whose investment was between US$ 1 million to US$ 2 million (including US$ 1 million), accounting for 14.8%; 36 companies whose investment was between US$ 2 million to US$ 10 million (including US$ 2 million), accounting for 10.6%; 18 companies' investment was more than US$ 10 million, accounting for 5.3%, an increase of 2.2 percentage points than that in the previous stage.

Among the 298 Taiwan-invested IT enterprises that were classified, 129 were in electronic components manufacturing, 43 belonged to software development and consulting industry, 40 were in the manufacturing of other electronic equipments, 27 in computer peripheral equipment manufacturing, and 11 in both IC manufacturing and other communications equipments manufacturing industries. There were 261 companies altogether in these six industries, accounting for 87.6% of the total. From the perspective of economics, the proportion of wholly Taiwan-owned enterprises was increasing gradually while the proportions of equity joint ventures and contractual joint ventures were in a rapid decline at this stage. In total, 66.9% of these enterprises were wholly Taiwan-owned, hiring 72.5% of the working staff, with the investment amounting to 78.4% of the whole (see Table 8-5). And the increases were 16.1, 15.5, and 33.0 percentage points, respectively, compared with those in the first stage.

It was shown from the geographical distribution of Taiwan-invested IT enterprises that their tendency to concentrate in the eastern region was quite obvious. There were 315 enterprises with 27,300 serving staff in the eastern region, and the initial investment reached US$ 619 million, accounting

Table 8-5 Economic Styles of Taiwan-invested IT Enterprises in the Mainland (1998.1–2001.12).

	Number of enterprises		In-service staff		Total investment	
	Number	Proportion (%)	Number	Proportion (%)	Sum (US$ 10 000)	Proportion (%)
Wholly Taiwanese-owned enterprises	227	66.9	20,379	72.5	50775.5	78.4
Equity joint ventures	87	25.7	6559	23.3	11243.8	17.3
Contractual joint ventures	25	7.4	1189	4.2	2773.97	4.3
Total	339	100	28,127	100	64793.2	100

Source: According to the foreign-funded enterprises directory database in Ministry of Commerce of the PRC and *Directory of Taiwan-invested Enterprises in the Mainland*.

Table 8-6 Distribution of Taiwan-invested IT Enterprises in the Eastern Region (1998.1–2001.12).

	Number of enterprises		In-service staff		Number of initial investment	
	Number	Proportion (%)	Number	Proportion (%)	Sum (US$ 10 000)	Proportion (%)
BSR region	53	15.6	1950	6.9	7260	11.2
YRD region	127	37.5	12125	43.1	40722.8	62.8
PRD and southeast coastal region	135	39.8	13238	47.1	13919	21.5
Eastern region	315	92.9	27313	97.1	61901.8	95.5
Total in China	339	100	28127	100	64793.2	100

Source: According to the foreign-funded enterprises directory database in Ministry of Commerce of the PRC and *Directory of Taiwan-invested Enterprises in the Mainland*.

for 92.9%, 97.1%, and 95.5% of the total, respectively (see Table 8-6). Within the eastern region, the proportion of Taiwan-invested IT enterprises increased remarkably in the YRD region while it decreased significantly in the PRD and southeast coastal region. Compared with those in the previous stage, there were 127 newly established Taiwan-invested IT enterprises (accounting for 37.5% of the total), the serving staff worked there were 12.1 thousand (accounting for 43.1%), and the initial investment added up to US$ 407 million (accounting for 62.8%) in the YRD region, with an increase of 7.3, 19.4 and 43.9 percentage points, respectively. In contrast, their investment in the PRD and southeast coastal region dropped to 21.5%, 38.1 percentage points less than that in the previous stage. Moreover, the average investment amount of Taiwan-invested IT companies in the YRD region was US$ 3.2065 million, almost 3.1 times of that in the PRD and southeast coastal region, where the average size was only US$ 1.031 million. Although the proportion of investment in the BSR region basically remained the same, the number of enterprises and the proportion of employees tended to decline. It can be seen from above that the Taiwan-invested IT enterprises were mainly transferring from the PRD region to the YRD region, and that their investment tended to centralize in the YRD region during this period.

In terms of distribution in provinces, most of the newly established Taiwan-invested IT companies in the mainland are concentrated in Jiangsu, Guangdong, and Fujian Provinces, the number of those enterprises in the three provinces adding up to 213 and accounting for 62.8%, serving staff reaching 23,200 and accounting for 82.4% and the aggregate investment being US$ 506 million and accounting for 78.2% (see Table 8-7). Especially in Jiangsu province, the number of enterprises accounted for 23.3% of the total, serving staff took up 35.3%, and the investment was as high as 56.8%, showing an increase of 10.9, 24.4, and 48.8 percentage points, respectively, over the previous stage. For Guangdong province, though the

Table 8-7 State of Taiwan-Invested IT Enterprises in the Major Provinces (1998.1–2001.12).

	Number of enterprises		In-service staff		Total investment	
Province	Number	Proportion (%)	Number	Proportion (%)	Sum (US$ 10 000)	Proportion (%)
Jiangsu	79	23.3	9924	35.3	36799.5	56.8
Guangdong	95	28.0	9892	35.2	8197.3	12.7
Fujian	39	11.5	3342	11.9	5621.7	8.7
Shandong	20	5.9	1020	3.6	4707.2	7.3
Shanghai	31	9.1	1392	4.9	2885.0	4.5
Chongqing	2	0.6	112	0.4	2097.0	3.2
Beijing	17	5.0	210	0.7	1673.6	2.6
Zhejiang	15	4.4	740	2.6	938.2	1.4
Liaoning	6	1.8	346	1.2	594.2	0.9
Tianjin	9	2.7	361	1.3	279.0	0.4
Hunan	5	1.5	297	1.1	271.3	0.4
Other	21	6.2	491	1.7	729.2	1.1
China	339	100	28127	100	64793.2	100

Source: According to the foreign-funded enterprises directory database in Ministry of Commerce of the PRC and *Directory of Taiwan-invested Enterprises in the Mainland*.

proportion of the number of enterprises and in-service personnel increased by 6.3 and 6.2 percentage points accordingly in this period, its proportion of investment decreased by 23.3 percentage points. As to Fujian province, these proportions decreased by 1.4, 16.1, and 14.7 percentage points, respectively. Jiangsu had surpassed Guangdong and Fujian provinces, becoming the favorite choice for Taiwan-invested IT enterprises. This revealed the fact that the investment of Taiwan-invested IT enterprises in the mainland was transferring from Guangdong and Fujian to Jiangsu province.

From the perspective of its distribution in cities, the new IT investment from Taiwan was highly concentrated in Suzhou, and the number of enterprises, aggregate investment, and in-service staff accounted for 15.6%, 47.3%, and 25.7%, respectively, in this stage, with an increase of 11.1, 42.7, and 19.6 percentage points, respectively, compared with those in the previous stage. In addition to Suzhou, Dongguan was another target city for the Taiwanese IT investment in this period, attracting 8.3% of such enterprises, 6.1% of the aggregate investment, and 9.5% of the service personnel (see Table 8-8). The Taiwan-invested IT enterprises attracted in Shenzhen and Shanghai accounted for 9.4% and 9.1% of the total number, respectively, but their aggregate investment took up only 2.0% and 4.5%, indicating that mainly small and medium-sized enterprises were attracted by these two cities . On the contrary, the average size of Taiwan-funded enterprises attracted in Suzhou and Wuxi was much larger. It was much clear from the average investment of each enterprise: it was US$ 5.780 million in Suzhou, US$ 5.370 million in Wuxi, only US$ 410 thousand in Shenzhen, US$ 470,000 in Guangzhou, and US$ 930,000 in Shanghai.

In short, Taiwan-invested IT enterprises carried out large-scale investment in the YRD region during this stage, with the characteristics of large number, large scale, diversification, and centralization. Those enterprises located in Shanghai were mainly some R&D organizations belonging to upstream sectors of IT industrial chain, while a large number of IT manufacturers preferred the surrounding areas, especially South Jiangsu. What's more, Kunshan was their favorite location, considering the price of land, labor, and other production factors, which was also in line with the custom that the distance between production and supply companies of IT material should be less than 200 km. At the same time, the investment scale of Taiwan-invested IT enterprises in the YRD region had

Table 8-8 State of Taiwan-invested IT Enterprises in the Top 10 Cities (1998.1–2001.12).

	Number of enterprises			Total investment			In-service staff		
City	City	Number	Proportion (%)	City	Sum (US$ 10000)	Proportion (%)	City	Number	Proportion (%)
	Suzhou	53	15.6	Suzhou	30617.9	47.3	Suzhou	7220	25.7
	Shenzhen	32	9.4	Wuxi	4295.8	6.6	Dongguan	2683	9.5
	Shanghai	31	9.1	Dongguan	3924.1	6.1	Canton	2358	8.4
	Dongguan	28	8.3	Fuzhou	3199.0	4.9	Shenzhen	2317	8.2
	Beijing	17	5.0	Zaozhuang	2980.0	4.6	Shanghai	1392	4.9
	Canton	14	4.1	Shanghai	2885.0	4.5	Zhangzhou	1209	4.3
	Fuzhou	13	3.8	Chongqing	2097.0	3.2	Xiamen	988	3.5
	Xiamen	13	3.8	Beijing	1673.6	2.6	Zhenjiang	958	3.4
	Jinan	9	2.7	Shenzhen	1303.0	2.0	Jiangmen	935	3.3
	Tianjin	9	2.7	Quanzhou	1206.1	1.9	Huizhou	780	2.8
	Total	219	64.5	Total	54181.5	83.7	Total	20840	74.0

Source: According to the foreign-funded enterprises directory database in Ministry of Commerce of the PRC and *Directory of Taiwan-invested Enterprises in the Mainland*.

significantly expanded and diversified in this period, with the investment on the high-grade products such as CD-ROM driver, motherboard, LCD monitors and new components emerging gradually.

8.3.3 *Market Expanding Stage (January 2002–February 2006)*

With the continuous expansion of Taiwan-invested IT enterprises in the mainland, the local IT companies also developed rapidly. A comprehensive IT industrial chain had been established in some coastal cities, laying the foundation for the further development of IT industry. More importantly, the consumer market of IT products had been steadily improved, effectively pushing the development of IT industry. The Taiwan-invested IT enterprises, on one hand, carried out export-oriented processing activities by using the superior resources in mainland China, on the other hand, they actively expanded their market in the mainland, starting a new round of investment boom.

Due to a serious lack of economic indicators and absence of investment records, the data from January 2002 to February 2006 were incomplete and had to be grossly substituted with registered capital. During these four years, there were 942 Taiwan-invested IT enterprises registered in the mainland, the registered capital reached US$ 4.198 billion, and serving staff were 62.4 thousand,[2] leading to the average registered capital of US$ 4.457 million and serving staff of 66 per company. Thus, compared with that in the second stage, the investment size of Taiwan-funded IT companies in mainland expanded significantly in this period.

Among the 921 Taiwan-invested IT enterprises that were industrially classified: 312 doing software development and consulting, 234 in the electronic components manufacturing, 54 in electronic and communication equipments manufacturing, 52 in the manufacturing of other electronic equipments, 44 belonging to electronic computer peripheral equipments manufacturing, those in radios and tape recorders manufacturing numbering 28, integrated circuit manufacturing 24, and computer manufacturing 23. The total number in the eight sectors reached 771, accounting

---

[2]Statistically incomplete, this figure is quite smaller than the real one, due to the lack of employment indicators.

for 83.7%. Having an absolute advantage, 936 wholly Taiwanese-owned enterprises had US$ 4.142 billion registered capital and 62,000 workers, accounting for 99.4%, 98.7%, and 99.3%, respectively, much higher than those in the second stage, which showed that, in recent years, almost all the Taiwanese IT investments in mainland China preferred sole proprietorship.

From January 2002 to February 2006, Taiwan-funded IT companies continued to move towards the eastern region. There were 913 Taiwan-funded IT companies in the eastern region, with the registered capital being US$ 4.056 billion, accounting for 96.9% and 96.7%, respectively, which indicated that almost all the Taiwan-invested IT enterprises were in the eastern region in this period. Within the eastern region, they tended to highly concentrate in the PRD region and YRD region, of which the enterprises in the PRD and southeast coastal region accounted for 61.4% of the total, with registered capital accounting for 49.9% and on-job workers accounting for 44.1%. The three proportions in the YRD region were 30.1%, 40.1%, and 41.9%, respectively (see Table 8-9). All of these proportions in PRD and southeast coastal region were much higher than those in the YRD region by 31.3, 9.0, and 2.2 percentage points, respectively. Compared with those in the previous stage, the proportion of the number of enterprises increased by 21.6 percentage points in the PRD and southeast coastal region, with an increase of 28.4 percentage points in the registered capital (compared with the total investment, similarly hereinafter), while the proportion in the YRD region decreased by 7.4 and 21.9 percentage points.

In province-level distribution, the newly established Taiwan-invested IT enterprises were highly concentrated in Guangdong, Shanghai, and Jiangsu, 789 altogether accounting for 83.7% of the total; while registered capital and workers highly centered in Guangdong, Zhejiang, and Jiangsu provinces, taking up 83.6% and 75.5%, respectively (see Table 8-10). Above all, in Guangdong province, where 57.3% of Taiwan-invested IT enterprises are located with 45.9% of the registered capital and 38.8% of the serving staff, increased by 29.3, 33.2, and 3.6 percentage points, respectively, compared with those in the previous stage. These proportions in Jiangsu province decreased by 12.2, 44.8, and 13.7 percentage points than the previous stage, respectively. The proportion of the registered capital of Taiwan-funded companies in Zhejiang province was up to 25.7%, higher than that of Jiangsu, and 15.3% of such newly established companies in the mainland

Table 8-9   Distribution of Taiwan-Invested IT Enterprises in the Mainland (2002.1–2006.2).

Region	Number of enterprises		Registered capital		In-service staff	
	Number	Proportion (%)	Sum (US$ 10 000)	Proportion (%)	Number	Proportion (%)
The BSR region	51	5.4	24493	5.8	2048	3.3
The YRD region	284	30.1	171822	40.9	26198	41.9
The PRD and southeast coastal region	578	61.4	209238	49.9	27537	44.1
Other regions	29	3.1	14255	3.4	6659	10.7
Total	942	100	419808	100	62442	100

Source: According to the foreign-funded enterprises directory database in Ministry of Commerce of the PRC and *Directory of Taiwan-invested Enterprises in the Mainland.*

were in Shanghai, though not large in scale. These findings indicate that, during this period, Taiwanese IT investment in the mainland went back to Guangdong province once again, and it begun to move from Jiangsu to Zhejiang in the YRD region, while some small- and medium-sized R&D, marketing, and service-providing companies were "flocking together" in Shanghai.

Considering their distribution in cities, the top five cities attracting the most Taiwan-invested IT enterprises were Shenzhen, Shanghai, Dongguan, Suzhou, and Zhuhai, a total number of 679 and accounting for 72.1%. Arranged in order of registered capital, the top five cities were Shenzhen, Hangzhou, Dongguan, Wuxi, and Shanghai, attracting US$ 3.001 billion altogether, accounting for 71.5% of the total (see Table 8-11). In the PRD region, these enterprises were gathering toward Shenzhen and Dongguan, while in the YRD region, the trend of diversification became obvious

Table 8-10 State of Taiwan-invested IT Enterprises in the Major Provinces (2002.1–2006.2).

Region	Number of enterprises		Registered capital		In-service staff	
	Number	Proportion (%)	Sum (US$ 10 000)	Proportion (%)	Number	Proportion (%)
Guangdong	540	57.3	192, 538	45.9	24210	38.8
Zhejiang	35	3.7	107, 797	25.7	9411	15.1
Jiangsu	105	11.1	50, 200	12.0	13463	21.6
Fujian	35	3.7	16, 490	3.9	3306	5.3
Shanghai	144	15.3	13, 825	3.3	3324	5.3
Beijing	21	2.2	11, 225	2.7	462	0.7
Shandong	14	1.5	10, 975	2.6	618	1.0
Total	894	94.9	403, 050	96.0	54794	87.8

Source: According to the foreign-funded enterprises directory database in Ministry of Commerce of the PRC and *Directory of Taiwan-invested Enterprises in the Mainland.*

with Suzhou's status decreasing significantly and Shanghai, Wuxi, Ningbo, Changzhou, Hangzhou, and Jiaxing becoming the new hot cities for investment. As an important gathering place of the Taiwan-invested IT enterprises in the past, Suzhou attracted only 3.3% of the total registered capital in this period, ranking the sixth in the mainland, right after Hangzhou, Wuxi, and Shanghai in the YRD region.

In summary, in recent years a new trend came up in the investment of Taiwan-invested IT enterprises in the eastern region as the PRD and southeast coastal region became their favorite areas again. That is, a large number of Taiwan-invested IT enterprises turned to the PRD region once again, rather than continue their northward expansion as was expected initially, which was quite different from the relocation pattern of Taiwanese investment moving from the PRD region to the YRD region in the mainland. IT investment in the BSR region still lagged behind, with the number of enterprises increasing even slower than that in the past two stages. Having maintained the rapid growth rate in the YRD region, the number of enterprises was much larger than that in the previous stage. However, a

Table 8-11   State of Taiwan-invested IT Enterprises in the Major Cities (2002.1–2006.2).

City	Number of enterprises		Registered capital		In-service staff	
	Number	Proportion (%)	Sum (US$ 10 000)	Proportion (%)	Number	Proportion (%)
Shenzhen	387	41.1	131,105	31.2	11133	17.8
Shanghai	144	15.3	13,825	3.3	3324	5.3
Dongguan	71	7.5	41,906	10.0	6334	10.1
Suzhou	51	5.4	13,667	3.3	5175	8.3
Zhuhai	26	2.8	5082	1.2	1594	2.6
Canton	22	2.3	4498	1.1	853	1.4
Beijing	21	2.2	11,225	2.7	462	0.7
Wuxi	20	2.1	18,695	4.5	4834	7.7
Fuzhou	14	1.5	6652	1.6	690	1.1
Ningbo	13	1.4	6413	1.5	923	1.5
Changzhou	11	1.2	4295	1.0	936	1.5
Hangzhou	10	1.1	94,576	22.5	2323	3.7
Zhaoqing	10	1.1	2206	0.5	1783	2.9
Jiaxing	9	1.0	5608	1.3	5805	9.3
Total	809	85.9	359,753	85.7	46169	73.9

Source: According to the foreign-funded enterprises directory database in Ministry of Commerce of the PRC and *Directory of Taiwan-invested Enterprises in the Mainland.*

more substantial increase in the number of enterprises appeared in the PRD and southeast coastal region, with its proportion rising to over 60% and the registered capital accounting for nearly 50%. It was very obvious that the Taiwan-invested IT enterprises favored the PRD and southeast coastal region again, which was closely related to the complete IT industry chain and service facilities in these areas.

In recent years, multi-pronged measures have been taken to further improve the IT industrial chain and local industrial supporting service system in the PRD and southeast coastal provinces by making full use of its advantageous location and the existing industrial foundation. In consideration of the soaring costs of raw materials, land, and labor, the local governments have taken multifaceted compensation measures to exclude Taiwan businessmen's worries to expand investment, such as encouraging investments relating to the existing enterprises and striving to enhance local infrastructure. However, from investigation results, we have to admit that although the IT industrial chain in the PRD region has been significantly improved, the majority part of the industrial chain are still confined inside the Taiwan-funded enterprises, having little connection with local industries and very low investment spillovers effects. The "non-embedded" situation may indicate another potential remigration of these enterprises if time is good.

8.4 Location Choice and Relocation Determinants of Taiwan-Invested IT Enterprises

Generally speaking, the many determinants affecting the location choice of investment and its relocation can be divided into two aspects: on the one hand, pressure from external environment, namely, the strategic adjustments made by Taiwan-invested IT enterprises that have integrated into the global industrial chain, in order to cope with all kinds of competition and seek their development chance; on the other hand, the local promoting effect, that is, the favorable conditions of different regions in mainland China to adapt to the development of these Taiwan-invested IT enterprises. According to the survey results of Taiwanese Ministry of Economic Affairs on the investing motivations of Taiwan-funded enterprises in the mainland and combined with the characteristics of the Taiwan-invested IT enterprises, these determinants are grouped into the following points as shown in Table 8-12.

8.4.1 *External Pressures*

With a quite long history of development, Taiwan's IT industry has made rapid strides since the establishment of the Hsinchu Science and Industrial Park in 1980 following the example of "Silicon Valley" and has become a competitive industry in Taiwan nowadays. However, due to the increasingly fierce competition in the international IT industry, Taiwan's IT industry needs to find a broader investment location and sales market to ensure its long-term development.

Table 8-12   Determinants of Location and Relocation of Taiwan-Invested IT Enterprises.

External factors	Local promoting factors
Needs of foreign customers	Location advantages
The impact of the international environment changes	Market potential
The effects of the adverse business environment in Taiwan	The cost of land, labor and other production factors
The investment of similar or related Taiwanese enterprises in the mainland	Personnel and technical conditions
Trying to continue exerting the capital and technology potential of these companies	Public services, supporting industries and local environment

Source: According to "Report of the Survey results of Investment Outflow in Manufacturing Industry" by Taiwanese Ministry of Economic Affairs, quoted from doctorial dissertation of "Study on Growth of Taiwan-invested Small and Medium Size Enterprises in Mainland China" by Dr. Xu Wenzhong (2007).

8.4.1.1 *Taiwan-invested IT Enterprises Turned to Mainland China for its Cheap and Abundant Production Factors due to the Intense International Competition*

The development of Taiwan's IT industry was facing various kinds of pressure: first, with the internationalization of economy, many local processing industries had been badly affected by the substantial imports of foreign products due to the opening-up of Taiwan; second, the profit had been redistributed as a result of the surging of new Taiwan dollar (NT$), which was caused by the huge trade surplus since 1980s, affecting the comparative advantage of practitioners in different type, size and processing levels of industry. Taiwan's economy was faced with a new round of transformation under such circumstances. IT enterprises began to turn their attention to mainland China and Southeast Asia, for the rich and cheap labor, raw materials, land, and other production factors could help reducing the competing cost in the international market. At this point, the PRD region became the first choice of Taiwan-funded enterprises in the mainland due to its various advantages in location; neighboring Taiwan, Hong Kong, and Macao; convenient transportation; favorable climate; and cultural and kinship ties to Taiwan.

8.4.1.2 *The Internal Business Environment in Taiwan Further Promoted the Investment into Mainland China*

The high degree of opening-up resulted in relatively higher risk for the business environment in Taiwan, which was worsened by the Asian financial crisis through tightening the constraints on land and human resources to the industry development. At the same time, desktop computers and related industries were mature enough to get restructured and upgraded, such as industries manufacturing monitors, scanners, optical drives, motherboards, and other components and peripheral products. Therefore, the IT industry, mainly the manufacturing of electronic and electrical products, began to move its investment and production to mainland China. A large number of Taiwan-invested IT enterprises increased their investment in mainland China in the late 1990s, continuing to invest in the good-foundation PRD and Southeast coast region. In the meantime, some large Taiwan-funded enterprises and consortia established "Taiwanese Investment Zones for High-Tech Industries" in Guangdong to develop high-tech projects. With the increase in foreign-invested enterprises, the Taiwanese businessmen gradually changed their investment mentality instead of trying to make a profit through tricky ways in a short time; many large enterprises even launched large-scale investment. The YRD region also became another hot investment place for Taiwanese businessmen.

8.4.1.3 *The Shrinking Industrial Profit Margins Encouraged Taiwanese Businessmen to Explore the Mainland Market Actively*

With the prices of computer products decreasing globally, the development pattern of Taiwan's IT industry, mainly original equipment manufacturing and design (OEM/ODM), came across new challenges, and their international competitiveness and returns on investment encountered crisis. That's why an increasing number of IT companies chose to invest in the mainland, following either their peers or related enterprises, so as to continue to give play to their potentials in capital and technology. At the same time, the demand for IT products continued to expand in mainland China, attracting the attention of these Taiwan-funded enterprises who were suffering from the ever-shrinking profit margins in the world market. Many famous enterprises such as FIC, MSI, and Mustek started their investment in Dongguan, while others like Liteon and CyberTan transferred their production line from Southeast Asia or Taiwan to the mainland. At this time, IT industrial chain began to take shape in areas with relatively fast growth speed. For example, in Dongguan, the Taiwan-invested IT enterprises had gradually formed a completely supported IT enterprise cluster with the upstream and downstream sectors linking perfectly, large-, medium-, and small-sized enterprises working in cooperation with a due division of labor, and more than 95% of the parts and components that needed in installing computers could be found there (Yang and Feng, 2002). The perfect supporting system of IT production attracted many IT enterprises transferring from Taiwan to the mainland.

8.4.2 *Local Promoting Effect*

Along with the actual needs of Taiwan IT industry in different development stages, the comparative advantages of each region in the mainland reveal themselves gradually. Six main factors have been chosen to analyze on the basis of the existing literature and the characteristics of the Taiwan-invested IT enterprises.

8.4.2.1 *The Location Advantage*

Compared with Taiwan, the PRD and Southeast coastal region have an unparalleled location advantage, which primarily determines the investment location of Taiwanese businessmen, especially in the initial stage of Taiwan IT enterprises trying to explore the mainland market. It is one of the closest areas to Taiwan in mainland China, sharing the same humanities and geopolitical characteristics with Taiwan. Moreover, Taiwan's textile, food, plastics, and other industries have invested in this region and formed a certain scale after the reform and opening-up, so when the development of IT industry comes across dilemma in Taiwan, transferring it to the PRD region in the mainland becomes inevitable.

Being adjacent to Hong Kong and Macao, the PRD region is very convenient for exporting, which is a great advantage for Taiwan-funded IT enterprises which take orders in Taiwan while production is done in the mainland. The Taiwanese businessmen make use of not only the convenient aviation and shipping facilities in Hong Kong but also its function as the international financial center to provide transport, ordering, purchasing, marketing, financing, and other services for Taiwan-funded companies in the mainland, so as to improve efficiency and avoid financial risks. Being a hot investment spot for Taiwan-invested IT enterprises, the PRD region has attracted much capital from foreign countries and rapidly formed an IT industrial belt with Shenzhen and Dongguan as the radiation centers, thanks to the industrial supporting advantages of foreign-invested enterprises and the enterprises engaged in "three-processing and one compensation" in the electronics, hardware, accessories, and other fields.

8.4.2.2 *Price of Production Factors*

With the continuous development of new technologies and products, the application area of computers continues to expand, together with a sharp increase in the demand for personal computers globally, which offers a golden opportunity for the development of IT industry. However, the shortage of labor and land and the soaring wage and land prices in Taiwan force IT companies to find suitable places for industrial transfer in the mainland China and Southeast Asian countries.

The cost advantage of production factors is very common in mainland China. Compared with that in Taiwan, the labor cost in the mainland is very low. For example, the minimum wage set in Taiwan is NT$ 15,000, equivalent to RMB 3000–4000, while that in the mainland is about RMB 800 (Ni and Li, 2005). Besides, mainland China also has a huge labor supply chain. Various preferential policies in land and taxation are great attractions for Taiwan-funded enterprises in the PRD and other regions. As to the YRD region, the cost of production factors is still favorable; for example, there is still cost advantage in Shanghai's surrounding areas though the cost of land, labor, and other production factors has been raised to a certain high level as an international metropolis (see Table 8-13). Therefore, transferring the high standardized production processes to the mainland will significantly reduce cost and increase profit for Taiwan-funded enterprises.

8.4.2.3 *Market Potential*

After China joined WTO, thanks to the gradually opening-up of its domestic market and improved market mechanism, it is much easier for

Table 8-13   The Average Cost of Essential Factors in Some Areas of the YRD and PRD.

Item	Kunshan	Pudong development zone	Ningbo	Wenzhou	Shunde
Land transfer price (Yuan/mu)	80,000	80,000	135,000	400,000	142,000
Wages of workers (Yuan/month)	1000	1083	1386	1527	1150
Salary of managers and technician	2000	2705	2705	2700	—
Average electricity price (Yuan/kWh)	0.53	0.78	0.63	0.68	0.71

Source: Liu and Ai (2005).

Taiwan-invested companies to sell their products in the mainland. In the meantime, the decreasing production costs due to the sharp drop in import tariffs and the improved tax system of sales in domestic market are quite beneficial to their competition. According to a survey by the Ministry of Commerce in Taiwan, "the local market potential" has risen to the second important factor that attracted Taiwanese investment to the mainland only after "cheap and abundant labor" (Feng, 2002). In order to maintain the sustained growth of the information hardware industry, Taiwan's IT manufacturers adjusted their production and management strategies rapidly to accelerate transferring IT production bases to the mainland China and expand the mainland sales market, in an attempt to recover their cost and make a profit in a short time.

The huge market advantage of the YRD region is unmatched to Guangdong and other places. Famous for its economic strength, the YRD region has always been the main base of the electronics and the petro-chemical industries in China, with a good economic foundation and transferring platform. Moreover, the YRD region has better access to the mainland market than the PRD region, thus holding a larger appeal to the relocation of Taiwan's IT industry. Besides competing for the Asia-Pacific re-exports port in the world with Hong Kong, Shanghai is quite convenient for the direct sales of Taiwanese products to Europe and America, with its rapid expanding transportation capacity. The Taiwan-invested high-tech industry corridor "Shanghai–Kunshan–Suzhou–Wuxi–Nanjing" is considered as a perfect way for Taiwan's IT industry to explore the mainland market and connect America and European countries at the same time. Being another potential economic region in mainland China, BSR region is the ideal base for Taiwan's IT industry to seize the Northeast Asian market, and that's why they will definitely invest in the BSR region if they are to develop new markets.

8.4.2.4 *Human Resources and Technology*

Human and technical resources are another important factor in the site selection. In Taiwan, not only is the labor cost particularly high but also the high-tech talent is quite scarce. According to statistics, the R&D talent gap of the semiconductor industry had reached 3349 by 2005. While as the main talent sources for technology industry in Taiwan, the four universities, National Taiwan University, National Cheng Kung University, Taiwan Tsinghua University, and National Chiao Tung University, who are famous for their prestigious electronic and motor majors, only cultivate graduates less than 4000 in total each year, almost leading to "a dogfight" of manufacturers to get the talent they needed. In the process of participating in the international division of labor, improving the technical level and the R&D capacities have become the key for the enterprise development, so to establish production institutions and R&D centers in the talent and technology-intensive areas has also become a major feature of the corporate relocation (Zheng, 2005).

The YRD region, surrounded by colleges, universities, and talents, has become an attractive investment place for many Taiwan-funded enterprises. Many enterprises have established R&D centers in Shanghai and cooperate with Fudan University, Shanghai Jiao Tong University, and other research institutes there to further expand their base and form an IT industrial chain with the production bases in the surrounding areas with specialization and cooperation in different sectors. The BSR region is even better with developed culture, education, science and technology, and a large number of universities and talents surrounded there with more than 1.3 million scientific and technical workers altogether, accounting for 27% of the total in China (Duan, 2006). The well-known IT brand Lenovo stems from here. IT workers in both Taiwan and the mainland need to seize the commanding heights of the market in order to survive in the intense competition in the future, which should need the help of the intellectual superiority in the BSR region. To take full advantage of the local talent and technology resources, Taiwan-invested IT enterprises may further increase their investment in the BSR region.

8.4.2.5 *Industrial Chain and Supporting System*

At present, almost 53% of laptops chips and 25% of desktop computer chips in the world are produced in Taiwan, and about a quarter of the laptops and 38% of the desktop computers are sold to the US, not to mention a greater proportion of the global supply of IT peripherals (Ma and Yang, 2001). However, the majority of Taiwan IT industry is the Original Equipment Manufacturer (OEM) at the end of industrial chain; therefore, improved industrial supporting facilities and reducd production costs are necessary conditions for its production. During the 10-year development in the PRD region, Taiwan businessmen have established a relatively complete industrial supporting system in the local cities and towns; some have even established R&D institutions and scientific and technological experiments parks in the support of local governments, with increasing profits in all the links of the IT industrial chain.

Similarly, there are certain potentialities for division of labor among the YRD region, the BSR region, and Taiwan-invested IT enterprises in R&D field. But due to the long time needed to form the industrial chain and supporting system, the relatively complete supporting system in industrial chain becomes one of the advantages of the PRD and southeast coastal region again.

8.4.2.6 *Public Service and Social Environment*

With high technological content, the IT industry has more stringent requirements on the external environment, in regard of which, the PRD region clearly is not as good as the YRD region. According to a survey result in Taiwan, the YRD region has been named the best area of investment in the mainland by Taiwan businessmen, while the southeast coastal region, where most of the Taiwan-funded enterprises concentrated at the earliest stage, such as Dongguan, Shenzhen, and other regions, is considered as poor investment areas with high risk. All of the seven "A" cities whose overall investment environment is regarded as the best in the YRD region, while all the cities in the southeast coastal region are rated as class C or D. Although the hardware condition of these cities is not bad, the soft environment and legal order there are not accepted by Taiwanese businessmen. Considering the long-term development potential, the Taiwanese IT industry starts "moving northward" (Zha, 2002).

Located between Shanghai and Suzhou, Kunshan is a good example. The brand services of "efficiency Kunshan" launched by the Kunshan municipal government, including simplified procedures, reduced administrative fees, and standardized administrative examination, have been highly appreciated by Taiwan businessmen. However, the Kunshan government also has sensed that the single industrial structure cannot maintain sustained economic development due to the tendency of Taiwan-funded enterprises transferring from the south to the north. Kunshan should adjust its development strategies, besides providing good services to the existing Taiwan-funded enterprises, vigorously develop the local private economy, improve the missing and weak links in the IT industrial chain, and cultivate a number of local private enterprises with independent intellectual property and brand, so as to maintain the competitive advantage of the IT industry in Kunshan.

To sum up, the Taiwan-invested IT enterprises choose target regions with favorable conditions in mainland China according to its own needs in different stages of development. On the basis of the three stages of the investment and relocation of Taiwan-invested IT enterprises in the mainland, the six local promoting factors attracting Taiwanese IT enterprises are summarized, as shown in Table 8-14.

8.5 Suggestions on the Localization of Taiwan-Invested IT Enterprises

Based on the analysis of the changes in the distribution and relocation determinants of Taiwan-invested IT enterprises in the mainland, we can

Table 8-14   Effect of Local Promoting Factors on the Investment and Relocation of Taiwan-Invested IT Enterprises.

Local promoting factors	Target regions	Time stage effected investment and relocation
Location advantages	The PRD and southeast coastal region	The first stage
Cost of production factors	The YRD region, PRD and southeast coastal region	The first stage, the second stage
Market potential	The YRD region and BSR region	The second stage, the third stage
Personnel and technological condition	The BSR and the YRD regions	The third stage
Industrial chain and supporting system	The PRD and southeast coastal region	The third stage
Public service and social environment	The YRD region	The second stage, the third stage

Source: Collected and arranged by the author.

know that, on one hand, these Taiwan-invested IT enterprises have played an active role in promoting the development of local economy, in particular the IT industry and IT industrial chain; on the other hand, although the local governments have introduced a large number of preferential policies so as to attract Taiwanese investment, Taiwan-invested IT enterprises still keep "footloose" in order to make full use of the favorable conditions. In order to attract and retain the Taiwan-funded enterprises, local governments compete with each other in introducing preferential policies, which is clearly not a permanent solution. We believe that fundamental measures should be taken to enhance the localization of Taiwan-invested IT enterprises and reduce the risk brought about by the transferring of these enterprises. Therefore, suggestions are proposed in three levels as shown in the following section.

First, the development of local advantageous links in the IT industrial chain should be encouraged on the basis of regional advantage. From the strategic perspective of the Taiwan IT industry, whether its moving into the PRD and southeast coastal region initially or transferring northward to the YRD region, are to make full use of the cheap production factors and explore the mainland market, resulting from the strategic consideration of fully enjoying various preferential policies continuously introduced by local governments competing with each other. The local policy competition may be more likely to push their relocation than to retain foreign-funded enterprises. The governments of the YRD region and PRD region should reconsider the local advantages in the development of the IT industry instead of blindly following the requirements of Taiwan-invested IT enterprises to establish science and technology parks, so as to encourage local enterprises to develop their advantageous links in the industrial chain. As for the BSR region, which is still likely to get the favor of the Taiwan-invested IT enterprises currently, more attention should be given to the development of high-tech fields with the local talent and technology advantages.

Second, the Taiwan-invested IT enterprises should be introduced to the principle of differentiation, forming a complementary investment and development pattern between local enterprises and foreign-invested enterprises. In the long term, both the PRD region and the YRD region are actually just one of the links of industrial chain restructuring for foreign-funded enterprises currently, acting as the outsourcing processing and manufacturing bases for foreign-invested enterprises. After the foreign-funded enterprises formed their industrial cluster, there is no need for them to connect and cooperate with the local products and industries. Even some local industries related to these "high-tech industries" are cultivated, but the local production capacity cannot be improved if these supporting industries are only restricted to the periphery of Taiwan-funded enterprises, carrying out standardized production of low value-added products or components, for it is still difficult for foreign technology to spill over in this condition (Xiang, 2004). Complementary industries associated with the local industrial structure should be given priority in the introduction of foreign investments in order to make them take root there. Therefore, the local governments should consider the requirement of differentiation in attracting foreign investment, based on the local strengths and long-term development, so as to establish a complementary industrial cooperation with Taiwan-invested IT enterprises to promote the overall development and improve the innovation capability of the IT industrial chain.

Third, an open regional environment with orderly and fair competition is needed. Taking full advantage of its special status in the global IT industrial chain, Taiwan's IT enterprises attract capital, technology, and sales orders from the US, Japan, and other developed countries and then produce in the mainland to make a profit, which is actually the result of the extension of global IT industrial chain and the spread of conduction effect. In this open industrial chain, capital, technology, labor, information, and other resources are being rearranged in different regions continually. The IT industrial cluster and the labor division in Taiwan are quite unique in the international community, owing some world-class large-scale enterprises as well as many small- and medium-sized enterprises with close specialization and cooperation with one another, ensuring the flexibility and efficiency in all links of IT production (Cao, 2003). With the continuous deepening of IT industrial chain's division, in order to ensure a high degree of flexibility and risk resistance capacity of the industry as a whole, the Taiwan IT industry needs to scatter these different types of production in different areas in search for greater profit, which inevitably leads to such relocation of foreign investment. Therefore, the fundamental development of regional economy should not blindly rely on foreign capital, but on strengthening the competitiveness of local industries. Local governments should give the same or even more attention, as that paid to the foreign capital, to the development of local enterprises. In order to attract foreign investment and develop the local economy at the same time, it is important to strive to establish a good environment, where foreign, state-owned, and private companies can carry out fair competition and achieve development together under the same rule, which is effective and essential way to keep foreign-invested companies in the target regions.

References

Cao, X. (2003). *The New Tendency of Taiwanese Investment in the Mainland in 2003. Relations Across Taiwan Straits*, (1), 47–48.

Duan, X. (2006). The Regional Characteristics and the Future Tendency of the Taiwanese Investment in the Mainland. *Asia-Pacific Economic Review*, (3), 72–75.

Feng, B. (2002). Taiwanese Investment and its Prospects in the Pearl River Delta Region in Guangdong Province. *Special Zone Economy*, (6).

Liu, H. and B. Ai (2005). Research of Motives for Enterprise Relocation. *Journal of Changsha University of Science & Technology (Social Sciences)*, (4), 50–53.

Ma, F. and J. Yang (2001). The Formation and Evolution of IT Industry Chain Across Taiwan Strait. *Journal of South China University of Technology (Social Science Edition)*, 3(4), 63–66.

Ministry of Commerce of the PRC (2008). *Report of Foreign Investment in China (2007)*. Available at: http://www.fdi.gov.cn. Accessed March 14th, 2008.

Ni, H. and Y. Li (2005). The Center of Taiwanese IT Industry Transferred to Mainland China. *Tai Sheng*, (10), 32–33.

Ren, Y. (2004). Discussion on the Current Investment of Taiwan-funded Enterprises in Mainland China. *Coastal Enterprises and Science & Technology*, (S1), 4–5.

Xiang, H. (2004). Research on the Migration and Rooted Issues of Foreign-funded Enterprises — Taking Taiwan-funded Enterprises for Example. *Zhejiang Social Sciences*, (3), 66–71.

Xu, W. (2007). *Research on the Development of Small and Medium-sized Taiwan-funded Enterprises in Mainland China*, PhD Dissertation, Graduate School of the Chinese Academy of Social Sciences, Beijing.

Yang, J. and G. Feng (2002). An Analysis of Industrial Structure of Cluster of Taiwan IT Firms in Dongguan. *Chinese Industrial Economy*. (8), 45–50.

Zha, Z. (2002). Research on the Reasons why Taiwanese IT Industry Lags Behind the Yangtze River Delta. *World Economy Study*, (5), 58–62.

Zheng, J. (2005). Research on Enterprises' Headquarters Transfer Motivation Mechanism. *Journal of Guangdong Business College*, (3), 46–50.

Chapter 9

Corporate Headquarters Relocation of Listed Companies and Wealth Transfer in China

Wei Houkai and Bai Mei

9.1 Introduction

Corporate headquarters (HQs) is the management control center of a company (Wei, 1998); the central nervous system of a whole company's normal operations; and also the brain, heart, and symbol of the whole company (Zhao, 2004). Despite these descriptions of corporate HQs having different functions, the core message is that the HQs is the management control center. By researching HQs relocation of listed companies, this chapter hopes to achieve the following objectives: (1) To understand the general nature of Chinese-listed companies HQs relocation; (2) To determine what the results are of the policy of industry relocation from east to west; and (3) To determine the effects of the policies employed by all of the major cities targeted at competing for the resources that corporate HQs bring.

Corporate HQs can be relocated, and in actuality, HQs relocation of companies is extremely common. On one hand, the location of a company's HQs is not invariable. As a company expands and changes take place in its management environment, changes will also occur in the location of its HQs. For example, since 1975, Boston was a popular place for Fortune 500 companies to locate their HQs, but by 1999, only 2 of the original 15 companies remained (Horst and Koropeckyi, 2000). On the other hand, the relocation of corporate HQs actually occurs more frequently than we know. According to analysis of data published by the China Securities Regulatory Commission (CSRC), by November 2007, out of the 104 securities companies, 7 had changed the location of their HQs, the rate of relocation was high to 6.73%. Furthermore, according to statistics from the Italian Business

Registration database, in 1999, a total of 10,198 companies relocated their HQs (Mariotti, 2002). Then, what about the situation of Chinese-listed companies' HQs relocation? This chapter will explore the results of the policies employed by all of the major cities targeted at competing for the resources that corporate HQs bring.

With competition among China's major cities to attract corporate HQs being extremely fierce, not every city has been able to realize its goals. It is well known that Beijing has proposed measures to vigorously develop HQs economy, attract transnational companies to locate their regional HQs, R&D centers, accounting centers, procurement centers, and operational centers in Beijing. Shanghai has also proposed measures to vigorously develop HQs economy, ensuring it becomes a gathering place for transnational companies' HQs, R&D centers, operational centers, and procurement centers. Guangzhou has also made it known that it will encourage transnational companies to set up their corporate HQs, operational centers, and R&D centers. Chongqing, Shenzhen, Tianjin, Dalian, Shenyang, Qingdao, Jinan, and other major or regionally important cities have also put forward proposals for the development of HQs economy and have launched preferential policies to attract large domestic and international corporations to relocate their HQs to their cities. It is obvious that only Beijing and a few other cities have an edge on the competition because of HQs' special request for location. Does this means "HQs economy" policies will weaken the effects of the "promoting east enterprise going west" policies?

China has implemented strategies for development of western region, revitalization of the northeast region, and rising of central region, and the most important point of these policies was a promotion of East–West industry transfer, encouraging eastern coastal enterprises to move to central, western, and northeastern regions. Under the influence of these types of policy, many manufacturing businesses indeed relocated to less developed areas. However, having conducted research into listed companies' HQs relocation, there is one fact that cannot be ignored: the listed companies' HQs are moving from one region to another, but a majority is moving from west to east, from under-developed to developed areas, particularly toward Beijing. If the total profit is calculated in the name of corporate HQs locations, then the profits as much as RMB 24.201 billion have flown out by HQs relocation, of which RMB 23.854 billion has flown into Beijing, accounted for 98.6%

of the total. At the same time, of those listed companies moving to central and western region, most are making financial losses. In other words, with listed companies relocating their HQs, highquality corporations will move their HQs and resources to Beijing, while those corporations operating at a loss will move their HQs and resources to the central and western region. Therefore, we can make a preliminary assumption that East–West industry transfer is mainly the shift of production capacity, whilst the HQs relocation is mainly the shift of the control and decisionmaking center. Furthermore, in East–West two way migrations of industries, it could be said that the central and western region does not necessarily have more to gain than to lose.

9.2 Advances in Domestic and Foreign Research

Since the 1970s, the relocation of corporate HQs has been a contentious topic in international academic circles. Semple (1973), Semple and Phipps (1982), Semple *et al.* (1985), Wheeler and Brown (1985), Holloway and Wheeler (1991), Lyons (1995), Horst and Koropeckyi (2000), Klier and Testa (2002), Strauss-Kahn and Vives (2005), and other researchers have all taken a great interest in researching corporate HQs relocation. Research into the US corporate HQs relocation has found that, in the last several decades, there has been a tendency for the US corporations to move their HQs away from large cities, such as New York and Chicago, toward second-tier cities. Semple *et al.* (1985), Holloway and Wheeler (1991), Lyons (1995) all have observed this emerging pattern of the US corporations moving away from metropolises, such as New York, Chicago, and Los Angeles. In 1975, almost 150, or 30%, of the Fortune 500 companies' HQs, were located in New York. But by 2003, that number had dropped to 80, accounting for 16% of the total. Therefore in less than 20 years, almost half of these companies had moved their HQs out of New York. The rate with which these corporations moved out was truly surprising. Holloway and Wheeler (1991) used data on the HQs of Fortune 500 companies to describe the location and changes of the US corporations' HQs in the years between 1980 and 1987. The research found that the number of corporate HQs located in the Sunbelt was gradually increasing, while the number of those in the Frostbelt was declining. It reveals that HQs in US was spreading from Frostbelt to Sunbelt. They concluded that both within individual industries and between separate industries, corporate HQs would continue to spread out.

By use of a database of more than 25,000 HQs in the continental US, Strauss-Kahn and Vives (2005) found that the locations of the HQs tend toward a greater concentration between 1996 and 2001. New York is a declining dominant center, but, excluding New York, the top 5, top 10, and top 20 centers show gains in share (sales-weighted). Meanwhile, among the sample, about 1,500 HQs moved between 1996 and 2001, the rate of relocation is about 5%. In view of the direction of relocation, there exist net changes that HQs moved away from the largest centers (such as New York, San Francisco, Los Angeles, Philadelphia, and Seattle) toward what Holloway and Wheeler (1991) call "second-tier" centers (such as Houston, Phoenix, Washington, and Atlanta). Besides, there was also a movement from "rust belt" traditional centers (e.g., Philadelphia, Youngstown, and Cleveland) in the north toward "sun belt" centers (e.g., Houston, Phoenix, Atlanta, Dallas, San Antonio, and Charlotte) in the south associated with emerging markets.

With respect to research into location characteristics of corporate HQs, scholars usually use data from Fortune 500 companies worldwide to conduct analytical research. As time passes, it is possible to discover the changes occurring and the spatial distribution characteristics of these Fortune 500 companies. Horst and Koropeckyi (2000) and Holloway and Wheeler (1991) used data on the HQs of Fortune 500 companies to carry out relevant research. Horst and Koropeckyi (2000) used the data spanning from 1975 to 1999 (in intervals of 5 years), and found that, in the 1990s, the number of Fortune 500 companies' HQs located in large cities was falling. A series of different papers have analyzed cross-sectional data. Shilton and Stanley (1999) conducted observational research into 5189 exchange-listed companies with over 2,500 employees. They found that 40% of the nation's HQs were located in 20 counties in the US, and their spatial density patterns take on three traditional urban forms: core, ring, and wedge. Their explanation of this phenomenon was that a city's relative superiority meant that it could support the operating methods of corporate HQs. The data that Davis (2000, 2003) used came from the Census Survey of Auxiliary Establishments. Klier and Testa (2002) used a mixture of documents and current information, employing panel data to trace the HQs location of all large listed companies since the 1990s.

There are also many Chinese articles on corporate HQs in recent years. Works carried out by Zheng (2002), Zhao (2005a, 2005b), Shi and Shen (2005), Zhang (2006), and Wang (2005) have generally targeted its research at transnational companies' HQs located in China. After sorting through pre-existing documentation, it was discovered that research into Chinese corporation's HQs relocation was still uncommon, and there was no specializing research conducted into the HQs relocation of Chineselisted companies.

9.3 Characteristics of HQs Relocation among China's Listed Companies

9.3.1 *Types of Listed Companies' HQs Relocation*

The data used in this research was from Guangfa Securities and China Merchants Securities market quotation software, listed companies' profiles and relevant websites.

At the end of September 2007, there were 1,481 listed companies altogether; 835 of them were in Shanghai Stock Exchange and 646 were in Shenzhen Stock Exchange. In investigating the HQs relocation of listed companies, five main types of HQs relocation were determined. The first type is moving HQs from one province to another. It means that a corporation moves its HQs to a city in a different province from its prior location, for example, Blue Star Cleaning moved its HQs from Lanzhou, Gansu Province, to Chaoyang, Beijing; Hubei Bothwin Investment Co., Ltd moved HQs from Jingzhou, Hubei, to Chaoyang, Beijing. The second type is moving HQs from one city to another within the same province. It means that a HQs' new location is in the same province as its prior location, for example, Yunnan Malong Industry Group Co., Ltd. moved HQs from Qujing, Yunnan, to Kunming, Yunnan. The third type is moving HQs within one area. This is generally a corporation moving its HQs from a county or town to a city in an administrative region and the moving distance is usually over 30 km. For example, Henan Oriental Silver Star Investment Co., Ltd. moved its HQs from Minquan County, Shangqiu, Henan, to Shangqiu, Henan, a distance of 52 km. The fourth type is moving HQs into a development zone or from a development zone to an urban area. For example, Shanxi Yabao

Pharmaceutical Group Co., Ltd. moved its HQs from Yuncheng, Shanxi to Fenglingdu economic development zone, Yuncheng, Shanxi. The fifth type: moving HQs within a city. For example, Beijing CCID Media Investments Co., Ltd. after floating in 1992, changed address from Changping, Beijing to Haidian, Beijing. Similarly, since Shanghai Forever Co., Ltd. floated in 1994, it relocated its HQs from Nanhui, Shanghai, to its current location in Pudong New Area, Shanghai.

The impact that the third, fourth, and fifth types of scenario can have on a city is far less than the first two types. Therefore, this chapter will only discuss the first two scenarios: corporate HQs relocating in a different province or in a different city in the same province.

9.3.2   The Rate of HQs Relocation among China's Listed Companies

Out of the 1,481 listed companies in existence up to September 2007, we identified 86 examples of corporate HQs relocation (see Table 9-1). This showed that in the 13-year time span between 1994 and 2007, the rate of relocation was 5.81%, with the yearly relocation rate being 0.45%.

Table 9-1   A Comparison of Corporate HQs Relocation Rate.

Studies	Sample	Sample number	Time	Number of relocations	Yearly relocation rate
Strauss-Kahn and Vives (2005)	US continental companies	more than 25,000	1996– 2001	1500	0.83
Mariotti *et al.* (2004)	Italian registered companies	All companies	1999	10,198	0.29
Our Study	Chinese listed companies	1481	1994– 2007	86	0.45*

*A relocation rate of 0.45% is an underestimation; the number of HQs relocations is actually higher than this figure.
Source: The author summarized and calculated the information supplied in the mentioned documents.

The instance of Jingwei Textile Machinery Co., Ltd. is an example of corporate HQs relocation; it was originally located in Jincheng, Shanxi, but after merger and acquisition, the HQs were moved to Beijing. However it was not identified by the market quotation software and therefore was not used as a research sample. Similar examples are Furen Medicines Group moving its HQs from Zhoukou, Henan, to Shanghai, and Henan Taloph Pharmaceutical Stock Co. relocating its HQs from Zhoukou, Henan, to Zhengzhou, Henan. According to the author's research, there were altogether 14 instances of corporate HQs relocation that were not identified from the same data pool. Because of this, they were not used as research samples. So in reality the rate of relocation was a little higher, and after the adjustment was made, the rate of listed company relocation was 6.75%, with the yearly relocation rate being 0.52%.

The average yearly relocation rate of the HQs for Chinese-listed companies is 0.52%, whilst in 1999 in Italy, the rate was 0.29% (Mariotti *et al.*, 2004), and yearly rate in the US is about 0.83% between 1996 and 2001 (Strauss-Kahn and Vives, 2005). Compared with manufacturing, the relocation rates of corporate HQs are relatively low. In a timeframe of less than 10 years (1990–1999), Japanese electronics companies located in Asian countries have a relocation rate of 33%, with an approximate yearly relocation rate of 3% (Belderbos and Zou, 2006).

9.3.3 *The Flow of Corporate HQs Relocation between Regions*

9.3.3.1 *Corporate HQs Relocation Flow in the Four Regions of China*

According to examination of the four regions, 54 listed companies moved their HQs over to eastern China, whilst 38 moved away from the east, leading to a net increase of 16 listed companies with HQs located in the eastern region. Three companies relocated their HQs in northeastern region, while nine left, creating a net decrease of six listed companies' HQs located in the northeastern region. A total of 18 companies moved HQs into the western region, and 28 left, leading to a net decrease of 10. The number of listed companies with HQs in central region remained constant. With regards to the destination of HQs relocation, relocation to the eastern region accounts for 62.79%, the western region 20.93%, the central region 12.79%, and the northeastern region 3.49%. In terms of the regions being left by corporate HQs, relocation away from the eastern region accounts for 44.19%, the western region 32.56%, the central region 12.79%, and the northeastern region 10.47%. As can be seen from Table 9-2, HQs relocations are most frequent in the eastern region, accounting for 53.49% of the total relocation. Overall, the eastern region is more often the destination for relocations, unlike the west and northeast, from which companies generally moved away.

9.3.3.2 *The Flow between Provinces of Chinese Listed Companies' HQs*

According to an examination of 31 provinces (autonomous regions and municipalities), 25 listed companies relocated their HQs in Beijing, whereas only one moved out of Beijing, giving a net increase of 24 HQs and making it the most popular city for HQs relocations. A total of 12 HQs were moved to Sichuan while 9 left, giving a net increase of 3. Nine HQs were moved to Guangdong and six left, giving another net increase of three. Five HQs moved to Shanghai and two left, also giving a net increase of three. The number of HQs in Shandong, Anhui, Jilin, Fujian, and Shanxi remained constant. Jiangsu, Yunnan, Guizhou, Ningxia, Xinjiang, Inner Mongolia, Qinghai, Zhejiang, Hainan, Guangxi, Hebei, Hubei, Heilongjiang, Gansu, Liaoning, Tianjin, and Tibet all experienced a net decrease in their number of HQs. Of them, Tibet and Tianjin saw the biggest net decrease. In terms of HQs relocations, 29.07% of the total number moved into Beijing, 13.95% into Sichuan, 10.47% into Guangdong, and 9.3% into Zhejiang, whereas 11.63% moved out of Zhejiang, 10.47% out of Sichuan, and 6.98% out of Guangdong. As can be seen from Table 9-3, Beijing is the most active target city, with the secondary band being made up of Sichuan, Guangdong, and Zhejiang. Meanwhile Zhejiang, Sichuan, and Guangdong are the most common areas to relocate away from. The areas with the most frequent relocation activity are Beijing, Sichuan, Zhejiang, and Guangdong.

According to an examination of cities, 25 listed companies relocated their HQs into Beijing, whereas only one moved out of Beijing, giving a net increase of 24 HQs and making it the most popular city for HQs relocations. Second was Chengdu, where 8 HQs moved in and two left, giving a net increase of 6; third was Shanghai, with 7 moving in and 2 leaving, leading to a net increase of 5 HQs. There were no relocations to

Table 9-2 Listed Companies' HQs Relocations by Region.

Region	Relocation into		Relocation away from		Net amount of relocations into	Amount of relocations	
	Number of companies	Percentage of whole (%)	Number of companies	Percentage of whole (%)		Number of companies	Percentage of whole (%)
Eastern region	54	62.79	38	44.19	16	92	53.49
Northeastern region	3	3.49	9	10.47	−6	12	6.98
Western region	18	20.93	28	32.56	−10	46	26.74
Central region	11	12.79	11	12.79	0	22	12.79
Total	86	100	86	100	—	172	100.00

Source: Author's calculations according to listed companies' data.

Table 9-3 Listed Companies' HQs Relocations by Province.

Province	Relocation into		Relocation away from		Net amount of relocations into	Number of relocations	
	Number of companies	Percentage of whole (%)	Number of companies	Percentage of whole (%)		Number of companies	Percentage of whole (%)
Beijing	25	29.07	1	1.16	24	26	15.12
Sichuan	12	13.95	9	10.47	3	21	12.21
Guangdong	9	10.47	6	6.98	3	15	8.72
Shanghai	5	5.81	2	2.33	3	7	4.07
Hunan	4	4.65	3	3.49	1	7	4.07
Shaanxi	1	1.16	0	0.00	1	1	0.58
Henan	1	1.16	0	0.00	1	1	0.58
Shandong	3	3.49	3	3.49	0	6	3.49
Anhui	2	2.33	2	2.33	0	4	2.33
Jilin	2	2.33	2	2.33	0	4	2.33
Fujian	1	1.16	1	1.16	0	2	1.16
Shanxi	1	1.16	1	1.16	0	2	1.16
Jiangsu	2	2.33	3	3.49	−1	5	2.91
Yunnan	2	2.33	3	3.49	−1	5	2.91
Guizhou	1	1.16	2	2.33	−1	3	1.74
Ningxia	1	1.16	2	2.33	−1	3	1.74
Xinjiang	1	1.16	2	2.33	−1	3	1.74

(Continued)

Table 9-3 *(Continued)*

Province	Relocation into		Relocation away from		Net amount of relocations into	Number of relocations	
	Number of companies	Percentage of whole (%)	Number of companies	Percentage of whole (%)		Number of companies	Percentage of whole (%)
Inner Mongolia	0	0.00	1	1.16	–1	1	0.58
Qinghai	0	0.00	1	1.16	–1	1	0.58
Zhejiang	8	9.30	10	11.63	–2	18	10.47
Hainan	1	1.16	3	3.49	–2	4	2.33
Guangxi	0	0.00	2	2.33	–2	2	1.16
Hebei	0	0.00	2	2.33	–2	2	1.16
Hubei	3	3.49	6	6.98	–3	9	5.23
Heilongjiang	1	1.16	4	4.65	–3	5	2.91
Gansu	0	0.00	3	3.49	–3	3	1.74
Liaoning	0	0.00	3	3.49	–3	3	1.74
Tianjin	0	0.00	4	4.65	–4	4	2.33
Tibet	0	0.00	5	5.81	–5	5	2.91
Total	86	100.00	86	100.00	–	172	100.00

Source: Author's calculations according to listed companies' data.

Lhasa or Tianjin, companies only relocated away from these two cities, and the duo experienced a respective net decrease of 5 and 4 (see Table 9-4).

9.3.4 *The Relocation Distance of Chinese Listed Companies' HQs*

9.3.4.1 *Average Distance of Relocation*

The average relocation distance of listed companies' HQs is 1,108 km, and the average of those moving from one province to another is 1,728.77 km, while those relocating within the same province have an average relocation distance of 363.65 km (Table 9-5).

With regards to the target cities, those companies relocating to Guangzhou on average traveled the longest distance, with a figure of 2,267.33 km. The average for those moving to Chengdu was 2,145 km, whilst those relocating to Beijing traveled 1,512.12 km. The figure for Shanghai was 1,336.43 km, those heading for Shenzhen racked up 1,081.5 km, and Hangzhou's was 563.6 km. The average relocation distance to Changsha was 556 km, while those traveling to Wuhan averaged 201 km.

When examining the results in terms of rank of target cities, the average distance of those companies moving their HQs to a municipality was the longest, coming to 1475 km. Second were those moving to provincial capitals, with an average distance of 1057 km, and behind them was 923 km averaged by those moving to sub-provincial level cities. Finally, those relocating to normal cities travelled 387 km.

When examining the results in terms of regions the target cities are located in, then those relocating in the western region averaged the longest distance of 1,493 km. Those moving to a city in the eastern region came second with an average of 1,127 km, while those relocating in the central region and northeastern region had only the average distance of 577 km and 408 km, respectively.

9.3.4.2 *Distance Decaying*

There were 35 listed companies that elected for a long-distance HQs relocation, whilst 51 were chose as short-distance relocation, leading to a ratio of 41:59. Therefore it is very clear that among listed companies, short-distance relocation is more common than long distance. This illustrates that

Table 9-4 Listed Companies' HQs Relocations in Major Cities.

City	Relocation into		Relocation away from		Net amount of relocations into	Overall activity	
	Number of companies	Percentage of whole (%)	Number of companies	Percentage of whole (%)		Number of companies	Percentage of whole (%)
Beijing	25	29.07	1	1.16	24	26	15.12
Chengdu	8	9.30	2	2.33	6	10	5.81
Shanghai	7	8.14	2	2.33	5	9	5.23
Hangzhou	5	5.81	1	1.16	4	6	3.49
Changsha	4	4.65	0	0.00	4	4	2.33
Shenzhen	4	4.65	3	3.49	1	7	4.07
Lhasa	0		5	5.81	−5	5	2.91
Others		—		—	—		—
Total	86	100.00	86	100.00	—	172	100.00

Source: Author's calculations according to listed companies' data.

Table 9-5　The Distance of Listed Companies' HQs Relocation in China.

	Average distance of relocation by target city				Average distance of relocation by target province				
Target city	Number of relocations	Average relocation distance	Longest relocation distance	Shortest relocation distance	Target province	Number of HQs	Average distance of relocation	Longest relocation distance	Shortest relocation distance
Beijing	26	1512	3768	137	Beijing	25	1422	3768	137
Chengdu	8	2145	3360	61	Sichuan	12	1702	3360	60
Shanghai	7	1336	2915	314	Guangdong	9	1532	3647	57
Hangzhou	5	564	2217	63	Zhejiang	8	409	2217	28
Changsha	4	556	1501	147	Shanghai	5	1305	2915	314
Shenzhen	4	1082	2939	57	Hunan	4	556	1501	147
Guangzhou	3	2267	3647	147	Hubei	3	201	334	109
Wuhan	3	201	334	109	Shandong	3	234	338	73
Changchun	2	462	523	400	Anhui	2	570	1076	64
Hefei	2	570	1076	64	Jilin	2	462	523	400
Jinan	2	206	338	73	Jiangsu	2	201	202	200
Kunming	2	364	571	157	Yunnan	2	364	571	157
Acheng	1	300	300	300	Fujian	1	263	263	263
Chishui	1	155	155	155	Guizhou	1	155	155	155
Deyang	1	232	232	232	Hainan	1	363	363	363
Dongguan	1	2596	2596	2596	Henan	1	2106	2106	2106

(Continued)

Table 9-5 (*Continued*)

Average distance of relocation by target city

Target city	Number of relocations	Average relocation distance	Longest relocation distance	Shortest relocation distance
Dujiangyan	1	500	500	500
Haikou	1	363	363	363
Jiaxing	1	28	28	28
Jiangyin	1	200	200	200
Linfen	1	274	274	274
Luzhou	1	60	60	60
Nanjing	1	202	202	202
Qingdao	1	291	291	291
Sanming	1	263	263	263
Shaoxing	1	63	63	63
Shunde	1	60	60	60

Average distance of relocation by target province

Target province	Number of HQs	Average distance of relocation	Longest relocation distance	Shortest relocation distance
Heilongjiang	1	300	300	300
Ningxia	1	300	300	300
Shanxi	1	274	274	274
Shaanxi	1	1509	1509	1509
Xinjiang	1	3768	3768	3768

By target region

Target region	Number of relocations	Average distance of relocation	Longest relocation	Shortest relocation
East	54	1127	3768	28
Northeast	3	408	523	300
West	18	1493	3768	60
Central	11	577	2106	64

(*Continued*)

Table 9-5 (*Continued*)

Average distance of relocation by target city

Target city	Number of relocations	Average relocation distance	Longest relocation distance	Shortest relocation distance
Wuzhong	1	300	300	300
Xian	1	1509	1509	1509
Zhengzhou	1	2106	2106	2106
Total	86	1108	3768	28

Average distance of relocation by target province

Target province	Number of HQs	Average distance of relocation	Longest relocation distance	Shortest relocation distance

By rank of target city

Target city rank	Number of relocations	Average relocation distance	Longest relocation distance	Shortest relocation distance
Sub-provincial level city	5	923	2939	57
Normal city	13	387	2596	28
Provincial capital	35	1057	3647	61
Municipality	33	1475	3768	137

Source: Author's calculations according to listed companies' data from Wind information database.

Table 9-6 The Quantity and Distance of Different Types of Relocation.

	Long- and short distance relocation					Inter-provincial and intra-provincial relocation			
Relocation type	Amount of relocations	Average relocation distance	Furthest relocation	Shortest relocation	Relocation type	Amount of relocations	Average relocation distance	Furthest relocation	Shortest relocation
Long distance	35	2341	3768	1076	Inter-provincial	49	1785	3768	137
Short distance	51	262	927	28	Intra-provincial	37	211	571	28

Source: Calculated according to Wind information.

the relocation of Chinese-listed companies' HQs has the characteristic of distance decaying (in other words, most companies prefer to move short distances rather than relocate far away). When listed companies are determining the strategy for their corporate HQs, their information about the target location always decreases as the distance prolongs, moreover they are prejudiced in favor of more proximate locations, and biased away from further locations. However, the number of inter-provincial relocations is 49, while relocations within the same province is 37, with a ratio of 57:43. This seems to contradict the aforementioned distance-decaying characteristic. In fact, many of the inter-provincial relocations actually occur between neighboring provinces, municipalities, or cities, and are in fact quite short distances. For example, the move from Tianjin to Beijing is only 137 km, and relocating from Ningbo to Shanghai is a distance of only 362 km.

The average long-distance relocation was 2341 km, the shortest was 1076 km, and the furthest was 3768 km. The average short distance relocation was 262 km, the shortest was 28 km and the longest was 927 km. The average inter-provincial relocation distance was 1785 km, while the average of those relocations occurring within one province was 211 km (Table 9-6).

9.4   Reasons and Target Locations for Chinese Listed Companies' HQs Relocation

9.4.1   *The Target Location for Chinese Listed Companies' HQs Relocation*

Instances of corporate HQs relocation can be divided into three categories according to the scale of the city moved away from and the scale of the target city. These three categories are up-going, parallel, and down-going relocations. Up-going relocation refers to a corporate HQs moving from a lower ranked city to a higher ranked city; down-going relocation refers to the move from a higher ranked city to a lower ranked city; parallel relocation refers to a corporate HQs moving to a city with the same rank as the city it moved away from. This type of categorization is mainly used to examine the type of corporate HQs relocation. Sometimes up-going especially refers to moving from underdeveloped areas to developed ones, and this can also be referred to as west–east relocation. Here, the "west" represents underdeveloped areas and "east" represents the economically developed areas. This west–east relocation shows that corporate HQs relocation will often consist of companies moving away from underdeveloped areas. Up-going is the most common form of China's HQs relocation, and west to east relocation is most frequent.

9.4.1.1 *Up-going Relocation*

Amongst China's listed companies, there were 56 up-going relocations, accounting for 65.1% of all relocations. There were 18 parallel relocations, occupying 20.9% of the total; down-going relocations numbered 12, or 14.%. In other words, the direction of the relocations was toward central cities, mainly toward municipalities and provincial capitals which numbered 49; while there were 71 relocations moving away from normal cities and provincial capitals, occupying 82.6% of the total (see Table 9-7).

Up-going relocations occupy the largest proportion in the central region, as high as 90.9%. In the eastern region, up-going relocations are also the most common, numbering 22, and occupying 61.1% of total relocations — similar to the overall proportion within the country. Although in the western and eastern regions, up-going relocations are the most frequent of any relocation type, the proportion of up-going relocations in these two regions are relatively lower in the country (see Table 9-8).

The main target cities of up-gong relocations were Beijing, Shanghai, Hangzhou, and Shenzhen, but there is a large difference in the numbers of HQs moving into these cities: 21 up-going companies relocated in Beijing, whereas Shanghai only had 7 and Hangzhou and Shenzhen numbered 4 each. Parallel relocations into Beijing and Chengdu were both 5, with 4 of the

Table 9-7   Listed Companies' HQs Relocation Types.

Rank of city being left \ Relocation type	Up-gong relocations	Parallel relocations	Down-gong relocations	Total
Sub-provincial level city	7		1	8
Normal city	35	4		39
Provincial capital	14	9	9	32
Municipality		5	2	7
Total	56	18	12	86
Percentage of total (%)	65.1	20.9	14.0	100

Source: Author's calculations having sorted through listed companies' information.

Table 9-8 Listed Companies' HQs Relocation Types by Region.

Relocation type Region moving-out	Up-gong relocations	Parallel relocations	Down-gong relocations	Proportion of up-gong relocations (%)	Total
Eastern region	22	8	6	61.1	36
Northeastern region	6	2	1	66.7	9
Western region	18	8	4	60.0	30
Central region	10		1	90.9	11
Total	56	18	12	65.1	86

Source: Author's calculations having sorted through listed companies' information.

Table 9-9 Listed Companies' HQs Relocation Types by City.

HQs relocation target city \ Relocation type	Up-gong relocations	Parallel relocations	Down-gong relocations	Total
Beijing	21	5		26
Shanghai	7			7
Hangzhou	4	1		5
Shenzhen	4			4
Changsha	3	1		4
Chengdu	3	5		8
Wuhan	3			3
Hefei	1		1	2
Guangzhou		2	1	3
Changchun, Jinan, Kunming	2 each			2 each
Haikou, Nanjing, Qingdao, Zhengzhou	1 each			1 each
Jiangyin, Hongtong county (Linfen), Luzhou, Qingzhou town (Sha county, Sanming), Zhuji city (Shaoxing), Wuzhong, Xian, Acheng, Chishui, Dongguan			1 each	1 each
Shunde, Deyang, Dujiangyan, Jiaxing		1 each		1 each
Total	56	18	12	86

Source: Author's calculations having sorted through listed companies' information.

parallel relocations into Beijing coming from Tianjin and the others coming from Shanghai. All of the parallel relocations into Chengdu came from Lhasa. That means that the enterprises of Tibet are used to take Chengdu as the management base (Table 9-9).

9.4.1.2 *West to East Relocation*

Even with three listed companies moving their HQs away from the eastern region — one going to the western region and the other two moving to the central region — China's eastern region still reaps the most benefits from listed companies' HQs relocation. Out of the 25 examples of inter-regional HQs relocation, 21 moved into the eastern region of China, accounting for 84.0% of all inter-regional relocations. 6 companies from the northeastern region, 13 companies from the western region, and 3 companies from the central region all but one moved to the eastern region. The western region felt the largest impact of HQs relocation away, as altogether 13 companies' HQs left. In terms of relocations within one region, the most active regions were the eastern region and the western region. 33 companies moved HQs within the eastern region; 17 moved within the western region; and only

3 and 8 moved within northeastern region and central region respectively (Table 9-10).

On an average, the eastern region's relative level of economic development is higher, so are the labor and land prices. The average cost of labor in eastern region in 2006 was RMB 25,048, which was the highest of the four regions, as can be seen in the Table 9-11. Therefore, Chinese-listed companies' HQs obviously are not moving eastward for the absolute cost of labor. In fact, what companies are always concerned with is never the absolute wage level but the efficiency wage, or relative cost rate of labor, with respect to productivity of labor. When the relative cost rate of labor is indicated by the ratio of total work reward to total added value, it can be seen in Table 9-11 that, in spite of the highest average labor cost, the eastern region has the lowest relative price level of labor benefiting from the highest productivity of labor, which means that, given the different productivities of labor, the eastern region has the lowest relative cost rate of labor, western region has the highest, and central and northeastern regions stays in the middle level.

There is a big difference between relocation of corporate HQs and relocation of manufacturers. The cost of labor has a large impact on the relocation of manufactures, such as the instance of Japanese electrics companies whose main reason for relocating was the cost of labor. China's low manufacturing cost was the main reason behind relocation of the Japanese electrical companies from Singapore, Taiwan, and Korea towards mainland China. For the HQs of company, the choice of location is not so affected by the explicit cost like wages, rents, and prices of land, as the implicit cost born of advancement in information science, external links, and exchanges; the efficiency of the government; the talent market; professional and efficient service, and so on. With the growing importance of the implicit cost, the central cities of eastern region will demonstrate their expanding advantage.

9.4.1.3 *West to East Transfer of Wealth*

There were 17 companies who moved their HQs from the northeastern, the western, and the central regions to the eastern region, and yet those moving out of the eastern region only numbered 2 (one moved to the central region while another one moved to western region). This means that the number of companies moved toward the eastern region is 8.5 times that of the left.

Table 9-10 Listed Companies' HQs Relocation Matrix in China.

| | Inter-regional relocation matrix | | | | | Overall relocation matrix | | | | |
| | Destination | | | | | Destination | | | | |
Origin	East	North-east	West	Central	Subtotal	East	North-east	West	Central	Subtotal
East	0		1	2	3	33		1	2	36
Northeast	6	0			6	6	3			9
West	12		0	1	13	12		17	1	30
Central	3			0	3	3			8	11
Total	21		1	3	25	54	3	18	11	86

Source: Calculated according to Wind information.

Table 9-11 Cost of Labor in 2007 by Region.

Region	Average cost of labor (Yuan/Year)				Relative cost rate of labor*			
	Total wages (RMB 1 billion)	Employee number (thousand)	Average wage (Yuan per year)	Relative level	GRP (RMB 1 billion)	work reward (RMB 1 billion)	Relative cost rate of labor	Relative level
Eastern region	1227.22	48,995	25,048	120	12859.31	4988.23	0.388	96
Northeastern region	212.01	11,951	17,740	85	1971.52	799.06	0.405	100
Western region	460.54	25,386	18,141	87	3952.71	1747.30	0.442	109
Central region	426.82	25,273	16,888	81	4321.80	1847.69	0.428	105
National	2326.59	111,606	20,846	100	23105.33	9382.28	0.406	100

*Relative cost rate of labor = total salary/GRP.
Source: Calculated according to *China Statistical Yearbook 2007.*

Table 9-12 Comparison between "West to East" and "East to West" Relocation.

		Total assets (RMB 100 millions)	Main business income (RMB 100 millions)	Total profit (RMB 100 millions)	Number of corporate HQs
West to east relocation	Northeast-East	650.3	167.7	28.2	4
	West-East	536.7	123.6	44.4	10
	Central-East	62.8	16.3	2.2	3
	Subtotal	1249.8	307.6	74.8	17
East to west relocation	East-West	38.9	5.1	0.6	1
	East-Central	5.8	5.5	−2.4	1
	Subtotal	44.7	10.6	−1.8	2
	Multiple	28.0	29.0	—	8.5

Note: Total assets, main business income, and total profit are the figure of 2007. The following tables are same as.
Source: Author's Calculations.
Source: Calculated according to Wind information.

If examined from the perspective of total assets, main business income, and total profit, the total assets that moved away from the northeastern, western, and central regions into the eastern region come to a total of RMB 124.98 billion. Whereas, the value of assets that left the east only amounts to RMB 4.47 billion. The value of the assets coming in is 28 times the value going out. As for main business income, the value moving in is 29 times the value moving out, and the total profit of listed companies moving away from the east was negative (Table 9-12).

In fact the predominance of this type of "west to east" relocation also exists within the individual regions of the west and the east. To take Tibet as an example, of the 8 listed companies, 5 moved their HQs to Chengdu, a proportion of 62.5% of all relocations away from Tibet. Within this high relocation rate of 62.5%, there is also another phenomenon that necessitates research: most of those companies leaving Tibet were making financial losses. Do these companies, which were at a deficit before they relocated, continue to make losses after their move? Are these relocations driven by a non-listed company purchasing shares from the listed company to

Table 9-13 The HQs Relocations of Tibet's Listed Companies.

	Corporate HQs		Total assets		Main business income		Total profit (RMB 100 millions)
	Amount	Proportion (%)	Amount (RMB 100 millions)	Proportion (%)	Amount (RMB 100 millions)	Proportion (%)	
Relocated	5	62.5	34.01	53.0	18.67	75.5	−0.71
Not relocated	3	37.5	30.10	47.0	6.06	24.5	0.66
Total	8	100	64.11	100.0	24.73	100.0	−0.05

Source: Calculated according to Wind information.

acquire control and achieve listing indirectly? These questions are pending on further research (Table 9-13).

9.4.2 *Target Cities and Wealth Transfer of HQs Relocation among Listed Companies*

9.4.2.1 *Geographical Concentration of Listed Companies' HQs*

The concentration of listed companies' HQs is increasing, and continuously congregating toward Beijing, Shanghai, and Shenzhen. The HQs of listed companies in China are mainly located in Beijing, Chengdu, Shanghai, and 29 other cities, while the cities being moved away from include Lhasa, Tianjin, Harbin, and 58 other cities. In 2005, the proportion of China's top 100 listed companies with HQs located in Beijing, Shanghai, or Shenzhen was 37%, and by 2006 this number had increased by 8 percentage points to 45%. The largest proportion of Chinese top 100 listed companies' HQs concentrated in Beijing: in 2005 there were 14; by 2006 it increased to 20 with the concentration ratio of 20%. Whereas, the proportion of China's top 100 listed companies with HQs located in Shanghai actually experienced a decrease of 2 percentage points, falling from 15% in 2005 to 13% in 2006 (see Table 9-14).

In these three cities, China's top 100 listed companies' concentration ratio of total assets, main business income, total profit, and market value is increasing; in 2005 they were respectively 84.%, 67.6%, 66.7%, and 65.8%, and by 2006, they had increased to 95.%, 75.9%, 80.2%, and 85.2%.

As China's top 100 listed companies congregate toward Beijing, the total assets are also being concentrated in Beijing. This is even clearer in terms of the change in asset concentration of the top 100 listed companies. The proportion of top 100 listed companies with HQs located in Beijing was 40.9% in 2005, which increased to 86.6% in 2006 — an increase of around 45 percentage points. At the same time, Shanghai's went from 36.2% in 2005 to 6.1% in 2006 — a fall of around 30 percentage points.

9.4.2.2 *Probability Analysis of Transfer of Wealth toward Beijing*

Corporate tax payment is a complicated process, and the transfer of wealth and tax revenue is equally complicated, therefore the following references to wealth transfer in reality refers to probability of wealth transfer.

Table 9-14   Concentration of China's Top 100 Listed Companies Between 2005 and 2006.

Year/City Indicators		2005				2006			
		Shanghai	Beijing	Shenzhen	Total	Beijing	Shanghai	Shenzhen	Total
Corporate HQs	Number	15	14	8	37	20	13	12	45
	Changes	—	—	—	—	6	-2	4	8
Total assets	Amount (RMB 100 Million)	16141	18230	3115	37486	161631	11303	4480	177414
	Proportion (%)	36.2	40.9	7.0	84.0	86.6	6.1	2.4	95.0
Market value	Amount (RMB 100 Million)	2481	4723	735	7940	51453	6857	3366	61675
	Proportion (%)	20.6	39.2	6.1	65.8	71.1	9.5	4.7	85.2
Main business income	Amount (RMB 100 Million)	3152	10816	535	14504	19956	3411	1093	24460
	Proportion (%)	14.7	50.4	2.5	67.6	61.9	10.6	3.4	75.9
Total profit	Amount (RMB 100 Million)	461	959	86	1505	3158	448	179	3785
	Proportion (%)	20.4	42.5	3.8	66.7	66.9	9.5	3.8	80.2

Source: Author's calculations having sorted through listed companies' information.

Table 9-15   Gains of Wealth Caused by Listed Companies' HQs Relocation into Provinces (RMB 100 Millions).

Relocation destination	Total assets	Total profit	Profit post-tax	Income tax
Anhui	5.84	−2.42	0	—
Beijing	3604.02	238.54	174.75	63.78
Guangdong	33.62	0.53	0.48	0.05
Henan	3.94	−0.07	−0.07	0
Hunan	10.79	−0.42	−0.43	0.01
Jiangsu	10.25	0.54	0.41	0.13
Shaanxi	38.9	0.63	0.37	0.25
Shanghai	141.28	5.3	3.89	1.41
Sichuan	34.01	−0.71	−0.17	—
Zhejiang	7.85	0.09	0.03	0.06
Total	3890.52	242.01	179.26	62.75

Source: Author's calculations having sorted through listed companies' information.

The income tax received by Beijing from companies moving their HQs into the capital is RMB 6.378 billion. Companies moving their HQs into Shanghai have brought RMB 141 million to the Shanghai Government, while Shaanxi, Jiangsu, Guangdong, Hunan, and Zhejiang all received income tax between RMB 1 million to 25 million. Companies moving into Henan, Anhui, and Sichuan do not contribute toward local tax (Table 9-15).

In terms of income tax lost due to companies moving their HQs elsewhere, Guangdong lost RMB 3.23 billion, which was the most of any province, over 50% of their tax transfer. Second was Tianjin, where RMB 770 million was lost in income tax due to corporate HQs relocations. Xinjiang, Liaoning, and Gansu lost RMB 730 million, 660 million, and 220 million, respectively (see Table 9-16).

From examination of the relocation matrix, one can observe that Beijing has seen the biggest increase in tax revenue due to HQs relocations. According to the rules of China's tax revenue system, the income tax of any given company should be paid in the location of its HQs. In 2006, those HQs relocating into Beijing brought a total profit of RMB 23.854 billion; and

Table 9-16   Losses of Wealth Caused by Listed Companies' HQs Relocations Out of Provinces (RMB 100 Millions).

Type Province left	Total assets	Total profit	Profit post-tax	Income tax
Beijing	5.8	−2.4	−1.8	−0.6
Gansu	200	8.9	6.7	2.2
Guangdong	2132.2	129.2	96.9	32.3
Guangxi	57.6	2.7	2	0.7
Heilongjiang	56.5	2.2	1.7	0.6
Hubei	62.8	2.2	1.6	0.5
Jiangsu	103.5	3.9	2.9	1
Liaoning	606.9	26.3	19.7	6.6
Shanghai	49.1	1	0.8	0.3
Tianjin	126.4	30.9	23.1	7.7
Xinjiang	233.4	29.2	21.9	7.3
Yunnan	26.9	3.2	2.4	0.8
Zhejiang	94.7	3.6	2.7	0.9
Total	3890.52	242.01	179.26	62.75

Source: Author's calculations having sorted through listed companies' information.

their total income tax was RMB 6.378 billion. Even though some companies relocated away from Beijing, those companies were actually making losses and so in terms of income tax, it did not have a large effect on Beijing; however it did reduce the sales tax.

9.4.3 *The Reasons for HQs Relocations of Listed Companies*

Why are listed companies so clearly favoring relocations toward Beijing and other central cities in the eastern region? This is because the HQs of listed companies are thought of as the core of the decision-making structure, so there is greater attention paid to the location and regional environment. There is also higher demand to be located in high-density metropolises areas, in order to facilitate the obtaining of information, senior managerial and technological talent, and the provision of specialized and efficient service, which thus helps corporations to rapidly and ably determine strategies.

9.4.3.1 *High Demand for Mobility of Capital and Convenience of Financing*

The research illustrates that in, more economically developed areas, there is greater mobility of capital whilst in economically underdeveloped areas, there is less mobility of capital. Mobility of capital is positively correlated with the convenience of financing. Compared with the central and western region, the eastern region has much greater mobility of capital and much more extensive and convenient financial channels.

First, the distribution of loans and deposits in banks among different regions is extremely unbalanced; the total amount of the eastern region's loans and deposits is far higher than that of the central and western region and northeastern region. At the end of 2007, of the total amount of deposits of local and foreign currency in all financial institutions in the entire country, the eastern region accounted for 61.2%, the central region was 15.0%, the western region was 16.3%, and northeastern region was 7.5%; of the total amount of loans, and the four regions were, respectively, 61.3%, 14.8%, 16.6%, and 7.3% (Monetary Policy Analysis Group of the People's Bank of China, 2008).

Second, non-governmental capital is far more active in the eastern region than it is in the central and western region, especially as it moves via the capital markets toward the eastern region and away from the central and western region. The eastern region has two stock exchanges (Shanghai and Shenzhen), and the great majority of funds flow toward joint-stock companies and the stock exchanges via the capital market; and local companies can then conveniently conduct financing through employing information advantage. In 2007, of the total amount of financing in the domestic stock market, the eastern region accounted for 81.2%, while the central, western, and northeastern regions were, respectively, only 5.5%, 8.5%, and 4.8% (Monetary Policy Analysis Group of the People's Bank of China, 2008).

Third, FDI in China is principally focused on eastern region, while the FDI into the central and western region and northeastern region is extremely limited. Between the years 1979 and 2006, 82.6% of FDI actually utilized throughout the entire country was focused on the eastern region, while the central, western, and northeastern regions were, respectively, 7.1%, 4.2%, and 6.1%.

In summary, owing to abundant capital strength, more financing channels, and greater capital mobility in the eastern region, financing will be far more convenient if enterprises located their HQs in central cities of eastern region.

9.4.3.2 *High Demand for a Rich Level of Technology and Talented Workforce*

Beijing and the YRD region, where there are numerous universities and scientific research centers, are the areas with the greatest density of talented people in the entire country. These areas have an outstanding competitive advantage in terms of technology and talent to other areas. Some companies relocate their HQs and R&D departments toward these areas so as to effectively use the abundant resources of technology and talent there and to ensure they are on the frontier of new technology and management concept within the country. Generally, technology and talent resource is the main reason for relocation of knowledge-based HQs and R&D departments.

9.4.3.3 *High Demand for Convenience of Information Acquisition*

For companies in the information era, information is vital, and companies in possession of huge amounts of information are usually the most able to seize prior opportunities. This is especially true since China entered the WTO; companies now face globalized markets and play part in global competition, giving acquisition of information even greater importance. In eastern region, where the foreign investment companies in central cities are numerous, information has developed and is now closely linked to overseas markets. For those companies that want to expand into overseas markets and become international corporations, relocating their HQs toward these central cities is the most convenient way to acquire information and monitor the movement of the overseas markets at any time. Examples of corporate relocation also shows that large corporations usually choose to relocate toward the two international cities, Beijing and Shanghai. The motivation for management-type HQs relocations is the ability to effectively use the information advantage to rapidly react to fast-changing international markets.

9.4.3.4 *Great Market Potential in Beijing and other Eastern Central Cities*

The eastern region has a large population and great purchasing power, and it has formed a large and effective market. Inland companies spend many years operating within their original location, and when the local market approaches saturation and if companies wish to expand their scale, they have to focus the gaze on the large eastern market. In the process of expansion, many companies choose to adopt the strategy of locating close to markets. This strategy not only means they can benefit from policies such as preferential taxing in the relocation destination but they can also adapt even faster to changes in the target market, and adjust accordingly the company's operating policies without delay. Enterprise relocating enabled companies to reduce transaction costs while entering the new market. Furthermore, they can use the effects of radiation outwards from central cities such as Shanghai, Beijing, and Shenzhen to enter the national market. The main motivation of marketing HQs' relocations is to obtain a great degree of market effect. In addition, as the capital of China, Beijing has many advantages of capital. Some listed companies relocated their HQs toward Beijing in order to make full use of the capital advantage.

9.5 Concluding Remarks

In recent years, with China's sustained and rapid economic growth, some home-grown companies with rapid scale expansion attempt to relocate their HQs to seek more convenient habitats for the ideal of growing from regional companies into national, or even global companies. China is running in the times of HQs relocation, and it is necessary for the rising power to have a flood of world-influential conglomerates, to the HQs of which are hosted at central cities as Beijing, Shanghai, etc. Therefore, some powerful central cities will stay in a better position in the new round competition for the entry of these huge conglomerates.

This chapter systematically investigates the relocation of Chinese-listed companies' HQs and once again provides evidence for the fact that "the strong will be strong forever". As has been analyzed, the relocation of listed companies' HQs is still market behavior, and the impact of "HQs Economy" policies is very small at present. However, with the increasing economic globalization and market-based reform in China, impetus from market may lead to even more companies relocating their HQs toward and assembling in central cities such as Beijing, Shanghai, etc. In this case, the HQs and R&D centers f high-end industrial chains like will be barely influenced by the national policy of industrial transfer from East to West, whereas industrial transfer going west will mainly focus on the links of processing and manufacturing. That may further strength the division of "mental and manual labor" between the east and the west.

References

Belderbos, R. and J. L. Zou (2006). Foreign Investment, Divestment and Relocation by Japanese Electronics Firms in East Asia. *Asian Economic Journal*, 20(1), 1–27.

Davis, J. C. (2000). *Headquarters, Localization Economies and Differentiated Service Inputs*: Brown University mimeo.

Davis, J. C. (2003), *Headquarter Service and Industrial Urban Specialization With Transport Costs*. PhD dissertation, Brown University, Providence, RI, USA.

Holloway, S. R. and J. O. Wheeler (1991). Corporate Headquarters Relocation and Changes in Metropolitan Corporate Dominance, 1980–1987. *Economic Geography*, 67(1), 54–74.

Horst, T. and S. Koropeckyi (2000). Headquarters Effect. *Regional Financial Review*, 2, 16–29.

Klier, T. and W.Testa (2002). Location Trends of Large Company Headquarters During the 90s. *Economic Perspectives, Federal Reserve Bank of Chicago*, 12–26.

Lyons, D. (1995). Changing Business Opportunities: The Geography of Rapidly Growing Small US Private Firms, 1982–1992. *The Professional Geographer*, 47(4), 388–398.

Mariotti, I. (2002). Methodological Problems in Firm Migration Research. The Case of Italy, In Cucculelli and M. R. Mazzoni (Eds.), *Risorse e Competitivia. Franco Angeli, Milan*, 208–229.

Mariotti, I., G. Micucci and P. Montanaro (2004). *Internationalisation Strategies of Italian district SMEs: An Analysis on Firm-level Data*, ERSA conference papers, European Regional Science Association.

Monetary Policy Analysis Group of the People's Bank of China. (2008). *2007 China Regional Financial Performance Report*. 30 May 2008.

Semple, K. R. (1973). Recent Trends in Spatial Concentration of Corporate Headquarters. *Economic Geography*, 49(4), 309–318.

Semple, R. K., M. B. Green and D. J. F. Martz (1985). Perspectives on Corporate Headquarters Relocation in the United States. *Urban Geography*, 6(4), 370–391.

Semple, R. K. and A. G. Phipps (1982). The Spatial Evolution of Corporate Headquarters within an Urban System. *Urban Geography*, 3(3), 258–279.

Shi, Z. and H. Shen (2005). A Study on Form of Headquarters Economy and Development in China. *China Industrial Economy*, (5), 58–65.

Shilton, L. and C. Stanley (1999). Spatial Patterns of Headquarters. *Journal of Real Estate Research*, 17(3), 341–364.

Strauss-Kahn, V. and X. Vives (2005). *Why and Where do Headquarters Move?* CEPR Discussion Paper No. 5070.

Wang, J. (2005). *Multinational Corporation's Region Headquarter in Shanghai and Its Influence*. Master's Thesis, East China Normal University, Shanghai.

Wei, H. (1998). *Location Decision*. Guangzhou: Guangdong Economic Publishing House.

Wheeler, J. O. and C. L. Brown (1985). The Metropolitan Corporate Hierarchy in the US South, 1960–1980. *Economic Geography*, 61(1), 66–78.

Zhang, J. (2006). *Study on Transnational Corporation Regional Headquarters' Location Factor*. Master's Thesis, Capital University of Economics and Business, Guangzhou.

Zhao, H. (2004). *Headquarters Economy*. Beijing: China Economic Publishing House.

Zhao, H. (2005a). Headquarters Economy and Its Development in China. *Jianghai Academic Journal*, (1), 61–64.

Zhao, H. (2005b) (Ed.). *The Development Report of China's Headquarters Economy (2005–2006)*. Beijing: Social Sciences Academic Press.

Zheng, J. (2002). Study on the Function of the Regional Headquarters of Multinational Corporations (MNCs) and the Location of Asian Headquarters. *World Regional Studies*, 1(11), 8–14.

Chapter 10

Relocation Mechanism and Spatial Agglomeration of Enterprise R&D Activities

Liu Changquan

With the acceleration of industrial transfer and corporate relocation in China, relocation of R&D enterprises and R&D activities of enterprises is increasing as well, clustering in such national centers as Beijing and Shanghai or to regional centers like Nanjing and Chengdu. Compared with the relocation of general enterprises, relocation of R&D activities is getting increasing attention, but the research perspectives and subjects are to be extended. Currently, most researches focus on the relocation of R&D activities and R&D centers of multinational companies, and analyze its effects on the company, and on regional or national economy, such as technology diffusion and technological progress, etc. However, few researches have been performed on the inter-regional relocation of R&D activities in China. Moreover, most of them mainly focus on the relocation of R&D centers of multinationals, which is considered as a part of the relocation of foreign direct investment. In this chapter, we first explore the mechanism of R&D relocation and the factors influencing the process from the micro perspective, and then analyze the characteristics and trends of spatial agglomeration of R&D activities in China at macro level, so as to get a more general understanding of the rules of R&D relocation and the characteristics of R&D agglomeration in China.

10.1 Characteristics and Types of Enterprise R&D Relocation in China

10.1.1 *Background and Characteristics of Enterprise R&D Relocation in China*

10.1.1.1 *Relocation of R&D Activities of Multinationals to China is Accelerating*

With the advance in economic globalization since the 1980s, R&D activities of enterprises are becoming increasingly globalized. Multinationals started their R&D investment in China in early 1990s, and accelerated the process later. In recent years, they have established a variety of R&D institutions such as research institutes, centers, and laboratories. According to a survey, 82 R&D institutions have been set up by 65 multinational corporations by the end of August 2002, and this number was increased to 750 by the end of 2004, and to 1200 by October 2006. So far, over 400 Fortune Global 500 multinational corporations have set up R&D institutions in China (Guo and Kong, 2009).

10.1.1.2 *R&D Activities of Multinationals in China Keep Upgrading*

According to the stage of their R&D activities within the global R&D systems of the multinationals, the R&D institutions can be divided into three categories with rising importance, i.e., technical support, application development, and basic research. At first, the R&D institutions established in China by multinational corporations mainly provided technical support instead of developing new technologies, and only assumed the responsibility of solving the technical problems within the manufacturing procedures, for instance, provision of manufacturing technical guidance, product testing, manufacturing process improvement, etc. Nowadays, the R&D institutions of multinational corporations in China mainly focus on the localization of products and technologies. Based on the core technologies developed in their home countries, they principally work on the application and development of products tailored to the demand of Chinese customers. With the upgrade of domestic market and the increase of excellent talents, some multinational corporations begin to establish R&D centers engaged in basic research gradually, for instance, Microsoft Research Asia, Nokia Hangzhou R&D center, Alcatel-Lucent Shanghai Bell R&D center, etc., technological achievements of which are being applied in global market.

10.1.1.3 *R&D Activities are Geographically Concentrated*

Nowadays, in China, R&D workers are mostly concentrated in provinces including Jiangsu, Guangdong, Shandong, Zhejiang, Liaoning, Henan, Hubei, Sichuan, etc., while the regions attracting the most R&D investment are Guangdong, Jiangsu, Shandong, Shanghai, Zhejiang, Liaoning, Beijing, Tianjin, and other developed areas. Although the majority of R&D personnel and investment concentrate in the eastern developed regions, central cities in the central and western regions of China also attract comparable volume of R&D projects. In recent years, a growing number of R&D institutions of multinationals, including more than 10 R&D centers mainly in IT and software industry, have been set up in Xi'an, Chengdu, Chongqing, etc.

10.1.1.4 *R&D Relocation of Local Enterprises is Accompanied with Scale Expansion*

Local enterprises with R&D relocation tend to be large scale, having the desire of expansion and the capability to establish R&D institutions in developed cities. Li *et al.* (2004) investigated the relocation of private enterprises in Leqing city of Zhejiang Province and found that, among the 110 studied corporations, only three had relocated their R&D institutions. All of the three enterprises were large- or medium-sized, two of which possessed more than RMB 400 million of total assets. Local enterprises usually relocate their R&D institutions to Shanghai and Hangzhou, which have gained a comparative advantage over other regions in scientific research, industrialization of new technology, and attracting talented personnel.

10.1.2 *Major Types of R&D Relocation of Enterprises in China*

According to the geographical scope of the involved areas, R&D relocation can be roughly divided into international relocation and regional relocation. International relocation refers to the relocation of R&D activities across nations generally by multinational corporations,[1] while regional relocation refers to relocation across regions within one country, generally by local corporations. After a period of development in China, some multinational corporations were confronted with the demand of strategic adjustment, and they preferred to relocate their R&D activities in China to different regions. Such relocation will be denoted as international relocation in view of the similarity in driving mechanism and decision-making characteristics.

According to the economic disparity between the destination and source areas, R&D relocation falls into two categories, horizontal relocation and vertical relocation. Horizontal relocation refers to the move of R&D activities between two regions with the same level of economic development, both of which being either developed or underdeveloped. Vertical relocation is denoted as the move of R&D activities between economically unbalanced regions, either from developed areas to underdeveloped areas, or vice versa. Benefiting from the economic and social development, especially the improvement of transportation and communication, an increasing number of R&D activities have been relocated from developed areas to underdeveloped areas, for instance, the move of R&D activities of multinational enterprises to China. Yet, R&D activities of local corporations are generally moved from less developed regions to developed regions.

There are three types of R&D relocation according to the patterns of investment: the establishment of new R&D facilities; on-site expansion, including increasing R&D facilities on the basis of non-R&D operations and/or increasing R&D projects by acquiring and merging local companies; the last one being the so-called R&D outsourcing, which, also known as "R&D agreement", means that enterprises give the R&D activities from the whole value chain to other organizations through contract and thus acquire innovations relying on these external forces (Fang, 2005). According to the investigation by the Economist Intelligence Unit (EIU) on over 50 top enterprises worldwide in 1993, most corporations confirmed that, almost,

---

[1] Strictly speaking, international relocation of R&D activities should also include R&D offshoring.

or even more than half of their competitive technologies come from external organizations (Xie *et al.*, 2001).

Impelled by different motivations, enterprises may relocate R&D to seek for technical or strategic breakthrough. In the former case, with limited research capabilities, enterprises hope to acquire advanced technologies through the establishment of new R&D institutions in regions with adequate resources and favorable environment for R&D activities. And in the latter case, equipped with strong technical force, enterprises relocate their R&D facilities outward to occupy the market. Taking one example, a majority of multinational corporations transfer their R&D activities to China in order to develop more localized products, reduce cost, and capture the market share by utilizing local resources, which is an important part of business strategies of those multinational corporations.

10.2 Micro Analysis of R&D Relocation: Mechanism and Influencing Factors

10.2.1 *Mechanism of Enterprise R&D Relocation*

An important part of production and operation as R&D is that its relocation is a significant strategy for enterprises to achieve profit and growth targets. Selecting location for R&D activities serves for business goals, which is decided by the forces of "push" and "pull". Along with changes in the market and resource distribution, the composition and strength of the push and pull forces in each region are changing. Then the chance for each region, as an alternative location for R&D activities, to fulfill a company' strategic objective is uncertain. R&D relocation will occur only if another region is better in achieving the strategic goals of a company, while the benefits of the relocation is able to compensate for the cost.

10.2.2 *Influencing Factors of R&D Relocation*

The pushing and pulling effects of a location for R&D activities is the combined results of various factors, which can be summed up from four dimensions, namely: product markets, innovation level, current location conditions, and R&D inputs (Figure 10-1).

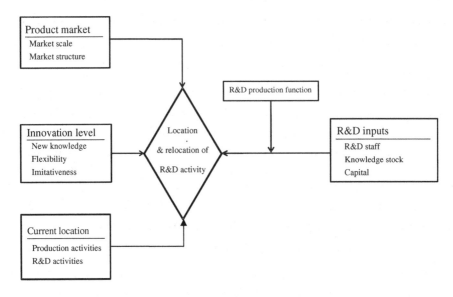

Figure 10-1   Location Choice and Relocation Decision of R&D Activities.

10.2.2.1 *Product Market*

The impact of market on the distribution of R&D activities comes from two aspects: market scale and market structure. Autant-Bernard (2006) studied the factors affecting the location choice of corporate R&D centers and laboratories using the data of 2024 French R&D centers and laboratories, and found that market scale had a positive impact while the intensity of competition exerted a negative impact. Due to the existence of big regional differences and rapid changes in consumers' preferences, R&D relocation can help discovering and better understanding market, so as to develop products adapted to local demands. For international R&D relocation, many specifications and technical standards in some fields of the target market may be different from those in the world market, therefore, multinational companies should carry out re-development based on these standards to adapt to and maximize the market. Market scale acts as an important determinant of R&D relocation (Zejan, 1990; Fors, 1996; Kumar, 2001; Odagiri and Yasuda, 1996; Belderbos, 2001, 2003; Chung and Alcácer, 2002). Therefore, developing adaptive technology is an important feature of the market-oriented R&D relocation. From the perspective of market competition, companies often follow their rival firms who have newly entered the market to maintain their market positions in some cases. According to the model of strategic R&D localization made by Belderbos *et al.* (2008), the R&D relocation of a multinational company would affect the relocation decision of the R&D activities of their rival companies, and the strategic impact depended on the structure of the product market.

10.2.2.2 *Level of Innovation*

Innovation can be divided into three types: original innovation, adaptive innovation, and imitative innovation. Original innovation is derived from basic R&D activities of the enterprises, composed of new disciplines and technologies; adaptive innovation stems from applied R&D activities; imitative innovation refers to technologies acquired through imitating. Both the original and adaptive technologies are new, that is new-to-market, while imitative technologies are new technology for the enterprises, that is new-to-firm, but not for the market (Leiponen and Helfat, 2006). Empirical research carried out by Leiponen and Helfat shows that R&D relocation will promote the innovation of enterprises by increasing their access to external R&D resources, but this effect is only limited to imitative innovation and not much in promoting original innovation.

10.2.2.3 *Conditions of Current Location*

Conditions of current location are the geographical distribution of existing R&D activities or production activities that may affect the location choice of new R&D activities. Cornet and Rensman (2001) studied the R&D relocation in the Netherlands and found that previous location choice (either for R&D or non-R&D activities) would influence the R&D relocation when companies tended to choose "non-greenfield investments" to carry out R&D investment, because the scale and scope effects of doing R&D investment in current location were much bigger than otherwise. In addition, Cornet and Rensman believed that the transfer of R&D activities in multinational companies was often along with the transfer of production, so as to meet the need of product localization. Autant-Bernard (2006) found that foreign-funded companies tended to layout their R&D activities in the border areas or major industrial regions, while single plant firms preferred areas with strong core–periphery features due to the effect of production layout. Under this circumstance, the production cost played a more important role in attracting firms than knowledge spillovers.

10.2.2.4 *R&D Inputs*

Regional factors related to R&D inputs include R&D personnel, knowledge stock, intellectual property protection, capital supply, etc. According to a study of Thursby *et al.* (2006), R&D personnel differ in quality, price, accessibility, and other aspects, which have important impacts on the location choice of corporate R&D activities. Knowledge stock refers to the stock of similar or complementary technologies and overall knowledge in the area. Companies are more inclined to engage in R&D activities in areas with high knowledge stock due to knowledge spillovers. Franck and Owen (2003) studied the impact of national knowledge stock on R&D location choice and pointed out that enterprises would have incentive to move their R&D activities abroad if the domestic and foreign knowledge was complementary; on the contrary, if the two were substitutive, such incentive would disappear. Autant-Bernard (2006) agreed that the stock of knowledge had a positive impact on promoting the agglomeration of R&D activities and also found that the knowledge spillovers attracted R&D activities but exerted no significant effect on public R&D activities. The protection of intellectual property is another important factor affecting the distribution and relocation of R&D activities. According to Thursby J. and Thurby M. (2006), inadequate intellectual property protection hindered the move-in of R&D activities in developing countries.

10.3 R&D Relocation in China at Macro Level: State and Trends

10.3.1 *Data Sources, Statistical Classification and Analysis Methods*

Most of the data in this section are from *China Statistical Yearbook* and *China Statistical Yearbook on Science and Technology* from 1997 to 2011. The indicators that reflect the scale of science and technology (S&T)

activities are: fund raised for S&T activities, internal expenditures for such activities, the number of personnel involved in, etc. In statistics, the indicator reflects the total spending a company or an organization dedicates to S&T activities, termed as expenditure in S&T activities, which can be further divided into internal expenditure and external expenditure. Internal expenditure refers to the full cost in implementing these activities within the organization or its executive departments, regardless of the source of the fund. External expenditure represents the actual cost of S&T activities outside the organization or its executive departments. The fund an organization allocated to others for S&T activities is regarded as external expenditure for the former organization, while internal expenditure for the latter. To avoid double counting in the summarized data, the total expenditure of regional S&T activities is the total internal spending of all agencies in the region, including all the cost of such activities of the organizations within this region and those located outside but belonging to this region. It can be seen from the statistical coverage that, the costs, irrespective of whether they are trans-regional, remain a part of the total expenditure of local R&D activities, as long as the enterprises' S&T activities are still within the executive departments after relocation. Therefore, the relocation scale of S&T activities and R&D activities cannot be calculated directly at the macro level. Only through analysis of the distribution of expenditure and R&D personnel can we determine the relative concentration of S&T activities, as well as the impact of economic development on the investment in S&T activities.

Part of corporate R&D activities is carried out within the enterprises, while some is fulfilled by research and development institutions, universities, and other non-business organizations, with the fund transferred through contracts, donations, or other forms. That's why, the relocation of corporate R&D affects not only the distribution of S&T activities in enterprises but also the distribution of all the S&T activities directly. Therefore, the analysis of the relocation of R&D at the macro level needs to begin from the distribution of the entire S&T activities. In the sections below, analyses are carried out in the perspectives of the whole region and large- and medium-sized enterprises, to learn the relative distribution, relative concentration, and outsourcing of S&T (R&D) activities by making use of data such as fund raised for S&T activities and the number of personnel involved (staff full-time equivalent), etc.

10.3.2 *Distribution and Relocation of S&T and R&D Activities*

10.3.2.1 *Changes in the Distribution of S&T Activities*

Figure 10-2 shows the distribution and its change of the fund raised for S&T activities in the four regions from 1997 to 2008, which tells that the investment in S&T activities is inclined to concentrate in the eastern region. The proportion of the eastern region kept increasing, until it surpassed 65% in 2005, and then stabilized at this level. Proportions of the western and northeastern regions continued to decline, and a sharp decline in the proportion of the central region occurred before 2005, afterward it increased rapidly. By 2008, the fund raised for S&T activities in the central and western regions accounted for less than 15% of the total, while 7 percentage points lower than the northeast region. Similar characteristics appeared in the distribution and its changes of R&D personnel involved: the proportion of the eastern region rose while those of the other three regions declined steadily. However, the concentration of personnel was still increasing while

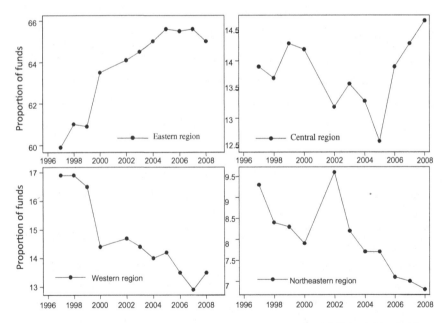

Figure 10-2   Changes in the Proportion of Fund Raised for S&T Activities in Four Regions from 1997 to 2008.

the concentration of funds tended to stabilize. Overall, the proportion of personnel had been lower than the proportion of raised-fund in the eastern region, while it is the opposite in the other three regions. In 2008, the personnel involved in the eastern region took up 57.7% of the total, the gap being 7.3 percentage points, while the adverse gap was 3.4 percentage points in the central region, 2.5 percentage points and 1.4 percentage points in the western and northeast regions, respectively.

The relocation reflected in the changes of regional distribution is a relative one. It can be seen from Table 10-1 that, though the proportions of fund raised in the central, western, and northeast regions have been declining, the absolute amount in these regions have increased substantially. The fund increased from RMB 65.47 billion to RMB 592.65 billion in the eastern region from 1997 to 2008, with an increase of 817.8%. The average annual growth rate was 22.3%. Moreover, the average annual growth rates of the other three regions were also higher than 17%.

In the perspective of provinces and municipalities, the coefficients of variation (CVs) of the fund raised for S&T activities, internal expenditures, and personnel involved in such activities are calculated to measure the unevenness of distribution or degree of agglomeration of inputs in

Table 10-1 Changes in the Regional Distribution of Funds Raised for S&T Activities from 1997 to 2008.

	1997		2008		1997~2008		
	Raised-fund (RMB 100 million)	Pro-portion (%)	Raised-fund (RMB 100 million)	Pro-portion (%)	Growth of fund (%)	Average annual growth rate(%)	Changes in pro-portion (%)
Eastern region	645.7	59.9	5926.5	65.0	817.8	22.3	5.1
Central region	149.7	13.9	1344.5	14.7	798.2	22.1	0.8
Western region	182.2	16.9	1232.7	13.5	576.5	19.0	−3.4
Northeastern region	100.6	9.3	620.1	6.8	516.2	18.0	−2.5

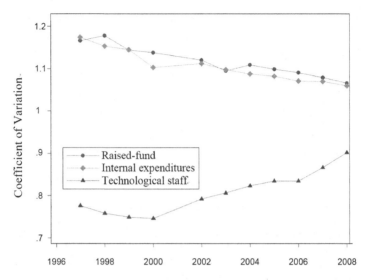

Figure 10-3   CV of Investment in S&T Activities at Province Level from 1997 to 2005.

S&T activities. It is shown in Figure 10-3, the spatial agglomerations of raised-fund and internal expenditures are much higher. CVs of the fund and internal expenditures were 1.066 and 1.060 respectively, while it is only 0.902 for the personnel involved. However, the agglomeration of raised-fund and internal expenditures has declined slightly in recent years, while that of the personnel involved keeps increasing gradually. CV of the distribution of personnel rose from 0.776 to 0.902 during 1997 to 2008, while those of raised-fund and internal expenditure decreased from 1.166 to 1.066 and 1.174 to 1.060 respectively in the same period.

10.3.2.2 *Changes in the Regional Distribution of R&D Activities*

Similar to the distribution of the fund raised for scientific and technology activities, the proportion of internal expenditure in the eastern region had increased from 59.4% to 66.5%, with an increase of 7.12 percentage points; while for central region, the increase was only 0.95 percentage points, and a decrease of 5.03 percentage points and 3.03 percentage points appeared for the western and northeastern regions, respectively. In the view of absolute amount, the fund increased from RMB 28.86 billion to RMB 469.94 billion in the eastern region, with an average annual growth rate of 26.2%, and the average annual growth rates of the western and northeastern regions were 21.5% and 21.2%, respectively (see Table 10-2).

Table 10-2 Changes of Regional Distribution of R&D Investment from 1998 to 2010.

		1998		2010		1998~2010		
		Amount	Proportion (%)	Amount	Proportion (%)	Growth of amount (%)	Average annual growth rate (%)	Proportion change (%)
Internal expenditures (RMB 100 million)	Eastern region	288.6	59.4	4699.4	66.5	1528.4	26.2	7.12
	Central region	64.3	13.2	1002.6	14.2	1458.4	25.7	0.95
	Western region	84.6	17.4	874.3	12.4	933.8	21.5	−5.03
	Northeastern region	48.2	9.9	486.3	6.9	909.5	21.2	−3.03
Full-time equivalent (10,00 manhours)	Eastern region	33.3	45.6	160.6	62.9	382.5	14.0	17.31
	Central region	12.7	17.4	41.7	16.3	228.1	10.4	−1.07
	Western region	17.5	24.0	33.9	13.3	93.3	5.6	−10.74
	Northeastern region	9.5	13.0	19.2	7.5	101.9	6.0	−5.50

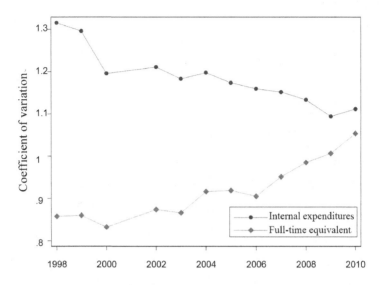

Figure 10-4   CVs of R&D Inputs in China from 1998 to 2010.

CVs are calculated to measure the distribution of internal expenditures and full-time equivalent of R&D staff at province level, and the results are shown in Figure 10-4. Compared with the investment in S&T activities, R&D investment is more unevenly distributed. In 2005, CVs of the internal expenditures and full-time equivalent in R&D activities were 1.174 and 0.919, respectively, and both were higher than those of S&T activities.

Similar to the investment in S&T activities, the degree of agglomeration of the internal expenditures in R&D activities is much higher than that of R&D personnel, and CV of the internal expenditures has been declining while that of full-time equivalent of R&D staff has been increasing. Differences in the trend show that the agglomeration of R&D activities is strengthening, though the internal expenditure is comparatively scattered, while higher concentration of R&D activities could be discovered from the perspective of full-time equivalent of R&D staff.

10.3.2.3 *Agglomeration and Concentrated Areas of R&D Activities*

From the view of the distribution of R&D activities at province level (Figure 10-5),[2] the internal expenditures of Beijing accounted for the highest

---

[2]The above analysis shows the similarity of the distribution of S&T activities and R&D activities, which is not going to be mentioned here.

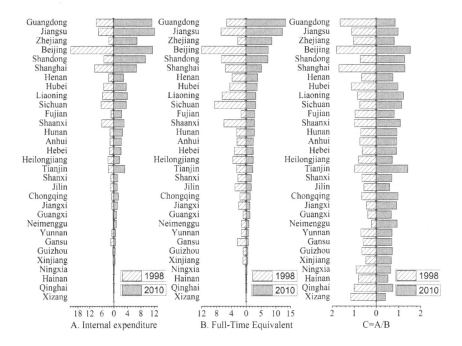

Figure 10-5   Regional Distribution of Investment in R&D activities and Its Change.

proportion of 21.1% in 1998, 12.9 percentage points higher than the second, Guangdong. However, after a decade's decline, the proportion had dropped to 11.6% by 2010, which is 0.5 percentage points lower than that of the first, Jiangsu province. In fact, it was the substantial drop of Beijing's share that led to the reduction of the overall coefficient of variation. With Beijing being not considered, the degree of agglomeration of internal expenditures in the other 30 provinces and municipalities would be much higher, with the CV increased from 1.008 in 1998 to 1.116 in 2005. The cumulative proportion of the five provinces with the highest or lowest proportion show that the cumulative proportion of the five highest was 52.7% in 1998 and fell to 51.7% in 2010 (Table 10-3), and that of the five lowest was 0.8% in both 1998 and 2010. On the whole, the dominant position of Beijing in R&D internal expenditures had been replaced by a few provinces and municipalities from 1998 to 2010.

In the aspect of full-time equivalent of R&D staff, the decline of proportion and position of Beijing was more apparent, with the proportion

Table 10-3   Cumulative Proportion of R&D Resources in the Areas with the Highest or Lowest Proportions from 1998 to 2010.

Region	Internal expenditures of R&D (%)		Full-time equivalent of R&D staff (%)	
	1998	2010	1998	2010
Top five	52.7	51.7	40.2	49.7
Last five	0.8	0.8	1.4	1.2
Top ten	76.4	73.4	65.0	69.3
Last ten	3.9	4.2	7.0	5.9

reduced from 11.9% in 1998 to 7.6% in 2010, and its ranking dropped from the first to the fourth. Its proportion of the full-time equivalent of R&D staff remained lower than that of R&D internal expenditure during 1998 to 2010, which meant that Beijing's advantages in R&D personnel were much smaller than that in funds. The provinces with the highest proportion of full-time equivalent of R&D staff were Guangdong, Jiangsu, and Zhejiang, whose proportion were higher than that of their own internal expenditures, suggesting more prominent advantages in personnel in these areas. From the cumulative proportion, it could be found that the concentration trend of resources towards advantageous regions was quite obvious, the cumulative proportion of the top five rising from 40.2% in 1998 to 49.7% in 2010 while that of the lowest five dropped from 7.0% to 5.9%.

Overall, the majority of R&D activities are located in provinces like Beijing, Jiangsu, Guangdong, Shandong, and Zhejiang, which are economically developed and where industries concentrated. Increasing agglomeration could make full use of both the adequate supply of fund and personnel and the strong demand for R&D.

10.3.3   Distribution and Relocation of R&D Activities of Large and Medium-Sized Industrial Enterprises

10.3.3.1   Changes in Regional Distribution

Similar to the characteristics of the distribution and its changes of S&T and R&D activities (as Table 10-4 shows), the internal expenditure and the

Table 10-4 Distribution and Changes of R&D Investment in Large and Medium-Sized Enterprises from 1998 to 2010.

		1998		2010		1998~2010		
		Amount	Proportion (%)	Amount	Proportion (%)	Growth of amount (%)	Average annual growth rate (%)	Proportion change (%)
Internal expenditures (RMB 100 million)	Eastern region	118.9	60.3	2686.4	66.9	2160.3	29.7	6.6
	Central region	27.3	13.8	635.8	15.8	2232.9	30.0	2.0
	Western region	27.7	14.1	393.4	9.8	1317.9	24.7	−4.3
	Northeastern region	23.2	11.8	299.7	7.5	1190.0	23.8	−4.3
Full-time equivalent of R&D staff (10,000 manhours)	Eastern region	14.4	43.3	33.3	65.3	130.5	7.2	22.0
	Central region	5.7	17.0	11.4	17.1	100.7	6.0	0.1
	Western region	8.2	24.6	9.4	10.6	14.3	1.1	−13.9
	Northeastern region	5.1	15.2	6.6	7.0	29.8	2.2	−8.2

full-time equivalent of R&D staff in large- and medium-sized industrial enterprises are also mainly concentrated in the eastern region, with a tendency to get further concentrated. The R&D internal expenditures of large and medium-sized industrial enterprises in the eastern region increased from RMB 11.89 billion in 1998 to RMB 268.64 billion in 2010, with an average annual growth rate of 29.7%, and an increase of its proportion of the total from 60.3% to 66.9%. Compared with the growth in the eastern region, growth in the central region was even slightly higher while those in the western and northeastern regions were significantly slower, and the proportion of the two regions decreased at different degrees.

Considering the full-time equivalent of R&D staff of large- and medium-sized industrial enterprises, the increase in the proportion of eastern region was quite obvious, which was from 43.3% to 65.3%, an increase of 22 percentage points. The average annual growth rate of the scale in eastern region was 7.2%, and the growth rate was up to 6.0% in central region, while for the western and northeastern regions, the growth rates were only 1.1% and 2.2%, respectively. Consequently, the proportion of the western and northeastern regions experienced a sharp decline, 13.9 percentage points for the western region, and 8.2 percentage points for the northeast region. So, the input of R&D staff of large- and medium-sized enterprises grow much slower compared with the input of funds, especially in the western and northeastern regions.

These data suggest that R&D investment in the large- and medium-sized enterprises is mainly concentrated in the eastern region and keep concentrating, with very clear trend of agglomeration; though the speed of agglomeration measured according to the full-time equivalent of R&D staff is a little lower, the speed of concentrating to the eastern region is becoming faster in recent years. In addition, the R&D investment in the large- and medium-sized industrial enterprises grows faster compared with the S&T activities, R&D activities of the society as a whole, indicating the rising dominant position of enterprises in the R&D activities.

10.3.3.2 *Concentrated Areas*

Table 10-5 shows the proportions and relative changes of R&D investment in the large- and medium-sized industrial enterprises in the most concentrated

Table 10-5 Distribution of R&D Activities from 1998 to 2010 (%).

| | Full-time equivalent of R&D staff | | | | Internal expenditures | | | |
| | 1998 | | 2010 | | 1998 | | 2010 | |
Ranking	Region	Proportion	Region	Proportion	Region	Proportion	Region	Proportion
1	Shandong	10.8	Guangdong	15.6	Guangdong	15.9	Guangdong	18.9
2	Sichuan	9.4	Jiangsu	13.7	Shanghai	10.0	Jiangsu	14.7
3	Liaoning	8.6	Shandong	13.1	Jiangsu	9.7	Shandong	8.8
4	Jiangsu	7.4	Zhejiang	6.8	Shandong	9.0	Zhejiang	8.5
5	Guangdong	6.3	Shanghai	5.9	Liaoning	6.7	Henan	5.0
6	Shanghai	4.7	Liaoning	4.8	Beijing	4.2	Shanghai	4.2
7	Shaanxi	4.4	Henan	3.7	Sichuan	3.9	Hubei	3.5
8	Hebei	4.2	Hubei	3.6	Hubei	3.8	Liaoning	3.2
9	Henan	4.2	Tientsin	3.5	Heilongjiang	3.7	Fujian	3.2
10	Heilongjiang	4.1	Fujian	2.9	Hebei	3.3	Hebei	2.8
Top five		42.5		55.2		51.3		55.8
Last five		64.1		73.6		70.2		72.7
Top ten		1.0		0.8		1.0		0.8
Last ten		6.6		4.1		5.1		4.5
CV		0.860		1.309		1.111		1.245

provinces, which were Guangdong, Jiangsu, Shandong, Zhejiang, and other provinces from 1998 to 2010. The investment is further concentrating to a few areas. In perspective of the full-time equivalent of R&D staff, Guangdong province took up the highest proportion, which was 15.6% of the total of the large- and medium-sized enterprises, followed by Jiangsu, which accounted for 13.7%. The top five provinces and municipalities with the highest proportions accounted for 55.2% altogether, with an increase of 12.7 percentage points from 1998. CV of the full-time equivalent of R&D staff also rose from 0.860 to 1.309 during this period. In respect of the internal R&D expenditures, the provinces with the highest proportions in 2005 were Guangdong and Jiangsu provinces, accounting for 18.9% and 14.7% of the total expenditure of large and medium-sized enterprises, respectively. Altogether, the top five provinces and municipalities accounted for 55.8%, 5.3 percentage points higher than that in 1998. As for the CV of internal R&D expenditures, it also rose from 1.111 to 1.245.

According to the analysis, the corporate R&D investment is concentrated to a few areas. And the degree of agglomeration of the full-time equivalent of R&D staff is higher than that of internal expenditure, which is quite different from the characteristics of agglomeration of R&D investment and research activities of the society as a whole, that is, R&D staff of enterprises are concentrated to advantageous areas faster.

10.3.4 *Causes for the Agglomeration Differences Between R&D Funds and Personnel*

The degrees of agglomeration of S&T activities and R&D activities measured in expenditures are generally much higher than that measured in personnel involved, but the gap narrowing in recent years. An important reason for such distribution and trend is the difference in mobility of capital and technological talents. Since the reform and opening-up, the mobility of funds is much higher than that of talents. Therefore, in the process of optimizing the allocation of resources, the agglomeration of R&D staff has lagged behind, while the R&D investment concentrates quickly with the imbalanced growth of regional economy. However, with the continuously improvement of the scientific management system and the marketization of S&T activities, the mobility of R&D staff has been improved, which cause a significant increase in its concentration level to approach that of fund. The marketization and mobility of R&D staff are much higher in corporate, and that's why the agglomeration of R&D personnel overtakes that of expenditure.

Another reason is the difference in the intensity of financial input and its growth rate among different regions. The intensity of R&D investment calculated by per capita expenditure needs to meet different requirements in different regions and different periods, thus leading to different growth rates of investment. On one hand, with great capacity to increase R&D investment, the per capita fund in the economically developed areas can grow much faster; on the other hand, a better economic structure requires a higher level of R&D activities, reflected on their needs for abundant fund, advanced equipment and high-tech talents. Generally speaking, the higher the economic structure and the greater the proportion of high-tech industry, the higher requirement is placed to per capita expenditure. Inevitably, there is a gap in the per capita expenditure of R&D personnel in developed areas and backward areas due to their structural differences, which leads to a more even distribution of personnel than that of expenditure statistically. However, if the per capita expenditure of the backward areas grows faster in a specific period, the degree of agglomeration of staff will increase and that of fund will decline relatively, resulting into the agglomeration measured in these two indicators merging gradually.

Figure 10-6 depicts the relationship between GRP per capita and per capita R&D expenditure at province level in 2010. It can be seen clearly from the figure that per capita internal expenditure of R&D personnel (full-time equivalent) exhibits a significant positive relationship with the local economy. A panel data is built, consisting of per capita internal expenditures of R&D personnel (full-time equivalent), per capita GRP, and the proportion of IT industry in total industrial output from 2002 to 2010, to analyze the influence of economic level and industrial structure on per capita internal expenditures. The proportion of IT industry in total industrial output measures the industrial structure. The expenditure of R&D activities in the past will affect current expenditure due to path dependence effect, so one-year and two-year lags of per capita internal expenditures are introduced as control variables, so are one-year lag GRP per capita and proportion of IT

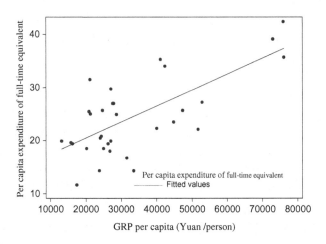

Figure 10-6   GRP per capita and per capita Internal Expenditure of R&D Personnel (Full-time Equivalent) in Different Regions in 2010.

Table 10-6   Estimation Results.

	Pooled OLS	RE	FE	SYSTEM-GMM
Ln(per capita expenditure) lag one phase	0.698*** (10.77)	0.698*** (10.77)	0.425*** (5.68)	0.403*** (4.36)
Ln(per capita expenditure) lag two phases	0.124* (1.96)	0.124* (1.96)	−0.011 (−0.15)	0.024 (0.32)
Ln(per capita GRP)	0.175 (0.90)	0.175 (0.90)	−0.014 (−0.06)	−0.058 (−0.22)
Ln(per capita GRP) lag one phase	−0.093 (−0.49)	−0.093 (−0.49)	0.477* (1.89)	0.661** (2.42)
Proportion of IT industry	0.004 (0.36)	0.004 (0.36)	0.009 (0.77)	0.029** (2.22)
Proportion of IT industry (lag phase one)	−0.005 (−0.46)	−0.005 (−0.46)	−0.009 (−0.73)	−0.024* (−1.79)
Constant term	−0.205 (−0.92)	−0.205 (−0.92)	−2.679* (−1.94)	−4.263** (−2.26)
Year dummy variable	No	No	Yes	Yes
Observed value	217	217	217	186

Note: ***, **, * Statistically significant at the 1%, 5% and 10%, respectively.

industry. However, the introduction of the lagged dependent variable makes it impossible to meet the requirement of the strict exogeneity. In order to obtain consistent estimates, the SYSTEM-GMM method is adopted, which could help estimate the dynamic autoregressive model and overcome the problem of endogeneity.

As is shown in the estimation results (Table 10-6), one-year lag of GRP per capita has significant effects on current per capita expenditure of R&D personnel, 1% increase of GRP per capita in the last year leading to 0.66% increase of per capita expenditure. While the impacts of current and one-year lag of proportion of IT industry are just the opposite, with the impact of the current being slightly higher, the industrial structure as measured by the proportion of the IT industry basically having no effect or slight effect on the per capita expenditure of R&D personnel.

10.4 Conclusion

R&D relocation is an important strategy for enterprises to achieve profit and growth objectives. For R&D activities, the push and pull forces of a district are the combined result of various factors, which can be divided into four dimensions: product market, innovation level, conditions of current location, and R&D inputs. The R&D relocation at micro level will lead to the redistribution of S&T and R&D activities at the macro level. The trends of agglomeration of S&T and R&D activities, especially industrial R&D activities, have been further strengthened along with R&D relocation in recent years. The proportion of internal expenditure on R&D of the eastern region increased from 59.4% to 66.5% during the period of 1998 to 2010, and the proportion of full-time equivalent of R&D personnel of the eastern region increased from 45.6% to 62.9%. During the same period, those proportions of the large- and medium-size industrial enterprises of the eastern region rose from 60.3% to 66.9% and from 43.3% to 65.3%, respectively. Measured with coefficient of variation, the degrees of concentration of fund raised for S&T activities and of the internal expenditure are much higher than that of personnel involved in S&T activities. But between 1997 and 2010, the level of the latter tended to increase while that of the former two declined, so did the agglomeration of total R&D investment. R&D activities are mainly concentrated in Guangdong, Jiangsu, Zhejiang, Beijing, etc., and the decline of the proportion of internal expenditures in Beijing is the dominating reason for the decrease in the degree of concentration of internal expenditure as a whole. The dominant position of Beijing in R&D internal expenditures has been gradually replaced by a few provinces and municipalities, as the proportions of Jiangsu and Guangdong provinces increased. The proportions of full-time equivalent of R&D staff remain to be the highest in Guangdong, Jiangsu, Zhejiang, and Beijing, but their advantages in personnel are relatively smaller than their advantages in financial aspect.

The distribution characteristics of R&D activities in large- and medium-size enterprises are similar to total R&D activities: investment mainly concentrates in the eastern region with increasing degree of agglomeration, and the input measured in full-time equivalent of R&D staff is being relocating to the eastern region at high speed. The degree of agglomeration of expenditures on R&D activities is significantly higher than that of staff, but the gap is keeping narrowing gradually in recent years. Such characteristics and changes of distribution could be attributed to two reasons: first, the difference in mobility between capital and scientific and technological personnel; second, the differences of intensity and growth rates of investment in different regions.

References

Autant-Bernard, C. (2006). R&D lab location. Evidence from the French case. Working Paper, CREUSET — University of Saint-Etienne.

Belderbos, R. (2001). Overseas Innovations by Japanese Firms: An Analysis of Patent and Subsidiary Data. *Research Policy*, 30(2), 313–332.

Belderbos, R. (2003). Entry Mode, Organizational Learning, and R&D in Foreign Affiliates: Evidence from Japanese Firms. *Strategic Management Journal*, 24(3), 235–259.

Belderbos, R., E. Lykogianni and R. Veugelers, (2008). Strategic R&D Location by Multinational Firms: Spillovers, Technology Sourcing, and Competition. *Journal of Economics & Management Strategy*, 17(3), 759–779.

Chung, W. and J. Alcácer (2002). Knowledge seeking and location choice of foreign direct investment in the United States. *Management Science*, 48(12), 1534–1554.

Cornet, M. and M. Rensman (2001). The location of R&D in the Netherlands: Trends, determinants and policy. CPB Netherlands Bureau for Economic Policy Analysis, The Hague.

Fang, H. (2005). Analysis of the Motives and Risks of Outsourcing of Corporate R&D. *Studies in International Technology and Economy*, (4), 21–25.

Fors, G. (1996). *R&D and Technology Transfer by Multinational Enterprises*. Stockholm, Sweden: Industrial Institute for Economic and Social Research.

Franck, B. and R. Owen (2003). *Fundamental R&D Spillovers and the Internationalization of a Firm's Research Activities*. Cowles Foundation Discussion Paper No. 1425.

Guo, T. and X. Kong (2009). R&D Strategy of Foreign Investment in China and our Countermeasures. *Red Flag Manuscript*, (8), 21–23.

Kumar, N. (2001). Determinants of Location of Overseas R&D Activity of Multinational Enterprises: The Case of US and Japanese Corporations. *Research Policy*, 30(1), 159–174.

Leiponen, A. and C. E. Helfat (2006). *Geographic Location and Decentralization of Innovation Activity*. Mimeo.

Li, W., S. Zhu and C. Wang (2004). A Survey of Private Enterprises' Relocation and Expansion Phenomenon: Evidence from Leqing City in Zhejiang Province. *On Economic Problems*, (9), 30–32.

Odagiri, H. and H. Yasuda (1996). The Determinants of Overseas R&D by Japanese Firms: An Empirical Study at the Industry and Company Levels. *Research Policy*, 25(5), 1059–1079.

Thursby, J. and M. Thursby (2006). *Here or There? A Survey of Factors in Multinational R&D Location and IP Protection.* Report to the Government/University/Industry Research Roundtable (December 1, 2006). Marion Ewing Kauffman Foundation, Washington, DC.

Xie, W., H. Lan, L. Jiang, and H. Xie (2001).Various Options of Technology Innovation in Enterprises. *Corporate Economy*, (6), 9–11.

Zejan, M. (1990). R&D Activities in Affiliates of Swedish Multinational Firms. *Scandinavian Journal of Economics*, 92(3), 487–500.

Chapter 11

New Industrial Division and Conflict Management in Metropolitan Area — Based on the Perspective of Industrial Chain Division

Wei Houkai

11.1 Conflicts Growing in Intensity in Metropolitan Area

Since the reform and opening-up, the fast-growing Chinese economy and the rapid process of industrialization in particular has expedited the process of urbanization. From the year 1978 to 2011, China's urban population increased from 172 million to 691 million, the urbanization rate increasing from 17.9% to 51.3% (see Figure 11-1). With the rapid increase of urban population and process of urbanization, a crop of metropolitan areas is emerging in recent years. The most typical ones are those metropolitan areas such as the Pearl River Delta (PRD), the Yangtze River Delta (YRD), the Beijing–Tianjin–Hebei region, Shangdong Peninsula, Wuhan, as well as Changsha–Zhuzhou–Xiangtan, Chengdu–Chongqing, and Zhongyuan. Measured by total population in the municipal districts of cities on a prefecture-level or above, China boasts 14 giant cities whose population exceeds four million, 30 super-large cities with a population of two to four million, 81 especially big cities with a population of one to two million, and 109 big cities with a population of 500,000 to one million in 2010. As it were, China has marched into a new era of overall competition among metropolitan areas. In other words, competition among regions in China is mainly manifested in overall competition among metropolitan areas, instead of intercity competition in the past.

With increasingly fierce competition, conflicts inside the metropolitan area are assuming increasing severity. Conflicts here refer to that in the metropolitan area, where the measures and action one side takes have

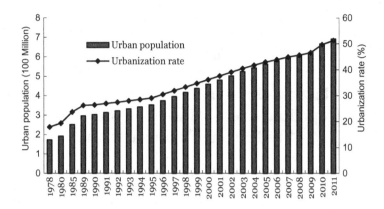

Figure 11-1   Change of China's Urban Population and Urbanization Rate.

exerted or will exert bad influence on the other side. Such conflicts are mainly of three types: economic, social, and environmental. The economic conflict, which is mainly reflected in all aspects of local economic activities, is a common phenomenon. For example, in October 2002, Shanghai decides to transfer all international and Hong Kong and Macao flights of Hongqiao Airport to Pudong International Airport, which directly increases the time and cost of logistics transportation among Shanghai and its surrounding cities (such as Suzhou and Wuxi), and thus impacts upon the industrial development of these cities. Upon that some cities propose to construct their own international airport (Tang and Li, 2005). For instance, a few years ago, for the purpose of taking on the industrial shift of the downtown and promoting suburb economy, Shanghai set up large industrial zones in the suburb, including nine municipal-level zones and a passel of county-level zones. For cities in Southern Jiangsu province, it seems that Shanghai builds an "anti-diffusion circle" on the border. In the Beijing–Tianjin–Hebei region, Beijing and Hebei cooperated to construct the Jingtang Port, and also Shenhua Group Corporation Ltd and Hebei made joint efforts to construct the Huanghua Port, which will exert a negative influence on the development of the Tianjin Port. In the aspect of industrial development, various regions racing to develop a certain industry causes heated fights for resources, market, and trained personnel, and even superfluous production capacity, which inevitably affect the earlier developed regions. All these are concrete conflicts in the metropolitan area. Also, social and environmental conflicts are quite common. For instance, the continuing spread of metropolitan area and the construction of industrial zones are gradually engulfing the peripheral fertile land, and thus results in environmental degradation.

It is to be remarked that the notion of regional conflicts is neutral. It has two sides, in that it may not only have damaging effects and but also arouse competition, which raises the resource allocation efficiency. The former is generally regarded as the destructive function, while the latter called the constructive function (Huang, 2002). Therefore, we should not consider regional conflicts only in a derogatory way. For example, some scholars define regional economic conflicts as "the subject of regional economy takes certain measures for the sake of regional interests to the detriment of other regions or even the whole society, which may leads the regional economic relations to violate from the ideal inter-regional balance" (Xu, 2003), which is derogative understanding as such. To a certain extent, although regional conflicts may affect one certain part inside the system negatively, the influence on the entire system might be negative or positive. The former is called malignant conflict, while the latter is called benign conflict. Malignant conflicts should be curbed and eliminated or at least solved by taking measures as they may exert a bad influence on one part of the entire system or the system itself. Benign conflicts are allowed in that it will not harm the entire system though it may jeopardize parts of the system. In such conflicts, if one side causes serious damage to another side, corresponding economic compensation should be offered or otherwise certain measures must be taken to solve it, according to the concrete condition.

In addition, regional conflicts may occur not only in the competition but also either in competition or cooperation. Even in the condition of a planned economy, regional conflicts have an objective existence. From the perspective of competition and cooperation, regional conflicts can be divided into four types: competitive conflicts, cooperative conflicts, competitive-cooperative conflicts, and non–competitive-cooperative conflicts. Here competitive and cooperative conflicts refer to conflicts that occur under the condition of competition or cooperation among different regions. Competitive-cooperative conflicts refer to conflicts occuring among the regions that both compete and cooperate with each other. And non–competitive-cooperative conflicts refer to conflicts that happen when different regions lack competition and cooperation. In some cases, although two different regions do not compete or cooperate with each other, they may also have conflicts, especially environmental conflicts and social conflicts.

11.2 To Adopt a Correct Attitude Toward Industrial Conflicts in Metropolitan Area

In metropolitan economic conflicts, the current prominent one is that different regions vie with one another to develop the same industry, or even the same product, which leads to identical industrial structure and reduplication of infrastructure. This is quite common in the PRD, YRD, Beijing–Tianjin–Hebei region, and so on, and cities (and even industrial zones) are competing fiercely with each other in bidding for investments and industrial development. To a certain extent, regional convergence of industrial structure may be regarded as the outcome of regional industrial competition and conflicts, and it is a neutral concept in that it can produce both positive and negative effects. However, in the previous discussion, the academia tends to be against the phenomenon of regional convergence of industrial structure and have a derogative understanding about it.

In recent years, although some scholars have made fine distinctions of normal and abnormal convergence (Wang, 1997) and desirable and undesirable convergence (Chen, 1998), or seen regional convergence of industrial structure as an objective economic law (Shi and Qi, 1999), but there are some other scholars or related government departments nowadays who still regard regional convergence of industrial structure as a persistent ailment that disturbs the sound development of the national economy. In their eyes, industrial structure convergence, which is a pronoun of withered regional industrial division of labor and specialization, seems only to be a kind of negative effect and merely leads to resources allocation efficiency loss. For example, some scholars believe that industrial structure convergence will not only cause malignant competition, wasteful investment, efficiency loss, serious duplicate construction, and surplus production capacity but also harm the overall quality of the national economy, affect the formation of scale economy, the upgrade of industrial technology, and the improvement of core competitiveness, which in consequence leads to violent ups and downs of the national economy (Han, 2001; Luo and Li, 2004). Obviously, such kind of a view is worth discussing. Next this issue will be analyzed from the following three aspects:

First of all, from the dynamic point of view, industrial structure convergence refers to a constantly rapidly rising tendency of industrial structural similarity among different regions. Currently, the domestic academia estimates the industrial structure convergence mainly by the structural similarity coefficient put forward by the United Nations Industrial Development Organization (UNIDO) in 1980 (Li and Chen, 2000; Yang and Bai, 2002; Hong, 2004). The computing formula is:

$$S_{ij} = \sum_k x_{ik} x_{jk} \bigg/ \sqrt{\sum_k x_{ik}^2 \sum_k x_{jk}^2} \qquad (11\text{-}1)$$

In the formula, S_{ij} is the structural similarity coefficient between the regions i and region j; x_{ik}, x_{jk} are respectively region i and region j's industry k economic indicator (such as output value, added value, sales income, employment, and so on) takes how much proportion in the entire industry. S_{ij} ranges from zero to one. When it is zero, it indicates that the industrial structures of the two different regions are completely different; when it is one, it indicates that the industrial structures of the two different regions are completely the same. The more similar the industrial structures of two different regions are, the similarity coefficient is larger, and conversely, the coefficient is smaller.

It can be seen that the similarity coefficient measures the difference of regional industrial structure. The implicit theoretical precondition is: inter-regional division of labor is also a kind of inter-sectoral division of labor. In other words, if there is only inter-sectoral division of labor among different regions, the rise of similarity coefficient indicates the convergence of industrial structure, which is accompanied by the weakening inter-regional division of labor. In fact, such hypothesis as "mere existence of inter-sectoral division of labor" is impossible in today's society. It is only applied to the initial stage of economic development when the industrial division of labor is much backward. Furthermore, the method of the similarity coefficient is a static analyzing method, which judges the rationality of the future structure on the basis of the old industrial structure, even though the old one is not rational.

Second, the industrial structural convergence measured by UNIDO's similarity coefficient is a kind of sectoral structure convergence. With the rapid economic and social development, the similarity coefficient of different regions will increase day by day, and the tendency of regional industrial structure convergence is inevitable. To a certain extent, the regional industrial structure convergence is an inexorable trend of the economic and social development, at least so seen from the larger territorial scope and the higher industry classification. Taking China's provinces and two-digit SIC industrial sectors for example, the industrialization of poor provinces in the western region had lagged far behind in the past. The industrial activity there mainly focused on mining and a few raw material industries, while processing industries, and even raw material industries, are highly concentrated in the more developed coast provinces. Under such unreasonable division of labor, the structural similarity coefficient is quite low. With the promotion of western industrialization, some economically backward provinces begin to develop metallurgy industry, chemical industry, mechanical industry, medical industry, and food industry as well, which may inevitably leads to the increase of the similarity coefficient of industrial structure. In fact, the convergence of sectoral structure is the demonstration of regional coordinated development. It complies with the thinking of the scientific outlook on development. Of course, from the perspective of protecting the vested interest of the minor developed regions, the convergence is kind of "unreasonable", since it has robbed away the cheese of some advanced regions via certain appropriate and reasonable regional competition, thereby breaking the previous unreasonable regional division of labor and benefit distribution.

Third, the domestic and overseas experience has shown that the convergence of the industrial structure does not mean the weakening of the division of labor and the specification among the regions. In recent years, with the promotion of the economic globalization and the rapid development of science and technology, the industrial division of labor transformed from the traditional inter-sectoral division to intra-sectoral division, that is inter-product division within the same industrial sector. It further developed to the industrial chain division of labor. Upon this new regional division of labor, on one hand, the tendency of convergence of industrial structure appears, on the other, the regional industrial division of labor and the specification deepens continuously. In other words, the convergence of industrial structure does not mean the weakening of the regional industrial

Table 11-1   Sectoral Specialization and Functional Specialization of US Cities.

Local population	Sectoral specialization			Functional specialization in management against production			
	1977	1987	1997	1950	1970	1980	1990
5,000,000–19,397,717	0.375	0.369	0.348	+10.2%	+22.1%	+30.8%	+39.0%
1,500,000–4,999,999	0.287	0.275	0.257	+0.3%	+11.0%	+21.7%	+25.7%
500,000–1,499,999	0.352	0.338	0.324	−10.9%	−7.8%	−5.0%	−2.1%
250,000–499,999	0.450	0.409	0.381	−9.2%	−9.5%	−10.9%	−14.2%
75,000–249,999	0.499	0.467	0.432	−2.1%	−7.9%	−12.7%	−20.7%
67–75,000	0.708	0.692	0.661	−4.0%	−31.7%	−40.4%	−49.5%

Note: In the table, the sectoral specialization is Gini coefficient, calculated according to 2-digit SIC manufacturing sectors. Its calculation equation is $\frac{1}{2} \sum_h |s_h - \bar{s}_h|$. In the equation, s_h and $\bar{s}_h$ are, respectively, the local and national shares of employment in sector h. The fuctional specialization is the percentage difference from the national average in the number of executives and managers per production worker (occupied in precision production, fabrication, or assembly).
Source: Duranton and Puga (2002).

division of labor. On the contrary, the convergence of industrial structure and the deepening of regional division of labor can exist together. A recent study shows that, in recent years, the sectoral specification of US cities is diminishing, namely there is the tendency of convergence of industrial structure, and the functional specification is increasing gradually. The industrial division of labor among cities is deepening (see Table 11-1). In other words, the management function of metropolis is strengthening. However, the medium and small cities are strengthening their production and manufacturing functions (Duranton and Puga, 2002).

Take the clothing industry of Zhejiang province as an example. At present, 85% of the textile and clothing industry of Zhejiang province is concentrated in Shaoxing, Ningbo, Hangzhou, Jiaxing, Wenzhou, Huzhou, and other places. Although these cities are all developing the clothing industry, there is great difference in the products. For instance, Ningbo emphasizes men clothing, which is China's manufacturing and sales base of shirting and suiting, with a large number of brand-name enterprises. Wenzhou pays more attention to men's clothing and casual clothing, Hangzhou highlights women's clothing, while Huzhou focuses on children's clothing, being the largest manufacturing and sales base of children's clothing in China. Its

Table 11-2 The Specialization of Clothing Production in Zhejiang Province.

Region	Specialized domain	Features of industrial development
Ningbo	Men's clothing	More than 1600 clothing factories, the manufacturing capacity of suite is 4.6 million, that of the shirts is 62 million. It's China's manufacturing and sales base of suites and shirt with a large number of brand-name enterprises.
Wenzhou	Men's clothing, casual clothing	More than 2000 clothing factories, more than 200 suite factories whose manufacturing capacity is above 50,000, 10 factories whose sales volume exceeds RMB 100 million.
Hangzhou	Women's clothing	More than 1000 factories, the number of women's clothing produced manually is more than 10 million, and the sales volume has exceeded RMB 1 billion.
Zhili, Huzhou	Children's clothing	The nation's largest manufacturing and sales base, of which the market share is 15%.
Chengzhou	Necktie industry	More than 1000 necktie factories, and the annual necktie production is 250 million, taking 80% of the nation's production and 33% of the world's production.

Source: Collected by the author.

market share takes up 15% of the national market, and the number of collars produced by Chengzhou reaches 0.25 billion, taking 80% of the national production and 33% of the world's production (see Table 11-2). In the YRD region, in recent years, there is the tendency of regional division of labor according to the different links and stages of industrial chains. The transnational companies and the enterprises in Zhejiang and Jiangsu gradually establish the headquarters, the regional headquarters, and R&D organization in Shanghai central area and build the manufacturing base both in the suburbs of Shanghai and in Jiangsu and Zhejiang provinces, forming an integrated pattern of industrial chain division of labor.

From this, we can see that the phenomenon of structural convergence caused by regional industrial conflict will not weaken the industrial division of labor, as presumed by some scholars. On the contrary, the structural convergence can exist together with the deepening of the labor division. Of course, if constructing repeatedly on a low level, various regions are racing to develop same industry and even same product by the self-established system, thereby causing excessive competition. The industrial structural convergence caused by malignant conflicts will lead to weakening interregional division and decreasing efficiency of resource allocation. That kind of structural convergence shall be prevented and resolved appropriately with corresponding measures. Besides the control of entry of market, the more important is to use the conflicts management means to lead the industries to become an integrated industrial division system. The new industrial division system can better solve the conflicts between the structural convergence and the deepening of the labor division.

11.3 New Industrial Division and Pattern of Metropolitan Labor Division

In recent years, with the rapid development of the communication technology as well as the quick promotion of economic globalization, there is great change, irrespective of the regional labor division within a country or the international labor division. The traditional labor division tends to change to the new labor division. With regard to the developmental process, the evolution of regional industrial division experiences three stages. The first stage is the inter-sectoral or inter-industrial division of labor, which means the specialized production by different industrial sectors in different regions. The second stage is the intra-sectoral or intra-industrial division of labor, which means that different regions develop the same industrial sector but the product's type is not the same. This specialization can be called the product specialization. The third stage is the industrial chain division of labor. That is to say, although many regions are producing one product, each region conducts the specialized production according to the different links, processes, and even modules of the industrial chain. Some scholars abroad call this the functional specialization (Duranton and Puga, 2002). Some scholars in China also call this industrial chain labor division as the intra-industrial labor division (Zhao, 2003). This is of course a misinterpretation. Because in the three major links of the industrial chain or the value chain of products, namely, the technology, production and sales, the activities of R&D, design, procurement, and marketing have expanded to other industries, belonging to the producer services. In fact, the industrial chain's labor division is the result of vertical disintegration and industrial merge. Therefore, it is not scientific to call the industrial chain's labor division as the intra-industrial division of labor, which usually means the labor division of the same industry and of the different products.

The so-called new industrial division is a concept as opposed to the traditional industrial division, being a theoretical summary of the new phenomenon and new tendency of international labor division since the 1980s. Although during the 1980s, there were some studies on the new industrial division of labor, the relevant study of China is very few (Meng and Li, 2000; Meng *et al.*, 2000). The studies at home mainly center around the new international labor division and the intra-product trade (Zhao, 2003; Tian, 2005a, 2005b), but they barely concern the new regional division of labor within a country. Up to now, the domestic academia lacks acknowledged definition of the new labor division. From the literature, new labor division is a relative concept, which relates to the traditional inter-sectoral division of labor and contains intra-sectoral and industrial chain division of labor. Table 11-3 has listed the basic features of each regional industrial division and their comparison. As opposed to the traditional inter-sectoral division, the new regional labor division differs widely with regard to the specialization pattern, labor division features, industry demarcation, labor division model, spatial differentiation, and dynamic mechanism.

In the literature of new labor division, at present, many domestic scholars have used the concept of "intra-product labor division", however, different scholars have different disintegration of it. For example, some scholars interpret the intra-product labor division as the labor division which is carried out according to the different procedures of the same product or the different technology content of the parts (Zhao, 2003), some just interprets it as the labor division whose different procedures, sections, and links of manufacturing and supply process are carried out in different spaces and then finally become the finished product at the same place" (Zhuang, 2005). The former one is a narrow interpretation, defining the "intra-product labor

Table 11-3 Basic Patterns and Features of Regional Industrial Division.

	Traditional regional labor division	New regional labor division	
Labor division type	Inter-sectoral labor division	Intra-sectoral labor division	Industrial chain labor division
Specialization pattern	Sectoral specialization	Products specialization	Functional specialization
Labor division features	In different industries	In different products of the same industry	In different links, procedures and modules of industrial chain
Industrial demarcation	Clear	Relatively clear	Weakened
Labor division model	Mainly vertical labor division	Mainly horizontal labor division	Mixed labor division
Spatial differentiation	In different industries	In different products of the same industry	In the different links, procedures and modules of the value chain
Dynamic mechanism	Regional advantage or the difference of resource endowment	Difference of product and consumer preference, overlapping demand, and economy of scale	Difference of resource endowment and technological level, economy of scale, and economy of industrial linkage

Source: Collected by the author.

division" from only the manufacturing link, however, the latter defines the "intra-product labor division" from the whole industrial chain. It is a comprehensive interpretation. Obviously, no matter its comprehensive or narrow interpretation, the industrial chain's labor division includes the "intra-product labor division". In the context of economic globalization and e-commerce, the technological development, production, sales, and other links of the products, the different procedures, sections, and modules of the manufacturing process and the different parts can be regarded as part of the industrial chain. Therefore, the "intra-product labor division" pointed out by some scholars belong to the realm of the labor division of the industrial chain.

However, from the perspective of the precision of the terms, the concept of "intra-product labor division" can easily be misunderstood. This is because any classification of the products is only relative. One product can be disintegrated into different parts or according to the manufacturing process, and it can be disintegrated into different procedures and modules. From the perspective of the assembly or integration, it's an integrated final product. However, as for the enterprises participating in the labor division, the procedures, modules, or parts undertaken by them can be also regarded as a product. Obviously, with the economic and social development and the scientific progress, the product types can be more specific, and product differentiation is inevitable. Under these circumstances, the scientific nature of the concept will be doubted. What's more important, when this labor division extends from the manufacturing link to the technological development and the sales link, it will break the boundaries of the industry, extending to the other manufacturing sectors or even the tertiary industry area. Under these circumstances, it is not accurate to define it as the "intra-product labor division". Therefore, from the angle of specification, the employment of the labor division of the industrial chain is more scientific.

In recent years, in some advanced regions of China, regional labor division has transformed from the traditional inter-sectoral labor division to the intra-sectoral division and to the labor division of the industrial chain. From the angle of the industrial chain labor division, we can see that the value chain of one enterprise can be divided into different links, namely from the headquarters, R&D, design of products, procurement of raw materials, manufacturing of parts, assembly, storage and delivery of finished products, and marketing to after sales service, and each link can be invested in different regions. In this context, with the quickening of the economic globalization and the integration of the regional economy, at present, the PRD, YRD, and Beijing–Tianjin–Hebei region will divide the labor according to different links, procedures, or even modules of the industrial chain. For example, in those metropolitan areas, the central area will emphasize the links of the

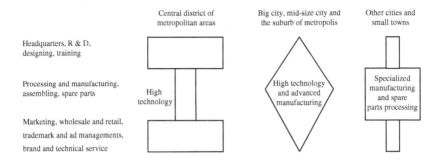

Figure 11-2   Labor Division System of Industrial Chain in the Metropolitan Areas.
Source: By the author.

headquarters, R&D, design, training, marketing, wholesaling and retailing, trademark and ad management, and technological service, thereby forming the structure of the "dumb bell", which is thick at both ends and thin in the middle. The suburbs (industrial zone) of the metropolises and other big and medium cities will develop the hi-tech industry and advanced manufacturing industry, thereby forming the structure of the shape of a diamond, which is big in the middle and small at both ends. The other surrounding cities and small towns will specifically develop some manufacturing industry and parts production, thereby forming the shape of "bar" which is thick in the middle and thin at both ends (see Figure 11-2).

In the system of labor division of industrial chain, the central area of the metropolis becomes the management control center since the headquarters, R&D, and design center, operating center and so on, are concentrated in this region. Since the senior administration, finance, law, advertisements, as well as R&D's functions are concentrated in the company HQs, the cities with concentrated headquarters naturally become the geographic "controlling point" of the regional, national, and the global economy. New York, London, and Tokyo are the three biggest global management control centers. Many companies set their headquarters or the regional headquarters there. The other major comprehensive international metropolis like Paris, Chicago, Los Angeles, Osaka, Hong Kong, and Singapore also concentrate the headquarters of the transnational companies or the regional headquarters. We can regard them as the international management control center of the world or of the region. In China, from the perspective of the developmental tendency, with the quickening of the regional integration and the economic globalization, the concentrating tendency of the companies' headquarters will be reinforced. In this way, some central cities with convenient transportation and advanced informational and financial services will gradually become important management control centers. Besides Hong Kong, Shanghai and Beijing can develop into national management control centers in the near future and into the regional international management control centers in the long run. However, Guangzhou, Qingdao, Dalian, Wuhan, Xi'an, Chongqing, Chengdu, and other cities can develop into the regional management control center in China.

11.4 Conflict Management Based on Industrial Chain Division in Metropolitan Area

From the angle of the management science, the American scholar L. D. Brown has investigated the relationship between conflict and organizational performance, finding that there exists an inverted U-shape interrelationship between the two. Namely, when the conflict level in organization is too high or too low, the organizational performance would decrease, and only when the conflict level in organization is moderate, would the organizational performance be highest (Tian, 2003). But this inverted U-shape relation is not entirely suitable for regional conflict, especially regional environmental conflict, since some regional conflicts *per se* are malignant and destructive and measures to controlling the conflict level within the "appropriate range" do not exist. For example, waste drainage from factories would pollute the water source area and the lower reaches of the river, exerting negative impact on other regions and overall interest. This is a typical malignant conflict. And this is also where significant difference between regional conflict and management conflict lies.

As for industrial conflict in metropolitan area, moderate regional conflict is inevitable. Especially in the environment with fierce regional competition, market competition inevitably brings about industrial conflict among all kinds of regions. For example, each district in Beijing tries to attract company HQs and R&D organizations to set up shop, CBD and Financial Street attract financial institutions, each zone of Zhongguancun Science Park (ZSP) attracts new and high-technology enterprises, and suburban counties in Beijing and cities and counties in Hebei around Beijing compete with each other in developing the manufacturing industry, which would certainly trigger off all kinds of conflicts of interest. These conflicts exist widely in real economy, and are the results of regional competition. In market economic system, moderate industrial conflicts among regions do not certainly exert negative impact on the whole. In many cases, the moderate conflict can be transformed into a kind of driving force, stimulating vitality of regions and strengthening regional competition. In the cases of Shanghai and Southern Jiangsu, in the metropolitan area, competition is the basis and premise of regional cooperation. In recent years, Shanghai industries spread toward Southern Jiangsu and their cooperation is strengthened, for which the key reason is the strong competitive pressure imposed by Southern Jiangsu instead of on a voluntary basis of Shanghai industries. In contrast, in Beijing–Tianjin–Hebei metropolitan area, the economic foundation of districts in Hebei around Beijing and Tianjin is too weak to impose competition threat to Beijing and Tianjin. Both Beijing and Tianjin take the mentality "not playing with you", thus industrial diffusion and cooperation are naturally impeded and the situation "there is no grass under big trees" arises. This phenomenon is very typical in Wuhan metropolitan area.

Of course, if this kind of industrial conflict is too fierce and exceeds a certain limit, regional division may be weakened and the overall efficiency of resources allocation may be decreased. For example, in some metropolitan areas, with or without conditions, each district is racing to develop the same industry, there is no division, and cooperation and system is established arbitrarily, giving rise to malignant competition. Thus the situation of low-level duplicate construction arises. In order to improve this situation, the key point is obviously to strengthen the idea of conflict management, exert sufficiently the function of market mechanism and government in planning and guidance, refer to advantageous conditions of each district in metropolitan area, and form a new nation-wide integrated industrial division system that is based on labor division of industrial chain, so that malignant conflict in industrial development of each district can be alleviated and eliminated. The industrial development pattern featuring overall competition advantages, positive interaction, and mutually beneficial and multi-win cooperation shall be formed. This philosophy of development is called conflict management strategy in the metropolitan area based on labor division of industrial chain. It can give full play to the basic role of market mechanism in resource allocation and also promote regional economic integration and form a good development pattern of complementary advantages, reasonable division, and reciprocity and mutual benefit. It should be pointed out that the conflict management in metropolitan area we emphasize is different from the management of organizational conflict in management science. Organizational conflict management put more emphasis on taking advantage of conflicts to manage and improve organizational performance, while here we emphasize the effective management and control of regional conflict.

Obviously this new industrial division pattern is the result of the autonomous location selection of enterprises under the guidance of market mechanism and government. The process of autonomous location selection of enterprises is influenced by the dominating function of market mechanism and the guidance and planning of government. Therefore, in the metropolitan area, in order to form a new integrated industrial division system, we shall first break the regional segmentation and administrative monopoly, give full play to the basic role of market mechanism, encourage rational movement of factors, and gradually form the integration of markets for land, capital, property rights, talents, technology, and labor. Second, the integration of regional planning, specify industrial development direction, and spatial distribution of each area must be developed and "double regulation" must be implemented, with the combination of industrial guidance and spatial guidance. Particularly, according to development conditions and functional orientation of different areas differentiated market access standards need to be formulated with regard to industrial type, technical content, land use efficiency, energy consumption and pollutant emission. Thirdly, in line with the new division principle, achieve functional complementation and staggered development. Apart from the staggered development of sectors based on traditional inter-sector division, this type of staggered development also includes staggered development of product and function based on the new labor division. In the staggered development of function, the central district of metropolis should put more emphasis on such links as headquarters, R&D, design, brand and marketing, and the suburbs of metropolis, and the small- and medium-sized cities shall attach importance to such links as production of parts, parts supporting, assembling, and procurement and storage, thus forming the integrated functional division pattern. Fourth, the guidance and coordination of policy need to be strengthened, the integration of investment information platform must be developed, the investment and capital attraction of industrial chain must be implemented, the formation of leading and competitive industrial chain must be promoted, and a bunch of internationally competitive industrial clusters must be formed. Fifth, around the construction of leading and competitive industries, the metropolis must be considered as the center; the construction of transportation network must be strengthened, especially inter-city fast tracks and railways; the formation of 1-hour or 2-hour industrial supporting circles must be accelerated; and industrial supporting ability in metropolitan area must be enhanced. This industrial support and complementation include the support from not only infrastructure but also production, residential conditions, and entrepreneurial environment. In the situation where regional competition becomes increasingly fierce, the local industrial support ability has become an important condition for accelerating development and attracting more investment and capital.

References

Chen Y. (1998). Estimate of the Convergence of the Industrial Structure as Well as the Desirability and Undesirability. *China Industrial Economy*, (4), 37–43.

Duranton, G. and D. Puga (2002). *From Sectoral to Functional Urban Specialization*. Cambridge, MA: National Bureau of Economic Research.

Han B. (2001). Getting Rid of the Misunderstanding of the Convergence of the Industrial Structure. *The Friend of Leaders*, (1), 27–28.

Hong S. (2004). An Empirical Analysis on the Similarization of Regional Industrial Structure in China. *Journal of FIEM & FSA*, (1), 57–61.

Huang S. (2002). *Modern Enterprise Management*. Beijing: Economy & Management Publishing House.

Li R. and J. Chen (2000). Convergence of Regional Industrial Structure and Countermeasures of Development. *Research on Financial and Economic Issues*, (8), 44–47.

Luo S. and M. Li (2004). Reasons and Countermeasures for the Convergence of China's Industrial Structure. *Journal of Changsha Railway University*, (4), 94–96.

Meng Q. and G. Li (2000). Progress in Studies on the New International Division of Labor. *World Regional Studies,* (2), 31–37.

Meng Q., G. Li and K. Yang (2000). The Dynamic of the New International Division of Labor: Conception and Mechanism. *China Soft Science,* (9), 113–117.

Shi K. and Y. Qi (1999). Convergence of Industrial Structure Obeys Objective Economic Rule, but Product's Structure's Convergence Disobeys Market Economy's Rule. *Economic Survey,* (1), 65–66.

Tang M. and Q. Li (2005). Policy Analysis of Regional Economic Conflict: A Case study of Competition for Airport Construction in Yangtze River Delta. *Municipal Administration & Technology,* (1), 7–8.

Tian H. (2003). Conflict Management. *Management & Fortune,* (6), 65–66.

Tian W. (2005a). Definition, Quantification and Comparative Analysis of Intra-product Trade. *Finance & Trade Economics,* (5), 77–79.

Tian W. (2005b). A Study of Determination of Intra-product Trade Model and Interest Distribution. *International Business,* (5), 9–13.

United National Industrial Development Organization (UNIDO). (1980). *Summary and Tendency of Each Country's Industrialization (Chinese edition).* Beijing: China Translation & Publishing Corporation.

Wang S. (1997). Judgment of the Two Values of Convergence of Regional Industrial Structure and Definition Criteria. *Journal of Zhongnan University of Finance and Economics,* (3), 40–45.

Xu Y. (2003). Short-term Behavior of Local Government and Conflict of Regional Economy. *Theoretical Research,* (3), 6–9.

Yang L. and F. Bai (2002). Industrial Structure Convergence across Regions. *Journal of Lanzhou University,* 30(3), 106–110.

Zhao W. (2003). On Comparative Advantage of China's Manufacture Industry Under New Worldwide Division Structure. *China Industrial Economy,* (8), 32–37.

Zhuang S. (2005). The Intra-product Division and Modularized Production in the Network Economy. *Journal of Nanjing University of Finance and Economics,* (4), 16–20.

Chapter 12

Analysis of Urban Industrial Relocation's Incentive, Approaches and Effects — Taking Beijing as an Example

Fu Xiaoxia, Wei Houkai and Wu Lixue

Since the 1950s and 1960s, with the rapid development of urban economy, most metropolises around the world have experienced enormous changes in demographic and industrial distribution, in line with the tendency that labor and manufacturing industries in large cities have relocated from central areas to the suburb, even the surrounding small towns. For instance, from 1960 onward, the enterprise relocation from central urban areas to the suburb account for one-third in all types of relocation in the UK (Keeble, 1976). In recent years, with the acceleration of urbanization and prosperity in large cities, China's industrial suburbanization is in acceleration mode as well (Jin, 2005), thus the industrial relocation issue is becoming increasingly important. For example, the metropolises such as Beijing, Shanghai, and Guangzhou, have renovated the old urban areas in succession by implementing the strategy of "retreating from the secondary industry and engaging in the tertiary industry", which has substantially regulated the original industrial distribution and land utilization, and promoted the transfer of industrial enterprises from central urban districts to the surrounding small-sized towns.

Since the reform from 1978, the market mechanism has begun to play more and more important role in China's resource allocation. However, China's industrial relocation is confronted with special contradiction, for that the market liberalization of land is still far behind others such as consumer goods. Therefore, the key issues, in both theoretical and practical sense, are how to deal properly with the relationship among city-dwellers, governments, and enterprises, especially how to find the optimal solutions to coordinate the partial land market and governments' guidance of urban land. Nevertheless, current domestic empirical studies on enterprise relocation are far from enough, and those on urban industrial relocation could rarely be found (Bai, 2003). This chapter plans to figure out the general mechanism of industrial relocation and changes in urban industrial location of China, which is in accordance with basic rules of urban industry's spatial distribution, by comparing industrial relocation and enterprise relocation under the market conditions. We study a typical case, the industrial relocation in Beijing since 1985, to serve the purpose of (1) analyzing effects on urban industrial distribution exerted by factors such as urban development and industrial structure change and (2) showing how the aims, approaches, and policies of relocation would affect the final efficiency of the migrations. By tentatively elaborating the special situations, influential factors, and undergoing experiences, this chapter plans to provide some policy basis for Beijing and other cities in their attempts to promote industrial relocation and regional economic development, and as well serve as a reference for further research on China's industrial relocation and enterprise migration.

12.1 General Theories of Urban Industrial Relocation

12.1.1 *Urban Industrial Relocation: Special Adjustments of Enterprise Locations*

The change in spatial location of enterprises, which provides the micro foundation for industrial transfer, is the main driving force for economic spatial distribution. In the modern economy, there are two types of changes in enterprise spatial location. The first one is enterprise migration, which means the enterprise would make adjustments in its whole or partial spatial locations, based on its development needs, room for expansion in the local area, location, and infrastructural conditions. The second type refers to forced relocation featured by governments' forcible promotion of enterprise location adjustments by administrative means such as planning and policy drive. In a market economy, most of the location adjustments are out of enterprises' own will, and forced relocations represent only a tiny proportion. On the contrary, in planned economy and transition economy, forced relocations are quite common. Take China for example, since the reform and opening-up, urban industrial relocations, namely the government-led adjustments of urban industrial distribution, have exerted substantial influences on the functional distribution, economic development, and urban residents' life in some large cities.

Theoretically, urban industrial relocation falls into the category of the change in enterprise spatial distribution. Nonetheless, in terms of incentives for relocation, approaches, and distance, it has great difference from general enterprise migration in a market economy. Thus we can conclude that it is a special kind of enterprise relocation. The uniqueness of urban industrial relocation, especially the distinctive feature that the motivations of relocation is government-dominated, results in the fact that it has particular formation mechanisms and relocation ways, along with the disparity in relocation effects from enterprises under the general market conditions. First of all, urban industrial relocation is part of governments' overall considerations of adjustments of original industrial distribution, especially land utilization of industries, for the purposes such as environmental protection, city landscape planning, and urban industrial development. Hence, urban industrial relocation is featured as passive, in which the enterprises often are put into an inferior position, in sharp contrast to those voluntary enterprise moves. Second, owing to the fact that this type of urban industrial relocation is predominated by governments, particularly the destinations are usually prescribed or decided by them, it is featured by inner-city short distance move which is mainly from central urban areas to suburbs and satellite cities. Further, urban industrial relocation is mainly an overall move, meaning that those medium- and small-sized companies, whose production, sales, management, and even staff and their homes all move from the original place to the new address. In addition, since urban relocation is forced by governments and most enterprises getting involved are state-owned, governments usually grant the enterprises relocation subsidies and land preferential policies at the in-migration destination. Table 12-1 summarized these characteristics above.

12.1.2 *Optimal Use of Urban Land: Theoretical Foundation of Industrial Relocation*

Land structure, a vital aspect of spatial location structure, refers to the spatial combination of land occupation as a result of various socio-economic

Table 12-1   Urban Industrial Relocation vs. Voluntary Enterprise Migration.

	Urban industrial relocation	Voluntary enterprise migration
Incentives	Government planning and adjustments	Enterprise development/market environment/government policy
Ways	Mainly overall	Overall/partial
Distance	Inner area, short distance	Inner area/outer area/multinational
Subsidies	Municipal governments/ emigrant and immigrant governments	Immigrant governments

Source: Author.

activities. With respect to the inner side of a city, production, life, trans-portation, and other types of economic and social activities need to occupy a certain amount of land in specific areas. Land utilization is featured by exclu-siveness, thus land occupation of various activities and its spatial layout in urban areas contribute to the structure of urban land use (Chen, 1993). The key to the realization of appropriate city planning and optimal use of urban land is the proper layout and use of various factors in economic activities, among which the decisive aspect is enterprise layout. The urban economic theory called bid rent model, which argues that spatial location can be based upon enterprises' different paying ability, can be viewed as a reference of urban land-use planning (Fujita, 1989).

The bid rent model depicts the fact that various economic activities will choose the right place near or far from the center of city, due to the different marginal paying abilities decided by their marginal productivity or profit getting from the location. Figure 12-1 illustrates the basic principles of this land-use scene. Assume the economy of a city could be simply categorized into agriculture, manufacture, and services, and their land utilization effi-ciency increases in sequence. Services are most sensitive to the enterprise's location and the distance to business central of the city; their production would be more efficient nearer to central areas. Agriculture is the most insensitive industry to location, namely, its production efficiency is least influenced by the distance to central areas. Therefore, the three sectors' paying ability varies a lot, with agriculture being the weakest, manufacture

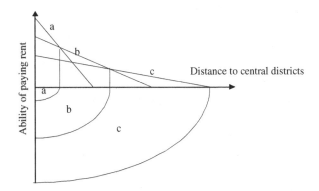

Figure 12-1   The Optimal Structure of Urban Land Utilization.

Note: a, b and c represent services, manufacture and agriculture industry, respectively.

industry in the middle, and services the strongest. No matter the result of market competition or demand for optimal use of urban land, the fact is that the most able payer, namely the service industry, should be located closest to city center, manufacture comes the second, and agriculture the farthest. Hence, urban land is distributed like circles, delimited by the crossing points of various industries with different paying ability.

Known from the above, enterprise are motivated to adjust their locations when failing to meet the demand of optimal land allocation. In a market economy, competition of different enterprises could spontaneously modulate their respective location in accordance with land prices. In contrast, in a planned economy, this modulation is achieved primarily by governments' city planning and land utilization planning. In China, though market mechanism has been gradually introduced to urban land exploitation, the government still has decisive influence on land utilization and urban industrial relocation. Specifically, the government takes three aspects into consideration when making firm relocation decisions. First, considering the necessity of improving residents' living environment, the dirty industries should be relocated to sparsely populated suburbs. Second, since services need more land near the central districts, some industries should be moved correspondingly to more peripheral regions, even when all the industries expand in the same proportion to the booming of urban areas. Third, during the process of urban economy development, different industries' paying ability would accordingly change with the upgrading of industrial structure, thus urban land use layout would not remain the same.

12.2 General Situations of Industrial Relocation in Beijing

Since the early founding of PRC, Beijing has chosen the industrial development pattern that placed more emphasis on heavy industry, in accordance with its aim of setting up independent industrial systems. Due to historical reasons, the manufacture industries occupying a large amount of land were dispersedly distributed in urban Beijing, leading to low efficiency of land utilization and poor living environment of the citizens. Statistics show that, in May 1999, there were 783 manufacture enterprises in the planned central area, occupying 28.34 million sqm and constituting 8.74% of the whole land, which was 324 sq km. Beijing failed to satisfy needs that highlight the city's functions of being the capital, having high land-use efficiency, and increase in land value as its industrial land is featured by large occupation and low land-use intensity and efficiency. With the development of the city, increasing conflicts have emerged between land for industries, especially the manufacturing industry, and that for other urban construction needs. In order to achieve reconciliation between industrial distribution and urban development, since 1985 the government has made a series of adjustments of geographical distribution of various industries in the whole city. Generally speaking, industrial relocation in Beijing has experienced three stages: (1) disturbance reduction, (2) distribution readjustment, and (3) Olympic preparation and new urban master planning implementation.

The first phase ranged from 1985 to 1995, when more attention was focused on pollution and disturbance problems brought by dispersed, small-sized, and high-pollution industrial enterprises. Thus the government set targets for those enterprises with time limits. For those failing to fulfill the target, forcible measure such as "closure, suspension, merger, shifting and relocation"[1] were implemented. Eventually, 294,000 sqm of land, worth RMB 1.228 billion were transferred in total 57 relocation programs. During this period, the relocated enterprises were featured by "tiny, dispersed, and small", namely, the transferred areas were tiny, transferred places were

---

[1]That is to close down, suspend operation, merge with others, shift to different line of production, and relocate the factories.

dispersed, and the transferred money was small. The enterprise relocation is basically operated in compliance with the simple model of "original scale and original plant site", which means that the area of new plant site and the size of new firms are roughly same as the old ones.

The second period lasted from 1996 to 2001, when the Beijing municipal government promulgated a series of documents and policies, including *Solutions to Polluting and Daily Life-Disturbing Enterprises Relocation of Beijing*, *Planning of Industrial Distribution Readjustment of Beijing*, and *Executive Solutions to Industrial Enterprise Relocation within Third and Fourth Ring Roads of Beijing, etc.* These measures have expanded the scope of relocated enterprises, and unfolded basic principles such as the strict adherence to products' restructuring, promotion of technical advance, improvement in the quality and efficacy of economic growth, and guarantee of the maintenance and appreciation of state assets value. Meanwhile, corresponding preferential policies relevant to enterprise relocation have been set out, such as land-transferring fees return and tax exemption. During this period, enterprise relocation work has stepped into the stage of integration of relocation and products' restructuring, when 112 relocation transfer programs are finished, with 4.211 million sqm land being transferred in total worth RMB 196 billion.

The third period lasted from 2001 onward. Taking the 2008 Beijing Olympics into consideration and putting *Urban Master Planning of Beijing (2004–2020)* into practice, the Beijing government broke the original concentric circle model of urban sprawl. Following the rule of "Two axle–Two belt–Multi-center" to reshape urban planning layout, Beijing shifted the priority of urban industrial relocation from curbing partial environmental pollution to the overall improvement of urban environments, from adjusting urban industrial layouts to optimizing functional layouts. It was planned that, before the 2008 Olympics, around 200 industrial enterprises within the fourth ring road would be relocated, and in the neighborhood of 4.5 million sqm urban land would be vacated. The Olympics and the new *Urban Master Planning* set more strict rules on the environment quality and industrial enterprises' site selection. With the increasing market and international orientation of China, higher needs are put forward to relocated enterprises' ability to survive and further develop.

12.3 Typical Cases of Urban Industrial Relocation in Beijing[2]

Case of Phase I: Beijing Third Factory of Chemical Technology

Beijing Third Factory of Chemical Technology was founded in the 1950s and was initially situated in the downtown areas. It is one of the best chemical factories in China during the planned economy era, but the company had to face declining competitiveness and revenues as a result of prominent problems, including heavy operational burden, backward management skills, obsolete equipment and technology, and high energy consumption, as China transited to market economy.

In order to adapt to the fierce competition resulting from market economy and fundamentally address the pollution and disturbance problems, Beijing Third Factory of Chemical Technology has been carefully preparing the relocation since the 1990s. The company remained discreet in selecting its property developers of original factory site's land, and the final decision was set after rounds of searches and negotiations. Even then, contract disputes surfaced after the property developer obtained the land and partial compensation for relocation was paid. Later, the developers terminated their payment for the remaining compensation, and since then the two sides were engaged in years of dissensions and lawsuits. The development of the enterprise and staff living were consequentially affected, with the shutdown of production and suspension of relocation, mainly because of the shortage of money and suspension of the construction of the new site.

Case of Phase II: Beijing Transformer Factory

Beijing Transformer Factory was also established in the 1950s and originally located in a downtown area with three sides facing the streets and one side facing a residential area. The development space of the factory was strictly restrained by surroundings, and local residents were at same time caught in problems of heavy pollution due to noise and waste gas. Eventually, the factory was relocated to the Changping site of Zhongguancun Science Park (ZSP) after objective authentication and investigation, with the powerful support of the industrial management authorities.

Aware of other's pitfalls of the state assets loss during the land transfer process, Beijing Transformer Factory took cautious attitude toward

---

[2] The cases below are based on the Industry Sector of Beijing Development and Plan Institute Commission & Beijing Economic and Social Development Research Institute (2002).

choosing land property developers. The company examined overall the candidates' certificates, credit and strength, for the purpose of ensuring the imperative funds needed after the relocation, such as the new site construction, product restructuring, structural reform and technology innovation. At the same time, the company adopted a series of forceful measures to ensure the management used the special funds for relocation. The construction work and equipment purchase were conducted through public bidding, and the prospective cooperators were selected through strict process, which was not so common at that time for state-owned enterprises in China. The relevant funds could be put into use only after the whole executive body reaching the final agreement. Therefore, compared with similar companies, the efficacy of fund use was substantially improved, with more than RMB 10 million being saved as a result of bidding.

In addition, Beijing Transformer Factory integrated its relocation with product upgrade, technology development, and structural reform. Viewing relocation as a historical opportunity, it aimed to fulfill the target of "Starting a Business for the Second Time". On one hand, it made the best use of foreign advanced equipment to improve products' quality and technology and vigorously seek potential enterprise clients and development opportunities from new markets; on the other hand, it actively shouldered corporate social responsibility by allocating part of relocation compensation to purchase and improve the environmental protection equipment and technology. Through adopting these measures, Beijing Transformer Factory managed to turn loss to gains during its relocation period.

Case of Phase III: Beijing Shougang Company Limited

Beijing Shougang Company Limited, endorsed by the Beijing municipal government, is a limited company initiated by Shougang Group with a public offering. It used to make great contribution to Beijing's construction and tax revenue, but its pollution kept bothering the local community residents. The relocation of Shougang Company was not put in schedule until the successful bid for the Olympic Games. In May 2004, the Beijing municipal government submitted the program on the restructure of reducing production and environment governance to the NDRC. After gaining approval of the State Council, the program was officially approved by the NDRC, agreeing in principle issues of reducing production, relocation, restructuring, and environment governance, and dispersing the parts relevant to the manufacturing of steel and iron out of urban Beijing to Caofeidian in Tangshan city, Hebei province.

The relocation of Shougang was classified into two strategies: the construction of new factory in Hebei and the reduction of output in the old factory in Beijing. At the end of 2005, the output was reduced by 2 million tons, and another 2 million tons in 2007. The production was completely stopped in 2010. Generally, the relocation of Shougang can be divided into three phases. In the first phase, accomplished in the end of 2007, Shougang reduced steel and iron production capacity of 4 million tons in Beijing factory and temporally retained steel production capacity of 4 million tons in Shijingshan District with 2 sintering machines and 3 coke ovens. In the second phase, Shougang ensured all the production of smelting and hot rolling to be terminated and retained only the HQs, R&D, and sales, logistics, and services without polluting Beijing. In the third phase, Shougang tried its best to complete the relocation of production system involving steel and iron in Shijingshan District, and to terminate the production capacity of smelting. If smelting production was not stopped, the sintering and production with coke ovens must temporally shut down during the Olympic Games.

Meanwhile, compared to the termination of production in Beijing, the program in the first phase of Shougang in Caofeidian, was to form the production capability of 4 million tons, which expanded into 8 million tons in the second phase of the program in 2010. The steel and iron project in Caofeidian is mainly directed by Shougang, which cooperates with Tangshan Iron & Steel and some other domestic and foreign private capitals to establish a factory with diversified ownership. The new steel factory is environmentally friendly, has recycling facilities, and is highly efficient. According to the idea of recycling economy, the factory imports international advanced technical equipments to construct an environmentally friendly, modernized fine iron and steel base with international competitiveness.

The relocation of Shougang, with a thorough plan, obtained great support from governments of all levels. The NDRC had called for a meeting with departments of finance, railroad, electricity, and environment protection to create solutions to the problems that emerged as a result of the relocation of Shougang factory, and approved to carry out a program of producing 1.5 million tons cold-rolled sheets (including zinc-coated sheets and color-coated sheets) in Beijing's Shunyi District, and preparing the arrangements for all the workers after the relocation of Shougang. They also agreed in principle on providing necessary support to Shougang on tax policies, loan subsidy, and enterprise equity deals. The developable land resources of Shougang in Beijing, which is the most developable land resources in the best location, with the largest area and the best infrastructure, can be developed for significant regional group programs.

12.4 Comparative Analysis of Industrial Relocation in Beijing

It can be seen that the impact of economic development, the upgrading of industrial structure, and municipal construction on the requirement of the distribution of industries in Beijing have lead to differences in its industrial relocation among different phases and different enterprises during this more than 20-year-old process. Especially in the three different phases, the ways of relocation and actual results are quite different from one other. Table 12-2 summarizes the characteristics of industrial relocation of Beijing in different phases.

According to the summary of Table 12-2, we analyze the typical cases of industrial relocation in Beijing based on the reasons, ways, and results of relocation.

12.4.1 *The Reasons of Relocation*

First of all, the preference change is the main reason that the Beijing municipal government made the decision of industrial redistribution. Since the reform and opening-up, the Beijing municipal government realized the original development strategy in the planned economy era can no longer meet the requirements to define the comparative advantage and city function of Beijing. Therefore, the government made significant transitions of economic development and city planning from constructing productive city and manufacture base with diversified industries to the economic development suitable for the characteristics of the Capital and constructing an international metropolis. These transitions did not only improve the decision of relocation but also made influence on the choice of key points of relocation. For instance, because of the redefinition

Table 12-2 Comparison on Industrial Relocation in Different Phases.

	1985–1995	1996–2001	2002–present
Purpose of relocation	Pollution	Pollution and redistribution	Structural adjustment, city orientation and international metropolitan construction
Scale of enterprises	Small	Small, middle and large	Small, middle and large
Ownership of enterprises	Municipal government owned	Mainly owned by municipal government	Multiple ownerships
Ways of relocation	Same location and same scale	Planning region, encouraging concentration	Confirm to the overall planning and encouraging cross-region relocation
Subsidy policies	Uncertain	Subsidies on relocation and encouraging technology reform	Relocation subsidy, support on technology reform and encouraging products upgrading
Land policies	Uncertain	Transfer through agreements	Bid, auction and public listing
Result of relocation	Worse operation of enterprises and polluting new environment	Better operation of enterprises and concentrated pollution	Improved operation of enterprises and controlling the pollution

Source: Author.

of economic development and city function, improvement of residents' awareness of environment protection and review of the scattered, disordered, and bad "Hutong industries", the government decided to relocate those small enterprises with backward equipment, low economic efficiency, noise, and pollution. This undertaking obtained support and understanding of most citizens and enterprises. Then the government gradually realized that spatial concentration is the requirement of industrial development with the improvement of economic level and the depth of the awareness to city development, so they made adjustments to the original scattered industrial enterprise distribution, directing enterprises to relocate in industrial park to achieve mutual improvement.

Second, it is the expansion of city size that requires the redistribution of industries and relocation of enterprises. With the development of economy, the population of Beijing kept increasing and the speed of urbanization accelerated. From 1978 to 2005, the average growth rate of total population was 2.12%, and the average growth rate of urban population was 3.73%, both obviously above the average rate of the country. As the city kept expanding, the Beijing municipal government had to expand the built-up area for further construction and development. The former peripheral areas of the city, from "the second ring", the inner city to "the third ring", "the fourth ring", even "the fifth ring", and "the sixth ring", once full of industries, including the manufacture, become the core area of the city now. Moreover, the expansion of the city economy is also the major reason that Shunyi District and Changping District, former suburban surroundings, make industrial development and the construction of those districts in turn provides space for the relocated enterprises from inner city.

And third, the upgrading of industrial structure of Beijing is the most important motivation to the industrial relocation. Since the 1980s, the Beijing municipal government has learnt the lesson from historical experience of economic development and paid more attention to improve and enhance the service function of the Capital. It is recognized that industrial development should follow the principle of pursuing high level and high efficiency, which expresses prominent characteristics of modernization. The economic structure soon developed into the structure with the tertiary industry ranking first, followed by the secondary industry, and then the primary industry, from the original structure of the secondary industry ranking first, followed by the tertiary industry, and then the primary industry. Especially in the mid- and late 1990s, the industrial structure of Beijing experienced enormous changes. The tertiary industry became the major drive of economic development and the proportion of finance, insurance, post and telecommunication, and some other sectors newly emerged with a high utility of land resource increased rapidly. The significantly increasing demand of land in the central region of the city made the government realize that it high time to make adjustment on the original industrial land utilization to spare more space for better development.

12.4.2 *Ways of Relocation*

The industrial relocation in Beijing is a "learning by doing" process. In the first phase from 1985 to 1995, due to the lack of overall view about the industrial development and distribution, the Beijing municipal government only commanded some state-owned enterprises to relocate because they disturbed residents nearby, and most were small firms in the inner city. Meanwhile, the method of relocation involved moving some factories outside, with little changes in the scale or operation of those enterprises. In the second phase, the Beijing municipal government integrated industrial relocation and development with the construction of the city. Through *Urban Master Planning of Beijing* and *Executive Solutions to Industrial Enterprise Relocation within Third and Fourth Ring Roads of Beijing*, the government defined the reasonable distribution of industrial land and the policies of relocation and gave guidance to the new location, the scale, the way of transfer, and the program about technological reform of enterprises.

After 2001, based on the experience and lessons learnt from the first two phases, the Beijing municipal government defined the orientation of the city and the direction of economic development, and the industrial relocation was then connected with industrial restructuring, old city reconstruction, and constructing international metropolis to put forward requirement of relocation to some industrial enterprises with other kinds of ownership, besides state-owned one. As to enterprises owned by the municipal government, the government changed the previous ways of transfers and adopted bid invitation, auction, and listing to promote the transfer of land. For example, in the relocation of Shougang, the government changed the old way of intra-city relocation and supported the cooperation between Shougang and Tangshan Iron & Steel (another large steel company in Tanshan, Hebei province) and inter-regional relocation. At the same time, Shougang made use of most of the original land in Shijingshan District to develop cultural innovation and recreation industries, which realized the aim of completing the transfer, exchange, and development under the rule of the market.

12.4.3 *The Results of Relocation*

The first phase of the industrial relocation of Beijing is basically simple spatial relocation. Most enterprises either went bankrupt or faced worse management state and eventually died out under the market competition as the result of relocation. In this phase, the relocation failed in improving economic efficiency. From the aspect of environment protection, although pollution in certain areas of the city was solved, the suburban areas now experienced more new pollution. Most enterprises faced many potential problems in the process of relocation for the lack of experience, legal knowledge, and necessary technical guidance, which led to the failure of many enterprises. For example, Beijing Third Factory of Chemical Technology failed mainly because the enterprise lacked the specialties and legal knowledge, which became a disadvantage and led to some ambiguous provisions against the partner in the negotiation regarding land transfer.

In the second phase, the government connected relocation with the construction of industrial parks, focusing on the technological reform and product upgrading through intra-city industrial relocation. The government also increased the support for the enterprises to move into industrial parks, including the relevant preferential policies of returning land-transferring fees and tax exemption to help enterprises improve their economic efficiency and environment protection, which made some enterprises rejuvenate in the process of the relocation. For instance, Beijing Transformer Factory took the strategy of "thorough planning and overall promotion" and insisted on the principle "relocation without impeding production, impact on the market and reducing profits", and meanwhile they stimulated the enthusiasm and creativity of employees, integrated relocation, construction, marketing and product structural adjustment with technological reform, and completed the stable transition from construction to production. Generally speaking, the relocation was quite successful and provided experience for other enterprises to share.

In the third phase, as the result of concluding all the relocation experiences, the capability of, production, technology level, and business practice of relocated enterprises have been improved through the collaboration of government subsidies and market direction, promoting the transition and development of enterprises and controlling the pollution to moving-in areas.

Furthermore, attempts at making use of land resources by the rule of the market, although not perfect, made a positive effect on avoiding the loss of state-owned properties. Typical enterprises in this phase like Shougang got great support of the governments in the relocation, which guaranteed successful relocation. At the same time, relocation with the help of the market ensured adequate funds to improve the productivity and technology, which predicted a better result of the ongoing relocation of Shougang than those in the first two phases. Taking the opportunities provided by the relocation, the enterprises can achieve the goals of technological upgrading and new development. They can not only solve the problem of pollution in the original location but also promote the economic development of moving-in areas through constructing new environmentally friendly enterprises.

12.5 Conclusion Remarks

The urban industrial relocation is a complex and tough systematic program, involving the reform of enterprises, city planning and construction, environment protection, and social development. It is so difficult in that it needs collaborations among the government, enterprises, and the society for promotion. In the past, relocation of some enterprises was an immensely successful experience through exploration and practice and resulted in the formation of diversified models of relocation, which can be great examples for those enterprises preparing for relocation. We should conclude and share the experience to avoid same mistakes in the past relocation, reduce the cost of relocation, and save social resources.

The method and policy are the most important factors to urban industrial relocation. The knowledge of relocation, specific policies, and practice of the government can also influence the result of relocation to a large extent. Industrial relocation is the demand of the development of the city. If the method is reasonable and the result is good, the relocation will make great contribution to the city. It is also a good opportunity for adjustment of product and industrial structure because of the inevitable equipment upgrading and technological reform in the process of relocation. If the subsidy and preferential policies are effective, most enterprises can carve out a new way and improve the capability of development. In addition, one of the main reasons of industrial relocation is the increasing return of spatial agglomeration mechanism. Therefore, if the government gives guidance and makes full use of this mechanism, better city industrial agglomeration can be achieved. However, if the relocation policies are not suitable to the ground reality, it will cause the enterprises to lose their previous development space. If they cannot adapt to the new environment, their business state worsen and they will be the new sources of pollution. Worsening business of enterprises and the shifting of pollution would impede the development of the whole city and increase the financial and social burden on citizens at the origin location and environmental pressure on citizens at the new location.

Meanwhile, we should realize that the autonomy of the relocation will increase with the development of market economy, and urban industrial relocation should not remain in the phase where the government is in charge of the whole relocation. Because of the economic development and the specialty of land utilization system in China, the government will continue to play a leading role in the relocation in short term. The marketization degree in the allocation of land resources remains low for now. There are many problems in land transfers, such as large difference of land policies between different industries. For example, the preferential land policy on manufacture industry in many cities has negative effect on the development of service industry. The government should improve the rule of land market and establish a land market with the principle of openess, fairness, and justice to ensure fair allocation of the profit made in land transfers among the government, relocated enterprises, and the developers.

References

Bai, M. (2003). *Research on Firm Relocation.* Doctoral Dissertation, Nankai University, Tianjin.

Chen, D. (1993). *Regional Economics.* Zhengzhou: China: Henan Renmin Press.

Fujita, M. (1989). *Urban Economic Theory.* New York: Cambridge University Press.

Jin, B. (2005). *Industrial Economics.* (New Edition) Beijing: Economic & Management Publishing House.

Keeble, D. (1976). *Industrial Location and Planning in the United Kingdom.* London: Methuen & Co.

The Industry Sector of Beijing Development and Plan Commission & Beijing Economic and Social Development Research Institute (2002). *Accelerating the Relocation to Prepare for the Olympic Games and Promote the Sustainable Development of Industries in Beijing — Investigation Report on Industrial Relocation of Beijing.* Internal Study Report.

Index